READING PRACTICES WITH DEAF LEARNERS

Reading Practices with Deaf Learners

Patricia L. McAnally
Susan Rose
Stephen P. Quigley

8700 Shoal Creek Boulevard
Austin, Texas 78757-6897
800/897-3202   Fax 800/397-7633
Order online at http://www.proedinc.com

© 1999 by PRO-ED, Inc.
8700 Shoal Creek Boulevard
Austin, Texas 78757-6897
800/897-3202   Fax 800/347-7633
Order online at http://www.proedinc.com

This book is designed in Goudy.

Production Director: Alan Grimes
Production Coordinator: Dolly Fisk Jackson
Managing Editor: Chris Olson
Art Director: Thomas Barkley
Designer: Jason Crosier
Print Buyer: Alicia Woods
Preproduction Coordinator: Chris Anne Worsham
Staff Copyeditor: Martin Wilson
Project Editor: Jill Mason
Production Assistant: John Means Cooper

Printed in the United States of America

1 2 3 4 5 6 7 8 9 10   03 02 01 00 99

CONTENTS

PART I: FOUNDATIONS

Part II: Instructional Management

Part III: Applications

P A R T

I

FOUNDATIONS

CHAPTER

COGNITION, LANGUAGE, AND READING

Preview

The title of this book indicates that its focus will be practical and centered on deaf students and instructional strategies in the area of reading. Before teaching and learning strategies for classroom use are discussed, however, the reader must first have a general understanding of the foundations of reading. In order to make good decisions regarding the teaching of reading, teachers must be familiar with the reading process and some of the current theoretical frameworks. Without this knowledge, the reading teacher's application of strategies can be little more than trial and error.

This chapter provides an overview of some of the important information in the foundations of reading. A discussion of the relationship of cognition and language emphasizes the impact of this interaction on deaf students as they begin the process of learning to read. Next, the reader will be introduced to the three major groups of reading theories, three popular models of reading, and the roles these theories and models play in instructional practice. As readers progress through the chapters of this book, they will see that almost all of the instructional strategies have their roots in one or a combination of two or more of these theories and models. The final discussion in this chapter focuses on the skills that hearing children and deaf and hard of hearing children bring to the task of learning to read. This section will provide some insight to readers on the enormity of the task faced by deaf and hard of hearing children as they embark on their reading journey.

Introduction

Historically, deaf and hard of hearing children have experienced enormous difficulties in learning to read. Their teachers will attest to this statement; the students themselves will proclaim that this is true; and, of course, countless research reports over the past 80 years indicate that deaf and hard of hearing children typically read at levels significantly below those of their hearing peers. Why is this so? What is it about the process that makes reading such a puzzle for these students?

Obviously, a major problem for many deaf and hard of hearing students is that they are trying to learn to read and comprehend English-language text when they do not yet have mastery of the English language. Reading is regarded as a language process and is closely allied to other language processes that children experience as they acquire expressive language (speaking, signing, writing) and receptive language (listening, seeing). Reading is also a cognitive process. It involves an array of complex mental activities such as processing information, constructing meaning, and storing and retrieving information.

Language and Cognition

Attempting to define the relationship between language and cognition is very much like trying to answer the age-old question "Which comes first, the chicken or the egg?" But however elusive, it is a worthy pursuit, as the nature of the relationship has both theoretical and practical significance, particularly for teachers of students who are deaf or hard of hearing. If cognition is dependent on language, then a language deficit would affect the development of cognition. If language is dependent on cognition, then a cognitive deficit would affect the development of language, including reading and writing. If neither is dependent on the other, then development in one area would not affect development in the other area (Paul & Quigley, 1990).

Language-Dominant Position

Several theories have been developed to try to explain the relationship of language and cognition. At one extreme is the language-dominant position characterized by Chomsky's (1968) nativist hypothesis, which proposes that children have an innate propensity toward the development of language. Perhaps the strongest version of this position is the theory of linguistic determination (Whorf, 1956), which asserts that the language of an individual determines the thoughts of that individual, thus proposing that there is a one-to-one relationship between language and cognition and that cognition is dependent on language.

Cognitive-Dominant Position

Constructivist hypotheses can be divided into two positions, one that is strongly cognitive-dominant and one that proposes a weaker cognitive-dominant position. The first hypothesis asserts that cognition provides the foundation for language development and that cognition can adequately account for children's ability to learn language (Karmiloff-Smith, 1979; Miller et al., 1977). The weaker position maintains that while cognition is necessary for language development to occur, cognition alone cannot account for children's ability to learn language (Cromer, 1976), suggesting that both linguistic skills and cognitive skills are necessary for children to acquire language.

Correlational Position

A fourth hypothesis, the correlational hypothesis (Miller et al., 1977), maintains that there is a strong and fairly equal relationship between language and cognition because they share similar underpinnings. As individuals engage in linguistic or cognitive tasks, the developmental changes that occur in the underpinnings can be observed, particularly in children's performances on various Piagetian tasks during the sensorimotor stage. A review of the literature reveals some support for this hypothesis, especially at the prelinguistic stage, the one-word stage, and the two-word stage (the emergence of syntax), implying that the influence of language and cognition is somewhat balanced at these beginnings stages.

Existing evidence does not fully support any one of the four hypotheses. While each hypothesis suggests and both language and cognition play important roles in language development theories, the degree and extent are not yet known. Continued study and investigations are needed to bring about an adequate understanding of the relationship between language and cognition.

Cognitive Functioning in Deaf and Hearing People

In the past, a popular research question was whether deaf children and hearing children developed similarly in their cognitive functioning, both quantitatively and qualitatively. According to Paul and Quigley (1990), from the early part of the century to the present, there have been three successive perspectives regarding the effects of delayed language development on the intelligence of deaf individuals: (1) deaf people are inferior individuals; (2) deaf people learn through concrete rather than abstract experiences; and (3) deaf people are normal. The subjects in the studies leading to these conclusions had hearing losses ranging from moderate to profound; thus, the word *deaf* referred to individuals with moderate to profound hearing losses (Quigley & Kretschmer, 1982).

Until the 1970s, most professionals in the field based their opinions on the language-dominant hypothesis, particularly linguistic determinism. Both Pintner (1918) and Myklebust (1964) believed that language deficiencies contributed to intellectual lag in deaf individuals. Myklebust argued that deaf people have difficulty understanding abstract concepts and that they perceive the world differently from hearing people.

The researchers who believed that deaf individuals were intellectually normal (Furth, 1966, 1973; Levine, 1976) disagreed with the dominant role of language in the development of cognition. Furth (1971) argued that Piaget's theory supported the development of normal intellectual abilities in deaf children. Indeed, the current view is that the range of intelligence for hearing and deaf individuals is similar. Paul and Quigley (1990) stated that a better understanding of the relationship of language and cognition in deaf and hard of hearing children requires the study of subgroups according to levels of language development, spoken and signed. They also suggested that the development of language "requires instruction in both language (e.g., vocabulary and syntax) and cognition (e.g., inferencing and reasoning skills)" (Paul & Quigley, 1990, p. 74).

Information Processing

Information processing refers to the ability of the mind to perform tasks such as remembering and comprehending. A general model of information processing explains how information is encoded, stored, and retrieved and consists of three mental structures: sensory storage, short-term memory, and long-term memory.

Sensory Storage

In the first stage of the information processing, the sensory storage takes in new, unanalyzed information for a very short period of time, which is, however, sufficient for other mental structures to do more extensive processing. Much of the information that is not relevant to the individual's needs disappears, while that which is relevant moves into short-term memory.

Short-Term Memory

Short-term memory (STM), or working memory, is the second stage and provides an important temporary storage for the information that the person is currently processing. To solve simple and complex problems, a certain amount of information must remain in the working memory. However, the working memory has a limited capacity; it can store only five to nine items. STM is critical for facilitating the flow of information into long-term memory, where it can be stored and retrieved for later use; STM has been extensively researched for both hearing and deaf and hard of hearing children as critical in the reading process.

Blair (1957) conducted the first major comparative study on the short-term memory processes of deaf and hearing children. The study compared the ability of the children to remember items presented sequentially and simultaneously (i.e., two or more items presented at a time). The scores on these tasks were related to the reading achievement levels of the children. The results indicated that the scores of the deaf children were lower than those of the hearing children on sequential memory tasks, but there were no differences in the scores of the two groups on the simultaneous memory tasks. Blair concluded that (a) the auditory memory ability of deaf children was inferior to that of hearing children, and (b) auditory memory ability was related to reading ability. Since Blair's study, several other investigations have produced similar conclusions (Greenberg & Kusche, 1989; Hanson, 1990; Rodda & Grove, 1987).

Short-term memory plays an important role in the development of language and reading skills. To understand this relationship, it is important to be familiar with the results of studies that have attempted to determine that mode(s) deaf individuals use for thinking and memorizing.

Several interesting research investigations have attempted to determine the form of information held in the short-term memory of deaf individuals. The data from these investigations indicate that many individuals with severe to profound hearing losses use a non–speech-based recoding strategy such as sign, visual or graphemic (print) information, or finger spelling (Bench, 1992; Greenberg & Kusche, 1989; Martin, 1985; Quigley & Kretschmer, 1982). The individuals in the studies exhibited a great deal of variability in the recoding strategies used, and they frequently used more than one strategy, especially during reading.

The findings of these investigations on recoding strategies used by deaf individuals in their internal mediating systems have a significant impact on the individuals' reading effectiveness. The mediating system of good readers who hear is predominantly speech-based; that is, the reader recodes printed words into their phonological equivalents to access meanings (Gough, 1985). In addition, it is thought that a speech-based internal mediating system plays an important role in the processing of syntactic structures and in developing inferential and metacognitive skills for connected reading (Paul & Quigley, 1990). It is interesting to note that a few investigations have found that some severely to profoundly deaf studies also predominantly use a speech-based code (Conrad, 1979; Hanson, 1985; Hanson & Fowler, 1987; Lichtenstein, 1984; Rodda & Grove, 1987). These investigations also indicate that deaf students who predominantly use a speech-based code are better readers than those students who primarily use nonspeech codes. It seems that speech recoders are able to retain more language information such as words and syntax in their short-term memories, enabling them to comprehend the meaning of sentences, particularly the underlying semantic relationships between the words in sentences. This ability allows the speech recoders not only to comprehend sentences written in literal word order (e.g., *The cat drank the milk*), but also to comprehend sentences with hierarchical structures (e.g., *The team that wins the game will get free pizzas*).

Kelly (1995) speculated that deaf readers who use a strategy less enduring than speech recoding for sustaining the contents of working memory are more likely to lose words in a sentence before their combined meaning can be constructed and stored in long-term memory. An interesting question that remains unanswered, however, is What is the nature of the speech-based representations, and How did the deaf students develop those representations (Leybaert, 1993; Paul, 1992)?

Working memory capacity appears to play a significant role in the reading process. Daneman, Nemeth, Stainton, and Huelsmann (1995) conducted a study investigating whether working memory capacity could account for individual differences in the reading achievement of deaf and hard of hearing children. Using three tests to assess the processing and storage capacity of working memory, they found that all three measures were good predictors of reading achievement in a group of orally educated 5- to 14-year-old deaf and hard of hearing children. In fact, working memory capacity was a better predictor of reading achievement than was the degree of hearing loss, even though the sample included children with hearing losses ranging from mild (27–40 dB) to profound (91+ dB).

Long-Term Memory

Long-term memory (LTM) is the third stage in information processing and contains a person's knowledge of the world. This stored knowledge (prior knowledge) is activated to interpret new experiences and knowledge, relate them to what is already known, and incorporate them into the already existing storehouses of information in long-term memory. This process of relating new information to that which is already known facilitates understanding.

Two types of long-term memory are episodic and semantic (Rumelhart, 1977). Episodic memory stores information that is related to a specific event, such as what a person did last year on the Fourth of July, or what a person ate for breakfast yesterday. Thus, episodic memory is different for each individual. The second type of memory is semantic memory, which contains general organized classes of knowledge. Carroll (1986, p. 47) gave examples of some of these classes, such as "motor skills (typing, swimming, bicycling), general knowledge (grammar, arithmetic), spatial knowledge (the spatial layout of your room or house), and social skills (how to begin and end conversations, rules for self-disclosure)." Episodic and semantic memory interact during the processing of information.

Investigations into the nature of long-term memory have mostly been concerned with the transfer of information from short-term memory and information retrieval in performing cognitive tasks such as answering questions and making inferences. The purpose of this research is to present a comprehensive model of knowledge that will account for what we know, how we know it, and where this knowledge is stored in the brain (Paul & Quigley, 1990).

Sachs (1967) and, subsequently, other researchers (Carroll, 1986; Rodda, Cumming, & Fewer, 1993) found that when subjects were asked to repeat a sentence after a short delay from when the stimulus was given, they did not remember the surface structure of the sentence but were able to convey an accurate meaning of the sentence. Hanson and Bellugi (1982) reported similar results in an investigation with deaf individuals in which the stimuli were presented in American Sign Language (ASL). These results seem to indicate that the long-term memories of both hearing and deaf individuals are semantically based, but it does not necessarily indicate that the encoding processes and storage of knowledge in the brain are also similar. If, as it appears, deaf individuals tend to process and store information visually and spatially in short- and long-term memories, and hearing people tend to process and store information auditorially and temporally, then it is likely that storage occurs in different hemispheres of the brain for these two groups of individuals. Paul and Quigley (1990) suggested that if environmental factors such as language and communication environments (sign versus spoken language, ASL versus English) influence hemispheric specialization, then the result may be differences in hemispheric development and processing in deaf and hearing people. It should be noted, however, that individuals with severe to profound hearing losses have been exposed to a variety of language and communication environments and are not a homogenous group in relation to hemispheric processing and storage; hence, no definitive conclusions can be made regarding hemispheric development and processing (Paul & Quigley, 1990; Wilbur, 1987).

Ursula Bellugi, in her work at the Salk Institute, has been studying the effects of stroke and brain injury on deaf signers since the 1980s. She was motivated by studies with hearing subjects who had brain lesions that indicated that visual–spatial processing occurred in the right hemisphere of the brain, while linguistic processing occurred in the left hemisphere. She was intrigued to know how the brain would handle a language that is also visual and spatial. In her studies she discovered that it was only with left hemisphere damage that sign language aphasia occurred, leading her to conclude that "the left hemisphere has an innate predisposition for language—whatever the mode of expression" (Dressler, 1997, p. 7).

Reading Theories

Three major groups of reading theories have been developed to attempt to explain the reading process. Each group of theories differs in the strategies believed to be used by children as they engage in the process of gaining meaning from printed text.

Bottom-Up Theories

Bottom-up theories (Gough, 1972; LaBerge & Samuels, 1974) are text-driven theories in which the major focus is on the text material as the predominant factor used by children to derive meaning from text. The elements of text that are emphasized are letters, words, phrases, and sentences. Bottom-up theorists believe that these elements are integrated from smaller to larger units to arrive at meaning. Instruction based on these theories emphasized decoding skills and the teaching of comprehension subskills, usually in some kind of sequential, hierarchical order (King & Quigley, 1985).

Top-Down Theories

Top-down theorists such as Smith (1988) and K. Goodman (1970) proposed that prior knowledge and its interaction with the processing of text is a more valid explanation of the reading process. They maintain that skilled readers construct meaning from text using only the most productive and time-efficient cues (K. Goodman & Gollasch, 1980). These theorists argue that skilled readers rely as little as possible on graphemic details and use prior knowledge and context as they strive for comprehension. Thus, instruction based on these theories deemphasizes the teaching of decoding skills and comprehension subskills and focuses instead on activities that will enable students to develop, activate, and apply prior knowledge to a text to effect comprehension.

Interactive Theories

In recent years, interactive theories have been replacing the bottom-up and top-down groups of theories of the reading process. Interactive theories emphasize that the reader is an active processor of information and strives to construct meaning from the text (Anderson, 1981). Two important premises of interactive theories state that (a) prior knowledge plays a central role in constructing meaning from text, and (b) readers develop and apply a large repertoire of processing strategies ranging from strategies for decoding print to complex metacognitive strategies. Interactive theorists maintain that the bottom-up and top-down theories fail to recognize that even very young children bring a large body of prior experiences to the task of reading and that skilled readers also use extensive graphemic knowledge and skills in their search for meaning. Skilled readers generally use a combination of these strategies, depending on their comprehension needs.

One group of interactive theories, schema theories, uses the concept of schemata as an organizing framework for prior knowledge. This concept of schemata provides a powerful tool for organizing knowledge; such ability to organize knowledge aids in its acquisition, storage, and retrieval, thus facilitating comprehension of text.

Reading and Cognition

Reading is not only a language function, it is also a cognitive function. Cognition refers to the acquisition and construction of knowledge and, of course, the act of thinking. When processing text, students are applying thinking skills that enable them to build their model of meaning as they read. Constructing meaning from the printed word requires a variety of cognitive processing strategies that will differ with the nature of the reading task and with individual differences in selecting and applying problem-solving strategies.

Schema Theory and the Reading Process

One cognitive model of reading is the concept of schemata and their role in the reading process as described by schema theories. *Schema* is the term used by cognitive scientists to describe how people organize and store information in their memories.

The Nature of Schemata

A basic premise of schema theory is that human memory is organized semantically—that is, that memory is organized more like a thesaurus than a dictionary. An individual can possess schemata for all kinds of things, ranging from simple objects, such as a car and a ball; to abstract entities, such as love and friendship; to complex events, such as a wedding or a basketball game (Taylor, Harris, & Pearson, 1988).

Schema activation is the mechanism by which readers access what they know and match it to the information in a text. In doing that, readers build on the meaning they already have and add to the information that is stored in the activated schemata. Rumelhart (1980) referred to schemata as "the building blocks of cognition" because they represent elaborate networks of information that people use to make sense of new information and events.

Schemata play a critical role in reading comprehension and learning. When readers can match their prior knowledge with the text, schema functions in at least three ways (Vacca & Vacca, 1996). First, it functions as a framework for learning that allows readers to seek and select information that fits with their purposes for reading. As they seek and select, readers are more likely to make inferences, that is, to anticipate content, make predictions, and fill in gaps in the material during reading. Second, schema helps readers to organize text information. The process of integrating new information into old information helps the reader to retain and remember. Third, schema helps readers to elaborate information. Vacca and Vacca (1996) suggested that when readers elaborate on what they have read, they engage in a cognitive process that involves critical thinking skills such as judgment and evaluation.

Selecting Schema

The process through which a reader determines what schema or schemata to select to comprehend material being read is complex and involves a great deal of inferring. Sometimes an author is quite informative and "sets the stage" for the reader with an opening statement such as, "This story is a murder mystery about the dark secrets of a small midwestern village." However, more frequently the reader has to rely on subtle clues and form hypotheses to begin to figure out what a story is about. Taylor et al. (1988) stated that often the reader must make great "inferential leaps" just to determine the nature of the text.

Once the reader has formed what seems to be a valid hypothesis about the overall nature of a story, the next task becomes one of filling slots, another task that requires inference. For example, if the story is a murder mystery, the reader knows from prior knowledge and appropriate schema selection that among the characters in the story will be one who is the protagonist and one who is the antagonist. When people read, they search for clues that will indicate the roles of the characters. As they gain more information about the traits of the characters in the story, they fill, at least temporarily, the various slots in their schema of "mystery story." As they continue reading and gaining more information, they may change the characters they have put into certain slots. Readers are constantly altering hypotheses, filling slots, and building meaning during the process of comprehending. These strategies that occur during the act of reading take place through inference. Inference is an essential part of schema selection and slot filling; in the process of working one's way through a text, tens, hundreds, even thousands of inferences are necessary (Taylor et al., 1988).

Changing Schema

Learning necessitates a change of some kind in a schema. A common kind of learning-within-schema theory is what Rumelhart (1980) calls *accretion*. The idea of accretion is similar to Piaget's (1952) concept of assimilation and to Smith's (1975) notion of comprehension. Accretion occurs when an individual experiences an example of an existing schema and the slot filling that occurs is committed to long-term memory. This process is what allows a person to recall specific circumstances from an experience, for example, a particular trip to a favorite park. While learning usually alters the structure of a schema, accretion does not; it merely fills some of the slots with new information.

A second kind of learning is *fine tuning* (Taylor et al., 1988). The notion of fine tuning would be included in Piaget's idea of accommodation and in what Smith calls learning. Through the process of fine tuning, the reader modifies the components of schemata in important ways; new variable slots may be added or changed. For example, a reader who has encountered only male villains in mystery stories might have a variable constraint that villains must be male. When a female villain is encountered, this variable slot must be modified to include females.

The third kind of learning is called *restructuring* and occurs when an old schema is replaced with a new schema necessary to accommodate existing and new information. Restructuring occurs continually in daily life; for example, very young children may label all four-legged animals as dogs; but as they gain new information, they develop new, specialized schemata for cats, horses, and cows. There are two aspects of restructuring: schema specialization and schema generalization. The previous example is an example of schema specialization— that is, an instance in which several new schema are needed to replace a single old schema. Schema generalization occurs when the learner realizes that several subschemata share some common variable slots and can be seen as components of the same schema; for example, myths and fables are both stories.

Two strategies that readers use to control their schemata during reading are top-down processing and bottom-up processing (Taylor et al., 1988). When readers apply top-down processing, they are usually actively engaged in the reading task, are generating hypotheses, and are applying new information from the text to already existing schemata. The match or lack of a match between the new information and prior knowledge determines whether a hypothesis is confirmed or disconfirmed, in which case it must be modified.

Sometimes readers are more passive and engage in bottom-up processing. In that case, the reader decides to wait before forming an opinion or making a judgment and reads on for more information before drawing any conclusions. This kind of processing frequently occurs when a reader first encounters a text, when a hypothesis has been disconfirmed, or when the reader simply is not understanding what the author is trying to convey. When readers are using bottom-up processing, they seem to be trying to operate within the author's schemata; when they are using top-down processing, they are operating within their own schemata. Skilled readers shift back and forth constantly between the two processing strategies in their attempts to comprehend text.

Using Schema Theory in Instruction Decisions

Schema theory not only offers a plausible explanation for at least some parts of the reading process, it also provides an explanation for some of the problems students exhibit when they fail to comprehend. Pearson and Spiro (1980) found that five kinds of problems that students exhibit can be explained within the framework of schema theory.

Schema Availability

If students are reading a selection on a topic about which they do not have a well-developed schema, they will have difficulty understanding the text. In, fact, Johnston (1981) and Johnston and Pearson (1982) determined that prior knowledge explains individual differences in comprehension better than measured reading ability does. To assess the extent of students' prior knowledge of a particular topic, a simple instructional strategy called *semantic mapping* can be used. This strategy, explained in detail in Chapter 7, can also be used for remediation to enable students to develop a more complete schema.

Schema Selection

Some students have the prior knowledge but fail to activate it and apply what they already know to the material they are reading. These students frequently rely too much on bottom-up processing and do not realize which of their schemata can be used to comprehend the text. In fact, many times students who fail to activate and apply prior knowledge fail to do so because they do not understand that they are allowed to use anything other than what is in the text to help them understand. Any prereading teaching strategy, such as semantic mapping, that focuses on appropriate schemata should help these students become more active processors of text.

Schema Maintenance

A reader may have available and select a schema for comprehending a passage but fail to maintain that schema through the reading, thus exhibiting a schema maintenance problem. One possible reason this happens is that readers rely too much on bottom-up processing and direct all their attention to decoding strategies, thus leaving little cognitive capacity for the integrative thinking that is necessary for comprehension (Taylor et al., 1988). Another possible reason is that the text does not make clear how different ideas should be connected; this is more of a problem for poor than for skilled readers. Skilled readers seem more able to create connections when none are offered by the author. No investigations have focused on which instructional strategies to use when students display problems with schema maintenance. Taylor et al. (1988) suggested that helping students develop schemata for the ways in which stories and expository text are organized may help overcome the problems of schema maintenance.

Overreliance on Bottom-Up Processing

Readers who rely too much on bottom-up processing will make reading errors because they are attending too much to graphic features and not enough to semantic concerns. They also tend to give verbatim answers from the text when inferences should be made and prior knowledge applied. Helping students change this reading strategy is not easy. Basically, they need to learn that reading should make sense and that comprehending often requires going beyond the text.

To help students focus on the idea that reading should make sense, strategies such as anomaly detection techniques can be used. Students are given texts that contain anomalous words, phrases, or sentences, and they must delete the parts that do not make sense. To do this, they must have a good idea of what the text is about. Helping students understand that they can go beyond the text is more difficult, but strategies such as teacher-modeling may help. In that strategy, the teacher reads passages to the students, modeling the comprehension process by explaining how he or she constructs meaning from the printed word. Another strategy that may help is the strategy known as question-answer relationships (QAR), which is discussed in Chapter 7.

Overreliance on Top-Down Processing

Sometimes students relay too much on top-down (schema-based) processing, which may lead to errors that are semantically appropriate. Students' answers to questions may seem sensible but reflect a cursory or careless reading. While a cursory reading (skimming) may be appropriate for some kinds of text, it is not appropriate if understanding details is important, such as in reading science text, directions, and poetry.

The question-answering behavior is similar to that of students who rely too much on bottom-up processing; the students need to develop an understanding that good answers to questions may come from within or outside the text. In this case, the students must realize that good answers can come from within the text. Having students supply answers to questions and then noting the pages and paragraphs where answers can be found may help to channel them toward more frequent use of this resource. For the careless reading problem, students can be given fill-in-the-blank exercises in which all answers are semantically correct (e.g., *smiled, giggled, guffawed*) but only one conveys the appropriate connotations for the sentence (*The little girl was so happy to see her new puppy that she _____ with delight.*).

Simultaneous and Successive Cognitive Processing

Simultaneous and successive cognitive processing is one model of dichotomous thinking that refers to *how* students solve problems, recognizing and restructuring information in a problem-solving situation such as reading (Walker, 1996). When students read, they vary their cognitive processing techniques depending on the nature of the reading task. For example, when determining a main idea from a text, readers organize the important topics (successive processing) while forming relationships among the topics (simultaneous processing). When reading requires a step-by-step analysis of a text, as in determining the sequence of events, readers use successive processing and sequentially order the information to solve the problem. When reading requires the analysis of several ideas at the same time, as in predicting the author's purpose and interpreting character motives, readers use simultaneous processing; they relate ideas according to a general category to solve the problem.

Students who have a preference for simultaneous processing of information tend to think about the multiple relationships among ideas, relating the most important characteristics (Kaufman & Kaufman, 1983). Such readers build their models of meaning using large, inclusive categories of meaning. This type of cognitive processing frequently precludes careful analysis of text. Simultaneous strength means that the student thinks first about the overall meaning and then organizes the parts as they relate to the entire meaning

(Walker, 1996). This type of cognitive processing seems to fit with top-down strategies.

Students who have a successive preference for processing information tend to develop models of meaning by arranging information in a logical, hierarchical sequence (Kaufman & Kaufman, 1983). They develop their model of meaning from precise words and look for the logical organization of the text to gain meaning. After reading a text, they can usually sequence the events but cannot tie the events together to form the main idea. A propensity for this type of cognitive processing frequently precludes using the overall meaning of the text to decode words, resulting in a reader who is word-bound. Successive strength means that the student thinks about the parts first and then orders the parts to form the general meaning (Walker. 1996). This type of cognitive processing seems to fit with bottom-up strategies.

Effective readers do not operate exclusively in either a successive or a simultaneous processing mode, but flexibly and fluently shift between the two to construct a model of meaning. They incorporate both a successive analysis of textual elements and a simultaneous connecting of textual and nontextual information to comprehend what they are reading. The teacher, when selecting instructional strategies, should be aware of the student's preferences for cognitive processing. The teacher should select techniques that will encourage the student to use areas of weakness that interfere with comprehension, as well as strategies that will utilize the student's strengths. It is clear that teachers cannot focus on a few favorite teaching techniques but must employ a variety of techniques; they must identify the key features of the techniques and determine how those features affect the reading process and meet the individual needs of the readers. It is unclear at this time how these two approaches interact for deaf and hard of hearing readers. It is also unclear whether skills in one approach can compensate for weaknesses in the other (Brown & Brewer, 1996).

Models of Reading

Teachers need to know what is currently understood about reading and reading comprehension to assess students' reading processes. Without an understanding of how good readers process and comprehend text, it is impossible to identify a reading problem or a potential area of development. A solid knowledge of the reading process is also a prerequisite for deciding what to do instructionally once a reading problem is identified.

Three popular models of the reading process have influenced current thinking about how the reading process develops and how it operates. These models represent the most important influences on reading practices, and on the whole language movement especially, over the last 25 years (Rhodes & Shanklin, 1993).

Transactional Model

Rosenblatt (1978) believed that readers bring to text all of their personal experiences and cultural learnings. The text is a black-and-white graphic display created by the author. The transaction that occurs between the reader and the text produces meaning, but this meaning is not the same for every reader because each reader brings different personal and cultural experiences to bear on the interpretation of the text. Consequently, readers may interpret the same text in different ways depending on their background knowledge. These interpretations are each equally valid, and what constitutes "knowledge" then is socially constructed among readers in a group (Rhodes & Shanklin, 1993).

Teachers frequently choose reading activities that exploit the social nature of the reading and learning processes. These activities include shared book experiences, literature discussion groups, partner reading, and dialogue journals. In all of these situations, the reader is clearly reading and performing transactions in a social context. They are sharing the act of reading with other readers, thereby providing opportunities for all participants to learn more about reading and to increase their knowledge through active participation in transactions with other readers. In such social contexts, readers provide demonstrations to each other of the strategies they use during the reading process, the personal perspectives they apply to their reading, and the ways in which they respond to and connect with text (Rhodes & Shanklin, 1993). These shared experiences offer opportunities for readers to create and confirm shared meanings of the text as they work with one another to clarify what they have read and understood.

Psycholinguistic Model

The psycholinguistic model of reading (K. Goodman, 1984, 1989) developed from Goodman's interest in analyzing the errors that readers make when reading. He looked specifically for evidence of an interrelated use of the four language cueing systems—semantics, syntax, graphophonics, and progmatics. Goodman believes that by studying these errors, or miscues, the investigator is provided with windows to the cognitive processing that occurs during reading. He maintains that miscues are natural to the reading process and that by monitoring for meaning, readers then make corrections. Goodman views reading as a process in which readers are constantly searching for meaning. The reading process requires that readers make predictions, confirm or disconfirm those predictions while reading, and integrate information from the text with their background knowledge to construction appropriate meanings from the text.

Socio-Psycholinguistic Model

Smith's (1988) socio-psycholinguistic model of reading incorporates some of the important premises of schema theory in that he argues that the more background knowledge (nonvisual information) a reader can apply to the reading situation, the easier the reading will be and the more likely the reader will comprehend and retain information. He also argues against phonics as the key to reading, pointing out that there are 166 different phonics rules to explain English pronunciation. He maintains that it would be virtually impossible for beginning readers to memorize all of those rules and to figure out when and when not to apply them. Furthermore, he argues that while many adults can articulate some phonics rules, they cannot articulate all 166 rules; yet they can still read. Therefore, something in addition to decoding has to occur for the reader to be successful.

One of Smith's most important contributions to models of reading has been his rethinking of how short-term memory and long-term memory relate to the reading process. Smith demonstrated that the short-term memory could take in and retain three to seven bits of information each second. Although the number of bits of information does not vary a great deal, the actual amount of information processed depends on the makeup of each bit. Smith found that readers took in fewer than 10 random letters in a section, but if those letters are organized into words, readers take in more "letters" because the brain can then process meaningful units. Subsequently, if the words are organized into phrases or sentences, still more letters can be processed because they are arranged in meaningful syntactic units.

Smith (1988) presented a diagram of how he perceives short-term and long-term memory working (see Figure 1.1). His diagram indicates that short-term memory exists within long-term memory. One important feature to note is that Smith suggested that while the STM processes incoming information into meaningful units, it is the LTM that guides and suggests the nature of those meaningful units. When the STM becomes overloaded, it cannot process information; hence, bits of information never get moved into long-term memory, where they can be stored and retrieved for later use. This phenomenon happens frequently when students do not have enough prior knowledge (or well-developed schemata) to apply to the text; hence, automaticity is obstructed, and the reader must spend time and assert cognitive energies toward figuring out meaning (Rhodes & Shanklin, 1993). This delay allows information to "drop out" of STM without ever reaching LTM; as a result, that information is not processed by the reader for comprehension.

This hypothesis, when applied to deaf and hard of hearing children engaged in the reading process, explains a great deal of the difficulty experienced by this population in the act of comprehending. Deaf and hard of hearing children frequently do not have adequate prior knowledge, or at least do not have adequate prior knowledge that has been linked to language, resulting in schemata that are not well developed or are not developed at all. In addition to lacking well-developed schemata, these children usually do not have a mastery of the English language, which creates additional "overload" on the short-term memory as it attempts to process incoming language into meaningful units. If, as Smith suggested, the STM cannot process information when it is overloaded and begins to lose bits of information, then it is not surprising that deaf and hard of hearing students have difficulties in comprehending English text. It is probably safe to assume that some or much of the information needed to construct meaning from text never reaches the LTM, where it can be processed for comprehension, stored, retrieved, and applied.

Smith (1988) also discussed the social nature of reading and his concept of learning to read through demonstration, engagement, and sensitivity. He suggested that parents, teachers, and peers are literacy models for children and demonstrate to them what reading is and what the strategies are for doing it. Through these demonstrations, the literacy models also demonstrate the social aspects of reading and learning to read. Engagement is the amount of time actually spent in a literacy task. Engagement can occur with one student alone, or

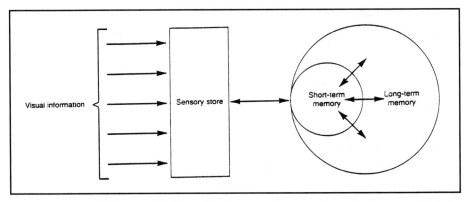

Figure 1.1. STM/LTM model. From *Windows into Literacy: Assessing Learners, K–8,* by L. Rhodes and N. Shanklin, 1993, Portsmouth, NH: Heinemann. Copyright 1993 by Frank Smith. Reprinted with permission.

it can involve others and thus become a social event. When it is social, some students will engage for longer periods of time and be more successful because they are assisting each other (Rhodes & Shanklin, 1993). Sensitivity refers to the extent to which the learner expects to learn. Sensitivity is also social, in that others can greatly encourage or discourage the act of reading. Smith states that these three terms can be defined separately, but they are best understood as acting together in real social contexts.

Although there are some differences in these models, they are more similar than not. All of them view reading as a constructive cognitive process and the reader as an active participant in the act of reading. They all reject the notion of a reader as a passive receptor of visual information acquired from moving the eyes back and forth across a page of print. All recognize that readers bring to the task of reading their prior knowledge, which is organized into mental structures called schemata. The nature of such schemata greatly influence the reader's ability to read and comprehend passages. And all of the models recognize the importance of sociological variables in almost all reading contexts.

Reading and Hearing Children

Reading is a complex skill and, as such, is composed of many components. Hearing children, when they begin the task of learning to read, are already familiar with many of these essential parts. In the first 5 or 6 years of their lives, they have developed a substantial vocabulary and have mastered most of the major syntactic structures of the English language (King & Quigley, 1985). They bring to the reading task a rich background of experiential knowledge with which they have developed various schemata, enabling them to manipulate prior knowledge and understand current information. King and Quigley stated that prereading hearing children generally have the strategies to link textual information, which indicates that they have already developed some inferential and figurative language skills that are critical to the comprehension process.

In summary, hearing children bring the following to the task of learning to read: a substantial vocabulary, experiential knowledge, a wide variety of developing schemata, cognitive development, linguistic competence in the English language, inference skills, and skills in figurative language. All of these attributes involve higher-order thinking skills and are complex components of the reading process. What hearing children do not bring to the task of learning to read is a repertoire of decoding skills; thus, a large part of a kindergartner's and first grader's reading instruction is devoted to the acquisition of those skills.

Figurative Language

Figurative expressions are elements of language that add interest and color to the message being communicated; at the same time, they are complex components of language that frequently confuse young readers. Some examples of figurative language include figures of speech such as similes (*She is as busy as a bee*), metaphors (*He's an old bear*), and onomatopoeia (*The constant varoom of the jets overhead*). Another form of figurative language is idiomatic language, including such examples as *You put your foot in your mouth*; *I looked over your report last night*; and *That noise drives me up a tree*.

Few investigations have been conducted on figurative language, probably because of the complex interactions of its components. For example, figurative language can involve interactions of grammar (vocabulary, syntax), meaning (semantics), and function (pragmatics) (Paul & Quigley, 1990). It should also be noted that geographical and cultural differences in figurative and idiomatic expressions influence the comprehension of those expressions by readers.

Inference

Inference is essential to reading comprehension once the reader moves beyond literal text material, which is at about the 3rd-grade level (King & Quigley, 1985). Anderson (1981) discussed functional, four-level classification of inferences that should be beneficial to reading teachers for organizing instruction. The first level is lexically based: inferencing depends a great deal on the reader's knowledge of language; understanding inferences is relatively independent of the particular context in which the lexical items occur. For example, in the sentence *She was so petite that she had difficulty buying appropriate clothes*, the reader must have some knowledge of the word *petite* to infer that the person was exceptionally tiny and beyond the age at which she could wear "little girl" clothes. At the second level, inferring occurs when the reader uses prior knowledge to figure out that two text propositions must be connected even though, objectively, there does not appear to be a connection. For example, in the sentences *One sunny day, Joe decided to go to the store. Fortunately, he looked out the window and then grabbed his umbrella before he left the house*, there is no apparent connection between the two propositions *he looked out the window* and *then grabbed his umbrella*. However, by applying prior knowledge (the sun may be shining, but black clouds could be approaching), the reader can make sense of the text and see the logical link between the two propositions. The third level of inferring occurs when the reader has activated schematic with unfilled slots and must supply the slot-filling information. The fourth level occurs when there is constant and repeated interaction of text and schemata to refine the schemata and provide an interpretive framework for the text. This last level of inferring occurs frequently in technical materials or advanced textbooks as the reader struggles to understand and, in doing so, brings to bear all prior knowledge and experiences (schemata) available to try to construct meaning. All of these levels of inferring occur automatically for skilled readers, to the point that, after reading a passage, they frequently cannot recall what they read from the page and what information they added through use of inferences (Brewer, 1975; Spiro, 1977).

Metacognitive Skills

Reading comprehension is a metacognitive process in which readers are aware of and have control over their comprehension. There are two components of metacognition; the first involves awareness of task requirements, and the second involves the ability to use self-monitoring skills (Searfoss & Readence, 1989). Awareness of task requirements implies that the reader must be aware of and know the skills, strategies, and resources that are necessary to complete a task successfully. Self-monitoring of metacognitive skills refers to the reader's use of self-regulatory activities such as checking the outcome of problem-solving attempts, planning and evaluating the effectiveness of any attempted actions, testing and reviewing strategies used in learning, and taking remediating action to overcome difficulties encountered (Baker & Brown, 1984).

Skilled readers of text generally understand that the purpose of reading is to read for meaning. They know how to use specific strategies to facilitate comprehension, and they monitor their own comprehension as they read, implementing "fix-up" strategies when they realize they are not comprehending. Readers who are not as skilled may have difficulty with reading comprehension for a number of reasons. They may not actively read for meaning, focusing on readings more as a decoding process than as a meaning-getting process (Taylor et al., 1988). They may not select and apply a variety of comprehension strategies to match the task requirements, and they are probably not as effective at monitoring their own comprehension. When they are not comprehending, they may not realize it; thus, they may not apply fix-up strategies.

Metacognitive skills become increasingly important in the later elementary grades and on through high school, when the emphasis in reading shifts from learning to read to reading to learn (King & Quigley, 1985). This can be a difficult transition for readers who focus on reading as a decoding process rather than a comprehension process. Sullivan (1978) reported that unskilled readers, even at the high school level, lacked the metacognitive awareness that text must be interpreted in relation to what the student already knows about the topic and were still viewing reading as a decoding process.

Reading and Deaf Children

Hearing children bring most of the high-order cognitive skills to the task of learning to read: they have a well-developed vocabulary, a substantial assortment of schemata, adequately developed cognitive structures, linguistic competence in the English language, inference skills, and skills in figurative language. What hearing children lack as they begin to learn to read are decoding skills. Unfortunately, the same is not true for most deaf and hard of hearing children.

Vocabulary

The vocabularies of deaf and hard of hearing students are far below those of their hearing peers (Anderson & Freebody, 1985; Paul & O'Rourke, 1988), and to compound the problem, deaf and hard of hearing students acquire new words at a slower rate than do their hearing peers (LaSasso & Davey, 1987; Paul, 1984). One reason for this is that while hearing students can acquire new words through context clues, deaf and hard of hearing students frequently do not have the skills (or the English-language facility) to use context clues to figure out meanings. Deaf and hard of hearing students quite likely have experiential backgrounds that are similar to their hearing peers; however, there is one important difference: For the most part, the experiences of deaf and hard of hearing children have not been linked to language because of the frequent lack of communication between the child and the rest of the family. Without the link to language, deaf children have difficulty connecting their experiences to the printed words.

Marschark (1993) proposed that processes at the word recognition level contribute to the difficulties that deaf children have in reading and suggested that when word recognition is not automatic, a greater demand is placed on the working memory. This greater demand on the working memory results in less capacity being available for integration of semantic information, which aids in syntactic processing.

Cognition

Earlier in this chapter, the discussion indicated that the cognitive structures of deaf and hard of hearing children and hearing children are probably similar, but whether they follow similar developmental patterns and timelines has not yet been determined. However, the linguistic competence of deaf children has received considerable attention (Quigley & Paul, 1984; Quigley, Wilbur, Power, Montanelli, & Steinkamp, 1976; Wilbur, 1987).

Linguistic Competence

Similar to the findings on vocabulary development, the results of investigations on the syntactic development of deaf students have indicated that most 18- to 19-year-old students performed at levels somewhat lower than 8- to 9-year-old hearing students (Quigley et al., 1976). Deaf students usually do not have highly developed inference skills. Although research on this topic is limited, all of the findings so far indicate poor inference skills (Wilson, 1979; see discussion in King & Quigley, 1985) and difficulty in answering nonliteral questions. The poor inference skills of deaf and hard of hearing students probably promote their use of inappropriate strategies such as word association, copying, and visual matching on vocabulary and reading tests (Davey & LaSasso, 1983; LaSasso, 1986; Wolk & Schildroth, 1984).

Figurative Language

Deaf and hard of hearing students have difficulty with many aspects of figurative language. This finding is not surprising in light of the fact that figurative language contains a great deal of interaction among linguistic components such as vocabulary and syntax, two areas in which deaf and hard of hearing students have considerable problems. Knowledge of some figurative elements requires more than knowledge of grammar and vocabulary, as in such examples as *He is knocking his head against a brick wall.* The sentence has a simple syntactic structure, and the vocabulary is not difficult; yet attention to vocabulary and syntax alone will not reveal the meaning of the statement. Fruchter, Wilbur, and Fraser (1984) found that deaf and hard of hearing students' knowledge of figurative language is related to their reading achievement levels.

Metacognitive Skills

Very few studies investigating the metacognitive abilities of deaf and hard of hearing students have been conducted. Quigley et al. (1976) conducted research in which students judged the grammaticality of English sentences. While they were not directly investigating metacognitive skills, through extrapolation they inferred that most deaf and severely hard of hearing students do not have effective metacognitive skills for reading. This finding should not be attributed to innate deficiencies in the cognitive structures of deaf and hard of hearing students; instead, it is probably due to the fact that the students had not been taught how to use metacognitive strategies during the process of reading.

Environmental Factors

Teachers have always known that nearly everything that happens in a student's home environment affects what happens to the student at school. However, in terms of the child's reading performance, some factors are more influential than others. The most important home environment factors affecting a child's progress in reading are the language environment of the home and the types of values that a child learns from the home environment (Taylor et al., 1988). While Taylor and her associates were referring to hearing children, the same is true for deaf and hard of hearing children.

Because the reading process is also a language process, it is not surprising that a great deal of importance is placed on the child's home language environment. The absence of a mutually shared communication system between the deaf child and the rest of the family has an adverse effect on the child's development of language and, subsequently, on the process of reading. Most deaf children with hearing parents who communicate using oral English are unable to develop a mastery of the English language before they begin the task of learning to read (McAnally, Rose, & Quigley, 1994). The same is true of deaf children with deaf parents who use American Sign Language for communication. The difference between the two groups is that deaf children of deaf parents have already acquired one language (ASL), making it easier for them to acquire a second language, in this case English (Israelite, Ewoldt, & Hoffmeister, 1992). In a study of the relationship between American Sign Language skills and English literacy among deaf children (Strong & Prinz, 1997), the results indicated that deaf children's learning of English appeared to benefit from the acquisition of even a moderate fluency in ASL.

Success in school is also facilitated when there is a match in home values and school values. Failure is more likely when the two sets of values do not match, thus causing a value conflict within the child. Some schools appear better able to accommodate differences in value orientation than others. If the school does not make accommodations for the differences, then the child must do so. Usually, the students who succeed are those who are able either to change their values or to accept the school's values, at least within the context of the school environment (Taylor et al., 1988). If academic achievement is not valued in the home, then it is usually difficult to motivate that child to devote time and attention to learning to read. The same is true if other more basic factors (such as lack of money to buy food, concern over gang and drug activity in the neighborhood) are taking precedence over a desire to learn to read. This discussion is not intended to imply that all children from lower socioeconomic environments are, or will be, poor readers. Socioeconomic levels are probably related factors, but if the parents in the home value reading; have high expectations for the child; and provide plenty of reading materials, encouragement, and assistance in reading, the child is highly likely to be successful in reading endeavors regardless of socioeconomic status (King & Quigley, 1985).

Diverse Student Populations

Changes in the composition of public school populations have been dramatic in the past 10 years. The same is true for schools and programs for deaf and hard of hearing students. Recent data from the U.S. Bureau of the Census indicate that the trend toward classroom diversity will continue. By the year 2020, 1 of 2 public school students will be from a minority background, and the number of children living in poverty will increase by 37%. Schools will probably be serving 5.4 million more children living in poverty in 2020 than they served in the early 1990s (Au, 1993). Classrooms, including classrooms for deaf and hard of hearing students, are not only becoming more linguistically, culturally, and economically diverse, they are also becoming more diverse in the disabilities and various types of learning problems exhibited by students. More and more students entering schools and programs for deaf and hard of hearing youngsters are being diagnosed with additional problems that affect learning. Some of the additional problems with which teachers are now trying to cope are attention-deficit/hyperactivity disorder (ADHD), specific learning disabilities (SLD), and a variety of behavioral and emotional problems. This change in the population has occurred rather rapidly, and no research has yet produced results that will help teachers deal with these complex students. In fact, it is not yet known what the interplay between the hearing loss and the additional disability might be and whether one compounds the effects of the other. Many of these students do not seem to respond to the "regular" instructional strategies employed by teachers; they seem to require instructional and behavioral strategies that have yet to be defined.

The different student population has made teaching more challenging and demanding than ever before (Vacca & Vacca, 1996). Diverse learners become quite academically and emotionally vulnerable when placed in instructional contexts that require them to engage in reading and writing. More often than not, students with diverse backgrounds become caught in a cycle of school failure that contributes to very marginal achievement and a sense of helplessness and frustration in learning situations.

Reading Achievement Levels

Studies conducted over the past 80 years have consistently indicated that deaf students have a great deal of difficulty in reading English text. As early as 1916,

Pintner and Patterson administered a reading test on following directions to deaf students who were 14 to 16 years of age and reported results indicating that the deaf students were reading at levels similar to those of 7-year-old hearing students. Unfortunately, investigators who have conducted studies since that time have reported similar results.

The accuracy of the results of earlier investigations has been questioned because deaf and hard of hearing students were not included in the norming samples. However, an adapted version of the *Stanford Achievement Test* was developed and normed on national samples of deaf and hard of hearing students. This adapted version, the *Stanford Achievement Test–Hearing Impaired* (SAT–HI), is now the most commonly used standardized assessment tool in programs for deaf and hard of hearing youngsters (Paul & Quigley, 1990). Despite the adaptations, the results using the SAT–HI consistently indicate that 18- to 19-year-old severely to profoundly deaf students are reading at levels similar to those of 9- to 10-year-old hearing students. These test results also show that deaf students increase their reading levels by only about .3 grade level per year and seem to plateau at about the 3rd- or 4th-grade reading level (Center for Assessment and Demographic Studies, 1991). It must be noted, however, that some deaf students do become adept at processing English text. Approximately 3% of profoundly deaf 18 year olds read at a level equal to that of their hearing peers (Center for Assessment and Demographic Studies, 1991). Kelly (1993) found that knowledge of English grammatical conventions, regardless of how difficult they are for deaf children to acquire, seem to make a significant contribution to reading competence in skilled deaf readers.

Clearly, educators must continue to search for reading approaches and instructional strategies that will prove to be a better match for the learning aptitudes of deaf and hard of hearing students. These students have the ability, the potential to learn to read, and investigators and teacher researchers must continue in their quest to find information that will answer the question "How?" In the meantime, teachers must strive to remain current in what is happening in reading—What are the most promising practices being used with hearing children, and how can these be used or adapted for use with deaf and hard of hearing students? Some of the most promising strategies being used today are interactive strategies, which are discussed in later chapters in this book.

Summary

Reading is both a language and a cognitive process and, as such, is closely associated with other language processes—listening/seeing, speaking/signing, and writing. As with language and cognition, reading deals with the subsystems of phonology, graphemes, semantics, and syntax. As a cognitive process, it involves the mental operations that comprise most kinds of thinking—attention, perception, encoding, memory, and retrieval.

In the research on information processing and the relationship of short-term memory to reading, it was found that most severely to profoundly deaf readers use a mediating system consisting of a combination of non–speech-based codes such as signing, finger spelling, and visual imagery to derive meaning from the printed word. However, readers who mediate primarily using a speech-based code were found to be much better readers than those using nonspeech codes. This advantage was attributed to the speech recoder's ability to hold more language information in short-term memory, and that kind of information may be necessary for comprehending hierarchical structures in the English language. This research on STM emphasizes the importance of the development of cognition and language to the development of reading.

The group of interactive theories known as schema theories probably provide the most convincing account of reading as cognitive process. Schema theory helps to explain five common processing problems frequently encountered by readers: schema availability, schema selection, schema maintenance, overreliance on bottom-up processing, and overreliance on top-down processing. Schema theories also emphasize the critical role that prior knowledge plays in comprehension.

When hearing children approach the task of learning to read, they have already developed most of the higher-order skills involved in reading. They bring to the task a substantial store of background experiences that have been linked to language, along with the development of cognition, language, and schema; inferring skills; and figurative language abilities. Subsequently, they are free to focus on a lower-order reading skill—decoding. Deaf and severely hard of hearing children are not as fortunate. They have not yet developed most of the higher-order skills that are prerequisites for reading, and they are trying to learn to read the printed form of a language (usually English) that they have not yet mastered in oral/auditory or any other form. So, there is no language base for reading. It is not surprising, therefore, that the reading achievement levels of deaf children are distressingly below those of their hearing peers.

Children's home environment also influence the process of learning to read. Two very important home environment factors are the language environment and the types of values that children learn from their families. Success in reading is more likely when there is a shared communication system in the home that gives the child access to language, and when there is a match between the home value system and the value system of the school. The lack of language access in the home or a mismatch between the value systems of home and school compounds the difficulties that deaf and hard of hearing children will encounter as they approach the task of learning to read.

LITERACY DEVELOPMENT

Preview

In response to society's concern for developing increased literacy proficiency among hearing and deaf individuals alike, widespread debate and reforms have occurred. Emphasis has been placed on the criteria used to define reading and writing skills as well as the processes used to achieve fluency in communication. Literacy programs have become popular avenues for philanthropy and volunteerism. "Literacy for all people" campaigns have become the penicillin of education. Illiteracy has been identified as one of the many "diseases" of our society that must be eradicated to fix our social and economic ills. Recognition of factors that can reverse illiteracy and our ability to implement practices that promote literacy will determine the achievement of goals and outcomes with deaf and hard of hearing children.

The interpretation of literacy and its implications regarding how and what to teach deaf children creates endless debate (Moores, 1996). While there is abundant literature documenting differences and delays in reading and writing abilities among deaf and hard of hearing children, there is evidence that deaf children can achieve functional and fluent literacy when the appropriate conditions and opportunities are provided. This chapter provides an overview of the construct of literacy and the evolution of perspectives in response to the condition of illiteracy. Specific focus is given to types of literacy that have an impact on the acquisition of reading and writing skills including cultural, social, and content literacy, as well as factors that influence the development of those skills. While this entire book focuses on research, practices, and processes related to reading and writing, this chapter provides an overview and perspective on the dimensions of literacy and their relationships to the product of communication through reading and writing with children who are deaf or hard of hearing. Specifically, this chapter includes historical aspects of literacy movements, types of literacy, and common factors that influence literacy development. Emergent literacy skills among deaf and hearing children are discussed, including the use of alternative languages and channels of communication. Skill development (e.g., phonological knowledge, comprehension), instructional strategies, and educational practices related to literacy appear in later sections of this book.

Historical Perspective

Literacy is frequently discussed as a tool that can provide individuals with knowledge, power, and independence. Morris and Tchudi (1996) noted that the repetitive concern for universal literacy is based on the notion that lack of literacy is at the core of poverty, unemployment, and general upheaval in society. Continual comparisons are made among students from various social, racial, cultural, and ethnic groups to demonstrate the associations of literacy with conditions such as teen pregnancy, drug use, and dropout rates. In his book *Illiterate America*, Kozol (1985, pp. 13–15) presented a series of facts associated with the condition of illiteracy:

- the estimated cost to businesses and taxpayers is in excess of 20 billion per year;
- over half of American adults are unable to read at the 8th-grade level;
- 85% of all juvenile offenders have reading problems;
- 60% of America's prison inmates are illiterate;
- 20% of American adults are functionally illiterate, and an additional 34% are only marginally literate;
- men (ages 25–34 years) with limited high school skills will lose more than $237 billion in earnings over their lifetimes.

Historically, illiteracy has had a stigmatic quality not unlike leprosy and AIDS. Illiteracy has been associated with the poor, inner cities, extreme rural cultures, immigrants, minorities, individuals who are cognitively deficient, and the disenfranchised, while high literacy levels have been indices of suburbanites and the well-educated, professionally employed, and empowered segments of our society. Deaf and hard of hearing people have been frequently deemed illiterate based simply on the quality of their oral and auditory communication skills. Roger Carver (1990) described the historical condition of deaf people as "being trapped in a literacy ghetto from which there was little hope of escape. Their poor literacy status ensured that they would remain in a vicious cycle of powerlessness, dependence and marginality, robbing them of their dignity and their rightful place in society" (p. 1).

Periodically, political and social movements have called for the elimination of illiteracy through crusades, campaigns, and legislative mandates. In recent decades, movements have exploded across the country, among them the 1964 Economic Opportunity Act, Title II-b, Barbara Bush's promotion for early reading initiatives with the goal to eliminate illiteracy during her husband's presidential administration (B. A. Quigley, 1997), and the 1997 Read America program on college campuses across the nation, as well as the Starbuck's coffee cup message announcing, "Read in order to live (G. Flaubert). Reading provides hope, discovery and opportunity. . . . Join the fight for literacy. Help others discover hope and opportunity." These causes, crusades, and slogans illustrate society's concern for universal literacy. B. Allen Quigley (1997, p. 34) chronicled 143 articles in the *New York Times* from 1980 to 1993 focused on issues of illiteracy and a search for the "cure" to society's problems through reading, writing, and effective communication skills.

Within the field of education for children who are deaf and hard of hearing, the concern for literacy is magnified by the challenge of achieving communicative and linguistic fluency. In their text *The Education of Deaf Children*, Quigley and Kretschmer (1982) stated that "the primary goal of education for typical (non-multiply handicapped) prelingually deaf children should be literacy" (p. xi). This position is reflected in approximately 40% of the articles published from 1990 through 1996 in the field of deaf education (in *The Volta Review*, *American Annals of the Deaf*, *Journal of Deaf Studies and Deaf Education*, and *Perspectives for Teachers of the Hearing Impaired*) that included "literacy" in the title or abstract (Rose, 1997). This growing emphasis on the development of literacy skills in children who are deaf or hard of hearing emanates not only from the demands and concerns of society in general but also from the consistently low English-based achievement levels repeatedly reported in the literature (Allen, 1986; Kelly, 1995; Moores, 1996; Paul & Quigley, 1994).

In 1965 the Babbidge Committee Report cited the critical underachievement in reading and writing among deaf children and adults. The report called for a major initiative in research related to literacy, and the training of educators to improve the conditions of unemployment and underemployment. The Commission on Education of the Deaf reported more than two decades later (1988) to the Congress of the United States that 200 years of research focusing on educational practices in achieving English literacy have been "remarkably unproductive: deaf students are still graduating from high schools coast to coast with third and fourth grade reading achievement scores." This urgency has been exacerbated by society's demands for higher levels of literacy among our youth, requirements for higher graduation standards in our high schools, and national testing practices for all students, including deaf, hard of hearing, and hearing students.

Defining literacy has occupied generations of educators, sociologists, and bureaucrats. In its most primitive definition, literacy may be considered synonymous with the ability to read and write (Teale & Sulzby, 1986). Fluency in oral communication has been an implied prerequisite within literate communities (Carver, 1990). An early measure of a literate person was the ability to write one's name on a piece of paper; later measures included the ability to read a simple familiar text (Graves, Watts, & Graves, 1994). Testing of literacy levels in the 1960s included measures of how well adults functioned in the real world, while some practitioners searched for grade levels as a literacy measure and others argued for the inclusion of IQ in the criteria of a literate person (B. A. Quigley, 1997). Reflecting the ideologies of the 1970s and 1980s for the inclusion of cultural literacy (Hirsch, 1988) and the application of contextual criteria and function in the definition of literacy, the 1988 Right to Literacy Conference extended the meaning of literacy to include the use of language to think critically, to synthesize judgment, and to form original perspectives (Padden & Ramsey, 1993). The U.S. Department of Education attempted to establish a baseline for literacy through the National Literacy Act of 1991 (*Highlights of the National Literacy Act*, 1991) and provided a definition that has more quantitative standards, including: "An individual's ability to read, write and speak in English, and compute and solve problems at levels of proficiency necessary to function on the job in society, to achieve one's goals, and develop one's knowledge and potential" (National Literacy Act of 1991, Section 3).

While definitions set standards, those definitions failed to meet the needs of social and political platforms among various advocacy groups (B. A. Quigley, 1997). Morris and Tchudi (1996, pp. 12–13) proposed a multifaceted definition illustrated through integrated circles to include three perspectives:

1. *basic literacy*—the ability to decode and encode, to pick up a book and not only recall the words but also say what they mean.

2. *critical literacy*—the ability to move beyond the literal meanings, to interpret texts, and to use writing not only to record facts but also to analyze, interpret, and explain, for example, when people discuss a movie, argue over political issues, analyze scientific data, or interpret a law brief or a contract.

3. *dynamic literacy*—the ability to go beyond text to encompass the use of related skills, for example, the skills and abilities associated with science literacy, historical literacy, computer literacy, baseball literacy, plumbing literacy, and so forth.

These integrated perspectives provide a wide range of skills that may impact on curriculum and instructional practices in school settings. Minimally, schools emphasize basic literacy, although students often achieve critical and dynamic literacy through home, school, and community experiences.

In the field of education with deaf and hard of hearing individuals, defining literacy is generally an implicit process rather than an explicit one. For example, the Center for Studies in Education and Human Development at the Gallaudet Research Institute conducted a national study regarding literacy in deaf adolescents with deaf parents and literacy in deaf adolescents in total communication programs (Moores, 1987). "Levels of literacy" were defined through measures of English-based reading comprehension and writing samples including a descriptive narrative and a business letter. Other measures that helped to define levels of literacy were academic achievement, and person-to-person communication incorporating oral language, English-based signs, and American Sign Language. In a theoretical review, Peter Paul (1996) discussed English literacy as a first or second language in deaf children. His definition focused on what Morris and Tchudi (1996) referred to earlier as "basic literacy," that is, the ability to read or write printed materials required by the mainstream environment. In another article focusing on the improvement of English literacy and speech communication skills, Nelson and Camarata (1997) implied that literacy includes communicative mastery, that is, normative, age-appropriate language fluency including spoken English, text, and sign language as indicators of literate achievement skills among deaf and hard of hearing learners. In an empirical study regarding the relationship between ASL and English, Strong and Prinz (1997) explicitly defined "English literacy" as reading and writing skills measured through the *Woodcock-Johnson Psycho-Educational Test Battery* and the *Test of Written Language*.

While no one definition of literacy is commonly accepted, the kaleidoscope of perspectives indicates that literacy extends far beyond the fundamentals of reading and writing. Literacy requires that deaf and hearing children alike be able to communicate—that is, respond to and interact with other people, as well as a variety of materials such as texts, novels, directions, documents, and computers, for the purpose of doing something as a result of reading, analyzing, reasoning, and problem solving. The complexity of determining literacy among children who are deaf is dependent on the expectations of society, demands of the environment, and inclusive perspectives on language and communication modalities. The challenge for educators is to formulate literacy goals in concert with the expectations of society and the personal goals, potential, and knowledge of the learner.

Types of Literacy

Literacy includes a wide range of definitions and perspectives that require the attention of professionals in the classroom. While the majority of literacy issues focus on the fundamental skills of reading and writing, other aspects of literacy influence the way an individual is evaluated as "being literate." The aspects of literacy that affect *what* is included in school curricula and *how* are cultural literacy, social literacy, and content literacy.

Cultural

Fluency and versatility in reading and writing are increasingly critical skills in today's society, particularly with computer-based communication and the exponential availability of information technology. Inherent in the process of acquiring cultural literacy is the anticipated acquisition of a common knowledge base or set of referents, frequently referred to as world knowledge. For example, the question *Is Paris close to Europe?* indicates the absence of what is considered common knowledge, or cultural literacy. Hirsch (1988) proposed that cultural literacy should include knowledge of literary, historical, and scientific facts that are commonly known in addition to assuming an automaticity in the recognition and production of text. Cultural literacy extends beyond the basic communication skills of reading and writing to include context and background information. Inherent in cultural literacy is the ability to communicate and participate in a standard language (McLaren, 1988). For traditionalists such as Hirsh, cultural literacy is considered a critical component for participation in "the political and cultural life of the nation." Concepts such as socialism, and rule of thumb are just a few examples included in his mandates for a culturally literate individual (Hirsh, 1988, pp. 152–215).

The idea of cultural literacy as a defined set of knowledge and skills has been severely criticized as elitism (B. A. Quigley, 1990). Critics suggest the inclusion of and adaptation to characteristics within various ethnic, racial, or religious environments, with an emphasis on the context of literacy including an array of settings, goals, and topics (Hornberger, 1989). Cultural literacy from a broader perspective includes knowledge about the culture in which an individual chooses to participate, as well as adaptation to the characteristics of that populace. The presence of functional knowledge and communication fluency in the social context is far more critical to cultural literacy than the specification of a predefined body of knowledge (Morris & Tchudi, 1996).

In a classic ethnographic study of literacy among African American and Anglo American working-class communities, Heath (1980) described the variations of reading and writing across contexts of use and the functions these variations have served across time and cultural communities. Literacy in the context of Heath's study extended beyond linguistic skills and achievement scores to include communication fluency and flexibility. She called for the recognition of cultural literacy as a basis for instructional planning and the provision of more appropriate learning opportunities for all children.

A number of researchers (Mather, 1989; Maxwell & Doyle, 1996; Schick & Gale, 1995; Schleper, 1997) are engaged in the ethnographic description of cultural literacy within deaf families and school settings in an effort to extend cultural literacy development to include the deaf and hard of hearing communities. Their findings may impact on the communication and literacy practices in home and school settings with deaf and hard of hearing children. Au and Mason (1983) illustrated the cultural variability of literacy through the superior performance of young children who are taught to read in situations that are compatible with those of their home culture, such as refrigerator notes, Bible passages, directions for preparing dinner, and TTY messages. Knowledge of communication and cultural practices among literate deaf and hearing parents and teachers may contribute to increased cultural literacy for all children who are deaf or hard of hearing.

Social

Becoming literate is a social process involving a complex set of experiences and expectations. As a social process, literacy affects our daily functioning and has a different meaning for each person. The process of becoming literate requires a myriad of social events, including interactions with the environment and adult role models. Literacy events such as reading, writing, and discussing storybooks, novels, and current events may be familiar to some children, while others may be more literate in accessing the Internet, using the TTY, the World Wide Web and JAVA; still others are experienced as storytellers and negotiators. Smith, Carey, and Harste (1982, p. 22) suggest a hierarchical social context of literacy as:

- *linguistic*—text that is visually represented on the page;
- *situational*—incorporating the linguistic text into the setting where reading and writing occur (e.g., in a classroom or dormitory) and the expectations

of the setting (e.g., leaving a note for the family, writing to a friend, making a kite); and

- *cultural*—the social and political contexts in which reading and writing occur (e.g., graduation proficiency exam, testimonial).

Each student comes to the classroom with a unique set of social literacy experiences that challenge the educator to use those experiences and that knowledge in the educational context of the classroom. Because it is a social process with a deeply rooted cultural base, literacy will necessarily differ among individuals in different contexts. Children arrive at school with linguistic, situational, and cultural experiences determined by the quantity and quality of their interactions including print, aural and oral, and signed interactions. The situational schemata and cultural knowledge of the world will structure the development of literacy both within the school setting and beyond it. Children who are deaf or hard of hearing resulting from significant medical trauma (e.g., meningitis, low birth weight) or whose families have immigrated from other countries experience distinctive socialization processes when compared to deaf children of literate deaf parents. While deaf and hard of hearing children are frequently described using homogeneous solutions for advancing academic achievement, linguistic, cultural, and situational distinctions influence the educational adaptations required for literacy development and proficiency.

Content

Content literacy incorporates the use of reading, writing, and communicating about different texts for different purposes. During the 1970s and 1980s, many secondary schools added explicit instructional programs to develop content-area reading skills. Much of the interest in this area has expanded to incorporate all aspects of communication on specific topics, such as mathematics, the sciences, and social and psychological studies, and includes the broad perspective of literacy instruction incorporating oral, reading, writing, and critical-thinking skills (Anders & Guzzetti, 1996). For example, English teachers team with social studies or science teachers to provide unified instruction in content literacy. For deaf and hard of hearing students, additional aspects of content literacy may be evident in the effective use of interpreters; content-related technical signs; aural, oral and sign communication fluency; and note taking.

Wells (1990, p. 4) identified three categories for content literacy. The first category was *directive* texts—that is, content material that encourages the reader to do something, such as directions on medication containers, bus schedules, and advertisements. The second category of content reading includes materials that contain *factual* information, such as dictionaries, science books, and office memos. The third category includes *interpretive* views or experiences as recorded by the author, such as poems, plays, novels, theories, and historical text. This classification scheme helped to arrange the types of instruction required for specific areas of content reading and writing.

The need for specific instruction in content literacy was illustrated through early studies that focused on reading and writing skills required "on the job" compared to those skills taught in school. Diehl and Mikulecky (1980) studied 200 occupations, identifying the demands for reading, the types of print material encountered, and the strategies used to complete the tasks. The authors reported that 99% of daily reading was done at work, for an average of 2 hours per day. The authors also reported that when asked why they read, 40% of the people interviewed responded that they read to do something with no learning, 26% read to do tasks, 23% read to do something with incidental learning, and 11% read to learn. In a study of reading activities in the community outside of the work setting, Guthrie and Seifert (1983) found that working adults spent an average of 2.5 hours per day reading. The time spent reading ranged from 1 hour for unskilled workers to 4 hours per day for professionals. The most frequently read materials included newspapers, newsletters, business documents, and directions, which consumed about 30 minutes per day. The second most commonly read content included news and business forms, which occupied approximately 20 minutes. Slightly less time was spent reading materials related to social issues. Utilitarian materials such as manuals, directories, and classified ads in newspapers ranked fourth in frequency, with 11 minutes per day. Fiction literature, short stories, magazines, and newspaper humor pieces were read for approximately 7 minutes, while printed information regarding sports and recreation received 4 minutes per day. Mason and Au (1986, p. 424) question the match between content literacy practices in school settings and those anticipated in the workplace. With the introduction of captioning, TTYs, and Internet communication in the workplace, home, school, and community settings, the requirement for content literacy is increasing at exponential rates.

As a means of facilitating content literacy, topical text materials were developed for use in educational settings with deaf and hard of hearing children (King & Quigley, 1985). A wide range of publications focusing on daily living skills (Olsen, 1984), science (Doblmeier, 1981; Fleury, 1982), money management (Kearney, 1981; Slater, 1981), and other content areas were commercially available. These specialized materials attempted to eliminate the process of "learning to read" while engaged in "reading to learn" by adapting and controlling the vocabulary, syntax, and amount of content presented. In a national survey of educational programs for deaf and hard of hearing children, King (1983) identified a minimum of 35 content-area texts written specifically for deaf students (King & Quigley, 1985, pp. 166–168). However, less than a third of these types of materials are available for use with deaf and hard of hearing people today. Research and special interests in the philosophy of "whole language" and other systems emphasizing implicit instruction have had a significant impact and have shifted the instructional approaches for literacy in the content areas away from "skill-specific" practices. In addition, economics and the "inclusive" movement in education have altered the availability of and demand for specialized content materials for deaf and hard of hearing students.

Factors Influencing Literacy

While an infinite number of events influence the development of literacy skills, three specific factors appear to have the greatest impact. Literacy research consistently identifies the family as the foundation for establishing motivation and values that include experiences in literacy development. The school, community, and social environments reinforce the values established through the family and create a setting in which becoming a literate individual is highly rewarding and desirable. Attitudes toward literacy are the third factor; they extend from the family to the school, community, and social settings.

Family

Because literacy is an interactive social process that is linked to cultural practices and expectations, the family is perhaps the most significant factor in the development of reading, writing, and communication fluency. Family literacy crosses the boundaries of socioeconomic and educational status. Heath (1983) compared literacy practices in the Carolina Piedmonts among working-class and middle-class families of Anglo American and African American cultures. She described a distinct difference in the parent-child interactions of middle-class and working-class families during storybook reading. Storybook reading was not a common practice among African American working-class families when compared to middle-class Anglo American families. While materials and topics of discussion differed between the African American and Anglo American cultural groups, the experiences in literacy development other than the practice of storybook reading were similar. Families' attitudes, practices, and values supported and advocated for literacy skills among their young children. However, teacher and school literacy expectations more commonly favored Anglo American middle-class families. The social, cultural, and content literacies within the African American families were either unknown or not recognized by the teachers or the school. Heath's documentary of family literacy practices has spurred a host of inquiries regarding typical behaviors that affect the development of dynamic literacy skills.

Taylor's (1983) study of six suburban parents identified specific literacy activities used in the home environment. She reported that parents of successful readers provide their children with storybooks at bedtime, paper-and-pencil activities, and other print materials in home and community settings. These families used written language, calendars, family correspondence, and other naturally occurring activities to provide opportunities for children to read a host of print materials, draw pictures, and write names of family members. Social interactions with family members included storytelling, frequently repeated readings of favorite books and family stories, writing notes to family members jointly with the children, "reading" children's attempts at writing, and posting messages for visitors. These types of activities provided children with a knowledge of literacy and the role of reading and writing in everyday functions. The frequency of events in which reading, writing, and general communications were used emphasized the value and importance of literacy to the children within their own homes. These home values were reaffirmed for the children when they experienced a high degree of success in reading at school.

Children who are deaf or hard of hearing are significantly influenced by family literacy and communication values in much the same way as children who are hearing. Whether the parents are deaf or hearing, children assimilate literate behaviors through the actions of and interactions with family members. Families who accommodate the child's need for visual, auditory, and experiential learning opportunities not only increase access to communication but also enhance the literacy learning process (Ewoldt, 1990; Truax, 1992). Maxwell (1985) reported literacy events among deaf families with a deaf child and hearing families with a deaf child. Through her interviews with and observations of 40 deaf and hearing adults, she concluded that opportunities for writing and reading were much greater within deaf families when compared to predominantly hearing families. These opportunities generally included the availability of TTYs in homes, as well as informational notes and messages. Albertini and Shannon (1996) revisited Maxwell's inquiry nearly a decade later and found greater synchrony between deaf and hearing families. In the latter study, nearly all of both deaf and hearing families had TTYs in their homes, with additional TTYs available at the parents' workplace. Communication through note writing also occurred across family settings, with the highest frequency occurring as *instrumental* writing, that is, reading or writing to convey information (e.g., what time parents would be home, where they were) and to give directives (e.g., clean your room, do your homework). *Social* writing (e.g., thank you notes, letters, greetings) was more common among hearing families with deaf children than among deaf families. The authors noted that this may also be a cultural func- tion, since a number of the respondents came from nonEurocentric cultures where social communication was defined in a variety of manners usually not including writing. *Expressive* writing such as in stories, diaries, and journals was practiced by only a few deaf students of hearing parents and not among children in deaf families.

Families, irrespective of hearing status, that spend time engaged in commu- nication by such means as reading and role-playing stories, writing letters, e-mailing messages, surfing the net, using the TTY, sharing discussions, using captioned TV and movies, and planning and negotiating family events provide foundations for literacy. Teachers who are able to create a fusion between home and school practices and recognize the diversity of experiences greatly enhance the opportunity for maximizing dynamic literacy growth in children (Barton & Ivanic, 1991).

Environment

The interpretations of literacy are consistently shaped by environmental expec- tations and demands. Internet chat rooms, TTYs, sign language interpreters, and captioning are creating new environments that shape the criteria for defin- ing literacy. Because communication is a social process, it is critical to incorpo- rate the larger contexts, including the situations where reading and writing are not only expected but required. Reading, writing, and communication for deaf and hearing individuals have changed as a result of new environmental demands. Educators are required to recognize those demands and to provide stu- dents with the skills to achieve literacy in an informationally explosive society (Hawisher & Selfe, 1989).

Literacy in the school environment differs considerably from that in home, work, and community settings. The match between the goals of the individual student and the environment and social expectations must be included in the instructional process if literacy is the primary goal of educators. Inclusion of deaf and hard of hearing students in general education classes creates a new and uniquely demanding environment for literacy functions. Communication with hearing peers may include passing of notes for social communication (Albertini & Shannon, 1996, p. 71) as well as for academic purposes. Communicating through computer-based technology (e.g., electronic note pads, e-mail) and interpreters, and use of real-time graphic displays, increases the environmental dynamics of literacy for deaf and hard of hearing youth.

Recognizing the critical influence that the environment has on experiences and knowledge of children, Gillespie and Twardosz (1996) surveyed residential schools for the deaf to identify common literacy practices in residences (dormitories and cottages). Twenty-six schools participated in the national survey. All of the schools reported that reading and writing materials including books, magazines, and newspapers, along with a variety of writing supplies were readily available in the children's residences. Adults read to the students one to three times per week, and letters home varied from three times per week to once a month. Included in several residential programs were a number of creative literacy activities including making posters for the dormitories, creative storytelling, discussion groups on current events, and library visits. The authors identified the need for a broader range of literacy materials, with diversity and rotation of stimuli, including books, magazines, and storyboards. The critical outcome of this study is the identification of the residential environment as having a vital role in the development of literacy skills, similar to the home and community experiences for hearing children, and the continuing emphasis that must be placed on providing opportunities for literacy development across environments that match with family, community, and career expectations.

Attitudes

Family and cultural attitudes regarding the function of literacy transmit critical values for school learning. Societal attitudes toward educational reform extend the need for a fully literate society including greater demands for reading, writing, oral communication, and computer-based communication, information storage, and retrieval. The resurgence of the desire for tougher educational norms and graduation performance standards, as well as national testing movements, has, once again, changed the criteria for achieving literacy. These criteria include the ability to express ideas effectively, the ability to identify propaganda and use reasoning and disciplined thought, and the ability to evaluate and not merely remember and recall information read. The attitudes of the family, the teacher, and the community toward literacy can be seen in the quantity and quality of time and effort spent on providing opportunities for the development of literacy.

As teachers engage in literacy instruction, it is important to recognize that students who are deaf or hard of hearing may differ significantly from each other in what they know and what they have experienced. The needs and goals of the learner—as well as the family, cultural norms, environment, and attitudes—must be considered in the development of literacy skills. With the implementation of the Americans with Disabilities Act and changing public attitudes to provide greater opportunities and mandates for "inclusiveness," the educational system serving deaf and hard of hearing children has been held more accountable for achieving increased proficiency in meeting the communication demands of the general society, including fluency in standard English reading and writing.

In contrast, Roger Carver's keynote address to the American Society of Deaf Children in 1990 admonishes the attitude among professionals that "deafness" and lack of access to spoken language is a cause of illiteracy: "If this were the case, there wouldn't be so many illiterate hearing persons" (Carver, 1990, p. 2). He proposed a change in attitude, that is, from the perception of literacy among deaf and hard of hearing children as a deficit to the perception of it as a difference. This change of attitude would emphasize building literacy through the child's strengths, using the child's experiences, the child's environment, and any and all cultural and linguistic skills the child brings to the educational setting as literacy development tools. This includes promoting more positive attitudes toward ASL literacy.

ASL Literacy

Whereas family, environment, and attitudes are the most commonly cited factors in determining functional literacy in the general population, several additional characteristics may contribute to literacy skill development among deaf and hard of hearing students. The cause of the hearing loss is frequently cited as having an impact on the reading and writing abilities of deaf and hard of hearing children (Marschark, 1993), particularly as it relates to the health and well-being of the child and the emotional response of parents to the presence of deafness (Corson, 1973; Meadow-Orlans & Steinberg, 1993). A second area that has received considerable attention in the literature, and in social and political arenas as well, is the deaf child's access to ASL. The critical factor related to literacy development has been early access to information through language. Deaf children who are born into an ASL environment develop language in a manner and at a rate similar to that of hearing children (McAnally, Rose, & Quigley, 1994; Petitto & Marentette, 1991). This early access to linguistic information is typically not available to deaf babies who are born into an oral-auditory environment.

Historically, education of deaf children has been viewed solely from the causal or biological perspective. Educational predictions and decisions were made using physical data such as those from audiograms, plus age at onset, age at diagnosis, causal effects of deafness, and adaptation to electronic amplification. Literacy was frequently determined by an individual's ability to speak intelligibly, while the ability to sign intelligibly went unrecognized. However, during the past decade there has been a significant movement away from the biologically based model to a culturally based model. Using the cultural perspective, the language of the deaf culture, American Sign Language, provides a foundation for literacy on which second-language learning (e.g., of English, Spanish) can be established. This shift in perspectives has emanated primarily from the frustration among deaf adults and parents of deaf children with the educational-biological model's failure to improve the literacy levels among deaf individuals (Johnson, Liddell, & Erting, 1989).

The ASL literacy movement builds on the foundation of the importance of family, environment, and attitudes as factors that influence literacy. ASL as a first language is established within the family, thus giving a deaf child *visual* access to language and participation in family matters, which provides the onset for emergent literacy skills. Access to ASL as a visual language can provide the young deaf child with literacy opportunities parallel to those of hearing children. Studies of deaf and hearing infants by Petitto and Marentette (1991) demonstrated that all children are born with the innate need to communicate through a variety of modalities, including hearing, speech, gestures, and facial and body expressions. Family communication and language patterns and the child's characteristics determine the extent to which language patterns will be developed. Deaf children of deaf parents and hearing children of hearing parents interacted in a similar manner during the early stages. However, although they tended to parallel each other in communication development strategies, there was a shift in modality. Deaf infants continued to develop their gestures into patterns of manual babbling while reducing their random vocalizations. Hearing infants decreased their random gestures and transformed random sound patterns into vocal babbling.

Environment has a strong influence on the development of literacy among deaf and hard of hearing children. The ASL literacy perspective has established environmental guidelines that provide deaf children with consistent access to and opportunities for communication patterns. Inherent among the environmental factors are the influences of social and cultural literacy. An environment that fosters development through social interaction with adult deaf role models and cultural practices promotes the growth of ASL literacy. The young child acquiring ASL literacy through the environment is provided with experiences in ASL literature (e.g., ABC stories, ASL poetry, deaf narratives, and ASL classifier stories), visual adaptations in communication, and opportunities to learn about English through ASL (Byrd, 1997; Kuntze, 1993).

Family, community, social, and cultural attitudes have significantly influenced the acceptance and nonacceptance of ASL literacy. While some educators view ASL literacy as a means toward the development of English-language literacy (Mayer & Wells, 1996; Strong & Prinz, 1997), others have supported the acceptance of ASL as a form of literacy equivalent to all other accepted languages (Lane, Hoffmeister, & Bahan, 1996). Attitudes toward the acceptance of ASL as a unique language, as a literate linguistic system, and as a potential means toward the accomplishment of fluency in English have been the result of extensive research (Klima & Bellugi, 1979; Siple, 1978; Supalla, 1990) and the accomplishments of generations of deaf individuals. Recognition of ASL as a second language by state departments of education; studies of ASL poetry, literature, and narratives by departments of rhetoric and linguistics in major universities; and the inclusion of ASL into the entertainment media are all examples of more recent perspectives and attitudes toward ASL literacy.

The argument regarding the primacy of ASL as a means toward the accomplishment of English literacy focuses on studies concerning bilingual-bicultural education and the theoretical model of second-language learners proposed by Cummins (1991). The development of a natural first language serves as the foundation from which a second language can be acquired through explicit instruction and practice (Mayer & Wells, 1996; Nover, 1995; Paul & Quigley, 1994). The intense interest in ASL as a first language and as a means of increasing literacy development in the socially dominant language has resulted in a number of studies focused on parent-child communication patterns, student achievement and literacy performance, and the implementation of bilingual-bicultural instructional programs for deaf children.

Strong and Prinz (1997) examined the relationships of English literacy, knowledge of ASL, and deaf and hearing parents. Children included in the study ranged in age from 8 to 15 years and attended a residential school for the deaf. Statistical analysis of English and ASL literacy measures as well as data collected through parent questionnaires suggested that "deaf children's learning of English appears to benefit from the acquisition of even a moderate fluency of ASL" (Strong & Prinz, 1997, p. 45).

An extensive North American study conducted with adolescent deaf students focused on those factors related to the development of sign and English-based literacy skills. The study examined the relationships between functional communication skills of deaf students and a wide range of characteristics, including the family and educational environments. Two research groups participated in the fact-finding study. The first group (Moores, 1987) focused on the literacy abilities of deaf adolescents attending residential schools for the deaf. Students participating in the study attended programs that used a "total communication system," that is, a combination of oral and aural and sign modalities as the primary means of communication both within and outside of the instructional environment. The participants were divided into two groups: (1) deaf youth with at least one deaf parent who used ASL in the home environment, and (2) deaf youth with hearing parents. A battery of 19 tests related to literacy skills included measures of reading and writing, general academic achievement, communication fluency in spoken and signed languages, cognitive development, and world knowledge (Moores, 1996, pp. 278–286). No comparisons were made between the two groups. Rather, the study focused on the identification of characteristics that were related to literacy. Moores (1996) summarized the correlations and analysis of factors within the tests as follows: "In general it appears that world knowledge . . . and measures of English grammar are the highest predictors of literacy in deaf adolescents in total communication programs" (p. 284). He also noted that there was no significant correlation between reading and writing skills and the early use of sign language.

Geers and Moog (1989) conducted a parallel study using the same battery of tests, differing most significantly in the criteria for the selection of participants. In this study, all of the adolescents were deaf and received their educational experiences in oral-auditory–only communication programs beginning in the preschool years. Students were recruited from programs within the United States and Canada. In contrast to Moores's (1987) study, 85% of these students participated in general education classrooms for all or part of the day, and a majority (68%) of the students came from middle- to upper-middle-class socioeconomic levels, with three-fourths of the families having at least some college education. Results of this study indicate that "the primary predictor of achievement is English language competence" (Geers & Moog, 1989, p. 69), with factors of hearing, early intervention, and spoken English contributing to literacy skills in deaf adolescents.

While the results of these studies do not suggest that one system of communication (e.g., auditory-oral, total communication), program philosophy (e.g., whole language, basal, phonics), or parental hearing status (e.g., hearing, deaf) is superior in determining the development of literacy skills, it is evident that early intervention; knowledge of a language, particularly the English language; and cultural or world knowledge are salient factors that are educationally significant to the development of literacy in deaf individuals. The opportunity for advancement of ASL-English literacy skills among deaf and hard of hearing individuals depends significantly on the degree to which each of these factors is achieved within the bilingual-bicultural and English as a Second Language (ESL) educational reforms today.

Emergent Literacy

The concept of *emergent literacy* evolved from the practice of teaching a set of skills that were commonly accepted as prerequisites for the proper development of reading and writing. Reading readiness instruction practiced in the 1930s included a hierarchy of tasks and characteristics such as interest in reading materials, ability to discriminate sounds visually and auditorily, picture identification, and rhyming-picture association (Durkin, 1989). While there was a dearth of research to support the theory of skill training as a prerequisite to reading and writing literacy, teachers persisted in the use of developmental materials and models well into the 1970s, adhering to the belief that early reading (prior to the age of 6) could place a child at risk both psychologically and physiologically (Durkin, 1989; Hefferman, 1960). Clay (1967) and Durkin (1966) conducted a number of studies refuting the notion that children were not ready to read and write until they were able to perform a set of phonic and visual tasks and display an appropriate attitude toward print. Emergent literacy, introduced in the mid 1960s, included a child's development in language, communication, reading, and writing as a continuous process in which culturally influenced experiences and interactions within the family and the environment determine the emergence of a literate individual.

Unlike traditional general education settings, nursery school and kindergarten programs for preschool children who were deaf modified the mandate for specific prereading skill inventories. In the early 1930s, Buell (1934) and her staff used storytelling, reading, and illustrations as part of the standard curriculum. In her book *Natural Language for Deaf Children,* Groht (1958) recommended "the method of using a great deal of lip reading and some silent reading before working on the development of speech sounds and writing and reading" (p. 21). Rather than training children to match geometric figures in preparation for reading, Groht stressed the use of naturally occurring experiences as a means of developing language through communication, including reading and writing with very young deaf children. She encouraged the use of pictures, print, and storytelling that was relevant and motivating to the child. Hart (1975) extended Groht's approach through her philosophy that reading begins at birth. Early intervention programs under her direction at the Lexington School for the Deaf incorporated language-enriched naturally occurring events, including storybook reading, as well as structured and creative writing activities. While the practices of Groht and Hart were labeled as *natural language,* the principles are implicitly similar to the concept of emergent literacy.

Emergent literacy is an inclusive term that refers to developing behaviors directly associated with reading, such as page turning, pointing to pictures, illustrating compositions, and inventing spelling. Sulzby (1989) defined emergent literacy as behaviors that develop into conventional literacy. Studies of emergent behaviors in young children demonstrate that language learning, reading, and written language develop in concert and "mutually reinforce one another" (Teale & Sulzby, 1986, p. 4). Emergent literacy extends from early childhood within the home to the child's formal exposure to print and the reading-writing processes at school. It is a time when children pretend reading and writing activities as part of their play and are willing to take risks and learn through trial and error. Within the construct of emergent literacy, a continuum of progress includes steady growth, dependent on social interactions within the family and the community, in an environment that provides meaningful and literate experiences.

This continuum of emergent literacy may vary considerably among children who are deaf or hard of hearing, extending from early childhood well into the elementary or middle school years. It is confounded by the multidimensional perspectives included in emergent literacy, that is, communication and language competence as fundamental components of reading and writing. The child's experiences within the family and community and school environments may range from isolation to full inclusion, varying in access to effective models and involvement in literacy events such as storytelling, leaving messages, telephone conversations, computer use, and television programs. For deaf and hard of hearing children, variables that appear to influence emergent literacy include hearing status, age of onset and identification of hearing loss, and the introduction of literacy experiences that are accessible and motivating to the child. For example, a conventional telephone conversation with Grandpa may not be highly motivating for a 3-year-old child who is deaf. However, a TTY message in which words and letters are rolling across the screen, "HI ANNA. PAPA SAYS HI ANNA," while Dad points with Anna to her name and to Grandpa's name and then returns the message by replying "HI PAPA" can serve as a stepping stone in emerging literacy. Ewoldt (1990) hypothesized that deaf children and hearing children who are provided with meaningful social, cultural, and interactive experiences will follow similar developmental literacy patterns.

While only limited research-based studies have been reported, the characteristics of early literacy experiences were documented by Taylor (1983) through her study of 6 hearing children who were identified as successfully learning how to read and write. Taylor observed each of the children within the family and home environments. She noted that early reading for young children begins with observing their parents and the opportunities for literate interactions. Parents read to their children regularly and had predictable patterns of behaviors with picture books and writing materials. Environmental print materials such as messages, thank you notes, and cereal boxes were routinely included in parent-child social interactions. The children accomplished a variety of reading and writing tasks before they acquired phonetic, alphabetic, or conventional writing styles. Taylor's observations indicated that "children learn to organize their environment through the use of print " (p. 54), developing schemata for beginning reading programs in school.

Williams (1994) observed 3 children (ages 3-5, 5-0, and 5-10) who were deaf and used a combination of oral-aural, total communication, and signs in social interactions at home and aural-oral communication at school. Using Taylor's categories of emerging literacy, each family was observed engaged in various types of literacy activities similar to those of the hearing children in Taylor's study. The children used writing in their preschool classrooms in ways similar to those of their hearing peers, including the use of left-to-right sweep across reading pages and distinguishing the tops and bottoms of pages. They were able to read their names and the names of family members, despite their language delay when compared to hearing peers. Williams generalized her observations and concluded that "poor literacy achievement may be attributed . . . to a lack of early, intensive experiences with print that are *personal, authentic, and meaningful*" (p. 150, author's emphasis) and to the instructional practices within school settings that focus on discrete skill development. However, Williams gave no evidence of instructional practices that may have inhibited the development of literacy skills with these 3 children.

Development of Literacy Skills in Hearing Children

Emergent literacy focuses on the child's ability to extract meaning from print, building on the schemata gained through related experiences. Learning to identify "words," "sentences" and "letters" and to construct meaning from those concepts is part of becoming a literate person (Cooper, 1997; Mason & Au, 1986). Clay (1985) identified four concepts about print that a child uses to construct meaning: books, sentences, words, and letters. The skills identified within each of these concepts are outlined in Table 2.1 (Cooper, 1997; Durkin, 1989). These skills are a critical part of the emerging literacy program and are the foundation for early reading programs in school settings. Concepts of print are developed through modeling, time, and experiences with print materials available in the environment. Cooper (1997) alerted educators to the fact that while some children develop these skills prior to formal schooling, many children may not have the same opportunities due to limited or inaccessible interactions with people and materials in their environment. It is important for teachers to assess the child's expertise with print materials, including factors of family, cultural, and attitudinal characteristics, and to develop the child's skills as part of the emergent literacy process.

Durkin (1989) recommended six basic guidelines for all teachers to follow in developing emergent literacy skills (see Table 2.2). These guidelines are based on common practices and applications to the school environment. Durkin's recommendations emphasize sharing literacy information with parents and including them in the development of beginning reading, writing, and communication skills to the greatest extent possible. Literacy activities at home may be the teacher's greatest asset. Parents should be made aware of the value of their

Table 2.1
Concepts of Print

Books	Words
Knows: • Cover • Title, author, illustrator • Beginning, ending • Left/right orientation • Top/bottom orientation • Print tells story, not pictures	Identifies: • Words (e.g., knows that *dog* is a word; does not sign/say it) • Empty space as marker of end of one word and beginning of another • Printed words as related to spoken or signed referents
Sentences	**Letters**
Identifies: • Sentence • Beginning, ending of sentence • Capital letter at beginning • Punctuation: period, comma, question mark, quotation marks, exclamation point	Knows: • Letters differ from words • Letter order • Capital and lower case

Note. From *Literacy: Helping Children Construct Meaning* (3rd ed.) (p. 167), by A. D. Cooper, 1997, Boston: Houghton Mifflin. Copyright 1997 by Houghton Mifflin. Reprinted with permission.

contributions to their child's process of becoming literate and should be provided with activities, strategies, and recommendations for materials that will assist their child's development. The teacher's flexibility and knowledge of alternative approaches (including reading and writing as a joint activity and sound-letter correspondence) are important components in the guidelines to meet the individual needs and interests of the child. Developing the concepts of print includes developing an understanding of the language of print, or *metalanguage*. For example, a child who has been directed to find the word *cat* responds by pointing to the letter *c* in *cat* and *cookie*, indicating that they are the same. The child's response demonstrates interest in developing the metalinguistic understanding of *letter* and *word*.

Allowing ample time for reading to children inherently means including frequent and fun reading episodes with children. These reading times should include pre- and postreading activities that will assist the emerging reader to develop comprehension skills as well as writing skills. Print materials used in the emergent literacy process should incorporate those things that are of primary interest to the children. This may include language-experience stories, notes from home, photographs, captioned movies, computer-generated illustrations, and comics, to name just a few resources (Durkin, 1989, pp. 110–123).

Table 2.2
Guidelines for Beginning Reading Instruction

1. Provide eclectic methodology.
2. Include basic elements of print awareness as prerequisites for beginning reading.
3. Verify that the children understand the language of instruction.
4. Provide time for reading to children.
5. Make generous use of experience materials.
6. Inform and include parents in literacy programs.

Note. Adapted from *Teaching Them to Read* (5th ed.) (pp. 110–123), by D. Durkin, 1989, Boston: Allyn & Bacon.

Development of Literacy Skills in Deaf Children

There is wide variation among educators in the methodology of programming for emergent literacy and beginning reading and writing programs. Likewise, no studies are available that demonstrate the best practices in programming with deaf and hard of hearing children. The review of methodologies in this section is provided as general information and to encourage the reader to pursue additional resources and to configure instructional opportunities in congruence with the needs of the child as well as the family. Any programming that may be beneficial for deaf and hard of hearing children must be child-centered, accommodate the interests and cultural experiences of the family and the child, and incorporate communication strategies that will promote fluency and access in communication, particularly between the child and family members. Principles and issues related to bicultural-bilingual literacy programming with deaf and hard of hearing children are presented in Chapter 4.

Studies of emergent reading with deaf and hard of hearing children are primarily based on models of hearing children. Andrews and Mason (1984) conducted a study using specific strategies of matching a child's internalized language base and knowledge to printed words. Using the results of the study, the authors hypothesized that parents of young deaf children who communicate manually using signs or finger spelling in the home environment can increase emergent literacy experiences. This can be accomplished when parents match known signs and finger spelling with print. Three levels of emergent literacy among the experimental group of deaf children were identified as follows:

1. The child knows about printed word symbols, can handle a book properly, begins to attend to stories, and begins to label pictures with manual signs.

2. The child recognizes words on food labels, cereal boxes, and road signs in picture context; recognizes the alphabet using finger spelling; reads and prints a first name; and attempts to sequence and recall stories.

3. The child actively breaks down letters in words, usually focusing on the initial letter. Sight vocabulary spelling and printing knowledge and reciting stories and sequencing abilities rapidly increase. (p. 27)

Equipping parents of deaf and hard of hearing children with the ways and means for encouraging early literacy experiences is critical to the development of the child. Acknowledging the need for early and consistent communication systems that are readily accessible to the child and the parents is an important first step. Recently, a number of studies have focused on the types of interactions that occur between deaf parents and their young children for the purpose of identifying strategies that can be transferred to hearing parents of deaf children (Akamatsu & Andrews, 1993; Lartz & Lestina, 1995).

Lartz and Lestina (1995) studied the behaviors of 6 deaf mother–deaf child dyads (children of ages 3–5 years) while reading a story. All the mothers used American Sign Language and some English-based signs. An analysis of the reading sessions indicated that there were at least six strategies that were commonly used among the deaf mothers while reading, including:

1. *Sign placement*—Mother signed certain words or phrases on the picture or used the book as part of the sign. This allowed the child to see the signs and the pictures in the book simultaneously.

2. *Text paired with signed demonstration*—Mother clarifies the text or picture by demonstrating the action pictured or represented in the text.

3. *Real-world connection between text and child's experience*—Mother signed an example of an event or experience in the child's life that related to the story text.

4. *Attention maintenance*—Mother physically secured the child's attention to her signing or to a picture in the book. Prompts used included tapping or nudging the child or moving the book up and down.

5. *Physical demonstration of character changes*—Mother used facial expressions and body posture to signal different characters in the book.

6. *Nonmanual signals as questions*—Mother used facial expressions to ask questions about a picture in the book. (p. 360)

For the most part, these strategies are accommodations unique to deaf mother–deaf child interactions in which ASL is used as the primary language form. Padden (1984) also noted that deaf parents explicitly teach their children to attend to the left-to-right sequence of letters in a word and a sentence, while hearing parents incorporate this practice into natural guided reading patterns.

Storybook reading was introduced as a strategy to enrich emergent literacy among deaf children at a residential school for the deaf (Gillespie & Twardosz, 1997). An experimental group of 9 children who were deaf or hard of hearing participated in storybook reading before bedtime twice per week. These scheduled reading sessions were in addition to the storytelling and book-reading events that occurred in the school and residential settings. Dormitory counselors or deaf high school students read the stories to the group of children using sign language, with occasional use of props, including videotapes of signed stories and puppets. The purpose of the study was to identify the emergent literacy behaviors demonstrated by the children in response to the storybook reading activities using Sulzby's (1985, 1988) system for measuring emergent reading ability. Gillespie and Twardosz (1997) reported that the children were more attentive and engaged in the reading process when the storytellers were more expressive and incorporated interactive strategies. The authors noted that the strategies used in storybook reading through sign language varied considerably among readers. A second outcome of the study indicated that these children were "more independent and reportedly showed more interest in books" (p. 329) when compared to the control group.

Using a case study approach and existing literature, Maxwell (1986) advocated for a reading program that emulated the six guidelines recommended by Durkin in the previous section. Maxwell recommends flexibility in strategies that include top-down and bottom-up processes. Reading and writing are integrated with experience stories and storytelling. Written language can be matched to signed or spoken words. ASL-signed segments can be matched with idea units. Concepts about print are experienced through the matching of finger spelling to words in print and letter identification.

David Schleper (1997) developed a set of 15 principles as part of the emergent literacy process based on practices among deaf parents regarding reading to children who are deaf. In his book and accompanying video *Reading to Deaf Children: Learning from Deaf Adults*, Schleper consistently emphasized the need for child-centered interactions, communication fluency, and an attitude of enjoyment in the process of emergent literacy. The principles proposed are based on studies and observations of deaf parents interacting with their children during storybook reading; however, they may be adapted to a variety of emergent literacy events—for example, trips to the grocery store, family conversations and debates, and reading environmental signs. Table 2.3 is an adaptation of Schleper's 15 principles following the practices of deaf parents. While American Sign Language is used across all of the studies cited in Schleper's work, the prin-

Table 2.3
Principles for Reading to Deaf Children

1. Deaf readers translate stories using American Sign Language.
2. Deaf readers keep both languages visible (ASL and English).
3. Deaf readers elaborate on the text.
4. Deaf readers re-read stories on a "storytelling" to "story reading" continuum.
5. Deaf readers follow the child's lead.
6. Deaf readers make what is implied explicit.
7. Deaf readers adjust sign placement to fit the story.
8. Deaf readers adjust signing style to fit the character.
9. Deaf readers connect concepts in the story to the real world.
10. Deaf readers use attention maintenance strategies.
11. Deaf readers use eye gaze to elicit participation.
12. Deaf readers engage in role play to extend concepts.
13. Deaf readers use ASL variations to sign repetitive English phrases.
14. Deaf readers provide a reinforcing environment.
15. Deaf readers expect the child to become literate.

Note. Adapted from *Reading to Deaf Children: Learning from Deaf Adults* (pp. 5–36), by D. R. Schleper, 1997, Washington, DC: Pre-College National Mission Programs.

ciples of reading can be used with virtually any system that provides consistency and fluency in the interactive communication process between mothers and fathers and their children who are deaf.

While the knowledge base regarding emergent literacy development among deaf and hard of hearing children is still relatively small, the work of Schleper (1997) and a host of other researchers is beginning to provide some avenues for advancement. It is widely recognized that the significant contributors to literacy include family, environment, and attitude. These three factors emphasize that school-family partnerships perhaps can make a difference in activating the unattained potential of deaf children in the areas of reading, writing, and communication fluency.

Summary

Literacy is a complex phenomenon. Socially and economically, it has been perceived as the root of failure and the foundation of success. While it is difficult to identify a single definition that is universally acceptable, literacy is basically the ability to read and write in the language of society to achieve one's needs and goals. The achievement of English literacy among deaf children has been a difficult and somewhat predictable journey. The inadequate achievement of literacy goals among deaf high school graduates has led to alternative avenues in pursuit of literacy. The recognition of ASL as a means of developing literacy skills is the most recent development in early childhood, elementary, and high school programs for deaf children. ASL provides the foundation for literacy and literacy-related experiences such as storytelling, acquiring world knowledge, and recognizing cultural expectations. Acquiring English as a second language, therefore, becomes dependent on instruction through ASL.

Achieving literacy is a process dependent on interrelated factors in a child's life, including the family, interactions with the environment, literacy events, and cultural or world knowledge. Attitudes within the family, the social setting, and the culture help to determine the level of literacy that is expected and the opportunities for development. The framework for understanding literacy is one of a multidimensional model that moves along a continuum. For the child who is deaf or hard of hearing, the emergent literacy process must be accessible—that is, children who are identified with a hearing loss early in their lives, whose parents establish a consistent communication system, and who are provided with enriched literacy experiences such as being read to, being told stories, using print in the environment, and captioning will have a head start in the stages of schooling. Teachers of young deaf children are responsible for developing the metalanguage of literacy, that is, concepts of words, letters, sentences, and symbol-sound associations. Teachers need to remain flexible in their approach to emergent literacy by incorporating a variety of methods, reading and writing events, and concepts of print in establishing the foundations of literacy and the development of literate individuals.

CHAPTER

VOCABULARY AND
COMPREHENSION

Preview

A product of reading and writing is comprehension. In a classic study, Davis (1944) identified two factors that significantly contribute to the reading process. The first component was word knowledge, and the second was reasoning, including the ability to integrate information and infer meaning from what is read. Several studies have demonstrated the relationship between breadth and depth of word knowledge, world knowledge, and reading comprehension. Durkin's (1978–79) studies of comprehension instruction in classroom settings revealed that minimal time (less than 1%) was dedicated to comprehension instruction. Rather, comprehension consisted of testing students' abilities to recall information by answering questions at the end of the story. As a result of Durkin's studies, greater emphasis has been placed on the development of explicit teaching of comprehension strategies and preparing students as strategic readers.

The knowledge base regarding vocabulary development and reading comprehension skills in children who are deaf or hard of hearing is limited. Marschark (1993, p. 203) pointed out that much of what is known through research has emanated from England and the United States and has been conducted with students who were educated primarily in auditory-oral programs. In addition, much of the research has been done with secondary and postsecondary deaf students; only a small number of studies include elementary-level deaf and hard of hearing students. However, the past decade has experienced a significant increase in research on comprehension, ASL, and deaf children (Strassman, 1997).

The process of comprehension is a complex set of interrelated events, including a wide range of perceptual, linguistic, and cognitive activities that cannot be described in a single text. This chapter briefly reviews word knowledge and comprehension from a variety of perspectives, as well as the principles that may be used to guide instruction with children who are deaf or hard of hearing. The underlying approach to comprehension assumes that reading occurs through an interactive process among the reader, the intentions of the author, and the text. The organization of this chapter focuses on the instructional needs and concerns of educators of children who are deaf and begins with the development of word meaning, including the characteristics of word knowledge and the relationship between vocabulary and text comprehension. The second part of the chapter provides highlights regarding text interpretation and comprehension.

Word Knowledge

From the very onset, a young child's communication, in which word knowledge is the core, becomes the foundation for reading and writing. As the child's communication skills increase from a select set of labels for primary needs and caretakers to an ever expanding set of named experiences, the relationships of concepts and words multiply. Hearing students enter school with approximately 5,000 words as part of their auditory-oral vocabulary and progress to the 6th grade with 20,000 words that can be read and understood (Nagy & Herman, 1987). The annual average growth rate for hearing children is estimated to be 3,000 to 4,000 words (White, Graves, & Slater, 1990) or 20 words per day in a 180-day school year (Graves, Watts, & Graves, 1994, p. 107). The direct relationship of vocabulary to reading comprehension has been demonstrated through numerous academic studies and is common knowledge to every literate individual.

Characteristics of Word Knowledge

Vacca, Vacca, and Gove (1995) define vocabulary as "the breadth and depth of all the words we know—the words we use to recognize and respond to meaningful acts of communication" (p. 229). The nature of vocabulary or word knowledge includes a set of dependent interrelationships. Figure 3.1 illustrates a partial conceptual map of the nature of these relationships and variables that impact on instructional practices. Using Menyuk's (1988) language development studies, Mason and Au (1990) described five fundamentally distinctive

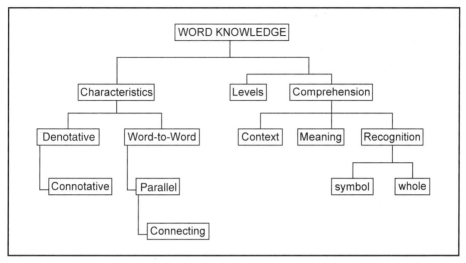

Figure 3.1. Partial concept map of word knowledge.

linguistic roles that words play in reading comprehension and writing: denotative meanings, connotative meanings, relationships among words, parallel relations, and causal and connecting relational terms. Each of these roles emphasizes the importance of language competence as part of the reading comprehension and writing connections. Linguistic, semantic, and pragmatic skills are intricately woven into the fabric of word knowledge and comprehension, as well.

Denotative Relationships

Words of all languages are used to identify or represent objects, events, and attributes, three categories that are considered to be distinctive and universal. As children acquire specific words for people, things, events, and activities and their characteristics, classification systems develop into hierarchical structures. The first area of denotative relationships is the process of *classification*, which denotes words as belonging to one of the three distinctive universal categories. Words may be further classified by experiences and perceived characteristics into subcategories (Mason & Au, 1990, p. 176).

A second area of denotative knowledge of words is the basic form class. All standard English words can be classified as either *function* words or *content* words. Content words may be subordinated into categories such as nouns, verbs, or adjectives and are generally defined as the words that carry the semantic value or the meaning of the message. Function words serve to provide the linguistic structure that links content words. For example, in the sentence *Henry waited in the car for a policeman*, "Henry," "waited," "car," and "policeman," are content words and carry the meaning of the sentence, while "in," "the," "for," and "a," are function words and provide the syntactic structure. Function words assume their meaning from the context shared with other words, for example, *Kelly is in love* and *Kelly is in Greece*. The contribution of function words to reading comprehension has been the subject of significant research programs. While there is general agreement that comprehension can be achieved without reliance on knowledge of function words, analytical and effective reading comprehension necessitates an understanding of the lexical structures, particularly function words (Mattingly, 1984). Kelly (1993) investigated skilled and average deaf readers' recall of English-based text. His findings suggest that skilled readers attend to and recall function words to a greater extent than average deaf readers.

Connotative Relationships

Mason and Au (1990) described connotative characteristics of word knowledge as "rules or sets of distinctions for deciding whether an object, event, or attribute is a member of a category" (p. 176). Words with multiple meanings, synonyms, figurative language, and pragmatic use of words denote basic class forms, universal characteristics, and distinctiveness based on context. Connotative criteria include the meaning of a word in context such as idioms, metaphors, and similes. Characteristic of connotative knowledge is the adaptive use of words determined by *where, with what, why, which meaning of,* and *when* the word is used. For example, selection of *hard* or *difficult, more* or *greater, happy* or *ecstatic* is dependent on connotative relationships within the context.

While some research has been conducted in the area of connotative meanings with deaf and hard of hearing individuals, the majority of these studies investigated word knowledge of figurative language and words with multiple meanings. Iran-Nejad, Ortony, and Rittenhouse (1981) focused on 9 to 17 year olds' comprehension of metaphors, while other studies investigated the text comprehension of idioms with deaf children. General results drawn from these studies suggest that deaf children are capable of comprehending figurative language (King & Quigley, 1985, pp. 63–65). Variables that appear to influence comprehension are explicit instruction, sufficient contextual information to support the meaning of the figurative expression, and linguistic match, that is, syntax and vocabulary that are accessible to the child's prior knowledge.

Word-to-Word Relationships

Words are labels that derive their meaning from experiences mentally stored as concepts. Words are then organized based on their experiential conceptual category or classification. The network creates an organizational pattern of concepts, or clusters of words. A number of theories and models have been used to describe the relationship among words, how they are used in the process of developing word knowledge, and how vocabulary may best be taught to young readers. Menyuk (1988) summarized three models of how words are related to other words: categorical, parallel, and connecting.

The categorical model includes networks of semantic relationships related to information-processing models. A hierarchical memory structure is established using the experiences and words an individual has retained over time. These organizational knowledge structures are referred to as *schemata* or *frames* in which vocabulary can be mapped into patterns of relationships. For example, a young child's schema for *games* may include denotative classifications such as cards, family activities, recess, and specific labels (e.g., "Old Maid" and football), as illustrated in Figure 3.2. Related concepts may include competition, winning and losing, prizes, and computer programs. Each member of the schema forms hierarchical structures that consist of ordered class relationships. As the child has more experiences, the connotative meaning of *game* (e.g., Mom bought a wild game cookbook; My big brother said, "Don't play games with me"; Dad wanted to know what the game plan was for the weekend) requires altering the schema to include related experiences and new word knowledge.

A number of studies report that the classification system of second-language learners and individuals who are deaf may differ from that of first-language and hearing learners, in part due to cultural, perceptual, and linguistic experiences (Bernhardt, 1993; Marschark, 1993). Deaf children are generally characterized as having unique classification systems since they may have fewer or different experiences with the subtleties of words. They are more likely to comprehend words that are specific or restrictive, such as concrete nouns and verbs that are related to familiar activities, rather than more abstract words (e.g., *justice, mystical*), words that provide "shades of meaning" (e.g., *fight for, struggle, strive*), or generic classification words (e.g., *paradigm, equestrian*) (King & Quigley, 1985). Yoshinaga-Itano and Downey (1986) suggested that young deaf children may have difficulty in the development of vocabulary and comprehension of reading and writing production because they have not had the opportunity to establish more complete concept-level schemata.

In addition to concept-word schemata, semantic features such as functions and topical relationships are considered as components of word knowledge (Mason & Au, 1990). Related to schema theory is the *semantic feature theory*, which classifies the relationships among semantic word characteristics. Features such as size, shape, and function of objects and events are thought to be the foundation for the organization of word knowledge. For example, *novel, storybook, biography, textbook, checkbook, Bible,* and *comic book* are all members of a

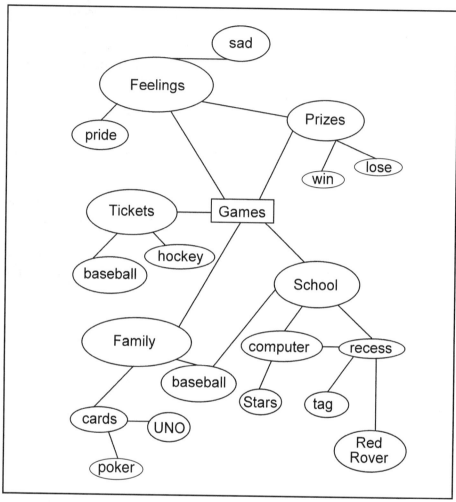

Figure 3.2. Young child's schema for "games."

semantic category called *books*. However, unique features create a variety of semantic relationships within the category of types of books. While researchers have long stressed ambiguity in the salience of various characteristics, there is general agreement that networking of words is based on word knowledge and semantic relationships (Clark & Clark, 1977; Johnson, Toms-Bronowski, & Pittelman, 1982).

Conway (1990) investigated the semantic relationships among known words with deaf students ranging in age from 6 through 11 years. The students were asked to tell everything they knew about a given word. Stimulus words included common nouns (e.g., *airplane, bird, book*) that were presented both in visual illustration and in the primary mode of communication used by the child. Conway reported that all of the students had a semantic understanding of the stimulus words used in the study. However, across age groups, students did not demonstrate growth or difference in the complexity of semantic relationships. For example, when defining the word/picture of an airplane, the students described the word with such phrases as something that flies in the sky, can go above the clouds. More complex semantic production may include such descriptions as jets, biplanes, helicopters, commercial, military, and cargo aircraft. These findings reinforced results of studies that describe semantic word knowledge among deaf children as underdeveloped or immature (Liben, 1979; Yoshinaga-Itano & Downey, 1986). Conway (1990) proposed that the reason for these differences may be related to the children's inability to express their knowledge or "tell all that they know" rather than the degree of knowledge among complex word relationships. Others have attributed the lack of growth in word knowledge among deaf children to strategies used in teaching (Paul, 1996).

Parallel Relationships

Familiarity with the parallel meanings among words, including synonyms, antonyms, and homophones, is a part of linguistic competence that contributes to word knowledge and comprehension. While few studies focus on deaf children's specific knowledge of such parallel relationships, LaSasso and Davey (1987) conducted a study in which the vocabulary comprehension subtest of the *Gates-MacGinite Reading Tests* (VOC) was administered to 50 deaf students between the ages of 10 and 15 years. The VOC subtest consists of a synonym identification task in which the student is given a key word and asked to select another word that has the same meaning from a four-choice set. The results included strong correlations between reading comprehension and the VOC scores. The implication of the study is that understanding word relationships— specifically parallel meanings—is strongly related to reading comprehension among deaf children.

Connecting-Word Relationships

The fifth area identified as fundamental to word knowledge is that of relational words that connect words, units, and ideas. These connectors convey conjunction (e.g., *and*), disjunction (e.g., *but, although, rather*), sequencing (e.g., *then, next*), time (e.g., *while, when*), and causal relationships (e.g., *because*). The effects of understanding connecting-word relationships on reading comprehension, particularly among deaf and hard of hearing children, has not been determined. King and Quigley (1985, pp. 139–140) summarized the results of early studies with a focus on connecting words as developmentally and linguistically related. They concluded that hearing children between the ages of 5 and 7 years were still in the developmental stages of forming an understanding of connective words, while older children with well-developed linguistic skills were more able to respond to variations among the relational words.

Word Knowledge and Comprehension

The relationship between vocabulary and comprehension is generally described from three perspectives proposed by Anderson and Freebody (1981). The first perspective is referred to as the *instrumentalist hypothesis*, in which the breadth of word knowledge is related to verbal skills and, subsequently, impacts on reading comprehension. The emphasis is placed on a causal chain relating the meaning of words to the comprehension of text without concern for the process of acquisition, for example, identifying the meaning of the word through dictionary definitions. The second perspective is referred to as the *aptitude hypothesis*, in which comprehension is enhanced by verbal fluency directly related to word knowledge. The distinguishing characteristic within this perspective is the verbal ability or aptitude an individual brings to the reading process that facilitates comprehension of text and enhances vocabulary development. The child's early literacy experiences as well as intellectual capacity are significant factors in determining the prospect for the development of competent readers. The third perspective is referred to as the *knowledge hypothesis*, in which emphasis is placed on experience and prior knowledge. Readers with extensive world knowledge tend to have greater word knowledge, which enhances comprehension. The knowledge hypothesis includes information-processing variables of conceptual acquisition and the schema approach to reading (Johnson, Toms-Bronowski, & Pittelman, 1982; Taylor, Harris, Pearson, & Garcia, 1995).

Each of these hypotheses has received considerable attention in the literature regarding individuals who are deaf or hard of hearing (Davey & King, 1990; Johnson, Toms-Bronowski, & Pittelman, 1982; LaSasso & Davey, 1987; Paul, 1996). While few researchers would disagree that the knowledge hypothesis has significant implications for reading comprehension, each perspective contributes unique guidelines for explicit vocabulary instruction and comprehension. The knowledge hypothesis illustrates the need for experiential learning and ready access to language. Meaning emanates from experiences and is stored through a network of semantic relationships to form concepts and schemata. Growth of vocabulary consists of increasing the number of concepts, words, and relational links within schemata (Pease, Gleason, & Pan, 1987). Emergent literacy experiences such as storytelling, reading to children, establishing effective communication channels, and writing are strongly supported by the knowledge and aptitude hypotheses, while the instrumental hypothesis supports the need to explicitly teach vocabulary words as a means of facilitating comprehension of text (Vacca, Vacca, & Gove, 1995).

Words and Meaning

Vocabulary development follows a predictive and sequential path—that is, moving from receptive to expressive vocabularies, from hearing words spoken or seeing signs used in meaningful contexts to reading words, speaking/signing, and writing. Word meanings are acquired in several different ways, including: explicit instruction; experience models or examples with the target word identified; analysis of structural components of the new word to identify its meaning; and identification of the meaning from the context surrounding the new word (Davey & King, 1990; LaSasso & Davey, 1987). All of these word development strategies are used by competent readers.

Words and meaning are interdependent entities—a word without meaning has no function, or connecting link for storage or recall, whereas meaning without a word has no avenue for expression. Meaningful words are established within a context connected to networks of stored concepts. Word recognition in print, then, is the mapping of a printed symbol into the network of what is already known. Pease, Gleason, and Pan (1987) describe the growth of vocabulary and meaning as an ever increasing semantic set of concepts and words with links expanding and extending between new and existing concepts and the linguistic system.

Word Recognition

Reading has been described as a process of problem solving in which printed letter codes and spaces are recognized as words and words are "problems to be solved" (Green, 1986). The recognition of words without having to think about the word or its components greatly contributes to the comprehension process (Durkin, 1989; LaBerge & Samuels, 1974). Adams (1990) summarized years of word recognition studies by stating, "The most critical factor beneath fluent word reading is the ability to recognize words, spelling patterns, and whole words effortlessly, automatically and visually. Moreover, the goal of all reading instruction—comprehension—critically depends on this ability" (p. 14). Skilled readers are able to demonstrate word recognition as a whole or through chunking letters into words, which may then be chunked into larger meaningful units.

Whole-Word Recognition. General agreement is found among educators that whole-word learning provides a mechanism for young children to develop a sense of reading and "wordness," especially as they are on their way to developing decoding skills. Durkin (1989) advocated for the progression of word recognition from large meaningful units of text to individual words and then to symbolic coding. During the emergent stages of reading, young children develop a wide range of logographic to whole-word vocabulary (e.g., *McDonald's, Mom, Dad*). These words are generally acquired through repeated exposure in meaningful and common situations. Familiar words such as the child's name and labels become so much a part of children's repertoires that they automatically recognize them. For example, while riding in the car, 2-year-old Anna's father routinely asked/signed, "What does that sign say?" Initially, Dad answered his own question, but after repeated exposures, Anna soon responded by signing, "Stop." While reading a book with her mother, Anna recognized the word *stop* in the context of a story and quickly read the statement "Mom said, 'Stop'." In this example, Anna moved from word recognition to word identification, at which time she was able to identify the word *stop* in context. While reliance on "sight-word" reading skills is inefficient and restrictive, the process of whole-word recognition is required for the identification of irregularly spelled words (e.g., *campaign, champagne*) and content-related vocabulary (e.g., *cochlea, thesis*).

Function words are typically learned by the fluent reader as whole words. Because they are high-frequency words that occur in the linguistic patterns of English, reading function words occurs with automaticity—that is, the reader does not stop to think about the meaning or the components that make up the word. The characteristics of function words are abstract and illusive to a young child and generally are the last to be recognized with automaticity in the sight vocabulary pattern (Malstrom, 1977). However, as discussed earlier, function words are significant to reading comprehension. Words such as *is, there, of,* and *nevertheless* serve as links among content words, sentences, and story structures. Durkin (1989) strongly recommended that function words be taught using a whole-word methodology and *in the context of other known words, sentences, and stories*. Practicing recognition of function words without contextual applications may be analogous to developing a golf swing without a club or a ball.

The selection of vocabulary to be taught through the whole-word methodology will vary within families, cultures, content areas, and environments. Durkin (1986) recommended that words of particular interest to the child be taught first through repeated exposure and function words added as the child begins to read text. As the child progresses, whole-word instruction may decrease and give way to decoding, at which time the reader can experience greater independence in the reading process. However, whole-word reading will continually be necessary, particularly in content areas (e.g., *tsetse fly, embalm*) where words that are important to comprehension of the text must be easily and quickly identified. Repeated experiences with these words will determine how efficiently and extensively a whole-word vocabulary is accomplished and how quickly recognition of these words becomes automatic.

Symbol Recognition. Symbol awareness is the ability to identify an arbitrary symbol (e.g., phoneme, grapheme, sign classifier) or set of symbols as different from another symbol or set of symbols. The critical nature of symbol awareness is to insure that children are able to decode words that are not recognized as whole words, rapidly and with meaning. The most common form of symbolic awareness is phonics, or speech sounds, followed by graphemes, that is, graphic or printed symbols (e.g., the sign for a curve in the road ahead) and the phonology (cheremes) of hand formations in ASL signs, including the letters of the alphabet. While studies regarding a child's awareness of ASL phonology are in the formative stage, Juel (1988) reported that emergent phonemic awareness is the best predictor of reading success for children. Young children becoming readers can often be observed playing with sound and nonsense words and rhyming patterns (e.g., *f-at* and *b- at*). This play with symbol awareness extends beyond the basic phonemes to letter-sound relationships, or phonics. Campbell (1991) refers to this process as "the three R's—rhyming, remembering and reading." Phonic skills are not considered a prerequisite to emergent literacy and reading comprehension; however, they appear to occur simultaneously as children engage in invented spelling and environmental reading. Teale and Sulzby (1986) suggest that phonic skills and oral written language occur simultaneously and "mutually reference one another in development" (p. 4).

Another way of defining letter-sound relationships is through the *alphabetic principle*, that is, the 26 letters of the alphabet as they correspond to the 44 phonemes of English. While isolated letters and phonemes are meaningless, they combine to form morphemes, or units of meaning. An analytic phonic approach builds on sight words already familiar to the student and identifies the sound-symbol relationship through an analysis of what the child knows about the sound of the word and the graphic symbols used to represent the word. In contrast to the analytic method, the synthetic method begins with naming the letters of the alphabet and associating the phoneme(s) with the letter. Once the sound-symbol relationships are easily recognized, rules and conventions of spellings and sound patterns (e.g., syllables, when vowels are long) are practiced. Finally, the sound-symbols are joined into words, building first on those words already familiar and then to new or unknown words (Vacca, Vacca, & Gove, 1995, pp. 278–279).

Illustration of ASL literacy and sign-symbol relationships includes finger spelling and sign play with cheremic or hand shaped rhyming patterns as described by Kuntze (1993). A chereme is a sign or ASL equivalent of an auditory phoneme. As a deaf child acquires chereme-sign relationships, a variety of symbolic finger spelling activities occur that indicate the recognition and comprehension of sign-symbol relationships. Symbol recognition may include a variety of invented sign-letter play, nonsense symbols, and rhyming of cheremes including the ASL-ABC story form, which has grown in popularity among deaf children.

The ASL-ABC story form is based on the cheremes or hand shapes of the ASL alphabet. Each chereme or symbol shape is related to a sign that conveys a concept in a meaningful context. For example, the hand shape or chereme V may be formed and used in sign/concept formation to indicate "watching something with great interest and intensity." The following is the English translation of an ASL-ABC story created by a student (Kuntze, 1993, pp. 272–273). The story illustrates the recognition of ASL phonemes presented in a meaningful context:

▶ A *I was driving*

   B *through a rolling countryside.*

   C *My car wheels were spinning.*

   D *Now the fuel gauge was inching*

   E *toward the E.*

   F *Worriedly, I moved my eyes searchingly ahead of me.*

   G *Finally, I spotted something in the distance looming closer.*

   H *With anxiety, I hurried to the place.*

   I *Now I saw an outline*

   J *With a J on it.*

   K *I got out of the car*

   L *and put the gas nozzle into the car.*

   M *sweat was pouring off my brow.*

   N *Looking here and there,*

   O *I saw nothing.*

   P *So I quickly got into the car*

   Q *and zoomed off.*

   R *With a cigar snug in my mouth,*

S *I was driving along.*

T *All of a sudden, an urge to relieve myself came over me.*

U *I had to hurry and find a way to do it.*

V *I looked about in increasing desperation.*

W *I became anxious.*

X *I simply must do it.*

Y *Now!*

Z *There was only one way: I reluctantly turned around to go back.*

Based on the work completed by Firth (1985), Vacca, Vacca, and Gove (1995) briefly described the three word recognition stages children pass through on their way to developing automaticity in word recognition:

> The first stage is the *logographic stage*. Children in this stage of word identification learn words as whole units, sometimes embedded in a logo, such as a stop sign. The second stage is the *alphabetic stage* in which children use the individual letters and sounds to identify words. The last stage is the *orthographic stage* in which children begin to see patterns in words and use these patterns to identify words without sounding them out. (p. 282)

Freebody and Byrne (1988) examined the relationship of comprehension, reading time, and phonemic awareness among second- and third-grade hearing children. A significant variable within the study was the identification of children as "sight-word" readers, that is, readers "who memorize associations between printed words and their pronunciations" (p. 450) and "phonetic" readers, described as those students who sound out words grapheme by grapheme. Freebody and Byrne further investigated the relationship of the strategies used by the children to comprehend text. Their findings suggest that sight-word second graders outperformed their peers who were phonic readers on all measures of comprehension. However, in the third grade the same students who relied on whole-word recognition had slower growth rates in reading comprehension and performed at significantly lower levels on recall of stories than their peers who were phonic readers. The results support the theory that phonemic awareness is a required skill to assist children in reading comprehension as they progress to more complex and varied reading tasks. Vocabulary increased in complexity from second to third grade, particularly in the depth of word knowledge, challenging those children who relied primarily on sight-based word knowledge.

The critical role of symbol awareness as a process in word recognition is illustrated in a number of studies including deaf and hard of hearing students. In his book *Psychological Development of Deaf Children*, Marc Marschark (1993) reviewed research focusing on literacy and reading comprehension. A number of studies demonstrated that deaf children who are fluent readers use some form of phonologic coding (Conrad, 1970; Dodd, 1980; Hanson, Goodell, & Perfetti, 1991). However, the majority of studies reported that deaf children use whole-word recognition and whole-word classification schemata more frequently than phonologic coding (Waters & Doehring, 1990). The question of how some deaf children develop phonologic coding systems remains unanswered. Conrad's studies in the 1970s indicated that some aspects of phonologic awareness may be associated with articulation patterns established by deaf children but are not the sole source of phonologic skills. Leybaert and Charlier (1996) suggested that other forms of coding are working in conjunction with articulatory patterns including finger spelling, speech reading, and consistent integration with printed information. Dodd (1980) noted that while hearing children directly connect graphemes to phonemes, auditory input was not a prerequisite for the development of phonologic awareness and coding skills. Building on Dodd's observations, Leybaert and Charlier (1996) conducted a series of studies in Belgium with deaf children ranging from 5 to 16 years of age. Their studies demonstrated the principle that deaf children who developed a system of internal phonologic recording were able to rhyme, remember, and use spelling conventions similar to their hearing peers. Some of the children in the study used a French cued-speech system, others used sign language at home and/or in school. The most salient variable that influenced the development of phonologic coding was early (before the age of 3 years) parental commitment to, and consistency in, the communication process from home *and* school settings.

The differences in word recognition proficiency between deaf and hearing children has been attributed to a wide range of factors. It is not uncommon to find teachers and parents who are impressed at the advanced reading levels among young deaf children but experience great disappointment when reading fluency begins to lag in the third grade and becomes a serious concern in the fifth and sixth grades. Given the reliance on visual input and limited access to, or absence of, auditory vocabulary experiences, deaf readers may not acquire decoding skills through symbolic recognition. Rather, the demand for word knowledge becomes more complex as the child encounters greater complexity in vocabulary. Repeated studies focusing on comparisons among deaf, hard of hearing, and hearing children demonstrate differences in word knowledge. Researchers have generally concluded that these differences are delays in word knowledge tasks and that the delays can be remediated through appropriate instructional strategies (Marschark, 1993; Paul, 1996; Quigley & Paul, 1990).

Context Clues

Everyone experiences unknown words in the context of known words. Whether those words are signed, spoken, or printed, the context in which the unknown word appears assists in developing some understanding of the target word. The ability to use context clues, that is, known contexts, is a critical component in the development of word recognition and reading comprehension. The use of context to discover meaning of an unknown word depends on the reader's prior knowledge or world knowledge and the existence of the word in the spoken or sign vocabulary of the child. Text variables also play an important role in context clues. If the context is to provide clues to the unknown word, a significant portion of the text must be known, that is, complex contextual information does not provide sufficient data. For example:

▶ *Una pajara calentaba un huevo. El huevo salto.*

A *pajara calentaba* her egg. The egg *salto.*

A mother bird *calentaba* her egg. The egg *salto.*

A mother bird sat on her egg. The egg jumped. (Eastman, 1960, pp. 3–4)

While context clues include a variety of formats, including photographs, illustrations, maps, graphs, and logographics, this section discusses the use of text clues subdivided into syntactic and semantic clues. Syntactic clues are derived from the role the word plays in the structure of a sentence. Using the rules and linear positional structure of the English language, the reader can determine some denotative information regarding the unknown word and its characteristics. These syntactic clues place constraints on the possibilities of word classifications that can be used. For example, in the sentence *Alex lost his* _____, syntactic clues place constraints on the possible word classifications that complete the statement.

Robbins and Hatcher (1981) studied deaf readers' comprehension of word meanings in context with varying syntactic text structure. They concluded that syntax is a critical variable prohibiting the use of contextual clues among deaf readers, even when the meaning of the targeted word is known prior to reading the passage. However, prior knowledge and familiarity with the topic or theme of the text can reduce syntactic barriers (Ewoldt, 1981; McGill-Franzen & Gormley, 1980).

Semantic clues provide a sense of meaning within the text. In concert with the syntactic clues, semantic clues place further constraints on the possible meanings of a word. For example:

▶ *There is no longer any need for the cowboy to carry a pistol, and so that part of his_____ has disappeared.* (Martin, 1967, p. 360)

The gap or missing word is restricted in function and meaning by the syntax and the semantics of the context. While hearing children may fill in the missing word (*equipment, tools, things,* or *paraphernalia*) through a process of matching the graphic-symbolic information with phonic or auditory codes already banked in memory, a deaf child may rely solely on knowledge of English language rules of syntax and semantics. Knowledge of phonics or graphonic coding helps the reader to decode the unknown word and associate the pronunciation with known oral vocabulary. The usefulness of contextual clues is dependent on the reader's knowledge of language structures, prior experiences, and vocabulary that can be used to provide decoding information.

Van Daalen-Kapteijns and Elshout-Mohr (1981) studied the acquisition of word meanings in context among adult readers. Their findings indicated that the more competent readers applied an analytical approach to discovering the meaning of a word through context; that is, competent readers used contextual information from a series of clues, altering the meaning of the new word as new clues were uncovered. Less competent readers relied on a holistic approach. The meaning of a word was determined by a sentence with little reliance on additional information that could alter the context or the meaning adopted by the reader in the initial clues. In a series of studies conducted by Strassman, Kretschmer, and Bilsky (1987), deaf adolescents did not use an analytical approach to word meaning and context clue tasks spontaneously. However, when provided with explicit instruction in the use of context clues to construct meaning, the students were able to deduce and infer meaning using both prior knowledge and contextual clues. DeVilliers and Pomerantz (1992) reported similar results where deaf adolescents acquired new vocabulary when the targeted words were presented in a rich context and when the new information was related to the prior knowledge of the reader.

Davey and King (1990) provided an overview of research regarding the factors that influence word meaning using context clues with an emphasis on the reading conventions of children who are deaf. The first factor focused on the *reader*, that is, characteristics of a reader's ability to acquire word meaning from context. These characteristics included (a) developmental differences—children appear to improve their ability to use context clues through practice and repeated exposure to word meanings; (b) knowledge of textual conventions— the reader must have an understanding of English linguistic structures and semantics associated with the context as well as ability to use context clues to help acquire meanings of words ; (c) prior knowledge—the reader's knowledge, concepts, and experiences with the topic greatly enhance efficiency in deriving word meaning from the context; and, (d) memory—the reader must have the ability to process and store information in working memory, thus, linking the reader's world knowledge, textual conventions, and practice with context clues.

The second factor related to word meanings and context clues includes the *task* or purpose for acquiring meaning of the word. If a student is directed to read a passage to learn more about the word *protest*, context clues will require considerably more attention than if the student were reading the sports column to find out who won the basketball game. In the latter example, unknown words may be ignored in favor of seeking specific information from the passage (Davey, 1987). The reading task also includes the reader's ability to fully use the text to construct meaning. This includes rereading and backtracking to check and connect the meaning of a new word from context. The task factor as an element of word comprehension appears to be enhanced through direct instruction and practice focused on the effective use of context clues (Graves, Watts, & Graves, 1994; Sternberg, 1987).

The final factor identified by Davey and King (1990) focuses on the *text* itself. Studies suggest that text construction can directly influence the reader's ability to derive meaning from context clues, including characteristics such as causal relationships, parallel and equivalent relationships, proximity of the clue to the target word, and multiple exposures to the target word. Another textual characteristic is the complexity of the unknown word. Words that are more commonly used are more conceptually salient, and words that have importance to the understanding of the text seem to influence the reader's ability to use context clues. However, the most critical text variable appears to be the ratio of known words—that is, words that are easily and efficiently accessed by the reader—to unknown words within the text.

Levels of Word Knowledge

The ability to say or sign, and use a word in context falls far short of word knowledge (Paul, 1996). Rather, a continuum expands from explicit instruction and memorization to a conceptual understanding by which the reader is able to construct meaning, with a median point along the continuum being a contextual level. This midpoint incorporates the reader's ability to extrapolate the meaning of a word from the context. For example, in the following sentence, the word *vaqueros* may be constructed by the reader from the context, assuming that the remainder of the context is within the reader's schema.

▶ Many vaqueros came north for jobs and soon were teaching American pioneers on the plains of Texas how to herd cattle. It was then that the cowboy was born. The cowboy, therefore, got his customs and paraphernalia from the Mexican vaquero. (Martin, 1967, p. 362)

Levels of word knowledge may also be described as having *breadth* and *depth*. Breadth involves the size or number of words known at any point along the definitional-conceptual continuum. It also includes the scope of vocabulary, that is, the array or diversity of words available to the reader across a variety of topics. Depth of word knowledge is the level of understanding of words, for example, an understanding of multiple meanings, syntactic and semantic relationships to other words, and contextual applications, including idiomatic and figurative functions (Vacca, Vacca, & Gove, 1995).

Using an instructional paradigm, Beck, Omanson, and McKeown (1982) identified three levels of word knowledge that determine the instructional objective and process: (1) unknown words; (2) familiar words—that is, at least one meaning of the word is recognized with some attention; and (3) established word knowledge—that is, meaning is known with ease and efficiency. Samuels (1988) illustrated this perspective of levels of word knowledge metaphorically as fluency in driving a car. At the first level, there is no familiarity with car driving skills. While parts and processes may be recognized, driving a car is unknown. The second level of acquaintance may be analogous to learning how to drive—that is, attention is given to each movement with great deliberation. The level of automaticity comes only after considerable experience behind the wheel, at which point the driver gives little or no thought to the tasks of driving; rather, the skills required to drive are present without explicit attention to the process. Graves, Watts, and Graves (1994) provide a framework (see Table 3.1) for the tasks students face when learning words in print that can be used as an instructional guide to selecting strategies and methods for instruction.

In summary, students who are deaf or hard of hearing differ considerably from each other in the word-learning task on a number of variables. Text-based variables are primarily focused on word recognition, including the relationship among words and the function that words have in the linguistic structure of the text. English, as the first or primary language, relies on word recognition through phonemic/graphic decoding. Students who are deaf or hard of hearing are challenged by the use of phonemic decoding skills, particularly of those words that have parallel relationships (e.g., same spelling with different meanings). Word recognition in a second-language model necessitates attributing meaning through translation from the first language to the second language. Knowledge regarding the relationships among ASL signs, finger spelling, or manual phonemic cues and the characteristics of English words may have a significant impact on the coding and decoding skills in the translation and read-

Table 3.1
Word Learning Tasks

Learning to Read Known Words	Good readers will have learned to read virtually all of the words in their oral vocabularies by 3rd or 4th grade.
Learning New Words Representing Known Concepts	Students have the concepts, but do not have the words for the concepts. They need to learn new words to label known concepts.
Learning New Words Representing New Concepts	Students do not have prior experience with the concept (e.g., *torque, endocrine*) and do not know the words necessary to discuss the concept. They need to learn both the concept and the words.
Learning New Meaning for Known Words	Students are familiar with a meaning for the word, but it is used with a meaning different from the one they know. They need to learn multiple meanings for words and how to apply them.
Clarifying and Enriching Meanings for Known Words	Students learn to expand and enrich the words they already know (e.g., *cabin/shed; brief/concise*).
Moving Words into Students' Expressive Vocabularies	Students must have exposure and reinforcement of new words and encouragement to use them when applicable.

Note. From *Essentials of Classroom Teaching: Elementary Reading* (pp. 108–110), by M. Graves, W. Watts, and B. Graves, 1994, Needham Heights, MA: Allyn & Bacon. Copyright 1994 by Allyn & Bacon. Adapted with permission.

ing processes. Paul and Gustafson (1991) stress the value of word knowledge instruction through the integration and meaningful use of new words in context with consistent exposure and practice. Instruction is a critical component in the word-learning process, particularly in the use of text variables and task factors to respond to differences among readers. While spoken English codes may be foreign to many young deaf children, providing experiences, a rich semantic context, links, and networking strategies with ASL signs, finger spelling, and English words may establish pathways to greater depth and breadth of word knowledge and facilitate reading comprehension. Instruction in phonetic and spelling conventions of English can equip students who are deaf or hard of hearing with the resources for word decoding and discovery.

Comprehension

Comprehension is the key to literacy. While vocabulary or word knowledge is a critical component of reading comprehension, the process consists of a complex set of interrelated tasks that have yet to be clearly defined. Graves, Watts, and Graves (1994) define the process of reading comprehension as relating the unknown to the known. Pearson and Johnson (1978) define the process as "building bridges between the *new* and the *known*" (p. 227). Comprehending text depends on the individual's ability to think and feel with the author—that is, the "reader's knowledge of the world interacts with the message conveyed directly or indirectly by the text. . . . The result is fully developed communication between the reader and the author" (Durkin, 1989, p. 10). Just and Carpenter (1987) defined comprehension as an active cognitive process that begins with information in the text, proceeds to the type of information applied during the process, and ends with information the reader has acquired from the process. Bernhardt (1993) built on that cognitive schema by describing reading comprehension as a "constructive process of relating new and incoming information to information already stored in memory" (p. 191). She distinguished reading among second-language learners as more of an associative than a constructive process, in which the reader uses conceptual schemata and multiple linguistic forms while interacting with the second-language text-based information.

The interactions that occur between the reader and the text are discussed as a set of skills or steps; however, reading comprehension is a series of complex interdependent systems including relationships among the reader, the text, and the task of reading that cannot be segmented. Palincsar and Brown (1984) identified six specific events that occur when readers are engaged in the comprehension process: (1) readers must have a purpose or motivation for reading; (2) readers must recall and apply prior knowledge that is relevant to the text and purpose for reading; (3) readers must distinguish information that is important from less important or irrelevant information; 4) readers must evaluate the text for cohesiveness and consistency with what they already know and with what is possible; (5) readers must monitor the process of comprehension to verify their ability to understand the information presented in the text; and (6) readers must bring their assumptions to the reading process, make inferences, and evaluate understanding of the text. Pearson and Johnson (1978) described the relationships among these sets of events as highly interdependent and overlapping, so that focusing on any one of the tasks means focusing on all of them: "The simple fact is that we cannot deal with the universe of comprehension tasks at once. We recognize that, for the sake of instructional convenience and sanity, you have to start somewhere and move toward something" (p. 227).

Prior Knowledge

As a reader engages in the reading process, factors such as word recognition, knowledge of syntax, and the ability to infer information provide meaning to the printed page only if the information can be linked to what the reader already knows and the reader has a purpose for reading. Each factor is influenced by the reader's prior or background knowledge and motivation. Reading comprehension is dependent on an individual's ability to relate the new information from the text to past experiences and knowledge (Graves, Watts, & Graves, 1994). Mason and Au (1990) identified two domains where background knowledge is critical: (1) knowledge of the topic of the text, and (2) knowledge of text structure (p. 38).

Topical Knowledge

Knowledge of the topic of the passage assists readers in comprehension by relating new information from the text with their own background knowledge. Prior topical knowledge is part of the schema a reader brings to the reading task. Anderson (1977) pointed out that writers assume that some degree of prior knowledge is common among their readers and intentionally leave gaps for readers to infer specific events. For example, in the opening statement of *Billy Had a System*, author Marion Holland wrote, "Billy Kidwell had a new ball, and Fats Martin had a new bat, so they were taking turns batting out a few on the vacant lot . . ." (1967, p. 52). The author assumed that the reader has topical knowledge about the game of baseball and chose not to provide detailed information regarding how the boys threw the ball, exchanged the ball and bat, or swung at the ball. The author implied a set of events and characteristics, which the reader must infer to reach comprehension of the passage (Mason & Au, 1986). Comprehension occurs when readers are able to use what they know about the topic, select what is relevant to the topic, and add to what is printed in the text (Anderson, 1977). Andrews, Winograd, and DeVille (1994) used an ASL retell strategy to increase students' topical knowledge of fables with a group of 11- and 12-year-old deaf students. Advanced knowledge of the topic, presented in the students' language of ASL prior to reading in English, significantly improved comprehension.

Alvermann and Boothby (1982) extended the importance of topical knowledge to the reader's interest in the topic of the text. A child's interest and purpose for reading (e.g., to identify the basketball champions, to solve a mystery) set expectations for the manner in which the child interacts with the text, the amount of attention given to facts and feelings, and the rate of reading. In fact, Alvermann and Boothby emphasized that interest in the text is, perhaps, of greater importance than knowledge of the topic. The critical points made are that students need to be interested in the topic and have a purpose for reading the text, and the topic of the text must be familiar. Unfamiliar topics should be taught or experienced prior to reading.

Text Structure Knowledge

Knowledge of text structure encompasses a broad category of factors sometimes referred to as global and local features. Included is a host of characteristics spanning word knowledge, coding, decoding, and text format, such as the use of headings and highlights, abbreviations, punctuation markers, illustrations, and story grammar. The reader's background knowledge and ability to recall and relate each of these factors to the text facilitates interaction between author and reader, resulting in comprehension. How much a deaf or hard of hearing student knows about the syntax and structure of English text, how English syntax relates to the student's language base (e.g., ASL, Spanish, Hmong), and the ability to integrate what is known to the printed page are key elements in the comprehension process.

Syntax

Readers bring knowledge of syntactic structures to the reading comprehension task with varying efficiency. Knowledge of how words and phrases are organized to convey specific concepts allows the reader to comprehend the intentions of the author with greater accuracy and fluency. A number of researchers have studied competent readers' use of syntactic background knowledge (Halliday & Hasan, 1976). There is general consensus that knowledge of how sentences and phrases are structured provides a network or cohesion for ideas within the text. Ideas can be combined with a structure such as a conjunction (e.g., *and*), ideas can be altered from one condition to another (e.g., with *or*), and a causal relationship can be developed between two ideas (e.g., with *because*) using syntax manipulations. The reader's background knowledge of syntax can affect text comprehension. For example:

▶ *Josh rode the bus to school, and Mom stayed home.*

Josh rode the bus to school because Mom stayed home.

Josh rode the bus to school, but Mom stayed home.

Reading comprehension is related to the reader's prior knowledge of syntax and complexity of text. DiStefano and Valencia (1980) matched reading passages to the reader's ability to read the text. Three levels of text difficulty were identified as being at the independent, instructional, or frustration level in concert with the reader's comprehension of the passage. Transformational structures in the reading passages were then simplified into basic sentence patterns. Students in the study demonstrated greater comprehension of the simplified text that was matched to the instructional level of the student. Passages that were at the independent level had no effect on comprehension since the readers were able to read the more complex structures prior to the syntactic modifications. Simplification of syntax in passages at the frustration level, however, did not increase reading comprehension. Rather, the text presented at the frustration level still contained a high ratio of unknown to known words or topical information unfamiliar to the reader.

A considerable number of studies examined deaf children's comprehension of text-based syntactic structures. Quigley and his associates (Quigley, Power, & Steinkamp, 1977; Quigley, Wilbur, & Montanelli, 1974) conducted a series of studies focusing on the comprehension of specific syntactic structures in deaf and hearing children ranging in age from 8 to 18 years. Results of extensive testing indicated significant delays among deaf children in the comprehension of syntactic structures presented in isolated sentences. Hatcher and Robbins (1978) conducted similar studies on a smaller scale with deaf children, controlling for word recognition and word knowledge. Their results supported the findings of Quigley and his associates. Sentences containing passive voice were the most difficult to understand, while active-voice sentences were the easiest (see King & Quigley, 1985, pp. 59–67). Additional research indicated that comprehension of some syntactic structures may not be fully dependent on the knowledge of syntax and may be facilitated through the use of context clues and connected discourse (Ewoldt, 1981; Gormley & Franzen, 1978). Fischler (1983) analyzed the patterns of responses among deaf and hearing college-level students on a cloze passage—a passage in which every nth word has been deleted—completion task. Fischler concluded that deaf and hearing students in the study differed in their specific prior knowledge of syntax and semantics. The identified inadequacies in syntax comprehension have significant implications on the background knowledge that deaf children can depend on in the reading comprehension process.

English syntax includes a variety of "nonrules"—syntactic structures that are "exceptions" and may not be taken literally. Prior knowledge is critical to the recognition of structures such as idioms, similes, proverbs, and platitudes. Wiig and Semel (1984) noted that the reader must interpret the form of figurative language through a process of syntactic and semantic reclassification to establish a variety of possible interpretations. Studies focusing on deaf readers' comprehension of figurative language forms when syntax and vocabulary were adapted to the proficiency level of the students resulted in high performance scores (see King & Quigley, 1985, pp. 63–65). Giorcelli (1982) investigated the comprehension of figurative language in single sentences and in enriched context. Deaf students demonstrated difficulty in comprehension when they did not have background knowledge of the syntax used in either the single sentences or the enriched context.

Text Organization

Experience with the organization of text-based information assists the reader in establishing a specific set of expectations that contribute to reading comprehension. Reviewing the layout of a document cues the reader into past experiences with smaller documents. The reader anticipates a different set of reading tasks with prior knowledge that a job application form is different from a personal letter, or that a novel is different from a poem. Having prior knowledge of text organization allows the reader to interact with the text and the intentions of the author with greater efficiency and effectiveness (Mason & Au, 1990).

Story Grammar

The structure of a story, or the way a story is organized, is referred to as *story grammar*. While text organization addresses the technical layout and format of print, story grammar has to do with the construction of the content. Prior knowledge or familiarity with the units or categories that make up a story assists the reader in comprehending the text through sensitivity to the priorities of the text—that is, readers with an understanding of story grammar infer causal connections between events, characters, and settings and attend to categories that are relevant. Competent readers develop a set of rules that govern implications and information within the text (Mandler & Johnson, 1977). Readers anticipate the story grammar of a mystery as being somewhat different from that of a biography. Vacca, Vacca, and Gove (1995) emphasized that children who are able to anticipate the story's structure are better able to focus on relationships within the text and to extract meaning from significant events and ideas. Children who have early experiences with storytelling acquire a familiarity with the grammar of stories and are better able to develop an implicit knowledge of constructs within the text.

Identifying a single set of elements that define story grammar or story schema has proved to be an extremely difficult task (Mandler & Johnson, 1977; Stein & Glenn 1979; Thorndyke, 1977). Vacca, Vacca, and Gove (1995) summarized six elements that appear to be most common: (1) the setting, including the main character, time, and place; (2) the initiating event; (3) the internal response, including the problem or goal of the story; (4) the attempt to address the problem or goal; (5) the consequence of the attempt; and (6) the reaction to the events (pp. 188–189). Instruction in identification of the elements of story grammar assists students in the development of a story schema. Pearson (1982) demonstrated the effectiveness of flow charting and teacher modeling as strategies for the development of story grammar, while Beck et al. (1982) used story maps to develop both implicit and explicit comprehension of structures. Hinchley and Levy (1988) reported that explicitly teaching children with reading comprehension problems about story grammar significantly increased their ability to recall and respond to questions when the stories were well organized. However, stories with poor grammar structure continued to be problematic.

Illustrations

Within the emergent literacy phase of reading, predictable books are frequently used with young children. Predictable books are well illustrated, with repeated and progressive sentences accompanying each illustration. With adequate and appropriate introduction to such a book, the young reader can use illustrations to make sense of the text and to note changes in the context. Some storybooks, such as Ellen Raskin's *Spectacles* (1968), integrate illustrations with text information, requiring the reader to extract and integrate meaning from both sources to acquire a sense of the story and to interact with the text. Illustrations within the text can also be helpful in developing comprehension and word knowledge through the use of rebuses or captions for cartoons (Taylor et al., 1995). However, the relationship between illustrations and comprehension is qualified by several variables, including "(1) artistic stylization; (2) amount of detail and relations to the text; (3) shifts in perspective from one picture to the next; (4) size and completeness of the picture; (5) proximity of the picture to the related text; and (6) whether or not the picture is placed within the text" (King & Quigley, 1985, p. 143). Beck, Omanson, and McKeown (1982) studied the use of illustrations as a part of the comprehension process in lesson delivery. They noted that illustrations should support the text and assist the reader in comprehending the main ideas or central theme conveyed. Illustrations that focus on irrelevant events or conflicts occurring in the text can create confusion in comprehension.

Joseph (1989) examined the relationship between the use of illustrations and reading comprehension with a group of 10- to 12-year-old deaf students.

Two types of illustration formats were used as advance organizers. Key words (e.g., *airplane, wings, propellers*) were simply illustrated in one format, while concepts (e.g., humidity, velocity) were depicted through illustrations, semantic maps, and graphic displays. Students demonstrated a small increase in reading comprehension when illustrations were used, with no advantage of key object illustration over the graphic semantic maps. Joseph noted that discussion with the students about the illustrations and their prior knowledge of the concepts were critical components in the comprehension process. Reynolds and Booher (1980) studied the comprehension of task-related text and illustrated information with college students who were deaf. The amount of information that was presented in text and pictorial information varied within the reading task and among different reading tasks. The results indicated that for this particular comprehension task (operation of machinery), the students relied to a greater extent on the illustrations and performed best when the maximum number of illustrations were used.

Inference

Developing comprehension of text requires that a reader be able to extract meaning from the words printed on a page or computer screen. Durkin (1989) defined knowing the meaning of the words and the order in which they are presented as "literal comprehension." However, reading comprehension requires that the reader have the ability to "go beyond the author's words by inferring" what the author implies (p. 7). Inference processes in reading require readers to integrate their prior knowledge or world knowledge with their word knowledge to extract meaning from text information that may not be explicitly printed or obvious within the passage. Comprehension of predictable events such as those in the example *The car came to a screeching halt, but the car behind couldn't stop in time* depends on readers' experiences as well as their ability to infer or use what they know about the event depicted in the passage. The author assumes a particular inferential match between reader and text. This match is particularly critical in the event of cultural uniqueness and second-language learners. Johnson (1981) pointed out that incongruency "between the text and the reader may pose a far more insidious problem—quite subtly causing the reader to build a completely inappropriate model of the text meaning without being aware of the problem. . . . Once the reader has begun to construct an inappropriate model, inappropriate inferences would be generated by virtue of the content of the growing model itself" (p. 31). For example, after reading an advertisement regarding "Free Checking Accounts," the reader rushed to the bank and opened an account. He began using his "free checks" with great delight. Several days later, he was dismayed when the bank returned his checks unpaid with a service charge for bad debits. The young consumer defended his actions by producing the advertisement for "Free Checking Accounts"!

Brown and Brewer (1996) reviewed studies regarding inferring skills among deaf readers. Based on a small set of studies conducted primarily with high school and postsecondary-level students, they concluded that students who are deaf are able to make inferences from the text. Sarachan-Deily (1985) noted that deaf students recalled inadequate inferences more frequently than their hearing peers. Pinhas (1991) noted that among deaf and hearing college students, inference was more likely to occur during questioning among the deaf students and during the reading process with the hearing students. A study addressing the predictable inference skills was conducted with deaf and hearing skilled and less skilled college students using reading passages that contained topical knowledge familiar to all of the readers (Brown & Brewer, 1996). The result supported earlier findings that deaf college students are able to make predictive inferences similarly to their hearing peers. Skilled deaf readers were less inhibited by word knowledge than less skilled readers.

Inferential aspects of the reading process are developed through experiences or world knowledge and are significantly influenced by the reader's ability to access the literal aspects of the text, that is, word knowledge, linguistic information, and text features. Hansen (1981) reported that by merely increasing the number of inferential questions asked of the students, comprehension scores increased. Based on her case studies in reading comprehension with deaf students, Ewoldt (1981) proposed that experience and word knowledge can be a powerful tool that can compensate for linguistic weaknesses. Readers who are reading in a second language have a knowledge base from which to infer or to make sense of the text; however, the reader may not be able to access sufficient information from the text to make appropriate inferences. For example, a young employee carefully read the employee handbook after his first month on the job, noting all the benefits, rules, and regulations. He noted that "each Level I employee receives 2 weeks' vacation per year." Excited about his job and the opportunity for benefits, he decided to take his 2 weeks' vacation the following week. Inference skills can be enhanced through experience and explicit instruction, particularly teacher questioning strategies prior to, during, and following reading.

Metacognition

Metacognition refers to knowing how we know or thinking about one's own thinking (Durkin, 1989, p. 365). Baker and Brown (1984) described metacognition as a means of evaluating one's own understanding of the text. Competent readers have a sense of control over their understanding of the text and are able to report when they do not comprehend the text. They are able to draw from a menu of strategies that can be applied to remediate the inability to comprehend. Paris, Lipson, and Wixson (1983) referred to this process as *strategic* reading. Table 3.2 describes some of the more common comprehension "breakdowns" that occur between the reader, the reading process, and the text. Developing an awareness of comprehension difficulties or breakdowns and the means to address these breakdowns is a developmental process that appears to occur as the reader develops fluency in reading comprehension. For example, children who are focusing their reading efforts on word meaning or decoding skills frequently experience difficulties in reading for meaning (Baker & Brown, 1984; Ryan, 1981). These young readers may not know how to apply strategies to monitor their own comprehension (Wagoner, 1983). Practice and direct instruction can assist a child in the development of metacognitive strategies related to monitoring his or her own understanding of the text.

Strassman (1997) conducted an extensive review of the research focused on deaf and hard of hearing students' metacognitive abilities. A summary of the studies suggests that students who are deaf generally are dependent on the teacher to assist in reading comprehension and have little knowledge of strategies that can repair breakdowns in comprehension (Andrews & Mason, 1991;

Table 3.2
Breakdowns in Comprehending

Understanding word meanings

A student reads the sentence, *The once beautiful garden was now filled with craters, and our house was a barren shell*, and skims over words because he cannot attach meaning to the words *craters*, *barren*, and *shell*. The student believes that the statement doesn't make sense.

Making sense of it

While reading the sentence *I loved to travel by train and snuggle to sleep in the cozy compartment while feeling the wheels snapping on the rails*, the student misidentifies *compartment* as *apartment*. After reading the entire statement, the student believes that it doesn't make sense.

Understanding the purpose of the text

The student is reading an editorial in the newspaper and assumes that the information contained in it is fact. As the student reads on, some of the information is in disagreement with what the reader already knows. The student realizes that an editorial is not always based on facts.

Note. Adapted from *Teaching Them to Read* (5th ed.) (p. 365), by D. Durkin, 1989, Boston: Allyn & Bacon.

Ewoldt, 1986; Ewoldt, Israelite, & Dodds, 1991; McCarr, 1973; Strassman, 1992). Strassman (1997) concluded that "current instructional practices used to teach reading to deaf children might actually hinder their development of mature knowledge and control" (p. 141). Erickson (1987) advocated that reading instruction at all grade levels should include comprehension tasks and explicit metacognitive strategies congruent with the maturity of the deaf readers' thinking abilities rather than their assessed standard English reading scores.

Research on the effectiveness of metacognitive interventions has escalated significantly since Durkin's (1978–79) report on the near absence of comprehension instruction in classroom settings. Studies with deaf children generally include small numbers of students and restricted designs with few conclusive observations. However, some insights into the instructional process can be gained from the observations thus far. The effects of summarizing stories or story recall following reading were reported by Akamatsu (1988), Griffith and Ripich (1988), and Andrews, Winograd, and DeVille (1994). Each of the studies demonstrated positive effects of summaries or recall following reading, particularly during the intervention phases of the studies. Rereading or "lookback" strategies are commonly used among readers when there is a breakdown in comprehension. Davey (1987) reported that the adolescent residential school deaf students she worked with did not report using lookback strategies to enhance comprehension. Rather, the students reported looking back to find an answer or a match to a question.

Taylor et al. (1995, p. 227) developed a basic checklist of metacognitive strategies that can be used by students. Taylor suggested that the following reminders could be posted in the classroom or placed on a "reminder card" that could be referred to as the student reads:

1. Get ready to read (i.e., read headings, look at pictures, think about what I already know).

2. Monitor my comprehension while reading (e.g., notice when I'm not understanding, use fix-up strategies).

3. Improve my comprehension while reading (e.g., ask myself questions, stop to assess where I am).

4. Check my comprehension and study after reading (e.g., create a summary, ask myself questions, create a story map or a graphic organizer).

5. Help myself answer questions (e.g., use lookbacks, question-answer relationships, or self-monitoring checklist).

Educators can see metacognitive strategies at work. Students' metacognition is reflected in reading when they begin to question themselves for clarification and word meaning, self-correct their recall, self-question their sense of the text, and interact with their peers and teacher to discuss the meaning of the passage. Bernhardt (1993) described evidence of metacognition in written passages as marked by question marks, blanks, and indirect or uncertain reports of information read, all indicators of self-monitoring strategies. Metacognition is a developmental process that requires time, instruction, and practice.

Summary

While little research is available regarding the processes used by deaf children in the development of word knowledge and reading comprehension, some evidence suggests a substantive difference in the reading process between deaf and hearing children. Whether the child has acquired ASL or English as a first language or a second language or is acquiring language through bilingual exposure, knowledge and experiences with language and the general concepts of language are part of the emergent reading-writing processes. Using the foundation of word knowledge and word meaning, comprehension of printed text begins. The continual growth and development of effective reading comprehension are dependent on access to and use of a variety of strategies that can assist ASL students who are bilingual and English-based deaf children to engage in and enjoy reading.

Pearson and Fielding (1991) summarized "consistently successful strategies" common to the task of comprehension. The first is establishing background knowledge. This strategy may include a variety of processes that are teacher directed, self-directed, or interactive among peers and with the teacher. Second is establishing a bridge between the students' prior knowledge and the text. Strategies may include developing a substantive schema of the story by discussing the students' prior knowledge of the topic and having them make predictions, draw inferences from questions posed by the teacher, and establish a purpose. The third successful strategy identified is developing and activating students' metacognitive skills so that they understand what is read and know when misunderstanding is occurring. This strategy includes making sense of the printed page or screen and is more frequently referred to as monitoring comprehension. The fourth and final strategy is summarizing—that is, recalling and retelling the text.

Limbrick, McNaughton, and Clay (1992) noted that deaf students who were observed as a part of their study spent small amounts of time actually reading. Teacher interactions, interruptions, and time schedules often interfered with the opportunity for reading with purpose and for meaning. The possibility that instructional practices may be linked to the inadequate literacy achievement among deaf and hard of hearing children has been raised by several concerned professionals (Erickson, 1987; Gormley & Franzen, 1978; LaSasso & Davey, 1987; Limbrick, 1991; Paul, 1996; Strassman, 1997; Williams, 1994). The response to this concern must include teachers and related professionals who employ effective systems and strategies for the development of strategic reading skills with deaf and hard of hearing children.

CHAPTER

ASL, English, and Reading

Preview

In the United States, many administrators and teachers of deaf and hard of hearing students have changed their traditional education programs to bilingual education programs (Strong, 1995), which are frequently referred to as bilingual-bicultural programs. These programs encompass not only an educational approach but a sociocultural approach as well. The bicultural component (referring mainly to the deaf and hearing cultures but usually credited with referring to all relevant cultures) is an important and integral part of these programs, as it is this aspect that focuses on developing deaf children's confidence, self-esteem, and pride in being a part of the deaf community, a focus that many consider necessary for the development of the whole child.

This chapter focuses only on the bilingual component and the pedagogy of bilingual instruction. A great deal of the information comes from the field of bilingual education and second-language learners who are hearing because not much literature is available on bilingual instruction with deaf second-language learners. Neither is there any published research on bilingual education with deaf and hard of hearing students; consequently, it cannot be said with any degree of certainty that this approach is or will be successful with that population. However, intellectually and intuitively, the principles and the strategies make a great deal of sense and, with some modifications, seem to fit the educational situation of many deaf and hard of hearing students.

If the reader desires a more detailed discussion of bilingual education than is offered in this chapter, there are many books that can provide that information; several are listed in the reference section of this book. The bulk of this

89

chapter provides information on strategies that have been found to be successful with hearing second-language learners and the modifications that can be made to adapt them to meet the needs of deaf second-language learners. Many of these strategies are already being used in classes with deaf children but perhaps not within the overall framework of a bilingual program. The final section of this chapter is a caveat to readers reviewing some of the differences in deaf and hearing second-language learners with a plea to implement programs responsibly by gathering data that will provide valid information for program evaluation.

Bilingual Instruction

Since its inception, education of deaf students in the United States has embraced a monolingual approach. In the United States, the language of instruction in this monolingual approach has been English, first in an auditory-oral mode and later in a signed-oral mode. Despite the high hopes of educators using a manually coded English system for increased academic achievement in their deaf students, they were disappointed to find that, even after 20 years of exposure to a signed English system, no significant gains were noted on academic achievement tests. Data from the Center for Assessment and Demographic Studies at Gallaudet University in 1991 indicated that approximately half the deaf students in the United States were reading below the fourth-grade level when they graduated from high school, results similar to those found by Furth in 1966.

In recent years, there has a been a movement toward the use of bilingual models of instruction in which the principal language of instruction is American Sign Language. This approach is regarded by many as one that will facilitate the students' language acquisition, learning, and expression of knowledge through both ASL and English. Bilingual proponents believe that if ASL is well established as the first-language, then English literacy can be achieved through reading and writing without exposure to English in its primary form, through speech, or alternatively through a manually coded English sign system (Israelite, Ewoldt, & Hoffmeister, 1992).

Defining Bilingualism and Bilingual Education

Language is commonly considered to encompass four skills: speaking, listening, reading, and writing. Proficiency in a language refers to a person's ability to process a language in each of these four skills, while being literate in a language refers to the person's proficiency in reading and writing skills at an appropriate level for a specific context (Williams & Snipper, 1990). Bilingual proficiency refers to the ability to process two languages in each of the same four skills and would therefore involve (1) understanding the message in each of the languages spoken, (2) being able to respond in each of the languages appropriately for the situation, (3) being able to read and understand a written message in each language, and (4) being able to write in each language. These four skills are not separate and unrelated; they are not hierarchical, nor do they progress sequentially in development. Consequently, most bilingual educators advocate instruction that integrates the language modes. Williams and Snipper suggested that it is possible for students to write even if they lack perfect speech or reading skills and that reading is possible even if the listening skills are not fully developed. The language modes interact reciprocally, so the more students read, the more vocabulary they acquire, thereby expanding their expressive language repertoire and improving their spelling from seeing words in print. The more students write, the more proficient they become at formulating clear and concise messages, which will, in turn, positively affect their expressive language.

Bilingual Education

In 1968 federal legislation was passed creating bilingual education programs, which were defined as educational programs in which two languages, one of which must be English, are used for teaching purposes. There are several different kinds of bilingual education programs, but two goals are common to all: (1) to teach English, and (2) to provide access to content-area curriculum through the home language while students are gaining English-language proficiency (Lessow-Hurley, 1990). Several kinds of bilingual education programs have been established (Peregoy & Boyle, 1993) and are briefly described in the following text.

Transitional Bilingual Education. Instruction in the student's primary language is provided for 1–3 years and is intended to serve as a bridge to instruction in the English language. After the transitional period is finished (1–3 years), all instruction is delivered in English. The goal is to develop English-language proficiency as quickly as possible.

Maintenance Bilingual Education. Instruction is provided in the primary language for an extended period of time with the intent to maintain proficiency in the primary language while developing proficiency in English. The program goal is for the students to become fully bilingual and biliterate.

Immersion Education. Canada established a bilingual program, referred to as an immersion program, to promote French-language acquisition by English-speaking students. Instruction takes place in the target language (i.e., French). In the

United States, immersion programs have been established to teach a second language to children who are already proficient in English. Instruction is provided in the target language (e.g., Spanish) in the early grades, after which there is a gradual introduction of English language arts. The goal of immersion programs in the United States is to develop full bilingualism and biliteracy in native English-speaking students.

Two-Way Immersion Programs. A two-way immersion program is a variation on the traditional immersion program. In the two-way program, two equal groups of students, one English speaking and one non-English speaking, are placed together for instruction. In the early grades, the non-English language (e.g., Spanish) is the language of instruction in an immersion approach, and instruction in English is gradually increased as students advance in grades. The goal is full bilingualism and biliteracy for all students; for example, the Spanish-speaking students will also be fluent in English, and the English-speaking students will also be fluent in Spanish.

Bilingual education programs that aim to develop children's bilingual and biliterate abilities fully are referred to as *additive*. These programs encourage the addition of a second language while maintaining or developing the primary-language abilities. In contrast to additive bilingualism, *subtractive bilingualism* occurs when an individual develops a second language fully while shifting away from identity with primary language and culture. This situation occurs frequently when people immigrate to a new country. Generally, school programs that do not aim for full bilingualism are most concerned with teaching the English language. It is then the responsibility of the immigrant family and community to help the children maintain and develop the home language. If the family does not consider the maintenance of the home language beneficial, then it will probably deteriorate over time and the child will no longer be bilingual.

ESL Programs

Bilingual education programs in which the students' first language and English are used serve only a small percentage of eligible students. Most students whose first language is other than English are enrolled in instructional programs that use only one language for teaching. The language used for teaching is English, and these programs are referred to as ESL (English as a Second Language) programs. Many classrooms, especially in large cities and suburbs, include students from several language groups, making bilingual instruction impossible. Peregoy and Boyle (1993) described several programs that fall in the category of ESL.

Sheltered English. In sheltered English programs, the language of instruction is English. Content-area subjects are organized to promote second-language acquisition while the students are learning concepts using grade-level materials. Special teaching techniques are used to help the students understand the instruction even though they are still limited in English-language proficiency.

ESL Pullout. In ESL pullout programs, second-language students spend most of their school day in the classroom with their monolingual (in English) peers. However, they are "pulled out" of the classroom on a regular basis to receive special instruction, usually from an ESL teacher, in English-language development activities and in reinforcement of the subject matter being taught in the classroom. The goal is to help second-language students "survive" while becoming proficient in oral and written English.

English-Language Development. In English-language development programs, second-language students learn all subject matter including English as a second language in a class taught by a teacher who has special training in or knowledge of second-language development. The majority of students in such classes are ESL or nonstandard English dialect speakers. The goal is full English-language and literacy development.

It is apparent that there are several different kinds of bilingual and ESL programs, and it is equally obvious that while the programs may differ philosophically in how a second language is acquired, the ultimate goal for all of the additive bilingual programs is the same. These programs aim to develop students who are bilingual and biliterate. In contrast, ESL programs focus on developing the English language and English literacy.

Bilingual Instruction and Deaf Children

Recently in the United States, a movement has developed to explore the potential for bilingual instruction in programs for deaf students. The basis for this instructional shift is predicated on several different areas of research.

One area of research that has influenced this movement focused on the differences between deaf children of deaf parents (DCDP) and deaf children of hearing parents (DCHP). The hearing status of the parents was found to be a good predictor of future linguistic and academic success, with the studies indicating that DCDP typically outperformed DCHP, at least in the early years (Meadow, 1968; Quigley & Frisina, 1961; Stuckless & Birch, 1966). Possible explanations for these results might be that (a) DCDP are better adjusted emotionally because of parental attitude; (b) the etiology of DCHP frequently is caused by trauma or disease, which may affect cognitive functioning; and (c) DCDP are more likely to grow up learning a natural language (ASL) in a natural manner. Lane (1990) maintained that this first language exposure is critical in preparing deaf children for future academic learning, particularly in English literacy. Braden (1994) attributed the advantage of DCDP specifically to the fact that they have had early exposure to a language and have been able to establish an internal language base, which facilitates their acquisition, storage, and application of academic knowledge.

Research in the use of bilingual instruction with hearing students has also influenced the movement of bilingual instruction in deaf education. Many educators believe that the same strategies that have been successful with hearing children can be applied to deaf students. Cummins (1981) stressed that there is a common underlying proficiency of languages, and Hakuta (1990) stated that native-language proficiency is a consistent and powerful predictor of second-language development. Some educators (e.g., Livingston, 1997; Moores, 1992) question using the bilingual approach with deaf children, asserting that ASL is not analogous to other first languages because it has no written form and pointing out that there is little research to indicate that ASL benefits the learning of English. Livingston has further stated that the majority of deaf children do not have a first language when they enter school, as do hearing students who are learning English as a second language. Thus, while the hearing student focuses on learning one additional language, the deaf student must learn two.

A study conducted by Strong and Prinz (1997) investigated whether or not a relationship existed between ASL skills and English literacy development in deaf children. The subjects in this study were 155 deaf students, 8 to 15 years old with no other known disabilities, who attended residential schools. In a pilot study conducted in 1995, Prinz and Strong validated their test instruments, refined data collection procedures, planned sampling procedures, and tested a small subsample of subjects (Prinz & Strong, 1995). In addition to the question stated above, they were also interested in a subsidiary question: Do deaf children of deaf parents outperform deaf children of hearing parents in ASL skills and English literacy skills?

The results of the investigation conducted by Strong and Prinz (1997) indicate a consistent and statistically significant relationship between ASL skill and English literacy. The data show that, when controlled for age and performance IQ, the subjects performed at a higher level of English literacy if their ASL skills were well developed than if those skills were lacking. This result was found in all age groups. They also found that English performance improves even with a moderate level of ASL skill. Similarly, students in the highest of the three ASL groups tended to achieve significantly higher English scores than students in the lowest ASL group and, in most cases, those in the intermediate ASL group. Thus, while acknowledging that additional similar research should be conducted to confirm their findings, Strong and Prinz stated that their data strongly indicate that expertise in ASL influences the acquisition of English literacy and supports the use of bilingual instruction for deaf students.

Applied to the second question, the data indicate that DCDP outperformed DCHP in both age groups (8–11 years and 12–15 years). That result supports and extends the conclusions of earlier studies done in the 1960s that concluded that DCDP outperformed DCHP, at least in the early years.

Bilingual Education of Deaf Children in Sweden and Denmark

The change to bilingual education for deaf children in Sweden was effected through a grassroots activism by deaf adults and parents of deaf children. In 1981, the Swedish Parliament passed a law stating that deaf people should be bilingual to function effectively in the family, in school, and in society. Schools were charged with the responsibility of educating deaf children bilingually, and since then, deaf children in Sweden have been educated in a way that fosters proficiency in both Swedish Sign Language and Swedish, with a focus on literacy (Mahshie, 1995).

No similar legislation was passed in Denmark; however, the idea of bilingual education is widely accepted there, and bilingualism in Danish Sign Language and Danish is the official aim of all schools for deaf children (Engberg-Pedersen, 1993). Currently, based on a regulation issued by the Danish Ministry of Education, Danish Sign Language is an academic subject that is a part of the curriculum for all deaf children in Denmark.

Both Sweden and Denmark have extensive early identification of and services for very young children, including deaf children, and their parents. The health care system has been restructured, and health care professionals have been retrained. Professionals who provide services for deaf children and their parents have been made aware that parents need the support of other parents with deaf children and that it is very important for the children and their parents to interact with other deaf children and deaf adults who know sign language. In addition, parent groups and deaf clubs help to ensure that these two things do indeed happen (Mahshie, 1995). The health care districts (which have jurisdiction over children before they enter school) have overcome many bureaucratic procedures so that young deaf children may cross district lines to attend the preschool where they will have access to the bilingual communication environment. While mainstreaming in regular-education classrooms remains an option for deaf children in Sweden and Denmark, Mahshie reported that almost none of the parents choose that option, having seen, during the preschool years, the educational and social benefits of placing their children with deaf peers and deaf adults.

The reported results of the bilingual education programs from those two countries have been impressive. Hansen (1990) reported that 55% of the deaf students in Denmark were reading at age-appropriate levels, 22% were reading at a "transitional stage," in which they were beginning to construct meaning from the text, and were expected to develop their reading skills to an age-appropriate level before leaving school. The remaining 23% (at age 12) were still functioning as word-by-word readers and were not processing the meaning of the text. Hansen stated that before the bilingual approach, more than 56% of deaf children left school functioning at that level. He credits the bilingual approach with the improvement in the children's reading levels. Neilsen (1991), a school psychologist in Denmark, reported that the first deaf students to start their schooling in bilingual classes in Sweden and Denmark graduated with reading and math levels comparable to hearing children. Heiling (1993), a Swedish psychologist, reported that a number of deaf children, whose hearing parents started to used signs when the children were 2 years old or younger, performed comparably to their hearing peers on a standardized reading achievement test given in all final classes of compulsory schools in Sweden.

In the bilingual education programs in Sweden and Denmark, a great deal of emphasis is placed on academic achievement. The texts that are used by the deaf children are the same texts that are used by the hearing children in public schools. During the early school years, much of the subject matter in the texts is conveyed to the children through sign language in much the same way that teachers of hearing children convey information through spoken language before the children can read. As children begin to read text, they depend more on the written word for information. The goal is that school achievement must not suffer while the children are learning the language of their textbooks; thus, the content is communicated, at first, through sign language.

Norden, Tvingstedt, and Heiling (1989) compared the results of tests administered to all deaf eighth graders at the School for the Deaf in Lund, Sweden, in the 1960s to the results of tests administered to all deaf eighth graders at the same school in 1989. They found that the average level of theoretical knowledge had risen substantially in the current eighth graders. The current eighth graders were also superior in all tests measuring ability to understand and use written Swedish, and they performed significantly better on tests of mathematical and numerical ability. The differences between the two decades were the most apparent, however, in the tests measuring language proficiency.

The results of the bilingual programs in Sweden and Denmark as indicated by achievement scores, particularly those in reading, are very encouraging and supportive of bilingual instruction, especially when compared to the achievement scores of deaf students in programs in the United States. However, it should not be overlooked that while these scores may very likely be influenced by the bilingual programs, they are probably also influenced a great deal by the early identification and follow-up services provided to the families, which encourage the development of sign language in all family members of very young deaf children. These two factors combined—early access to language and bilingual programs—may be the necessary ingredients for this claimed success, rather than bilingual instruction alone. In fact, several investigators have found that when the home environment of a deaf child of hearing parents closely resembles the home environment of a deaf child of deaf parents—that is, when it is full of visual language and acceptance of the deaf child—the more likely it is that the child will have higher-developed language and cognitive skills (Ahlgren, 1994; Erting, 1992, 1994; Spencer, Bodner-Johnson, & Gutfreund, 1992).

It should also be noted that the field of education of deaf children is subject to "sweeping enthusiasms." That is, new approaches are proposed periodically that are claimed to greatly improve the educational achievements of deaf students (e.g., finger spelling from the Soviet Union in the 1960s and total communication in the United States in the 1970s and 1980s). Unfortunately, some of these new approaches (including the two previous examples) have proved to have limited success in the long term. Cautions are being voiced at present concerning the approaches and successes of ESL and bilingual education with hearing students in the United States. The results claimed for the new programs for deaf students in Sweden and Denmark are noteworthy, but those programs should be subjected to rigorous research in the United States before being introduced wholesale in this country.

Second-Language Learners and Reading

Students entering school and learning English as a new language face many challenges as they attempt to make sense of the school environment. Perhaps their greatest challenge is learning how to read a language in which they have not yet achieved proficiency. Native-English speakers learning to read encounter words and grammatical structures that they can already understand orally. The second-language learner encounters an extraordinary amount of unfamiliar language even in beginning texts. Beginning readers who are native-English speakers expect to understand the text once they have managed to decode it; readers who are learning English frequently cannot comprehend the text even if they manage to decode it (Chamot & O'Malley, 1994).

Second-Language Readers and the Reading Process

During the past 20 years, several studies have been conducted in an attempt to determine how people process print when reading in English as a second language (Carrell, Devine, & Eskey, 1988; Goodman & Goodman, 1978; Grabe, 1991; Hudelson, 1981). Researchers have consistently found that the process is essentially the same whether reading English as the first or the second language. Both first- and second-language readers look at the page, sample the print, and use their knowledge of sound-symbol relationships, word order, grammar, and meaning to predict and confirm meaning. In the reading process, both kinds of readers activate and apply their prior knowledge to the topic of the text, as well as their linguistic knowledge and reading strategies to arrive at meaning. If their initial interpretation does not make sense, they may go back and read again or apply other repair strategies.

These studies of have concluded that second-language readers use an interactive process. They engage simultaneously in top-down and bottom-up processing of the text, shifting back and forth from decoding text to cognitive processing of meaning based on relevant background knowledge. This view differs from the traditional notion that the second-language readers' primary task is to extract information accurately from text (Nurss & Hough, 1992). Instead, the interactive model suggests that the reading process is a dialogue between the reader and the author, with the text activating a range of reader knowledge that can be used for comprehension.

Although second-language readers appear to use the same reading process as native-English readers, the task is usually more difficult for them. While the process may be the same, the resources that first- and second-language readers apply are different. The two most important influences are second-language proficiency and background knowledge (Peregoy & Boyle, 1993). First-language readers can anticipate grammatical structures, thus maintaining fluency in their reading, which facilitates comprehension. Second-language readers, including deaf students, do not yet have adequate English skills to be able to anticipate grammatical structures, which decreases fluency and adversely affects comprehension. Function words such as articles and prepositions, which lack content, are familiar to first-language readers, who easily recognize the words in text and continue reading without interruption in fluency. Second-language readers, including deaf students, are often baffled by function words and hesitate when they meet such a word in print, thus interrupting fluency and comprehension. Consequently, limitations in second-language proficiency affect second-language reading comprehension, causing it to be slower and more arduous.

Another powerful factor that influences a second-language reader's comprehension is the reader's prior knowledge of the topic of the text. For example, a first-language reader who is reading a fairy tale very likely has a great deal of prior knowledge about the text. First, the reader probably has heard the story many times before when it was read by family members and so is already familiar with the content. Because of prior experiences, the reader is also likely to be familiar with common narrative forms, story structure, and plot sequences. This background knowledge facilitates comprehension because it allows the reader to make predictions about future events in the story. Many second-language readers may not have had these same stories read to them, or in the case of most deaf children, may not have had stories read to them at all, at least not in a language that they could access. The extent to which second-language readers are familiar with the topic and structure of a particular text will greatly influence the difficulty or success they will have in comprehending. By providing reading material on content familiar to students, teachers can offset reading comprehension difficulties stemming from limited second-language proficiency (Peregoy & Boyle, 1993).

Developmental Phases in Second-Language Reading

Peregoy and Boyle (1993) maintained that second-language readers progress through two developmental phases or categories in learning to read. They labeled these two categories as beginning and intermediate second-language reading phases. They do not view these phases as identifiable, discrete stages but rather as general categories within a continuum. These two general categories are intended to facilitate teaching decisions as teachers help students move from one developmental phase to the next by challenging them to higher levels of performance.

In general, beginning second-language readers are very similar to beginning first-language readers. They are just beginning to arrive at meaning from reading short texts. They are still not completely familiar with the English alphabet and its several unusual combinations of letters and spelling patterns. They may recognize a number of sight words but need much more practice in reading to develop a larger sight-word vocabulary. Most beginners can read simple texts such as predictable books using word recognition strategies, language knowledge, and memorization but probably still have difficulty processing text beyond the sentence level. Regardless of age, second-language readers need a great deal of experience with written language. If they have never read in any language before, as is the case with deaf children, they need to see and experience the many ways people use reading and writing for everyday activities and for enjoyment. In summary, hearing and deaf beginners need to be immersed in reading and writing activities that have relevant and clearly understood purposes. They need ample time to practice so that they can develop their sight-word vocabularies, establish firmly some of the conventions such as reading from left to right and from top to bottom, and move toward successful, independent reading of simple texts.

The language experience approach (LEA) is one of the most frequently recommended approaches for beginning second-language readers (Tinajero & Calderon, 1988) and is an approach that is commonly used in preschool, kindergarten, and elementary classes for deaf and hard of hearing children. In this approach, the student provides the text through dictation; this text serves as the material for reading instruction, thus tailoring the material to the learner's own interests, background knowledge, and language proficiency (Peregoy & Boyle, 1993). Stories may also be dictated by small groups of children or by the entire class. The stories are written down verbatim on a whiteboard or a large chart, and the students read them back; even with minimal decoding skills, students are usually successful because they already know the meaning. With the LEA, students have many opportunities to see reading and writing as meaningful communication about their own interests and concerns. In addition, as they observe the process through which their messages are put into print form, they are exposed to important learning regarding the English writing system, thus preparing them for the writing process. Finally, when students read their own stories, they are able to experience the success of independent reading (for additional discussion of the language experience approach, see Chapter 5).

Several other literature-based strategies are also recommended for use with beginning-level second-language readers. Some of these strategies are listed below in a sequence from simpler to more complex:

- using patterned books with repeated phrases and refrains
- illustrating stories or poems
- using shared reading with big books
- using the directed reading-thinking activity (DR-TA)
- using readers' theater
- using story mapping

All of these strategies have been used effectively with deaf and hard of hearing children and are discussed in Chapter 7.

Intermediate second-language learners generally have a rather large sight-word vocabulary and the ability to comprehend various kinds of texts, such as stories, letters, and simply written magazine and newspaper articles. They have a fair amount of automaticity in their reading and so can read with some fluency (Peregoy & Boyle, 1993). Deaf second-language learners have difficulty achieving automaticity and, subsequently, fluency for several reasons, one being the lack of opportunities to practice. Both hearing and deaf students still have difficulty dealing with text that has new vocabulary, but hearing second-language learners need less assistance than beginning first-language readers in contextualizing lessons with graphic organizers and scaffolds (for a discussion on scaffolding, see Chapter 6), while deaf and hard of hearing second-language learners continue to benefit from as many graphic organizers and scaffolds as possible. Both groups will need to continue using the reading strategies they learned as beginning readers, as well as learning and applying new reading strategies to increasingly complex texts. Some of the strategies effective with intermediate-level second-language readers, both hearing and deaf, include the following:

- using cognitive mapping strategies
- using K-W-L strategy (see Chapter 7)
- using the directed reading-thinking activity (DR-TA)
- using semantic maps and webs
- using literature response journals
- developing scripts for readers' theater
- adapting stories into plays and scripts for videotapes and films

These strategies are also discussed in Chapter 7.

Cognitive Strategies in Reading Instruction

The Cognitive Academic Language Learning Approach (CALLA), developed by Chamot and O'Malley in 1986, is an ESL content-based curriculum that is derived from a cognitive model of learning. Although developed for hearing second-language learners, the procedures and strategies are applicable to deaf and hard of hearing learners also. CALLA instruction consists of three major components: (1) the use of high-priority content taken from the grade-level curriculum; (2) language activities added to the content that are designed to develop vocabulary, oral skills, and reading and writing skills that will allow students to think and reason about the knowledge presented; and (3) explicit instruction of learning and reading strategies that will aid in comprehension, storage, and retrieval of information. Some learning and reading strategies may be observable, as in note taking or outlining; some may be unobservable, as in monitoring comprehension, activating prior knowledge, or making inferences. A challenge for learning strategy instruction is to make the unobservable strategies observable to students through activities and materials that explain and foster their use (Chamot & O'Malley, 1994).

CALLA's method of reading instruction is based on cognitive theory, from which interactive reading strategies and instruction are derived. This interactive process operates most effectively when readers can independently apply comprehension and metacognitive strategies to facilitate their comprehension of text; therefore, this method of instruction is more appropriate with intermediate-level learners. Skilled readers use a variety of strategies, while less skilled or beginning readers do not have a large repertoire of strategies; either they do not use different strategies, or they use them less effectively (Pressley, 1988). A substantial body of research indicates that strategies that increase reading comprehension can be taught successfully to poor readers and that increased strategy use is maintained over time (Jones, Palincsar, Ogle, & Carr, 1987; Palincsar & Brown, 1986). Therefore, a strong focus in the CALLA curriculum is the development of learning and reading strategies.

Four categories of reading strategies are taught in CALLA to expand the students' repertoire of strategies. One group is the body of strategies that will aid in elaboration and in activating and applying prior knowledge. In acquiring and practicing these strategies, learners may work individually or cooperatively to list or illustrate their knowledge about a topic before reading. A second group of strategies enables the students to set a purpose for reading and to plan how to approach the text. Students learn to decide why they will read a text, and once that decision is made, then they must decide how to approach the text. For example, if they are reading a passage to recall a specific bit of information, will they read slowly or skim? Will they read the passage from beginning to end or first read the headings to guide their reading? The third category consists of the body of strategies that develop metacognitve awareness and monitoring skills. Readers learn to ask themselves questions such as: "Am I understanding this?" "Does this make sense?" They also learn "repair" strategies; for example, if the text does not seem to make sense, what strategy does the reader apply to get back on track. The last category consists of self-assessment strategies. The reader must learn to assess whether the purpose set for reading was achieved. Self-evaluation strategies can take a number of forms, including discussion in cooperative groups, oral/signed or written summaries (or retelling), self-ratings, and learning logs.

In CALLA, reading skills are practiced during reading experiences across the curriculum so that students are provided many opportunities to encounter authentic texts of differing types. A major emphasis of this curriculum is to provide students with authentic texts that include both content-area material and literature, to integrate oral/signed and written language skills so that students can develop all aspects of academic language, and to develop strategic reading and writing through explicit instruction in learning and reading strategies (Chamot & O'Malley, 1994). While this approach was developed for hearing second-language learners, the focus of CALLA appears also to be appropriate for deaf students who are learning English as a second language. Several researchers (Hanson, 1989; Hayes & Arnold, 1992; Paul, 1993) have concluded that the reading process is essentially the same for both hearing and deaf students, including ASL-using deaf students learning to read English as a second language. An interactive approach to reading instruction and the use of strategies derived from schema theories and other cognitive theories seem to hold the most promise for developing reading skills in deaf second-language readers (King & Quigley, 1985; Paul & Quigley, 1990), just as interactive approaches seem most beneficial to hearing second-language users (Carrell, Devine, & Eskey, 1988; Grabe, 1991; Hudelson, 1981).

Selecting Materials for Instruction of Second-Language Readers

All second-language learners, deaf and hearing, need a strong print environment in English, and, when selecting the materials to create this environment, teachers should give special consideration to the kinds of materials they choose. There are three general criteria that should be considered first (Allen, 1994). Print material in the classroom should vary in kind and should reflect the interests of the children. The material in the print environment should cover topics that are within the already developed schemas or prior knowledge of the children, and, finally, the structure of the text should be consistent, organized, and familiar to the reader. For example, beginning readers are usually more familiar with narrative text structure than with expository text structure and find text written in narrative style easier to comprehend. However, text written in expository style is easier to comprehend than text that shifts back and forth between a narrative and an expository style (Rigg, 1986).

Allen (1994) states that materials chosen for second-language readers should do the following:

- encourage children to choose to read;
- help children discover the values and functions of written language;
- permit children to use written language for a wide range of purposes;
- be appropriate for the age and interest level of the children;
- take into account the children's cultural background;
- make use of the children's native languages when possible;
- support the children's acquisition of English;
- offer a rich array of genres;
- have text structure that will support children's understanding; and
- take into consideration the children's background knowledge. (p. 112)

Other materials that can be used to support second-language learners' acquisition of literacy skills include materials written by the students themselves, as in the language experience approach. Because providing a print-rich environment is also important, the teacher should provide print materials such as newspapers, magazines, brochures, catalogs, poster, letters, and menus so that their students can explore print. Experiences with a variety of print materials encourage children to choose to read for different purposes and help them discover the values and functions of written language. Textbooks, including basal readers and content-area texts, should also be a part of the materials provided for second-language learners. For example, the three most important factors in reading comprehension (prior knowledge, linguistic competence, cognitive and metacognitive processes) have been addressed in two reading series specifically constructed for deaf and hard of hearing students and other second-language learners: *Reading Milestones* and *Reading Bridge*.

Reading Milestones (Quigley, McAnally, King, & Rose, 1991) addresses some of the problems of beginning readers. Through systematic exposure to and reinforcement of text-based variables such as vocabulary, syntax, and figurative language, *Reading Milestones* makes initial and continuing success in reading possible. Currently, *Reading Milestones* is reported to be the most commonly used reading series in educational programs for deaf and hard of hearing students (LaSasso & Mobley, 1997) and is widely used with other students. The purpose of *Reading Bridge* is to provide practice in the higher-level comprehension skills needed for understanding advanced reading materials. The objective is to bridge the gap between the demands of beginning reading and those of more advanced reading (Quigley, Paul, McAnally, Rose, & Payne, 1991).

Children's literature books should also be a part of the materials provided for second-language learners. Children's books provide a rich input of cohesive language made more understandable by patterned language, predictable structure, and, generally colorful and strong illustrations that support the text. In addition, these books provide reasons to communicate and offer a framework for writing.

In selecting books for beginning-level second-language readers, teachers may want to consider seven different categories: concept books, predictable books, well-illustrated books, books that invite discussion, books that offer a framework for writing, books that support the curriculum, and books linked to the children's cultures. These categories of books are briefly described in the following text.

Concept Books

Concept books describe the varied dimensions of a single object, a class of objects, or an abstract idea, as in a book about a house and its interior rooms, a book about toys, or a book about opposites.

Predictable Books

Predictable books have a predictable sequence of cumulative events (as in *The Napping House* by Audrey Wood), a predictable pattern of events (as in *Three Billy Goats Gruff* by Paul Galdrone), or repetitive language patterns (as in *Brown Bear, Brown Bear, What Do You See?* by Bill Martin, Jr.). These books provide cohesive chunks of language that invite children to participate and read along.

Well-Illustrated Books

Many good picture books have illustrations that not only convey what is in the text but also extend and enhance the message. Frequently, in books for young children, predictable books have excellent illustrations, and this combination makes the books more comprehensible for beginning-level second-language readers. The *Good Dog Carl* books by Alexandra Day are examples of well-illustrated books that delight children of all ages.

Books That Invite Discussion

Books that invite communication are also an important part of the print environment in the classroom. Too often, a good book is read aloud to the students and then put back on the shelf so that the student can get back to the "real work" of the classroom (Allen, 1994). However, the opportunity to respond to a book is very important for enabling students to become reflective readers. Frequently, book discussions are viewed as occasions for the teacher to "interrogate" the students to see if they comprehended what was read to them or what they read themselves. However, real book discussions are opportunities for the children to make a personal response to the book. Children's responses to literature can allow the teacher to observe the connections that each child is making (K. Smith, 1990). Every book read to students should provide opportunities for discussion and personal responses.

Books That Offer a Framework for Writing

Some books offer an excellent framework for writing, which children must be able to use for a wide range of purposes. Books can motivate students to write and provide language to support that writing; they can also serve as models to frame the written product. *Goodnight Moon* by Margaret Wise Brown is one example of a book that offers a framework for writing for young children, as does the story *The Little Red Hen*.

Books That Support the Curriculum

As children become older, the focus shifts from learning to read books to reading books to learn. Older students use books to help them acquire and organize new information. Content-area textbooks with technical vocabulary can be particularly difficult for second-language readers; thus, it is important to have a large number of books available that supplement and enlarge on the information in textbooks. Children should have access to large numbers of books, both content-based and children's literature books, that deal with what they are learning. These books should have a wide range of reading levels and offer children rich resources of information through print, illustrations, photographs, maps, diagrams, and drawings that will support the goals of the unit.

Books Linked to Children's Cultures

Every classroom should contain books that are about the children's own cultures. Acknowledging their cultures and providing print materials about their cultures will enhance the children's self-esteem. In reading and discussing these books, it is important for the children to focus on the similarities of the cultures as well as the differences. When selecting books that relate to the children's cultures, teachers should avoid books that portray sterotyped views.

Clearly, to maximize benefits to children, teachers must select an appropriate mix of materials to support the literacy development of their second-language readers. However, a good collection of books is not enough; books must be read and used appropriately. The teacher's role involves much more than making good book selections; it also requires that teachers provide time for children to choose books, read, and communicate with each other about books. Allen (1994) has stated that the teacher's role also includes the following:

- matching books with particular children to meet both their language needs and their interests;
- selecting books that support vocabulary development;
- exploring how books can help children develop specific aspects of oral and written language;
- choosing books that support understanding across the curriculum;
- helping children revisit books in significant ways;
- using books to support talk in book discussions and conferences;

- thinking of ways that books can be a springboard to writing for a variety of purposes; and

- using children's responses to books as one way of assessing children's developing language and literacy. (p. 126)

Using reading materials in these ways will allow teachers to integrate literacy development into the total curriculum of the classroom, meet the individual needs of the children, and help to develop an appreciation and enjoyment of books and reading.

Teachers of deaf and hard of hearing students almost never have homogeneous groupings in their classrooms. The students may differ in important instructional characteristics such as degree of hearing loss, age, degree of proficiency in American Sign Language and English, background experiences, and level of educational achievement. All of these characteristics will influence children's attitudes toward print and their responsiveness to reading instruction and almost insure that teachers will be challenged with a wide range of reading levels within their classroom group.

Because of this extraordinary diversity that teachers in deaf education frequently encounter in their classrooms, it is not feasible to identify a single set of activities that can be expected to work for all students. However, there are some basic instructional activities that frequently are effective with most students learning to read English; as is frequently the case, they may need to be adapted or modified to fit a particular group of students. Some of the basic instructional activities that have been used successfully with second-language learners are discussed in Chapter 7.

Second-Language Learners and Writing

The process approach to teaching writing has gained prominence in classrooms from kindergarten to college and has been applied with several diverse populations, including deaf and hard of hearing students. In recent years, the writing process approach has been used successfully with second-language writers and appears to be a more promising approach to teaching writing than the traditional methods (Peregoy & Boyle, 1993).

Research on Second-Language Learners and Writing

Current research indicates that writing processes for first- and second-language learners are quite similar. For example, both first- and second-language writers make use of their emergent knowledge of the English as they create texts for different audiences and purposes (Ammon, 1985). As students progress in their understanding of the English language, their writing begins to approximate standard English (Hudelson, 1986; Peregoy & Boyle, 1993). Additionally, when learning to write in their second language, very young children support their writings with drawings (Hudelson, 1986; Peregoy & Boyle, 1990), just as their first-language peers do. The problems that the two groups of writers encounter are also similar and include such stumbling blocks as spelling, grammar, choosing topics, and writing for a specific audience. Because the writing process for first- and second-language writers is similar and because the groups encounter similar problems in writing, it makes sense to use similar instructional strategies with the two groups of students.

Although the processes of English writing are essentially similar for first- and second-language writers, what the students in each group bring to the task of writing is not necessarily similar. Second-language learners, both deaf and hearing, will not be as proficient in vocabulary, syntax, and idiomatic expressions as their first-language peers will be. They probably will not have had the exposure to written English that their first-language peers have gained from reading and from having books read to them. As a result, deaf and hearing second-language learners will not have an intuitive sense for the way English translates into its written form.

In first- and second-language acquisition theory, errors are seen as positive signs, evidence of a productive process of testing and refining hypotheses about how the language works. Svartholm (1994) stated that educators of deaf children have historically compared the written language of their students to that of hearing children and labeled the written language of deaf students as deficient. However, if they compared the written language of second-language learners and deaf students, their perceptions of deaf students' writing would be quite different. Whether hearing or deaf, the second-language learner uses the information available about the new language, makes generalizations, and constructs inner, mental hypotheses about the language. The outcome may be different from the standard model, particularly if the learner has limited access to the standard model, but it is nevertheless the result of an active and creative language-learning mechanism. Svartholm maintained that the errors in the writing of deaf children are evidence of their language-learning capacity and should not be viewed as deficits.

Finally, several research studies have indicated that second-language learners can profitably engage in reading and writing English before they have gained full control over the phonological, syntactic, and semantic systems of spoken English (Goodman, Goodman, & Flores, 1979; Hudelson, 1984; Peregoy & Boyle, 1991). Ahlgren (1992) pointed out that because deaf children do not have access (or complete access) to spoken language, the learning of a written language, such as English, is like other language situations in which children learn to read and write without having a strong command of the underlying spoken form. This situation exists for deaf children as well as for speakers of some dialects and for children who learn to read Chinese characters. Other researchers have emphasized the importance of teaching composing processes to students, maintaining that providing students with opportunities to write not only improves their writing but also promotes second-language acquisition (Peregoy & Boyle, 1993).

Given the similarities between the writing processes of first- and second-language learners, it is not surprising that effective teaching strategies for the former group, with a few modifications, tend to be effective also for the latter group. In fact, process writing has been enthusiastically applied by bilingual and ESL teachers for the past several years (Peregoy & Boyle, 1993), as well as by teachers of deaf and hard of hearing students.

Process Writing and Second-Language Learners

The process approach to writing appears to be beneficial for second-language learners, both hearing and deaf, for several reasons: (a) learning takes place in risk-free environments (Law & Eckes, 1990); (b) children are allowed to write from their own experiences (Peregoy & Boyle, 1993); and (c) it does not require children to create content and simultaneously think about how to convey it correctly in a second language (Mather, 1990). Instead, the students are free to elaborate their ideas first and make corrections later, after they have their thoughts on paper.

The writing process approach allows for a variety of learning dynamics—from solitary learner activity to paired interactions to small group interactions. The cooperative and interactive nature of the writing process approach provides opportunities for second-language learners to benefit from discussions with peers when selecting, refining, and organizing a topic, and from peer assistance during both revising and editing. Effective cooperative groups will promote better writing, as well as provide numerous opportunities for group discussions, within which a great deal of positive interaction occurs, fostering continued development of language and social skills. And finally, when using the writing process, children do not have to focus on all aspects of writing at the same time, which can be overwhelming, especially to young writers who are deaf or hard of hearing. Instead, children can concentrate on each aspect of writing as they progress through the process. Chapter 8 contains a detailed discussion of the writing process approach and associated instructional strategies.

Developmental Phases in Second-Language Writing

Second-language learners progress developmentally as they gain control over the writing process, just as their hearing peers do. To become effective writers, children must develop and coordinate a broad range of complex skills, including clarity of thought and expression, knowledge of different genres and appropriate applications, and knowledge and application of conventions of spelling, grammar, and punctuation. Characterizing developmental levels is not easy because the traits exhibited by effective writers vary with the purpose for writing and the genre and also because individual development of those traits is apt to be uneven. For example, one child may write short, simple stories using appropriate spelling and punctuation, while another child writes more complex, action-packed stories but without appropriate spelling and grammar. Both writers are in the beginning phase of writing, but neither has consistent development in all aspects of good writing. Such variation among students is quite normal (Peregoy & Boyle, 1993).

Peregoy and Boyle (1993) developed the writing traits matrix in Table 4.1. This chart describes beginning, intermediate, and advanced second-language writing on the six trait dimensions listed in the first column: fluency, organization, grammar, vocabulary, genre, and sentence variety.

Comprehending Through Reading and Writing

Several researchers have conducted studies that have established reading and writing as mutually supportive language processes (Mason, 1989; Rosenblatt, 1989; Shanahan, 1990) that should not be taught apart from each other. Research findings also suggest that reading and writing processes function similarly for first- and second-language learners (Grabe, 1991). Both rely on the reader's or writer's background knowledge to construct meaning (Pritchard, 1990), and both make use of cueing systems (graphic, syntactic, semantic) to allow the reader or writer to predict and confirm meaning (Carson, Carrell, Silberstein, Kroll, & Keuhn, 1990). Edelsky (1982) found that when writing in a second-language, writers rely on what they know in their first language, which would account for much of the difficulty in writing experienced by elementary-age deaf children, who frequently do not have a well-established first language on which to rely. Carson (1990) concluded that reading experiences improved the writing of second-language learners more than grammar instruction or additional writing exercises. Consequently, it is not surprising to note that Stotsky

Table 4.1
Writing Traits Matrix

Trait	Beginning Level	Intermediate Level	Advanced Level
Fluency	Writes one or two short sentences	Writes several sentences.	Writes a paragraph or more.
Organization	Lacks logical sequence or so short that organization presents no problem.	Somewhat sequenced.	Follows standard organization for genre.
Grammar	Basic word-order problems. Uses only present-tense forms.	Minor grammatical errors, such as "-s" on verbs in 3rd person singular.	Grammar resembles native speakers of same age.
Vocabulary	Limited vocabulary. Needs to rely at times on first language or ask for translation.	Knows most words needed to express ideas but lacks vocabulary for finer shades of meaning.	Flexible in word choice; similar to good native writers of same age.
Genre	Does not differentiate form to suit purpose.	Chooses form to suit purpose but limited in choices of expository forms.	Knows several genres; makes appropriate choices. Similar to effective native writers of same age.
Sentence Variety	Uses one or two sentence patterns.	Uses several sentence patterns.	Uses a good variety of sentence patterns effectively.

Note. From *Reading, Writing, and Learning in ESL: A Resource Book for K–8 Teachers*, by S. Peregoy and O. Boyle, 1993, White Plains, NY: Longman. Copyright 1993 by Addison-Wesley Longman, Inc. Reprinted with permission.

(1983) found that good writers tend to read more frequently and widely and to produce more syntactically complex writing. She also found that reading experiences have as great an effect on writing as direct instruction in grammar and mechanics does. In applying this research to classroom practices, teachers will select strategies that capitalize on the interactive nature of reading and writing.

Reading and Writing
Across the Curriculum

Livingston (1997) stated that deaf students must be inundated with appropriate text in all subject areas to gain adequate exposure to English so that they can become bilingual. Exposure to reading and writing English only during the reading and writing period is far from adequate, and students will not develop an understanding of English language in such a limited setting. Reading and writing must be an integral part of all subjects throughout the school day for deaf students to be provided with enough exposure to English so that they can begin to understand it. Peregoy and Boyle (1993) listed six elements that create optimal content learning for second-language learners; reading and writing play significant roles in most of those elements.

• *Meaning and purpose*: For topics to be meaningful to the students, students should select them and help shape their development.

• *Prior knowledge*: All learning should be built on students' prior knowledge, which, if not adequate, should be developed before starting the unit. Developing prior knowledge should occur through direct experiences when possible.

• *Integrated opportunities to use reading and writing for learning*: Oral/signed and printed language should be used to acquire knowledge and to present knowledge gained to others.

• *Scaffolds for support*: Students should be provided with scaffolds, including group work, process writing, and direct experiences for learning.

• *Collaboration*: Students should be encouraged to collaborate with each other to build and organize knowledge for summarization.

• *Variety*: Variety should be built into each unit, with discussions, reading, writing, field trips, guest speakers, and other avenues of learning provided. (p. 153)

When students are involved in interesting content-area projects, they integrate and practice a number of important social, linguistic, and academic skills, such as posing questions, gathering data through reading, interviewing, discussing findings with peers, and organizing and summarizing information for a final presentation.

Currently, numerous teachers in programs for deaf and hard of hearing students are using thematically organized instruction, with student choices built in to create motivation and purpose. The six elements listed previously can be incorporated quite easily into thematic instruction, providing the added advantage of having reading, writing, vocabulary, and other learning efforts all focused on a single theme and thereby assuring reinforcement of important concepts and vocabulary throughout the unit.

ASL and English

When considering the use of a bilingual program for deaf students, teachers must first consider the significant differences between traditional second-language learners and deaf students. Most second-language learners have already developed a first language and have the ability to hear the second language that they are learning. Deaf students usually do not begin their school experience with a first language already developed. Most deaf students of deaf parents will have a first language, American Sign Language, but that group comprises only about 8% of the deaf children entering school. The other 92% have most likely not developed either English or ASL as a first language and so have the astonishing task of developing two languages in order to be successful in their academic achievements and in later life. Consequently, teachers have the astonishing task of providing a school environment that will nurture the develop of both ASL and English.

Deaf children entering school without a well-developed language base have a critical need to develop one as rapidly as possible to facilitate their cognitive development and their ability to acquire, store, and apply academic information. A language base is also important so that communication can develop and children can negotiate within their social environment, thereby developing their confidence and self-esteem. Because American Sign Language is the only language intended to be processed visually and, consequently, is the only language that young deaf children can receive in its complete form, it makes sense that ASL should be the first-language for most deaf children. If that is the case, then schools and programs for deaf children should emphasize the development of American Sign Language from the very beginning, at the preschool level. If ASL and literacy skills are emphasized within the preschool and kindergarten years, deaf children should have, at least, the beginnings of a language base and, subsequently, communication skills when they enter the first grade. At that point, bilingual instruction can begin, developing English as a second language while continuing the development of ASL as the first language.

In the bilingual education program, ASL should remain as the language of instruction. The learning of English should occur mainly from reading and writing, as those activities provide the most complete model of the English language for deaf students. However, the key to this approach is providing adequate exposure to the English language in print and, later, providing enough opportunities for deaf students to write. The only way that children can gain adequate exposure to print is if reading and writing are integral components of all aspects of the curriculum, from 1st through 12th grades. In all classrooms, from middle elementary grades up, ASL discussions, reading, and writing should occur in approximately equal proportions during each period if a traditional approach to education is used, or during the day if an integrated curriculum approach is used.

At this time, there is no research to support any particular approach to bilingual education. Limited research has come out of the programs in Sweden and Denmark, but those studies have not clearly defined the framework and strategies used in those bilingual programs. Much more research and information are needed in order to duplicate those approaches. What is certain, however, is that none of the approaches used historically has been successful with the majority of deaf students. A bilingual approach appears to be sound theoretically; however, a great need exists for some well-planned bilingual programs that incorporate sound research procedures so that appropriate data can be collected and programs can be modified, improved, and replicated. Only when a responsible approach such as this is undertaken can educators ascertain whether bilingual instruction truly makes a difference in the academic achievement of deaf students.

Summary

Bilingual education is claimed to be successful in Sweden and Denmark, with test results showing significant gains in the academic achievement of the deaf students in those countries. However, currently, there is not much information on specific strategies that have been used in these two countries. Several programs for deaf students in the United States have changed to bilingual-bicultural approaches and have adopted many of the strategies and techniques that are used in bilingual programs in this country for hearing students.

Most of the strategies that are successful with second-language learners are the same as those that are successful with first-language learners; however, they are used with adaptations that place additional emphasis on reading and writing. All of these are research-based strategies that are derived from the interactive group of reading theories known as schema theories. All of the strategies are interactive in three dimensions: (1) in using the strategies, students must shift back and forth between top-down and bottom-up processing approaches to promote flexible thinking and prevent rigidity that leads to the application of skills from only one approach; (2) all of the strategies promote interaction between the reader, the text, and the author; and (3) most of the strategies promote interaction among students, giving them opportunities to talk about strategies and how and when to use them.

Programs that are implementing bilingual instruction with deaf students will, perhaps, also incorporate sound research procedures so that much needed data can be collected to provide a source for evaluation of this approach. With the absence of appropriate research to determine the effectiveness of new philosophies and strategies—for example, when total communication programs were implemented—educators, students, and parents had to wait as long as 20 years and more before it became clear that students were not making the academic achievement that was expected. With good investigations of programs, perhaps appropriate evaluation of new approaches and subsequent changes and modifications will not require so much time.

P A R T

II

INSTRUCTIONAL MANAGEMENT

INSTRUCTIONAL SYSTEMS

Preview

The reading scores of students in the United States have historically been scru-
tinized by the public and used as indicators of the success or failure of school systems and educators. Because the public and educators have not been satisfied
with the scores achieved by students, controversy has prevailed in the area of
instructional systems for the teaching of reading and, subsequently, also for the
teaching of writing. The current debate about the best way to teach reading
centers on two instructional systems: skill-based (including phonics) and
whole-language, although other systems have been pitted against each other in
the past several years, for example, phonics versus whole word, and phonics versus the language experience approach. Although these various instructional systems have appeared to emerge and enjoy popularity in a somewhat cyclical pattern, curiously, a comparison of the National Assessment of Educational
Progress data indicates that American students' reading performance over the
past 25 years has remained nearly constant (Mullis, Campbell, & Farstrup,
1993; Williams, Reese, Campbell, Mazzeo, & Phillips, 1995), a statistic that
does not seem to support one system over another.

This finding becomes even more puzzling when one considers the fact that
the past few decades have produced some significant insights into the reading
process. Concepts such as the schema theory model of reading, the role of prior
knowledge, the interactive nature of reading, the importance of efficient decoding, the role of automaticity, the significance of metacognition, and the active,
constructive nature of learning in general—all of these are centrally important

concepts and have somewhat obvious implications for instruction. In addition to achieving better understanding of the reading process, many of the instructional implications derived from this new knowledge have been investigated. For example, substantial data support using repeated reading to increase automaticity; sustained silent reading has been shown to be more effective than worksheets in fostering reading proficiency; ways of engaging students with texts have been developed and validated; appropriate comprehension strategies to teach children have been identified; and effective approaches to teaching comprehension strategies have been documented (Graves, 1996).

Two well-recognized social factors increase the urgency for schools to improve the reading proficiency of American students—the increasing number of students entering schools for whom learning to read is likely to prove difficult (e.g., economically disadvantaged students, minority students, and students for whom English is not a first language) and the increasing literacy demands of society. Perkins (1992) and Bruer (1994) have stated that full participation in American society will require much higher levels of literacy than have ever been demanded before, and Resnick (1987) has argued that in the near future, entry-level jobs will require skills equivalent to those of today's college sophomores. Bruer has noted that these higher expectations present an unprecedented challenge to public education.

The challenge for teachers of students who are deaf and hard of hearing is perhaps even greater when one considers the low reading achievement levels of this population upon graduation from high school. If these students are to be competitive in contemporary society, strategic changes must be made in their educational programs that will afford them the opportunity to achieve higher reading levels. This chapter will describe some of the instructional systems currently used in the teaching of reading and will discuss available research findings on the effectiveness of those systems. The focus of the discussion is on whole-language, the language experience approach, the literature-based approach, basal reading programs, and a balanced approach.

Whole Language

The whole-language approach has been adopted by many teachers for use with deaf and hard of hearing children, sometimes completely and sometimes in part. It seems to be particularly appealing to some teachers because of its de-emphasis of phonics, or the sounds of language. Such de-emphasis would appear to fit the needs of deaf students, but research does not fully support that supposition. Neither does research indicate that whole language should be completely avoided or ignored; there are many sound principles and effective practices within the whole-language philosophy. Therefore, teachers should become knowledgeable about this instructional system, its principles, and its practices in order to determine which components are best to adopt or adapt for use in their own classrooms.

Whole language is used to describe a certain perspective on education. The term seems to have been derived from a belief that language should be kept whole during instruction rather than fragmented it into bits and pieces for isolated drill. It reflects the natural approach to language learning, which maintains that children learn language in natural social environments in which language is used for communicative and meaningful purposes—that is, children learn language through communication for the purpose of communication (McAnally, Rose, & Quigley, 1994).

Whole-language advocates believe that children learn to read and write in a similar manner—through the use of whole texts with natural language patterns rather than the "stilted and unnatural language characterizing the early levels of basal reading texts" (Weaver, 1994, p. 332). The focus of teaching is to help readers attend to whole text rather than to words, letters, and other bits and pieces of language. Reading materials should be meaningful, predictable, and authentic (Manning & Manning, 1989). Whole language is not a program or a method but is considered to be a philosophy of literacy development and of learning in general.

Philosophy and Basic Principles of Whole Language

The philosophy underlying the concept of whole language embraces beliefs about teachers and teaching and learners and learning. A strong premise in the whole-language philosophy is that students must have ownership over their learning and that teachers must trust in students' abilities to construct their own knowledge. Concomitantly, teachers facilitate and support learning that is largely student-determined, provide direct instruction based on students' needs and interests, and, in addition, commit to promoting individual growth rather than uniform mastery of a predetermined curriculum (Weaver, 1994). Several guiding principles are derived from the philosophy of whole language; Crafton (1991) defined six that characterize the intent of this instructional system.

Principle 1: Oral and Written Language Develop from Whole to Part

Principle 1 is probably the most central to the philosophy of whole language and is derived from the natural approach to language learning. From birth, young children are exposed to language wholes; parents communicate with their children using language that is a complex whole, with syntax, semantics, and pragmatics operating at the same time. The whole-to-part principle contrasts with the part-to-whole, skill-based view of literacy prevalent in basal reading programs, which promotes learning skills (parts) first and then puts the parts together into a whole (the actual act of reading and writing). This basic principle dictates that from the very beginning, children should read and write texts that have all the characteristics of real language. The focus of written-language exposure is on the students' construction of meaning, which will be learning that does not deteriorate, because it is constructed by the learner and is not imposed from an external source (Weaver, 1994).

Principle 2: Language and Literacy Are Social Learning Events

While reading and writing appear to be solitary events, they are not; they may involve interaction with one or several other people. Reading and writing are frequently part of an ongoing dialogue with an author, with oneself, or with other readers and writers. Change and progression can occur in comprehension and composition when a reader or author has the opportunity to discuss with others the possibilities of meaning found in a text. The perspectives gained from such interactions influence the reading and writing, as the reader/writer applies to the task the results of the social exchange. This process, negotiating meaning, can also occur between a reader and an author even when the author is not present. As readers try to construct meaning, they negotiate between what they interpret the author's intent to be and their own prior knowledge and experiences that influence their interpretations, reconciling any differences or mismatches to arrive at comprehension. Whole language promotes collaborative learning and encourages students thinking together. Crafton (1991) stated that reading and writing need to be looked at as extended activities, with each process beginning and ending in a social setting and with exchanges built into the process itself.

Principle 3: Literate Behaviors Are Learned Through Real, Functional Use

Language outside of the classroom always has a purpose; there is a personal reason for a person to speak/sign, listen/receive, read, or write. Children learn at a very early age that language, both oral and written, can be used to negotiate and to control their environment—to get attention, to get a cookie, to explore and understand a new event. Whole-language advocates believe that language and the purposes for language in the classroom should be just as authentic as language and its purposes are outside of the classroom. Teachers should think about all the ways that language is used in everyday life and provide opportunities for students to use language in similar ways in the classroom, thus ensuring that children are learning "real" language for "real" purposes and that the literacy they develop in school will benefit them outside of school.

Principle 4: Demonstrations Are Critical to Learning

Children see adults reading, and they see the finished products of adult writing; but they usually do not see the process that the adult has gone through to accomplish comprehension of printed text and a finished composition. Because all they witness is the finished product, they commonly develop the understanding that the ultimate goal of reading and writing is to get it right the first time. Therefore, demonstrations should be real engagements that show students the potential paths that can be taken (Crafton, 1991). Teachers should model for their students, explaining the mental negotiations they go through to arrive at meaning when reading and sharing the drafts and revisions that occur before a composition is considered to be finished. By sharing their thinking with students, teachers help students to understand and to participate in the processes of reading and writing.

Principle 5: All Learning Involves Risk Taking and Approximation

Classrooms must be safe environments for children; in order for learning to occur, children must feel secure enough to take risks. Goodman (1986) maintained that risk taking is essential to learning. Children must be encouraged to predict and guess as they try to construct meaning from text; as they write, they must be encouraged to think about what they want to say, to explore genre, to invent spellings, and to experiment with punctuation. Because children are trying things that they have never tried before, their paths toward learning will be filled with approximations. Their learning activities will be characterized by experimentation, approximation, and refinement as they move toward accomplishment. If they do not feel safe enough to try new experiences without fear of failure, learning will not occur. When children see their approximations treated as signs of growth, they will continue to take the risks necessary to grow as language users (Crafton, 1991).

Principle 6: Learners Must Take Responsibility for Their Own Learning

Whole-language advocates view the principle that learners must take responsibility for their own learning as the defining principle distinguishing whole-language classrooms from traditional, skill-based classrooms. They maintain that in traditional classrooms teachers feel responsible for the teaching *and the learning*, and students quickly learn to be passive and wait for others to initiate their experiences. With external direction of learning activities, students' motivation is decreased and their involvement in learning is diminished. When learning activities are self-initiated, students display a greater degree of owner-ship, involvement, and commitment to the activity. For this to occur, learners need opportunities to take responsibility for their learning, which means they should be given choices in reading and opportunities to select their own topics for writing. Schedules must be developed that will allow students time to read and reread, to write and revise, and to interact with classmates and teacher for the purpose of sharing their thinking and receiving responses from others. When there is shared decision-making and self-direction in learning, students are more likely to accept responsibility for their own learning, become more independent learners, and develop into life-long learners, one of the primary goals of education.

◇   ◇   ◇

These six principles, which define a perspective on language and learning, com-prise the basic beliefs underlying whole language. Whole-language proponents maintain that it is this perspective—not materials or activities—that exempli-fies the difference between their philosophy and that embraced by proponents of traditional, skill-based instruction.

The Role of the Teacher

One of the major differences in the role of a whole-language teacher and that of a traditional teacher is that the whole-language teacher relinquishes the role of being a director of learning and becomes a facilitator of learning. Whole-language teachers create classrooms that are child oriented and student directed and provide opportunities for learning to occur in a safe, risk-free environment. Crafton (1991) suggested that the major shift from traditional teaching to whole-language teaching "may all come down to issues of control and shared responsibility and teachers who are willing to allow students to direct their own learning" (p. 43).

Weaver (1994) listed five qualities that characterize a whole-language teacher. The first is that teachers are role models. They must demonstrate that they themselves are avid readers, writers, and learners in order to encourage stu-dents' development of literacy and learning. They also must demonstrate that they are risk takers and decision makers to foster these same characteristics in their students.

A second role of whole-language teachers is to be mentors and collabora-tors. They offer learning experiences and choices and help students consider and acquire the skills and resources needed to complete their projects success-fully. They guide students in learning the strategies that will enable them to be successful in reading and writing, frequently demonstrating and discussing those strategies with students so that the students become metacognitively aware of a growing repertoire of strategies for constructing meaning and dealing with text.

A third responsibility of whole-language teachers is to create a supportive community of learners in which everyone feels safe to take risks, make decisions, and try new strategies without fear of negative consequences. Teachers encourage student collaborations such as brainstorming ideas, responding to each other's work, working cooperatively on projects, and helping one another.

The fourth role of whole-language teachers is to present themselves as learners instead of authorities on learning. The former believe that all students can learn, and they respond positively to what students do while offering challenges to stimulate students' motivation to learn.

Finally, whole-language teachers share with students the responsibility for curricular decision making, thus allowing them to take ownership and responsibility for their own learning. By fulfilling these five roles, teachers empower students to become independent, self-motivated learners who will have the skills, abilities, and desire to become, eventually, life-long learners.

Crafton (1991) contrasted the roles of traditional teachers and the roles of whole-language teachers. She claimed that traditional teachers are transmitters of information, while whole-language teachers are facilitators of learning; traditional teachers focus on product and teach skills in isolation, while whole-language teachers focus on process and highlight strategies in functional contexts. She also described traditional teachers as emphasizing direct instruction and controlling learning and whole-language teachers as emphasizing demonstration, engagement, and reflection and placing responsibility for learning on students. She maintained that the traditional curriculum is built on student deficits and minimizes social learning, while the whole-language curriculum is built on student strengths and maximizes social learning.

These descriptions of the roles of teachers seem to underscore the centrality of whole-language teachers as educators who know how to develop effective learning contexts and have meaningful discussions with students, and who understand the importance of and can provide strong demonstrations of proficient literacy and skilled problem solving. While whole-language teachers are sometimes criticized for not teaching (in the traditional sense of the word), whole-language supporters maintain that teachers in this instructional system do indeed "teach," but their teaching takes a different form.

The Role of the Student

As the role of the whole-language teacher is described, the role of the student begins to emerge. Proponents of whole language perceive students in a traditional classroom as being passive learners, while students in a whole-language class-room are perceived as active, involved learners. Students in traditional class-rooms participate in what Crafton (1991) described as a "cognitive runaround," in which they jump from one story to the next, one chapter to the next, and one topic to the next, usually at a pace that is too fast for the students to grasp any of the deeper understandings that require an assimilation of information or to make the critical connections among content areas and their concepts. In contrast, students in whole-language classrooms along with their teachers *create* curriculum as they engage in exploring real-life questions through reading, writ-ing, talking, and research. They do not cover myriads of topics; rather, they explore themes in depth, creating their own paths of inquiry, exploring differ-ent perspectives, connecting concepts from many of the content areas, and relating their learnings to past and future experiences. Students are also involved in the assessment of their learning, which enables them to develop self-evaluative skills that will serve them in future years. Because students are actively involved with their teachers in determining the course of study and in the evaluation of their performance, they feel an ownership in the tasks they have set for themselves and accept responsibility for their own learning.

Curriculum Perspectives

Crafton (1991) suggested that four sources should be considered for identifica-tion of curricular content: student interests, teacher interests, the content required by the district or state, and incidental occurrences. When each of the first three sources is described, whole-language teachers find that there is usually a great deal of overlap, and it is this overlap of student and teacher interests and required content that determines curricular content. Cordeiro (1992) claimed that the curriculum in whole-language classrooms is a generative curriculum, in which teachers map out a general plan using grade-level curricula as guides. Teachers develop the goals and objectives for learning and the beginning activ-ities; however, subsequent activities and the linking of content areas evolve as a result of what happens in the initial activities, the students' interactions, and their interests and discoveries. The day-to-day activities are generated from the developmental needs of both teacher and learner, thus fulfilling a curricular requirement set forth by Douglas Barnes (1976), which stated that for a cur-riculum to be meaningful, it must be enacted by both students and teachers.

Weaver (1994) also maintained that the curriculum is negotiated among the teacher and the students. The teacher determines the general parameters within which the students may make choices. Negotiations occur on a daily basis in the give and take of the classroom. Weaver expressed support for the use of both direct and indirect instruction in a whole-language classroom but said that all instruction must occur based on student needs and in the context of the whole. Typically, instruction proceeds from whole to part and back to whole. Direct instruction may occur with the whole class if it is relevant to what many of them are doing or is what they will be doing in the near future. However, instruction frequently occurs with small groups or with individuals, depending on the skill or strategy needed. The important point is that instruction on a skill or strategy occurs not just because it is in the scope and sequence but also as a direct response to students' interests and needs.

Another curricular perspective supported by whole-language teachers is that of the integrated curriculum incorporating theme studies. Ken Goodman (1986) defined whole language as the integration of oral and written language for concept learning, which leads naturally to the integration of reading, writing, and literature across the curriculum. A detailed account of an integrated curriculum and thematic studies is presented in Chapter 6.

Strategies Used in Whole-Language Classrooms

It is not surprising that proponents of whole language do not use instructional strategies that focus on specific reading skills; instead, they apply what are labeled as global strategies, which are the major strategies that readers must eventually develop in order to be effective readers of a variety of texts. Global strategies include several broad categories that are important for readers to develop and include strategies for purposeful reading; activating and applying prior knowledge; predicting, confirming, and revising predictions; using graphics effectively; using all the language cueing systems together; and monitoring comprehension.

While these strategies are the same as those taught in a basal reading instructional system, whole-language advocates claim that it is the methodology that differs. Whole-language teachers claim to facilitate the development of these strategies in a manner that recognizes reading as a process in which the reader is constructing meaning. They do not "teach" reading strategies; rather, they demonstrate them and encourage students to use them. Teachers and students experiment with strategies in the context of authentic reading. They may collaborate and make lists of the strategies they use; thus, together the teacher and students both become authorities in the reading process, and the students develop increasing ownership over their learning (Weaver, 1994). Specific instructional strategies used in reading and writing are described in Chapter 7.

Assessment in Whole-Language Programs

With new research, subsequent theoretical understandings, and the resulting innovative practices in literacy instruction, educators have directed their attention to the assessment of literacy development in students. Instead of relying on standardized test scores, whole-language teachers use "authentic" assessment procedures to evaluate their pupils. Hart (1994, p. 9) defined authentic assessment as assessment that "involves students in tasks that are worthwhile, significant, and meaningful" and that resembles learning activities more than traditional tests. While there are specific strategies associated with assessment in whole-language instructional systems, this section discusses the concept of such assessment and its underlying principles. Information on assessment strategies can be found in Chapter 10.

Weaver (1994) suggested that assessment in a whole-language instructional system should consist of both formative and summative evaluations and described three major principles that characterize the concept of formative assessment in a whole-language classroom. The first of these principles stipulates that assessment must be collaborative (Anthony, Johnson, Mickelson, & Preece, 1991; Short & Burke, 1991; Weaver, 1994). Collaborative assessment may involve several different people in various roles. For example, the teacher evaluates the student; the student participates in self-evaluation; peers may evaluate each other's contributions to a cooperative learning project; and parents can be invited to evaluate their child. Parents may be asked to describe their child's strengths and needs at the beginning of the year, then later asked to describe the growth that they have seen. Parents may also be invited to attend and participate in conferences along with the student and the teacher in which they assess progress and determine learning goals, or children can plan for and conduct conferences with their parents. Each of these contributions to the assessment process provides valuable and unique perspectives from which a more accurate picture of the student's learning processes unfolds.

Another facet of collaborative assessment involves students and teachers evaluating themselves, each other, and the curriculum. The discussion and evaluation of curriculum then, in essence, becomes the classroom experiences that the students and teacher plan and develop together (Weaver, 1994). In this process, students consider their contributions to the classroom community and how well they have worked in their cooperative groups.

The second principle indicates that assessment is multidimensional, meaning that the people involved in the evaluations do not only look at the student's products but also consider the student's learning processes, such as those for reading, writing, math, and science activities. Other factors considered by the evaluators are the students' perceptions of themselves as readers, writers, and learners; the students' increasing enjoyment of a wider variety of learning experiences; and the students' growth in the social aspects of learning such as the ability to work collaboratively with others.

The third principle states that assessment is contextualized—that is, information for assessment purposes is collected primarily during regular classroom activities rather than through testing, which differs from normal learning experiences. Therefore, assessment data is rich and varied and the assessment process is ongoing and continuous. Assessment data consist of recorded teacher observations; periodic performance samples; and data from conferences, interviews, inventories, journals and learning logs, and student projects.

Summative evaluation should consist of three kinds of assessment data: individual-referenced assessment data based primarily on student growth, criterion-referenced data based on progress toward meeting externally imposed goals, and norm-referenced data based on comparison with others using whatever standardized tests are required by the district. Edelsky and Harman (1988) suggested that the individual-referenced and criterion-referenced assessment data may be kept separate from the norm-referenced assessment data, particularly if the latter consist exclusively of standardized test scores that are used as part of an aggregate of data for the entire school.

Related Reading Approaches

Before the instructional system known as whole language emerged in classrooms, there were two other approaches that many teachers used and that fit within the philosophical parameters of a whole-language classroom. These two approaches, language experience approach and literature-based instruction, continue to be commonly used within the whole-language framework. The language experience approach has been used in classrooms for many years and has been and remains a frequently used instructional approach in lower elementary grades in programs for deaf and hard of hearing children.

Language Experience Approach

The language experience approach provides children with the opportunity to use their own experiences, vocabulary, and language structures as the basis for learning to read. This approach is characterized by the motto "Anything I can say, I can write; anything I can write, I can read" (Weaver, 1994). Thus, the teacher begins with the experiences and language of the children, enabling them to begin an intensive use of printed language. Through this approach, children begin to develop and expand their listening/receiving, speaking/signing, reading, and writing vocabularies and develop an awareness of common vocabulary and high-frequency function words such as *the*, *a*, and *of*. In addition, this approach provides children with models of spelling and opportunities to experience the variety of meanings a word may take in different contexts (Searfoss & Readence, 1989). As children dictate their stories, they are also beginning to associate meaning with print, which facilitates their understanding of reading as a communication tool. Initially, children may dictate only one or two lines, frequently as a caption under a picture they have drawn. Later, as teachers and family members read to them and they encounter models from picture books with increasingly more print, their stories will become longer.

The language experience approach, while very effective, is not complex and contains six basic steps, which are flexible and can be adapted to meet the needs of the student. These steps are described briefly in the following text:

1. *The experience.* The experience may be one that the child has had individually or it may be a group experience in which all of the class has participated, such as a field trip, a cooking experience, or an art or science activity.

2. *Discussion.* The teacher and the student(s) discuss the experience for the purpose of establishing a sequence of events and clarifying ideas.

3. *Writing the story or account of the event.* If the children are deaf and they use ASL to dictate their experiences, the teacher should explain and emphasize that the message will remain the same but will be written in English. After the sentence is written, the teacher indicates that she or he is reading the sentence silently and then signs the sentence to the child in ASL, verifying that the meaning is the same as what the child intended. If it is a group experience story and there are also hard of hearing children in the class, the teacher should then read the sentence aloud for their benefit. If the student or the group is hard of hearing and uses spoken English as a communication mode, the teacher will record the message exactly as it was dictated. Working on grammar and wording while trying to elicit an experience may only repress a child's natural spontaneity and reduce the motivation (Searfoss & Readence, 1989). Also, the ownership of the story should remain with the child, and if the teacher begins editing at this point, ownership shifts to the teacher. Later, after the story is finished, the teacher and the child(ren) can begin the editing process, focusing on a limited number of English constructions that the children need to work on at this time. Focusing on changing the entire story to correct English grammar is too overwhelming and frustrating for the children and will greatly reduce their interest in the activity.

4. *Reading the story or account of the event.* With hard of hearing children, the teacher reads the story back to the child to make sure that what is written is what the child wanted to say. When this is confirmed, the teacher reads the story again so that the child can begin to become familiar with the printed

words. Then the child reads the story to the teacher. If the child is deaf and uses ASL, the teacher reads the story silently and then retells the story using ASL. (The story is read silently first so that the child understands that the message comes from the printed word and also so that the child can begin to develop bilingual skills. A part of these skills is understanding that the language of print is English, which is one language, that ASL is a different language, and that both languages are meaningful and have equal value.) The child then reads the story and retells it in ASL, or, if the story is fairly long, the child may read one or two sentences and restate those sentences using ASL, continuing until the story is completed. Then the child may try to read the entire story and retell it using ASL.

5. *Reinforcement and practice activity.* The teacher provides immediate reinforcement after the child reads (and retells) the story so that the words can begin to become part of the student's reading vocabulary. Searfoss and Readence (1989, p. 133) suggested several activities that children can do for reinforcement:

- read (and retell) the story or account to a friend;
- illustrate the story;
- think of a good title;
- practice reading (and retelling) the story to read it to the class.

6. *Opportunities for later reinforcement.* Later in the day or the next day, the teacher, an aide, a volunteer, or an older student should review the story or account with the child. With each reading, the printed text should be emphasized, particularly with a deaf child, who reads silently first and then retells the story. The child may also want to record a story or account for inclusion in the portfolio.

The language experience approach has enjoyed several peaks of popularity from the early 1900s to the present time. Today, it is used as part of a total approach rather than as a single approach to learning how to read and has been effective with older nonreaders and those whose reading is quite limited, as well as with children and adults learning English as a second language (Meek, 1983; Rigg, 1990).

Literature-Based Approach

Allington, Guice, Michelson, Baker, and Li (1996) noted that the most compelling finding of several large studies was the widespread implementation of literature-based instruction. Data from the 1992 National Assessment of Educational Progress (Mullis, Campbell, & Farstrup, 1993) indicated that half of all fourth-grade teachers reported a "heavy emphasis" on literature-based reading. These data also revealed that the students in the programs claiming to have a heavy emphasis on literature-based reading instruction achieved higher levels of proficiency on the assessments. A little over half of the fourth-grade students reported that they were given time daily to read a book of their choice, and teachers reported widespread use of children's literature. Hoffman, Roser, and Battle (1993) reported that three-fourths of the teachers in their 24-state study read aloud to children from literature, and Fractor, Woodruff, Martinez, and Teale (1993) found that almost 90% of the 183 teachers in their investigation had children's trade books available in their classrooms.

Allington et al. (1996) stated that the research literature does not provide a clear and consistent description of literature-based instruction, and Giddings (1992) came to a similar conclusion, stating that little agreement exists as to what constitutes this kind of curriculum other than providing children with the opportunity to read children's literature. However, Allington et al. suggested that several themes seem to characterize literature-based instruction: (a) an emphasis on integration of reading and writing instruction across the curriculum, (b) increased use of children's literature across the curriculum, (c) developing reading and writing skills and strategies within the context of actual reading and writing activities, and (d) attempting to provide all learners with access to the same high-quality curriculum. Each of these themes differs from the basic tenets of traditional skills-oriented curricula, in which reading and writing are taught through specially constructed texts and tasks that focus on practicing skills in isolation and different curriculum goals and experiences are presented to students of presumed different abilities.

Zarry (1991) claimed that a literature-based reading program is an individualized approach to reading, which is an alternative to using basal readers. He stated that important components of this approach are a classroom library that is well stocked with books that reflect the children's interests and good school and community libraries that supplement the classroom library. Librarians play significant roles, as they help to provide reading materials that appeal to children's interests and that provide curricular content appropriate to all grade levels.

Fisher and Hiebert (1990) examined the nature of tasks in literature-based classrooms and those in skills-oriented classrooms. They found that in literature-based classrooms library books had replaced basal readers and that students were given many more opportunities to write. Whereas students in the skills-oriented classrooms spent their time on relatively small, discrete tasks, students in the literature-based classrooms spent their time on larger tasks such as reading an entire chapter book and writing their own books. In addition, the latter students were given more autonomy in conducting and completing their tasks; for example, they could choose the topic and genre of their compositions.

Teachers in literature-based reading programs usually use different approaches to reading. In one approach, students choose their own reading materials and read at their own pace. A second approach involves thematic literature units that are developed by teachers and librarians and that mesh curricular requirements and students' interests with trade books. A third approach features a number of books that are usually supplied by the teacher and librarian and that are shared with the whole class. These books may be book sets in which several students read the same book and have periodic discussions with each other incorporating various responses to the book, such as relating the story from a character's perspective or dialogue journaling with a peer or teacher about feelings evoked by the story. Most teachers who provide a literature-based reading program usually combine these three approaches to create an effective reading program (Zarry, 1991).

The development and use of learning centers are another key feature of literature-based reading programs. Learning centers provide information and activities revolving around particular themes and encourage skill development as well as promote independent learning in children. Each learning center should have a prominent display of graphics that identify its theme, such as posters, photographs, and children's art, and should include a wide variety of print materials such as books, magazines, catalogs, and brochures. Task cards may be available to identify the projects and activities the children can do in that center. Learning centers should reflect the theme of the instructional unit and should reinforce and enhance what the students are learning.

Instructional strategies such as traditional questioning techniques must also change to respond to the literature-based approach. Following the five Ws (who, what, where, when, and why) tends to trivialize prose and poetry (Zarry, 1991) and should be replaced with strategies that engage readers in actively constructing meaning on their own and encourage their personal responses to the author's message. These strategies are essentially the same as those used by whole-language teachers and are discussed in Chapter 7.

Basal Approach

A second major instructional system for the teaching of reading is the basal reader approach, which is sometimes referred to as the traditional or conventional approach. This is the approach that has been used in schools for several decades, which started with the McGuffey readers, progressed to the "Dick and Jane" books, and is now characterized by multifaceted basal reading packages that generally include most of the materials that the teacher needs for the reading program.

Flood and Lapp (1986) maintained that basal series have played a key role and continue to play a significant role in reading instruction. They estimated that 98% of teachers in the United States used such series in the mid-1980s. One reason for the popularity and importance of such series is that they come as a package designed to address a wide range of reading-related skills from diagnosis to decoding and literary appreciation. In addition, instructional practices are suggested and opportunities are provided for guided practice within the text, in workbooks, and in supplementary materials. For coordinating reading instruction, they also provide a management system, which includes a scope and sequence of skills and evaluation and diagnosis through criterion-referenced tests. McCallum (1988) believes that most teachers do not have the time, energy, or expertise to develop all of the instructional materials and strategies needed to meet the expectations of parents, administrators, and legislators; consequently, basals are a necessary tool for successful teaching.

Philosophy and Basic Principles of the Basal Approach

Educators who support a basal approach believe in a skills and subskills view of reading and maintain that to become a fluent reader, the student must master a hierarchical series of skills; each skill is metaphorically thought of as a brick. These skills, when learned and orchestrated appropriately, become the building bricks that result in a total construction. It follows then that these reading skills and subskills must be identified and ordered in a logical sequence; lessons must be constructed to teach each of these components; and tests must be developed to assess whether the skills have been attained by the students. If they have, then instruction moves on to the next skill in the sequence. Basal readers usually present a scope and sequence of skills that are blended into the reading and discussion of stories and other selections.

Artley (1965) characterized the basal reading approach as comprehensive, concerned with all aspects of reading, and having three major features: scope, sequence, and organization. *Scope* refers to the range of skills that the fluent reader needs to acquire; *sequence* refers to the order of presentation of the skills; and *organization* deals with the integration of all the elements of the reading program in ways that will be most profitable for the students. The teacher's manual is the key to the organization of lessons and the overall program; in fact, basal reading series are sometimes chosen because of the clarity of the manuals.

In addition to the three features described by Artley, Searfoss, and Readence (1989), three features commonly are included in basal reading series: controlled vocabulary, teaching steps or lesson plans, and adjustments for above average and below average students. First, the selections in basals contain vocabulary that is carefully controlled—that is, the vocabulary in the early levels is suited to beginning readers and gradually increases in difficulty as children move from level to level. Second, the teacher's manual contains guides for step-by-step presentations of the reading lessons and usually includes suggestions for prereading activities, guided reading and discussion activities, and postreading skill development and enrichment activities. Finally, basal readers include adjustments for students who are reading above or below grade level. Basals are written for the average reader—that is, those readers who progress normally, moving from grade to grade each year. However, for those children who are above or below grade level in reading, adjustments must be made in the basal teaching procedures. Almost all basal reading series acknowledge and make provisions for meeting these differences, sometimes in separate sections at each level and sometimes by incorporating teaching suggestions for above and below average readers into each selection.

McCallum (1988) made a strong case for the use of basal reading instructional systems, arguing that they provide on-the-job training for teachers and serve as source books for reading instruction. A successful teacher must be knowledgeable and skillful in the complex task of systems management, which is what is required in the effective presentation of a reading program, regardless of which instructional system is used. Many teacher training programs require only one reading methods course, which is not sufficient to develop the competencies necessary to direct growth in reading. Therefore, many teachers turn to basals, where they can get the help they need to be reasonably sure that they are providing students with a consistent and effective program.

The Role of the Teacher

In a traditional, basal reading approach, the major role of teachers is to direct the reading lesson. They select the basal reader; they determine the selection (usually taking each selection in order as it is presented in the text); and they follow the teaching procedures suggested in the manual. Teachers plan each step with the help of the manual, reflecting carefully on the needs of the students and the adjustments necessary in activities to enable each student to be successful. They select the vocabulary to be pretaught and the teaching strategies to use in presenting the new concepts. During the reading of the selection, they ask questions to check student comprehension and determine passages to be reread for a specific purpose, such as to verify an answer. During the postreading segment, they conduct a discussion to facilitate comprehension of the entire selection; provide decoding skills lessons, practice, and assessment; and present enrichment activities to extend the comprehension of the selection.

This is not really an accurate description of what teachers do currently in the teaching of reading, however. Due to the influx of new information about the reading process and the influence and competition of the whole-language approach, basal reading series have undergone many changes, some for the better, some that are possibly premature. McCallum (1988) urged educators to be careful not to discard practices or materials that have been shown to produce results. Pearson (1996) has claimed that vocabulary control is now virtually gone in basals, even in the early readers that first graders use. Stories are no longer written to fit into a sequence or adapted to fit a particular level of difficulty. In addition, Pearson found that there are currently few opportunities for students to practice skills in independent learning situations; in fact, it is often difficult to find skill development and practice at all. It is not surprising that teacher behaviors have also changed to encompass many of the same roles as teachers in whole-language classrooms while maintaining some of the traditional roles assumed by teachers in basal reading programs. Therefore, it is common in classrooms today to see teachers using a basal reading instructional system but not assuming a totally directive role as was once associated with that system.

The Role of the Student

Similar changes have occurred in the roles of students. Traditionally, the role of the student was believed to be passive, accepting the direction of the teacher. Students did not expect to choose their reading selections but accepted the order of the selections as presented in their readers. They followed the teacher's directions, they read the stories, and they completed the assigned pages in their workbooks.

However, the changes in the teacher's role have also changed the role of the student. As do teachers, students maintain some behaviors from the traditional role while assuming some behaviors that have emerged from the influence of the whole-language movement. The latter reflect a more active role in the learning process in which students assume some ownership and responsibility for their own learning with guidance from their teachers.

Curriculum Perspectives

The most striking difference in curriculum perspectives is the pervasiveness of reading instruction in the content areas. Traditionally, while reading was always a part of other subject areas, the actual teaching of reading skills occurred primarily within the time frame designated as the reading period. In many basal programs, this perspective has remained, while whole-language classrooms adhere to a curriculum perspective that emphasizes reading and writing across the curriculum and includes the development of those skills in all subject areas.

However, the traditional curriculum has not remained static; it has evolved over time, specifically in content and instructional practices associated with reading that have changed to accommodate prevailing views.

Before the 19th century, religious content was prevalent, reflecting beliefs and the focus of society at that time. This focus gave way to one on morality and character development, which, by the 20th century, had changed to an emphasis on "good literature" (McCallum, 1988), which continues to the present day. Content changes in reading selections have included emphasis on minorities, women, and the disabled. Instructional practices have evolved from an emphasis on rote memorization and oral reading toward silent reading and the skills management systems of today. The last 20 years have produced an intense focus on comprehension, changing instructional practices from the sole use of questioning by the teacher to assess comprehension to teaching comprehension strategies to students so that they can learn *how* to comprehend. Current understanding of the reading process has been incorporated into the comprehension strategies offered in basal series. McCallum stated that such changes reflect the symbiotic relationship between theory and practice and the role that basal series play in the process.

Basal Approach Strategies

Many of the instructional strategies historically used in a basal reading systems approach are no longer used, due to the influence of new information regarding the reading process and how children learn. While strategies such as memorizing definitions of new words, oral reading, and rigid questioning techniques were once prevalent in the basal reading classroom, the emphasis has changed to the use of interactive and schema-based strategies, which are currently believed to be more effective. In fact, many of the strategies used in a basal instructional system today are the same as those used in a whole-language instructional system and are described in Chapter 7.

Assessment in a Basal Instructional System

As mentioned previously, the assessment programs provided in basal reading series focus on evaluation and diagnosis through the use of criterion-referenced tests. These tests usually are paper-and-pencil kinds of tests and include items that provide the teacher with information on the student's acquisition of decoding skills, comprehension of both direct and inferential information, and application of skills and concepts to related areas. The diagnostic tests provide the teacher with information on the student's knowledge and application of a variety of subskills.

However, it would be unfair to characterize all assessment programs in basal series in this manner, as perspectives on assessment have also changed with the influence of whole language. In classrooms currently using a basal approach, it is not unusual to see paper-and-pencil tests combined with performance assessment such as student presentations and portfolios.

Research on Whole-Language and Basal Programs

Controversy over the best way to teach reading to children continues in schools across the nation. Low test scores in reading on the 1994 National Assessment of Educational Progress indicated that students in the United States can decode, comprehend literally, and read at basic levels; however, they have difficulty thinking about and constructing meaning from the information they have read. Routman (1997) suggested that whole-language was blamed for the low scores in reading without taking into consideration other school problems that likely influenced the test results. These additional problems included such variables as large class sizes, low education funding, inadequate school and public libraries, great numbers of students whose primary language is not English, and insufficient staff development for teachers. However, in the past 10 years, several research investigations have focused on determining the effectiveness of whole language and comparing the results of whole-language and skills-based instructional systems, with findings that do little to settle the dispute. Some of the studies show a significant positive effect favoring whole language, and some of the studies indicate that there is little or no significant difference in the effects of the two instructional reading systems.

Weaver (1994, p. 323) summarized the investigations conducted with primary-grade children by Stephens (1991), Shapiro (1990), and Tunnell and Jacobs (1989) with the following general conclusions, which she qualified as being tentative.

Children in whole-language classrooms:

- show greater gains on various reading tests and subtests;

- show greater abilities to use phonics knowledge than did children in a traditional reading approach who learned and practiced skills in isolation (also see Cunningham, 1990);

- develop vocabulary, spelling, grammar, and punctuation skills as well as or better than children in more traditional programs (also see Calkins, 1980; Gunderson & Shapiro, 1987);

- are more inclined and able to read for meaning than just to identify words;
- develop more strategies for dealing with problems in reading;
- develop greater facility in writing;
- develop a stronger sense of themselves as readers and writers; and
- develop greater independence as readers and writers.

In contrast, Anderson (1996) stated that research on whole language has been inconclusive. Based on a meta-analysis of the United States Office of Education's first-grade studies and of 46 additional studies, Stahl and Miller (1989) concluded that "overall, whole language/language experience approaches and basal reader approaches are approximately equal in their effects" (p. 87). Because this meta-analysis was criticized for not distinguishing between whole-language and language experience approaches, Stahl, McKenna, and Pagnucco (1993) conducted a review of 45 studies that appeared after the first synthesis. However, the conclusions remained essentially the same. Both reviews found positive effects of whole language in kindergarten. Although the earlier review found slightly negative effects of whole language after kindergarten on word identification and basic comprehension, the trend in the recent studies was toward slightly positive effects on measures of these competencies but no difference on measures of writing, orientation toward reading, or attitude. Stahl, McKenna, and Pagnucco also noted that effects were variable from study to study, which prompted criticism by whole-language theorists, who claimed that the tests and experiments used were not appropriate to test the results of whole-language programs. The investigators maintained that rather than an inadequacy in testing and experimental procedures, the inconsistent results attained from the various studies may indicate that whole language has dysfunctional aspects or that the philosophy is being imperfectly realized in practice. However, whether this would have a significant influence on the test results becomes a moot point, as the same could be said for any instructional system to which whole language was compared.

Schleper and Farmer (1991) conducted a year-long case study examining high school deaf students who were reading 6 to 7 years below grade level according to standardized reading tests and who were receiving traditional instruction in the content areas. These students were considered to be at risk (75% were minority students, and 25% came from homes in which English was not the primary language). At the end of one year in an interdisciplinary English and social studies class, the students had made gains on various reading skills and had developed a more positive attitude toward reading and writing. Their independent reading level rose between 1 and 3 grade levels, with a mean gain of 1.1 grade levels on a reading/retelling task, a significant gain when compared to the findings by Furth (1966), which indicated that after the age of 10 deaf students typically increased their reading levels by less than one level in 5 years.

Kelly (1995) tried to determine possible differences between skilled and average deaf secondary readers in a study in which he compared the two groups on two categories of reading tasks: (1) the reader's fluency in processing the detailed, visual information of text, which requires bottom-up processing; and (2) the reader's tendency to engage in higher-level processes focusing on meaning, which require the use of top-down processing. Kelly hypothesized that a finding that indicated that skilled readers can be distinguished by their effective use of top-down processing would argue for increasing the use of whole-language strategies, which emphasize the reader's use of the semantic information that they bring to or construct from the text. However, if fluency in processing the visual information of text (bottom-up processing) was the skill category that distinguished the skilled from the average readers, then support for whole-language strategies would have to be tempered with instruction that develops efficient processing of visual information, a task accorded secondary importance by whole-language supporters. The results of Kelly's study indicated that the reading tasks that distinguished between the two groups of skilled and average deaf readers were differences in the efficiency of processing the visual information of text, which are skills requiring bottom-up processing. The average readers showed evidence of top-down processing similar to the skilled readers, leading Kelly to conclude that productive top-down processes may be necessary for comprehension but are not sufficient alone. Reasonable bottom-up fluency is also a necessary component of reading competence.

The findings of Kelly's study should not be interpreted as a reason to reject whole language in classrooms for deaf children, as many of the whole-language strategies focus on top-down processes, which are necessary for reading comprehension. However, the findings do present a strong case for direct and systematic instruction in basic, bottom-up skills. They also suggest that teachers in programs for deaf and hard of hearing students should ignore the controversy over whole-language versus skills-based programs and focus instead on the kinds of information and processing strategies that each student needs to become an effective reader, creating the balance of instruction in top-down and bottom-up processing that is needed by each student.

Dolman (1992) cautioned educators of deaf and hard of hearing students not to rush into educational trends such as the whole-language movement without thoughtful consideration of the educational implications of those trends. For example, research on the effectiveness of whole language up to this point indicates that whole-language classrooms may not be most effective for children whose English-language skills are weak. He also pointed out that Anderson,

Hiebert, Scott, and Wilkinson (1985) and Stahl and Miller (1989) found that practices consistent with the whole-language philosophy were not any more effective in promoting literacy in hearing children than more traditional practices were. Stahl and Miller, in their analysis of 46 investigations, noted that whole-language and language experience approaches produced weaker effects with disadvantaged children than with nondisadvantaged children. They suggested that disadvantaged children need direct instruction to catch up with other children who have had hours of incidental learning through listening to stories and engaging in other literacy-related activities.

In support of these findings, Chall, Jacobs, and Baldwin (1990) concluded that a combination of basal readers and other reading materials such as trade books leads to higher gains in word recognition and comprehension for children from disadvantaged families, and thus recommended early teaching of word recognition skills, systematic and explicit phonics instruction, and connected reading from a variety of sources for these children.

Dolman (1992) suggested that while none of these studies directly addressed literacy issues for deaf children, an analogy can be drawn between the knowledge base brought to the reading task by low-income or otherwise disadvantaged children and that brought to the reading task by deaf children. The decreased time spent in exposure to print, interaction with books, and experience with English is serious enough to warrant a more direct approach to literacy than is offered through the whole-language philosophy alone. King and Quigley (1985) stated that the severe deficits in experiential, cognitive, and linguistic skills typically imposed by deafness make direct instruction even more compelling for the prereading deaf child than for the hearing child from a disadvantaged home. Thus, based on the information from research findings, Dolman, as well as other specialists and investigators such as Pearson (1996), Lyon (1997), and Metsala (1997), has encouraged educators to consider balanced approaches in teaching reading, selecting principles and practices from both the whole-language and the skills-based philosophies that best meet the needs of each student.

A Balanced Approach

The whole-language movement has spread rapidly into American schools and has produced significant curricular changes in reading programs and in the way children are learning to read. Pearson (1996) views many of these changes as positive developments that all educators, regardless of their philosophical dispositions, should support. These universal principles of literacy learning are authenticity of text and task, curricular integration, student and teacher empowerment, the primacy of constructing meaning, and a recontextualization of learning within a community context (p. 266).

However, Pearson believes that there have also been casualties and that some practices have been deleted from reading programs that should be reinstated. Two of these casualties are the loss of vocabulary control and the direct teaching focus on skills. Without the vocabulary control in the early grades, many beginning readers are forced to struggle with text and stumble over words they do not know. Hiebert (1996) suggested that many children will not learn the alphabetic principle just from being immersed in print or by listening to others read aloud. The same is true for other basic skills in reading, as well as for comprehension strategies; many children, particularly those who have had little exposure to print and literature before entering school, will have considerable difficulty learning many of the basic reading skills and comprehension strategies without direct instruction.

Another casualty mentioned by Pearson (1996) is the emphasis on structure. This rejection of the study of structure seems to extend to any systematic analysis of infrastructure, such as the study of grammatical structures and story structures. Supporters of whole language do not claim that students should not learn these structural tools; rather, they believe those tools are best inferred from reading and writing authentic texts in the process of constructing meaning. However, many beginning readers and particularly those who are deaf or hard of hearing do not have the necessary skills in inferring to gain those strategic meanings.

The last casualty Pearson lists is reading in the content areas, which in the whole-language approach focuses extensively on related literature and the subsequent de-emphasis on reading expository text and the developing of study skills. The lack of attention to expository text will certainly prove to be counterproductive for the students as they enter middle school, high school, and the worlds of work and higher education. Thus, Pearson encouraged educators to implement a balanced approach in which the focus is on the needs of the learner, sound theory, and practice.

The National Reading Research Center at the University of Maryland supported a project that sought to characterize the nature of outstanding primary-level literacy instruction (Metsala, 1997). The project investigators studied 125 regular- and special-education teachers who were judged by their supervisors to be highly effective and whose classrooms were filled with many authentic and diverse literacy opportunities. One of the most striking findings was the consistency with which teachers reported integrating explicit skills instruction and opportunities to read and write whole, authentic texts. These teachers reported a great balance in the instructional practices they employed in their classrooms

(Pressley & Rankin, 1994; Pressley, Rankin, & Yokoi, 1996) by using both immersion in authentic literacy-related experiences and extensive explicit teaching through modeling, explanation, and mini-lessons, especially with respect to decoding and other skills such as punctuation, mechanics, and comprehension strategies. The project data strongly support the position that teachers should be educated to blend perspectives rather than to adhere solely to one perspective and, thus, be able to present an instructionally balanced approach to literacy development.

Summary

A question that is relevant to educators of deaf and hard of hearing students is whether the whole-language philosophy is suited to the needs of this population. There is no question that deaf and hard of hearing children must have access to real literature to achieve genuine literacy. However, a primary issue is how early literature should be introduced and whether these "authentic" materials should form the entire language arts program. Currently, research does not indicate that whole-language programs are any more effective in promoting literacy in hearing children than more traditional practices are (Anderson et al., 1985; Stahl, McKenna, & Pagnucco, 1993; Stahl & Miller, 1989). Other research indicates that less direct instructional methods may have a deleterious effect on reading abilities in disadvantaged children (Adams, 1990). King and Quigley (1985) suggested that the severe deficits in experiential, cognitive, and linguistic skills typically imposed by deafness make direct instruction even more compelling for the prereading deaf child than for the hearing child from a disadvantaged environment.

Many aspects of the whole-language philosophy intuitively make sense for deaf and hard of hearing learners, as well as for hearing students. The assumptions that students will succeed rather than fail and that reading and writing are done for real purposes (Goodman, 1986) are worthy principles for teachers to embrace regardless of the hearing status of their students. Other philosophical underpinnings of whole language that would enhance reading programs for deaf and hard of hearing children are the beliefs that students and teachers learn from and teach each other, that children must be active, involved learners, that students can play a part in curricular decisions such as selecting themes and texts, and that students can accept responsibility for their own learning, have ownership of their work, and become full members of the classroom community. The whole-language emphasis on creating literacy through a print-rich environment, through reading aloud, writing stories, and keeping journals is as beneficial to deaf and hard of hearing learners as it is to hearing students. Another valuable contribution of the whole-language movement is the integration of reading and writing in the content areas (Newman & Church, 1990; Schleper & Paradis, 1990).

While recognizing the contributions of whole language to literacy development in children, educators should avoid jumping from one trend in education to another searching for the "one best approach" to teaching deaf children. Particularly since some research indicates that whole-language classrooms may not be most effective for children with limited English proficiency (which is true of most deaf children), educators must explore this movement carefully and implement only those approaches and strategies that are successful with their students. Neither should all of the approaches and strategies of traditional reading programs be thrown out in favor of the "newer" approaches; rather, teachers should strive for a balanced approach, shifting the emphasis to meet the needs of the learner and focusing on the most effective practices for promoting literacy in deaf and hard of hearing children.

For these reasons, many teachers in programs for deaf and hard of hearing students have created a blend, utilizing sound practices from both instructional systems. It is not uncommon for teachers to use a basal series (such as *Reading Milestones*, with controlled vocabulary and syntax) as the foundation for the reading program and to enrich that foundation through the use of trade books and other authentic literacy experiences.

INSTRUCTIONAL DESIGNS

Preview

Instructional design refers to the way instructional materials are selected, structured, and managed to promote efficient and effective learning (Merrill & Tennyson, 1987). The teacher is the primary designer of learning environments, particularly of those activities that occur in the classroom. The ultimate goal is that each child will be motivated to learn, will enjoy learning, and will experience success in learning. Teachers have a wide range of options that can be developed and applied, or adapted and applied, in their instructional plans. They are not limited to using only one but are challenged to combine different instructional designs in creative ways that will motivate all of their students to become actively engaged in literacy experiences and maximize the opportunities for success. Generally, the principles of instructional design are applicable to all learners, while strategies used in a design may be adapted to match the unique characteristics of a child who is deaf or hard of hearing.

The first instructional design discussed in this chapter is *scaffolding*, which encourages teachers to plan and present instruction in ways that will ensure that the children encounter success as they learn to read. The teacher plays an active role in the children's learning by assisting, demonstrating, and sometimes doing parts of the tasks until the children are able to do them independently. One of the basic premises of this design is that a child who is successful in learning is motivated to continue learning. While scaffolding is discussed in this chapter as it relates to reading instruction, it applies to all areas of learning.

The second instructional design is *thematic instruction in an integrated curriculum*. This design emphasizes that children must be actively involved in learning experiences, and that, for maximum benefit to the students, these learning experiences should not be separated and categorized in single-discipline subject areas. Rather, they should be organized around themes that are relevant to the lives of the students, enabling students to connect their learning in the classroom to their lives outside of school and to connect concepts and ideas across disciplines. Integrated instruction applies to all curricular areas but is uniquely applicable to reading because it emphasizes the inclusion of reading and writing in all learning activities throughout the day.

Three early reading intervention programs are discussed in this chapter, including Reading Recovery, Early Intervention in Reading, and Shared Reading. Common design characteristics shared by these programs include modeling of reading behaviors, time on task, positive teacher–child and parent–child interactions, and monitoring of reading behaviors. The unique combination of proven strategies within each of the programs constructs an instructional design focused on proactive prevention of reading failures.

The last section of this chapter gives a broad overview of computer-based technology applications with deaf and hard of hearing students. While the topic occupies volumes, this section presents three perspectives on the application of computer-based technology to literacy: computers as tools that enhance instructional designs; computers as tools to adapt environmental learning conditions; and computers as bridges between the learner and what is to be learned.

Scaffolding Instruction

One of the goals for developing students who are literate is that they know how to read and learn from texts independently. Yet many students who are deaf and hard of hearing have a great deal of difficulty handling the conceptual demands inherent in reading material when trying to gain meaning from text on their own. All too frequently a gap exists between the ideas and relationships they are studying and their prior knowledge, language proficiency, cultural background, and reading ability. Teachers using instructional scaffolding can support readers' efforts to comprehend text while showing them how to use strategies that will eventually lead to independent reading and learning (Vacca & Vacca, 1996).

Bruner (1986) described scaffolding as a process in which an adult helps students do what they cannot do alone and then slowly encourages them to take responsibility for parts of the process as they are able. Applebee (1991) explained that instructional scaffolding provides the necessary support that students need as they attempt new tasks while modeling and leading the students through effective strategies for completing those tasks. Pearson (1996) maintained that thoughtful teachers scaffold the learning environment to help students cope with complexity. He stated that it is better to provide extensive scaffolding to enable students to complete difficult text than to break down the text into smaller, simpler components, which frequently reduces text coherence, thus making construction of meaning more difficult for the reader. Graves and Graves (1994) believe that scaffolding allows teachers to intervene in complex learning environments and to provide the cues, questions, and coaching needed to allow students to complete a task with help while they gradually gain control of it and develop the ability to complete it independently.

While scaffolding instruction in reading can be a very effective approach to help students to succeed and become increasingly more independent in their reading, it should not be misrepresented or misunderstood as being a complete reading program. Scaffolded reading instruction is an instructional design; it does not contain all of the components of a comprehensive reading program. For example, it does not deal with word identification skills, vocabulary instruction, inferring, or summarizing. Scaffolded reading instruction can be used within each component of the reading program to assist students in understanding, enjoying, and learning from the selections they read. Successful reading experiences will produce more students who want to read and, thus, who will become better readers.

Scaffolding is an instructional design that requires very little adaptation when used with deaf and hard of hearing students. As they read about scaffolding instruction, many teachers will realize that this is the kind of instruction they have been providing their students all along as they strive to program each student for success. However, it may be helpful to take a deliberate look at scaffolding, to understand its theoretical roots, learning principles, and instructional concepts. A good understanding of an instructional design allows teachers to plan and present learning activities in an organized, thorough, and consistent manner.

Student Success

Common sense dictates that if students are going to learn to read effectively, they must experience success in the majority of reading tasks they undertake. Students who frequently experience failure in the task of learning to read soon develop negative attitudes and an aversion to books and print. If the goal of the reading program is for students to become proficient readers who voluntarily engage in reading as a means to gain information, enjoyment, and personal fulfillment, then they must experience success as they strive to develop the skills that will lead to that goal.

Several benchmarks are indicators of successful reading experiences. First, and possibly the most important, is that readers understand what they read. Understanding may require more than one reading of the text; it may require assistance from the teacher or from other students; and it will require the reader to be actively involved in manipulating the ideas in the text, summarizing them, discussing them with peers, or comparing them to other ideas (Graves & Graves, 1994). Second, a successful reading experience is one that the student enjoys and finds informative. Finally, a successful reading experience is one that prepares the student to complete the postreading tasks satisfactorily.

Graves and Graves (1994) stated that children's success in reading is directly under the control of the teacher. The teacher selects or influences the selection of materials that they read and provides the necessary support (or scaffolding) before, during, and after they read that will allow them to meet the challenges presented in the text. The teacher also selects or helps them to select the postreading activities in which they can be successful. A word of caution may be necessary at this point. While a scaffolded instructional design promotes student success, it does not mean "spoon feeding" students. An effective learning environment requires that children be confronted with challenges so that they can develop needed strategies and become confident that they can meet the challenges they will encounter in the future. For learning to occur, students must be willing to take risks, to engage in learning activities whose outcomes are uncertain, and to accept feedback and use it effectively in their future attempts at learning. Therefore, to develop as readers, children need to be given some challenges; however, teachers must arrange and scaffold reading activities so that children can meet those challenges successfully (Graves & Graves, 1994).

Cognitive Learning Concepts

For the past two decades cognitive psychology has been the dominant orientation of education in this country. Cognitive psychologists focus on the study of learners' thought processes and view learners as active participants in learning rather than as passive respondents to their learning environments. Four major concepts that have emerged from cognitive psychology that have had significant influence on reading and on the development of the concept of scaffolded reading experiences are schema theory, the interactive model of reading, automaticity, and constructivism (Graves & Graves, 1994).

Schema theory has been discussed in detail in Chapter 1, and that discussion will not be repeated here. However, it is worthwhile to note that people generally interpret their experiences—real, vicarious, or representational—by comparing those experiences to an existing schema, thus assigning prior knowledge a very significant role in reading. What people learn and the ease or difficulty of their learning is influenced greatly by their schemata—their prior knowledge and their ability to activate that prior knowledge. Graves and Graves (1994) suggested that there are three kinds of schema that children are most often required to activate in reading and that teachers should consider as they plan reading instruction. These three kinds of schemata are world knowledge, text structure, and schemata for specific content areas.

World knowledge contributes significantly to a reader's understanding of narratives because that is the kind of information that narratives most frequently require. *Text structure* refers to the way a text is organized—as narrative material or as expository material. Children usually have more experience with narrative texts and are more familiar with their organization as materials that have a beginning, middle, and end; characters that are confronted with a problem; and problem resolution. Children usually do not have much experience with expository materials such as science, social studies, and math texts and do not have well-developed schemata for that kind of material. An additional complication is that expository texts can have a number of different structures; thus, teachers will frequently find that children need assistance in reading successfully in those areas. The third kind of schema that children need for success in reading is *schema for content areas*, which comes from formal schooling and which children develop from year to year as they progress through their schooling. Until they have had sufficient experiences with content-area information to build their schemata, they will frequently need assistance to read successfully.

While schema theory emphasizes the importance of the reader's knowledge in understanding text, the *interactive model of reading* emphasizes the importance of both prior knowledge and text. Readers must use both their schemata and text characteristics, such as letters, words, phrases, sentences, and punctuation to be effective readers, and they must use those sources simultaneously and in an interactive manner (Samuels, Schermer, & Reinking, 1992). Teachers should select texts and reading tasks that allow students to use their prior knowledge and text characteristics in such a fashion. If, for example, the text material is not familiar and contains difficult vocabulary, students may be forced to give the bulk of their attention to the individual words and neglect the application of prior knowledge to their understanding of the material. Additional problems may occur when students are required to do a lot of oral reading (or signing as they read), which forces them to put undue attention on the text and on words, rather than on gaining meaning. On the other hand, focusing only on silent reading may encourage students to neglect text characteristics, concentrate on top-down processing skills, and fill in missing information by guessing at the meaning. The goal for reading instruction should be to provide an appropriate balance of attention to text characteristics and to prior knowledge.

Automaticity refers to a person's ability to perform an activity automatically, without having to give cognitive attention to its completion. Riding a bicycle is an example of an activity that most people can perform automatically, that is, they do not have to think about each step as they get on the bicycle, pedal, guide, and balance. Automaticity in reading is a concept set forth by LaBerge and Samuels (1974) that proposes that the mind's attentional capacity is limited and can focus on only one major task at a time. If the task is complex and children are required to focus on several aspects of it simultaneously, they will fail to complete the task successfully. Reading is a complex task and includes several subprocesses that need to occur at the same time; these subprocesses involve such complex activities as decoding and comprehension. The amount of attention, or cognitive energy, that each person has available is limited, and decoding and comprehension both require a great deal of attention, especially in beginning reading (Samuels, Schermer, & Reinking, 1992). Ideally, when a person is reading, the demands of decoding and comprehension require less attention than that person has available; however, in beginning reading, the demands of decoding and comprehension are usually greater than the reader's attention resources. Readers need to develop automaticity in decoding—that is, in recognizing words and in assigning meaning to those words—thus allowing them to direct the bulk of their attention to the comprehension of the text. Samuels and his colleagues (1992) state that it is decoding that becomes automatic through practice and that comprehension almost always requires considerable attention, especially if the concepts are unfamiliar. The beginning reader can do only one task at a time—either decoding or comprehending—while the fluent reader, who has achieved automaticity in the decoding process, can do both simultaneously. Therefore, an important characteristic of effective reading instruction is the provision of many opportunities for practice on materials that children find relatively easy, interesting, and enjoyable, so that they can develop automaticity.

Constructivist theory is a theory about knowledge and learning that synthesizes current work in cognitive psychology, philosophy, and anthropology (Brooks & Brooks, 1993) and proposes that much of the meaning that a reader gains from text is constructed by the individual and is heavily influenced by the reader's social interactions (Gergen, 1985). Classroom practices that adhere to the premises of constructivist theory would use strategies that promote the readers' active engagement with the text—strategies that would encourage readers to think about what they are reading and link information they are gaining from the text with ideas and events that they already know. The role of social interactions in learning would support the use of cooperative learning, group projects, and group discussion. Graves and Graves (1994) explained that students should be given opportunities to work together in preparing to read, in writing about what they have read, and in completing projects pertaining to their reading. Working together also results in exposure to alternate interpretaions of a text. In addition, many educators maintain that group work allows students to develop skills in working with others and that those skills will serve them well when they enter the world of work (Johnson, Johnson, & Holubec, 1990; Slavin, 1987).

Instructional Concepts

When Graves and Graves (1994) developed their concept of scaffolded reading experiences, they drew heavily from Jenkins's (1976) *tetrahedral model of learning*, which states that learning will be influenced by four different factors: the characteristics of the learner, the nature of the materials, the learning activities, and the required tasks. The scaffolded reading experience consists of two phases: the planning phase and the implementation phase. The planning phase deals with the learner, the materials, and the task, while the implementation phase deals with the learning activities. This model emphasizes that when planning learning activities, the teacher must take into consideration all four of these factors.

A second instructional concept that greatly influenced the development of the scaffolding model is the concept of the *zone of proximal development*, which is attributed to Vygotsky (1978), and which emphasizes the social nature of learning. According to Vygotsky, children have a zone, or a range, in which they can learn. At the lower end of the range are learning tasks that they can complete independently; at the upper end are learning tasks that they cannot complete even with assistance; and between these two extremes, in the middle area, is the range that is most productive for learning. The tasks that lie within the middle range are the tasks that children can achieve if they are assisted either by adults or, in some cases, by each other.

A third instructional concept that plays a significant role in scaffolding is the *gradual release of responsibility model* (Campione, 1981), which promotes a progressive transference of responsibility from the teacher to the student. Initially, the teacher takes the majority of the responsibility for the student's successful completion of a reading task, perhaps even doing, or demonstrating how to do, most of the work. The student begins to assume increasing responsibility and finally takes complete, or nearly complete, responsibility for reading tasks. An important facet of this concept is that it is recursive and will occur repeatedly as students engage in new tasks throughout their school career.

A fourth instructional concept that needs to be considered within the model of scaffolding pertains to the different purposes for reading *informational* or *aesthetic* materials. Teachers will want to consider the different kinds of student responses invoked by different texts and make provisions for such in their instructional planning. In informational reading, students are focused on what they can learn from the text; their purpose is to learn new information, answer questions, or discover how to solve a particular problem. Most of the reading in content-area textbooks is informational reading. In contrast, when students are engaged in aesthetic reading, their primary concern is not with gaining information from the text but with experiencing the text—making associations and developing feelings, attitudes, and ideas (Rosenblatt, 1978). Literature is an example of aesthetic reading material. Students should be given opportunities to enjoy aesthetic reading as well as opportunities to become adept at reading to gain information.

The instructional concept of *generative learning* was developed by Wittrock (1986, 1990) and applies primarily to informational reading. According to this theory, meaningful learning occurs when readers generate relationships among the ideas in a text, and between the ideas in the text and the ideas with which the reader already is familiar. Wittrock (1990) suggested that such activities as composing titles and headings, writing questions, paraphrasing, writing summaries, making charts and graphs, and identifying main ideas will encourage the development of relationships among the ideas in the text. Some of the activities suggested for relating ideas in text to prior knowledge are to give personal examples and create new examples; give demonstrations; make comparisons; and create stories, plays, and other kinds of writing.

In summary, the instructional design of scaffolding was developed within a flexible framework influenced by diverse ideas from cognitive learning theory and from several instructional concepts. Graves and Graves (1994) explained that the sources for this design are diverse, as the approach itself is diverse and multifaceted since it was designed so that teachers could plan and develop activities for different students, texts, and reading purposes. They also believe "that a variety of perspectives offer useful ideas about teaching and that no single perspective . . . can offer all the ideas teachers need to meet the challenging goal of making reading experiences successful for all students" (p. 41).

Scaffolded Reading Experiences

As mentioned previously, a scaffolded reading experience consists of two phases: the planning phase and the implementation phase. In the planning phase the teacher considers the interdependent factors of students, texts, and purposes. Also interdependent are the components of the second phase, which are pre-reading, during-reading, and postreading activities. The scaffolded reading experience may appear to be similar to the directed reading activity (Betts, 1946) or to the directed reading-thinking activity (Stauffer, 1969); however, it is markedly different from those two instructional designs in that it is not a preset plan for dealing with any reading selection. Instead, it is "a flexible framework that provides a set of options from which teachers select those that are best suited for a particular group of students reading a particular text for a particular purpose" (Graves & Graves, 1994, p. 5). After teachers determine the skills, needs, and interests of the students, the "fit" between students and text, and the specific purposes for reading as stipulated in the planning phase, they consider the implementation phase and determine effective instructional strategies for the scaffolded reading experience.

Prereading Activities

Prereading activities prepare students to read the text selection as successfully as possible. These activities should motivate the students, activate their prior knowledge, and include the preteaching of any vocabulary or concepts in the selection that may be difficult. Graves and Graves (1994) suggested that prereading activities serve four major functions: (1) motivating the students and getting them interested in reading the selection; (2) building or activating prior knowledge, which should contain activities that relate reading to students' lives, activate background knowledge, build text-specific knowledge, and preteach vocabulary and concepts; (3) focusing attention, which should include prequestioning, predicting, and direction setting activities; and (4) suggesting strategies, in which teachers remind students of the strategies they already know and suggest the use of certain strategies when reading the selection. Instruction in new strategies does not occur during prereading activities. Teaching students about strategies and how to use them requires specific and intensive instruction and is not appropriate during the prereading stage.

During-Reading Activities

After the students have been prepared to read the selection, the next step is for them to read—that is, to interact with the text and construct meaning. During-reading activities include both the things the students do to comprehend text and the things the teacher does to assist them in that task. In this category, Graves and Graves (1994) included five categories: (1) silent reading, (2) reading to students, (3) guided reading, (4) oral reading by students, and (5) modifying the text.

Silent reading should be the most often used during-reading activity. Silent reading is required of independent readers throughout their school careers as well as in their after-school careers; thus, students should have frequent opportunities to develop and master this skill. Also, during silent reading readers can focus on decoding and comprehension and not have to devote part of their attention to the correct articulation of the word or sign.

Reading to students can be done occasionally if it serves to make the selection more accessible to the students. Reading the first few pages of a somewhat difficult selection may help to get some students started with silent reading and may serve to increase their interest and motivation. For hearing students and for some hard of hearing students, this activity can serve as a good model for oral reading; it becomes a slightly different activity when used with students who are deaf. However, if the purpose is to provide more incentive for the students to begin silent reading or to establish more familiarity with the topic and vocabulary, the teacher can read aloud and sign part of the selection. If the students receive ASL better than a manually coded English, the teacher will need to read silently a paragraph or other short section of the text at a time and then express the meaning of the English text in ASL to focus the students on the topic and concepts and ease them into silent reading.

Guided reading includes scaffolding activities used to focus students' attention on important aspects of the reading selection or to assist them in understanding, enjoying, and appreciating the selection. These activities should encourage generative learning—that is, they should lead the students to connect ideas within the text to each other and to connect ideas in the text with their own experiences. When planning guided reading activities, Graves and Graves (1994) have suggested that teachers consider such questions as what students should attend to as they read this text and what key concepts they should be looking for (cause and effect? author's perspective or bias? colorful language? characters' motives? sequence of events?). Guided reading activities should encourage students to consider and manipulate ideas and concepts in ways that will enhance understanding and enjoyment of the text.

Oral reading by students is a relatively infrequent activity for hearing and for some hard of hearing students; it is even more infrequent for deaf students. The purpose of oral reading is to allow students to experiment with language, enjoy the sound of language, and to focus on meaning. None of these goals is particularly relevant for deaf students even if they "read aloud" by using a manually coded English sign system. When they do attempt this activity, they frequently become so focused on translating the English word to the English sign that they lose a great deal of the meaning and, of course, do not experience the sound of the language. If they read the text selection and then sign the meaning of the English words using ASL, the activity is changed from reading aloud to story retelling, which is a different activity with a different purpose.

Modifying the text is sometimes necessary to make it accessible to students. Modifying the text may take the form of audiotape or videotape presentations or rewriting to simplify or shorten it. Changing the text in any manner is somewhat controversial, particularly if the selection is considered to be children's literature. However, if the choice is between the children not reading it at all and reading (or seeing) it in a different form, some exposure to the text, even though modified, seems preferable.

What the teacher plans and presents as during-reading activities depends on the students' needs and interests, the text selection, and the students' purpose for reading. Prereading activities and during-reading activities share the same goal—to provide a scaffold that will help students read successfully and become independent readers.

Postreading Activities

Postreading activities provide a variety of worthwhile opportunities for students, such as synthesizing and organizing information, evaluating the author's perspective in presenting a message, and responding to the text. In responding to the text, the students might reflect on the meaning, compare the ideas with those in different texts, engage in a variety of creative activities, and apply what they have read to their lives and to the world outside their classroom.

Graves and Graves (1994) have suggested seven categories of postreading activities:

1. *Questioning*—to encourage the students to use higher-order thinking skills such as interpreting, analyzing, and evaluating.

2. *Discussion*—to promote the active exchange of ideas, allowing students to clarify their own responses to the text and modify them according to the information they gain from their classmates.

3. *Writing*—to demonstrate understanding of the information and to apply, synthesize, and elaborate on information and ideas.

4. *Drama*—to involve students actively in what they have read.

5. *Artistic, graphic, and nonverbal activities*—to provide students with alternative ways to respond to text, allowing them to interpret and synthesize the information they gleaned from the text in a variety of ways that will accommodate different learning styles (e.g., by creating models, dances, videos, slide shows, graphs, charts, and diagrams).

6. *Application and outreach activities*—to encourage students to take the information they learned from a text and use, explore, and elaborate on it (e.g., reading an article on the homeless and then conducting a food drive at school for donation to a food bank or volunteering for work in a soup kitchen).

7. *Reteaching*—to enable the students to develop a better understanding of

the text if it becomes apparent that they have "missed" parts of the relevant material. Reteaching may consist of such activities as having students reread sections of the text, presenting mini-lessons on troublesome parts of the text, or having students assist each other.

Postreading activities emphasize the importance of *purpose* in reading and provide opportunities for students to realize that they can actually do things with the ideas in books. During postreading activities, readers should be engaged in motivating and thought-provoking activities that enhance the reading experience.

Balancing Reading Experiences

Most classrooms consist of students who have a wide range of abilities and therefore require activities at different levels. Teaching to the "average" student generally misses the mark for all students. Each student should have opportunities to engage in reading tasks that are both easy and challenging. Tasks that are easy for students enable them to develop automaticity, build confidence, and create an interest in reading. Challenging tasks enable students to gain new information, develop critical thinking skills, and become increasingly confident in their own abilities.

Providing a balanced reading program—one that provides tasks that are both easy and challenging—will foster the development of independent reading in all students. Because the tasks students face when they leave the school program, whether they enter college or the world of work, will require them to engage in reading at a variety of levels, a balanced reading program will provide them with the skills and the practice that will enable them to be as successful as possible.

Integrated Instruction

Integrated instruction is another instructional design that requires little adaptation for use with deaf and hard of hearing students. The concept of integrated instruction has emerged periodically in educational movements over the past 40 to 50 years; however, the current perspective on integrated instruction is more inclusive and has a different emphasis than previously. In the past, teachers planned topics and activities in their specific disciplines (or subject areas) to correlate with the topics and activities to be presented in the other disciplines. Currently, teachers are selecting a context and theme within which the knowledge and skills that used to be relegated to separate subject areas are now sub-sumed and connected to personal and social concerns of the students and their environment.

David Perkins (1986) wrote that all too often the skills and concepts taught to students are disconnected from the purposes and the arguments that make them meaningful, flexible, and functional and connect them to the real world. Teachers have frequently become discouraged because what they teach in the classroom seems to remain in the classroom and is not transferred or connected to the students' experiences in other classrooms or to their lives outside of school. In their search for more effective ways of teaching, many teachers have begun to implement the concept of integrated instruction, which they soon find necessitates a curricular change.

The Integrated Curriculum

The concept of the *integrated curriculum*, sometimes referred to as an interdis-ciplinary curriculum or core curriculum, has its roots in the curriculum designs of the 1930s and 1940s (Vars, 1991). Clark and Clark (1995) stated that a cur-riculum of this nature is well suited to the needs of students because of its emphasis on personal and social concerns and because of an organizational structure that blends concepts and topics from multiple disciplines. Many edu-cators (Beane, 1990, 1993; Clark & Clark, 1995; Jacobs, 1989; Perkins, 1991) believe that an integrated curriculum is particularly well suited to the learn-ing styles of young adolescents and strongly encourage its implementation, particularly in middle school programs. Beane (1990, 1991) asserted that the curriculum should be organized around themes dealing with early adolescent problems, needs, and concerns related to the world in which they live and that these questions and concerns should form the basis for the integrated cur-riculum.

The integrated curriculum does not simply connect two or more subject areas through a common topic, with the subject areas continuing to maintain their identities. Beane (1993) stated that the integrated curriculum "dissolves and transcends subject area boundaries, but does not abandon all of the knowl-edge and skills that have traditionally been defined within disciplines of knowl-edge." In addition, this curriculum structure opens opportunities for the inclu-sion of knowledge and skills such as problem solving, critical analysis, ethics, valuing, and inquiring that frequently are omitted because they do not fit neatly into the preconceived notions of any particular discipline. Figures 6.1 and 6.2

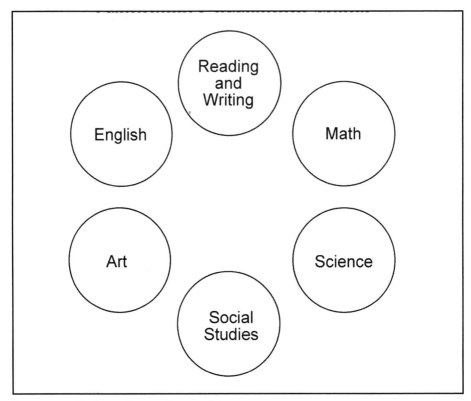

Figure 6.1. Traditional curriculum model.

show the differences in a traditional and an integrated curriculum model, respectively; Figure 6.3 shows two transitional stages.

Rationale

Clark and Clark (1995) maintained that the many benefits of the integrated curriculum have been demonstrated by research from more than 80 investigations. Vars (1991) found that students in integrated instruction did as well, and often better, on standardized tests when compared with students in traditional instruction. The results of two other studies indicated that the students in the integrated instruction groups outperformed the students in the traditional study groups on measures of knowledge acquisition (Brown, 1992; Gamoran & Nystrand, 1992). In addition, Clark and Clark (1994) found that the collaboration of teachers that is necessary in integrated instruction to develop learning experiences for their students created school climates that focused on student needs, instructional and curricular improvement, and reflective practice.

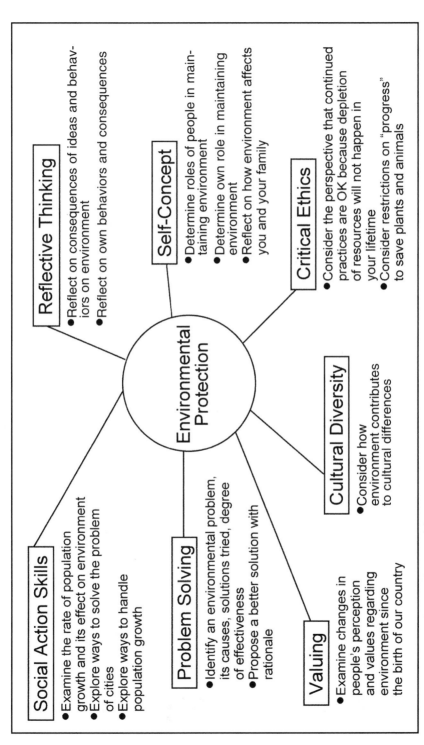

Social Action Skills

- Examine the rate of population growth and its effect on environment
- Explore ways to solve the problem of cities
- Explore ways to handle population growth

Reflective Thinking

- Reflect on consequences of ideas and behaviors on environment
- Reflect on own behaviors and consequences

Problem Solving

- Identify an environmental problem, its causes, solutions tried, degree of effectiveness
- Propose a better solution with rationale

Valuing

- Examine changes in people's perception and values regarding environment since the birth of our country

Environmental Protection

Self-Concept

- Determine roles of people in maintaining environment
- Determine own role in maintaining environment
- Reflect on how environment affects you and your family

Critical Ethics

- Consider the perspective that continued practices are OK because depletion of resources will not happen in your lifetime
- Consider restrictions on "progress" to save plants and animals

Cultural Diversity

- Consider how environment contributes to cultural differences

Figure 6.2. Integrated curriculum model.

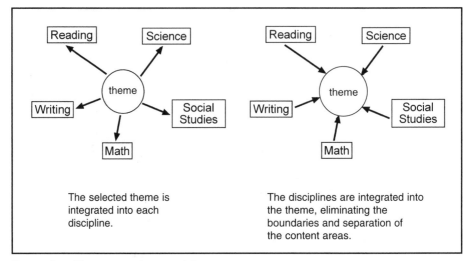

Figure 6.3. Two intermediate models.

Guthrie and McCann (1997) conducted an investigation in which they studied the effect of integrating language arts and science on the learning of third- and fifth-grade students. They found that the students in the integrated instruction groups were more motivated than the students in the traditional instruction groups to use strategies for learning. The students who applied the strategies that they had learned showed increased literacy engagement and gained conceptual understandings of science at a higher level than did students who did not apply them.

In her study of a program described as an interdisciplinary, thematic, team-based approach to teaching the humanities, Aschbacher (1991) found that it had several important, positive effects on the students enrolled. Using multi-dimensional forms of measurement, the investigators found that the program had a statistically significant effect on students' writing and content knowledge; that the longer the students spent in the program, the better their attendance was; that the drop-out rate decreased and remained lower than that of students in the traditional program; that the students liked school better even though they found it more demanding than the comparison students did; and that the students felt that their teachers and fellow students cared far more about them than comparison students thought that their teachers and fellow students did.

In addition, in this age of complex technological advances, knowledge is growing at an astounding rate. Teachers try to revise their curricula but find it more and more difficult to determine what should be added to and what should be eliminated from the courses of study. They are beginning to realize that it is impossible to teach all of the important facts from all of the disciplines and are now faced with decisions concerning what critical topics to include and what critical topics to throw out. And, to create more pressure on the schools and the teachers, knowledge will not stop growing. This realization forces educators to rethink the "what and how" of teaching; educating children so that they know content and facts no longer provides a satisfactory educational program. Young people must be taught how to learn, how to find information independently, how to investigate and analyze problems and develop solutions and plans of action. In addition, the critical topics selected must be relevant to them and to their world.

Finally, reading and writing profit immensely in an integrated curriculum, for no longer is there the "reading period" or "writing period" that frequently limits the students' opportunities for reading and writing throughout the day. In integrated instruction, reading and writing are an integral part of every activity, regardless of whether the focus is science, social studies, math, or health, and students gain exposure and practice in a variety of texts and genres.

Barriers

As with any program or curriculum, there are disadvantages as well as benefits. Some of the barriers to implementing integrated curriculum programs were compiled by Clark and Clark (1995); identified by Ackerman (1989), Beane (1991), Clark and Clark (1992), and Jacobs (1991); and included the following:

1. *Time*—Teachers have difficulty finding enough time during the school day for teacher collaboration and community networking.

2. *Lack of teacher preparation*—Teachers have not had training in collaboration or in developing and implementing integrated programs.

3. *Lack of appropriate resources*—Because textbooks and materials developed around integrated themes are not readily available, teachers frequently must develop their own materials.

4. *Professional concerns of teachers*—These concerns include the effort required to plan and implement integrated instruction, the feeling that their discipline will be compromised, and the pressure to reorganize curricula while continuing to be responsible for covering the material on standardized tests. (Clark & Clark, 1995, pp. 3–4)

While it seems that the advantages to both students and teachers offer a strong rationale for developing and implementing an integrated curriculum, it is also clear that this must be a concerted effort of all teachers with the full support of administrators. Administrators must be willing to be involved in the change, to learn about the benefits and the problems of the program, to address teacher concerns, and to support the students and teachers in their efforts.

Thematic Instruction in the Integrated Curriculum

One of the most prominent concerns of many teachers as they begin the planning and implementation of an integrated curriculum program is that the subject areas will be minimized or ignored, with a subsequent reduction of knowledge and skills on the part of the students. Beane (1993) argued that this should not occur, and that subject matter and skills are not diminished but rather are repositioned within the context of significant personal-social *themes*. To understand how this repositioning occurs requires a paradigm shift for most educators, who tend to think of units within the classroom as topic units, which are integrated into each of the subject areas, instead of as themes in which all of the subject areas are *integrated into the thematic unit.*

According to Shanahan, Robinson, and Schneider (1995), a topic is just a subject, such as birds, the food chain, or pollution. In topic units, the subject (e.g., birds) is incorporated into several or all of the content-area periods. In math, the students might count birds or use bird figurines for their manipulatives, or their word problems would be about birds and they might figure out how far birds fly if they migrate from Canada to Mexico. Social studies might include activities such as locating migration routes on maps and native areas for various species of birds, and science would include additional studies of birds.

Conversely, themes allow for a deeper examination of ideas. According to Shanahan et al. (1995), thematic teaching is a way of organizing instruction around themes instead of around subject areas. They maintain that a theme differs in that it states a point of view; for example, pollution affects both people and their environment. Themes are dynamic; the student can support the statement or argue against it. Beane (1993) views themes somewhat differently; he believes that instruction should be organized around themes rather than subject areas but that themes should name a personal-social concern of the students, thus connecting with the individual and with the "real" world. Themes that he has suggested include "Living in the Future," "Careers, Jobs, and Money," and "Environmental Problems." To fully explore themes such as these, students would need to apply a variety of skills, such as communication—including reading, writing, and researching. However, in addition, several other skills that are not often included in the subject areas on a regular basis should be emphasized, including reflective thinking, critical ethics, problem solving, valuing, self-concept, and social action skills. Beane (1993) has described these skills in the following manner:

1. *Reflective thinking*—both critical and creative thinking about the meanings and consequences of ideas and behaviors.

2. *Critical ethics*—identifying and judging the morality in problem situations.

3. *Problem solving*—including problem finding and analysis.

4. *Valuing*—identifying and clarifying personal beliefs and standards on which decisions and behaviors are based.

5. *Self-concept*—describing and evaluating personal aspirations, interests, and other characteristics.

6. *Social action skills*—acting on problem situations both individually and collectively. (pp. 40–41)

Learning Advantages for Students

The use of thematic instruction has been recommended for second-language learners by Peregoy and Boyle (1993) for several reasons. Since many deaf students are second-language learners, or are learning two languages (ASL and English) at the same time, these reasons apply also to their educational programs. First, thematic instruction creates a meaningful, conceptual framework that provides many opportunities for students to develop and practice their reading and writing skills. Second, the meaningful content established by the theme increases both content learning and second-language skills. Third, because all disciplines are woven into the theme, similar vocabulary and concepts are repeated throughout the day, thus giving reinforcement for new information in meaningful and relevant situations. An added benefit is that only a reasonable number of new vocabulary words are introduced to students since every subject area is not discussing completely different topics; therefore, the student is not overwhelmed with too many new vocabulary words to try to learn. Another reason is that thematic instruction includes projects in which students participate, thus creating student interest, motivation, involvement, and purpose. Finally, as students work cooperatively on their projects, they have more opportunities to use language for communication, reading, and writing as they question, inform, problem solve, negotiate, and interact with their peers.

Educators supporting thematic teaching also point to a fact that reports on education have repeatedly stressed—that student knowledge is frequently quite superficial and that students lack a depth of understanding of what they learn. National assessments of student achievement have concluded that American students can state their opinions clearly in writing but have great difficulty in supplying evidence to support their arguments. Appraisals of student knowledge in science and social studies indicate that students, while having reasonable awareness of content, lack an understanding of the meaning of the content and the relationship among ideas (Shanahan et al., 1995). These assessments seem to imply that while students are exposed to many topics, their knowledge seems to be limited to facts without an understanding of the ways in which this knowledge affects their lives, their community, and their world. Learning is thereby relegated to an educational exercise rather than equipping students to use their knowledge to shape their thinking about events occurring in their environment and to make intelligent decisions about their own lives.

Peregoy and Boyle (1993), in recommending the use of thematic instruction for second-language learners, also stated that thematic instruction creates a meaningful conceptual framework within which students are provided many opportunities to use language (oral and signed), reading, and writing and to explore various content areas in depth, thereby increasing both content learning and second-language acquisition. In addition, collaborative projects provide numerous opportunities for students to develop and use critical thinking skills and the language to support those mental activities, for example, questioning, informing, problem solving, negotiating, and interacting with peers. Through such engagement, both social and academic language development is challenged and promoted. Thus, Peregoy and Boyle concluded that thematic instruction creates optimal language and literacy learning opportunities for both first- and second-language learners.

Kinds of Thematic Instruction

In the literature, references are made to labels that refer to some type of thematic instruction such as topics, themes, thematic units, and theme cycles, to name but a few. The authors' exact meanings are sometimes unclear, and the reader is left trying to decipher the differences among the terms. Weaver (1994) supplied clear explanations of several of the terms using the labels *theme unit, theme exploration,* and *theme cycles.* These terms delineate three levels of thematic instruction through which many teachers progress as they begin to shift from a traditional teaching approach to a thematic approach, starting with thematic units and moving into theme exploration and ultimately into theme cycles. One of the important common characteristics of these three concepts of theme study is student participation in making decisions regarding the learning process, with the student's responsibilities progressively increasing from the theme units to the theme cycles.

A *theme unit* is planned mostly by the teacher, who determines the topic, plans and organizes the information, and identifies the goals. The theme unit may look very much like the skills curriculum that is superficially organized around a topic, or it may reflect a much more creative integration of writing, reading, and language activities into a study of a chosen topic. Weaver (1994) gave the example of teaching a thematic unit on the American Revolution by using a core book such as *Johnny Tremain* by Esther Forbes and using a variety of activities that would help students appreciate the novel and understand the Revolution and that period of time in our country's history. Some of the activities suggested included timelines of pictures showing major events of the Revolution, acting out some of the important scenes or sections from the novel, writing letters to the editor either for or against the Boston Tea Party, learning songs and dances from the Revolutionary period, preparing foods according to colonial recipes, and producing an edition of the *Boston Observer* newspaper as it might have appeared in the days of Johnny Tremain (Weaver, 1994, p. 431). Even though units of this type have high teacher input, they also have high student involvement as the variety of activities is challenging and meaningful enough to motivate and engage the students in active learning. Theme units do not provide many opportunities for student choice; generally, the teacher sets the problems, identifies the major ideas, organizes the materials and activities, and finds the resources.

In *theme exploration*, the teacher determines the topic beforehand and presents it to the students, soliciting their input on the subtopics (Weaver, 1994). For example, the teacher might present the theme *relationships* and carry out an initiating activity explaining the theme and its different facets and parameters. Then the students identify the major subtopics—for example, family relationships, peer relationships, dating relationships—and what to pursue within these subtopics. In theme studies, students should have a significant degree of ownership, and for that to occur, there cannot be a prepackaged unit. The theme exploration must evolve as teachers and students together negotiate the curriculum.

Edelsky, Altwerger, and Flores (1991) stated that *theme cycles* provide the opportunity for pursuing a line of inquiry. In theme cycles, teachers and students together brainstorm possible topics for extended study during the year. Together, they form the questions, find the resources, and pursue their line of inquiry. As students delve into their extended study tasks, they frequently come up with more questions, which lead them in different directions to study about different subtopics; however, all are connected to the original theme or initiating question, thus producing the effect of a chain or a *cycle*.

Edelsky, Altwerger, and Flores (1991, pp. 64–68) maintained that in theme cycles, students do not do science *activities*; they do *science*, as a scientist would. They do not do social studies activities; they investigate social phenomena, as a social scientist would. Through theme cycles, they are involved in authentic and relevant learning experiences that are generally not included in theme units but may be included in theme explorations. In theme cycles, teachers involve students in determining which lines of inquiry to pursue and encourage them to continually raise new questions to guide their inquiry. When one line of inquiry is completed, the teacher and students begin another in the theme cycle (Short & Burke, 1991).

Teachers frequently are uncomfortable with an integrative emphasis on theme study instead of on separate subjects such as social studies and science; they fear that students will not learn the information to be gleaned from centuries of history. However, with the information explosion that has occurred within the past few decades, it would be impossible for students to learn all of the facts and events from the past, as well as keep up with what is occurring in their contemporary world. When this kind of traditional teaching approach is used, the students do not remember the information or apply it in any meaningful way to their own lives. Many teachers find that in a thematic approach to teaching it is quite acceptable to abandon the fact-based lessons in favor of concentrating on key events and periods, the people involved, their way of life, and their motivations and actions (Weaver, 1994). A major advantage is that what appears in textbooks to be an intimidating amount of factual information to be memorized can often be replaced by a few topics, explored extensively during thematic study.

Organization of Thematic Instruction

Peregoy and Boyle (1993) offered six criteria for organizing thematic instruction to promote language development, critical thinking, independence, and interpersonal collaboration, all of which are important factors in the instruction of students who are deaf and hard of hearing. All of these criteria represent basic learning principles, as described by Enright and McCloskey (1988).

The first criterion states that all thematic instruction must have *meaning and purpose*; it must be relevant and interesting to the students. One way to ensure this is for the students themselves to participate in selecting the theme, activities, and projects that become a part of the unit of instruction. When students have opportunities to make choices, they assume ownership of their own learning, thereby creating self-direction and purpose.

The second criterion is that thematic instruction should build on the *students' prior knowledge*. This prior knowledge should reflect the students' school and home experiences, thus allowing varied cultural experiences to be incorporated into their schoolwork, providing an understanding of themselves and others.

The third criterion stipulates that the teacher create *integrated opportunities for the students to use oral and written language and literacy for learning purposes.* These opportunities should be determined and planned with input from students. The students are thus provided with activities to broaden their experiences, with different forms and functions of print that coincide with their interests and goals.

The fourth criterion emphasizes that the planning of thematic instruction includes *scaffolding for support*—that is, the teacher structures instruction so that it supports students' efforts and values their accomplishments. One way to do this is to use the scaffolding techniques discussed earlier in this chapter to assist students in participating successfully, even if their language or literacy proficiency is limited. Another way is to allow students to display their learning and share it with others.

The fifth criterion encourages *collaboration* by providing students with many opportunities to work together on theme-related projects and activities. Collaboration in pairs and small groups gives students opportunities to process complex information actively with a minimum of risk and anxiety. In this way, language and content-learning are productive and are used purposefully, promoting acquisition and retention of learning.

The last criterion emphasizes that the learning process must promote *variety*–variety in study themes, in learning strategies, in the functions of oral/signed and written language used, and in task difficulty. Variety and flexibility also should characterize the learning groups (pairs, small groups, and whole class), thus ensuring that interest remains high for all students.

Developing thematic instruction is a dynamic process that should include input from the students at all levels of decision making. The first step is to choose the organizing theme—that is, the theme that will serve as the focus of interest. There are several sources for identifying themes, including state and local curriculum guidelines, personal interests expressed by the students, and special interests of the teacher. However, the organizing theme should not be so general that it is beyond the scope of definitive investigation, nor should it be so narrow that it restricts the parameters of study (Jacobs, 1989). Themes can be focused on concepts (e.g., patterns, revolution, flight, pioneers), events (e.g., historical events such as the Holocaust, current events such as outer space excursions, and future events such as productive habitation patterns within the limits of earth's resources), issues (e.g., protecting the environment), and problems (e.g., teen pregnancy, substance abuse). The theme selected should cross discipline lines and be relevant and interesting to students.

Once a theme is chosen, the next step is to brainstorm ideas related to the theme. One way to organize the brainstorming is to create a cluster or word web on a chart or chalkboard using the organizing theme as the topic in the center of the cluster or web. The teacher and students generate ideas around the theme, accepting and recording all ideas on the chart or board. When that is completed, they can then begin grouping together related ideas, resulting in a map of the major subtopics to be investigated. At this point it is worthwhile to create another web, grouping all of the subtopics around the discipline fields, so that teacher and students are aware of the disciplines included in the exploration. This step also provides them with an opportunity to add subtopics, which would include any field of discipline inadvertently overlooked, that would fit comfortably within the exploration of the theme. The aim is not to have the same number of subtopics under each discipline but to promote deliberate examination of the theme through all discipline perspectives (Jacobs, 1989).

Another graphic organizer that can be used effectively in this step is the K-W-L structure, which is a strategy using three columns. Under the first column the teacher and students list *what they already know* about the organizing theme; under the second column they list *what they want to know*; and under the third column, as their investigation proceeds, they list *what they have learned*. A fourth column can be added, of subtopics related to the theme that they still want to explore, thus providing continuing topics for exploration in their theme cycle.

The next step in developing thematic instruction is to establish guiding questions to serve as a scope and sequence. The teacher and students develop these questions for each subtopic, arranging them in an order from fundamental issues to more complex ones. Developing these questions for each subtopic provides a structure for the unit of study and aids in the development of strategies and timelines. After the questions for investigation have been determined, a plan for the execution of each investigation should be developed. Clark and Clark (1995) suggested four steps in the planning process:

1. Identify strategies, activities, and experiences to be used in each investigation.

2. Determine resources needed and their availability.

3. Determine assessment and evaluation procedures.

4. Determine tasks that must be completed and assign specific responsibilities to each member of the team. (p. 21)

Clark and Clark also suggested that the teacher compare the concepts and skills to be taught in each content area with state and district requirements. With students who are deaf and hard of hearing, the teacher will also want to provide an appropriate emphasis on language-learning activities; therefore, one of the teacher's major responsibilities is to make sure a variety of functional language and literacy uses are incorporated into the projects and activities undertaken by the students. In addition to exposing students to a variety of literacy forms and functions, the teacher will want to make sure that scaffolding activities are provided to facilitate student participation, even if English-language proficiency is limited. Therefore, as one of the final steps in developing a theme cycle, the teacher will examine the project and activity plans and consider the students involved in each to assure that they have the appropriate materials and supports necessary to be successful in their tasks.

Jacobs (1989) suggested that the final step in theme cycle development should be undertaken by the teacher. In this step the teacher checks to make sure that critical and creative thinking is encouraged in each investigation. One model of cognition that can be used for this check to ensure the inclusion of opportunities for higher-level thought processes is Bloom's *Taxonomy of Educational Objectives* (1956). One way to accomplish this step is to develop a matrix of six columns, each column headed by one of the thought processes in Bloom's taxonomy: *knowledge, comprehension, application, analysis, synthesis*, and *evaluation*. Each of the activities planned should be placed under the appropriate column, and, when completed, the teacher should look at the distribution on the matrix. If most of the activities are listed under the first two levels of thought processes, for example, then it is a clear indication that the thematic instructional unit will promote only recall of information. The matrix serves as a graphic picture of the actual design focus for thinking that is built into the integrated instruction design.

Integrated instruction has been used at all levels in school programs. It has been used for various time frames: semester courses at a university, modular schedules at a high school, and team teaching in middle schools and elementary programs (Jacobs, 1989). Careful planning can avoid two key problems: lack of organization and coherence, and unbalanced focus on content areas. By determining a scope and sequence of guiding questions, a scattered sampling of activities can be avoided. By graphing the guiding questions and activities under discipline lines and thought processes, a balanced disciplinary approach and an appropriate array of thought processes can be included, thereby ensuring that all of the students benefit from the substance of an interdisciplinary, integrated instruction.

Emergent Literacy Intervention Programs

Identifying the importance of early intervention in the reading process has led to the development of a host of programs addressing the need for early and systematic reading programs for young children. The emphasis on early literacy experiences is largely motivated by Stanovich's (1986) report indicating that children who are classified within the "at-risk" or lower group of readers in the first grade will remain in the lower groups in fourth grade with little hope of advancing in later years. To change this momentum of failure, specific instructional programs have been designed to reverse the trend and to provide literacy learning experiences that promote success. Three specific instructional designs are reviewed in this section: Reading Recovery, developed and explained by Maria Clay in her book *The Early Detection of Reading Difficulties* (1979); Early Intervention in Reading, developed by Taylor, Short, Frye, and Shearer (1992); and the Shared Reading Project, developed by David Schleper (1996a). The first two of these programs emphasize phonemic awareness and the relationship of reading and writing, and have been used almost exclusively with hearing children. However, the number of deaf and hard of hearing first graders receiving Reading Recovery instruction is rapidly increasing. The Shared Reading Project is specifically designed for families of young deaf children as an emergent or early literacy experience focusing on storytelling, reading, and emergent literacy experiences.

Reading Recovery

This effective and increasingly popular approach to literacy originated in New Zealand in the late 1970s, with implementation in North America in the 1980s. Maria M. Clay (1979) developed the Reading Recovery program to provide first-grade children who had the greatest need for literacy development with experiences that would place them at level with their more literate peers. She did this by developing a highly systematic, intensive, and short-term, instructional design that was delivered by well-trained, experienced teachers. The focus of the program is on comprehension through connected text and the development of fluency before poor reading habits are established. The Reading Recovery program aims at developing a positive attitude toward reading through the use of materials that support student success and reading enjoyment. The program uses a set of prescriptive principles in which individualization, support, and success are carefully constructed into each lesson. Students who are eligible to participate in the program must be identified by their classroom teachers as being in the lower 20% of their class. Four fundamental principles of effective instruction provide the foundation in the design of Reading Recovery: (1) time on task, (2) individualized instruction and strategies, (3) consistent monitoring of student progress, and (4) teacher–student interactions.

Time on Task

Reading Recovery uses a pull-out model of instruction, in which each child receives instruction from a uniquely trained teacher for 30 minutes per day.

During the one-to-one tutorial session, the teacher and the student follow a routine of instructional activities designed specifically for the child, maximizing the reading and writing time on task. The intensive tutorial sessions occur daily for an average of 12 to 20 weeks; however, students continue in the tutorial sessions until they have achieved a reading level comparable to or above that of their class peers (Swartz & Klein, 1996). Time spent engaged in reading has been identified as a significant factor contributing to reading fluency with hearing children (Taylor, Frye, & Maruyama, 1990) and also with deaf children (Strassman, 1997). Poor readers spend considerable time attending to nonreading or off-task behaviors such as relying on the teacher's directives, defining vocabulary, or simply attending to assignments such as worksheets. Good readers spend greater amounts of time engaged in reading, have free time to read, and use strategies that promote continuous reading (e.g., lookback, question-answer relationships). Reading Recovery motivates and engages the child in time that is dedicated to reading and writing.

Individualized Instruction and Strategies

The typical Reading Recovery lesson consists of seven prescriptive instructional activities that are adapted to meet the individual needs of the learner. Stimulus materials include colorful and well-illustrated storybooks for beginning readers. Each child-centered story includes repetitive syntactic patterns so that immediate success can be experienced by the reader. Predictable syntactic refrains are closely related to the illustrations; sounds, rhyming of words, and alliteration are used within the story, emphasizing the development of sound-symbol awareness through repeated exposure in context (Spiegel, 1995). Storybooks are selected at the child's instructional level to provide maximum opportunities to use reading strategies.

Each tutorial session is segmented into seven daily activities. The opening activity is the rereading of one, two, or three familiar storybooks that are of interest to the child and vary in selection and difficulty. Rereading gives the child experiences with fluency in familiar contextual settings, expands word knowledge, and extends opportunities for comprehension and practice in metacognitive strategies (Pinnell, 1989; Spiegel, 1995).

The next segment is the rereading of a book that was introduced in the previous lesson. During this second activity the teacher records the child's reading behaviors, including words read correctly, words not read at all, and words the child is attempting to decode. The teacher notes the types of strategies the child uses to discover meaning and to make sense of the text, such as using illustrations or rereading.

The third phase includes instructional strategies based on data from the previous activity, including word and letter identification practiced within contextual events. The teacher may develop word awareness through the use of letter cards, word frames, and dictation of short story summaries.

Next, the child writes a story or a message of one or two sentences, with the teacher and the child talking about sound-letter relationships. During the writing activity, the teacher assists the child in developing the context and composition of the story and guides the child in discovering the spelling of words on their own through phoneme cues and phonemic awareness activities. The teacher scaffolds the writing activity through word frames or illustrations. The fifth activity is an editing experience and extends from the writing activity. During this time, the child rearranges or expands the written story and reads it for the teacher.

During the sixth phase of the lesson, the teacher introduces a new story that has been selected specifically to take advantage of the child's strengths and developing skills. Finally, the child reads the new storybook to the teacher, incorporating available reading strategies (Spiegel, 1995; Swartz & Klein, 1996). The daily routine of the instructional design begins and ends with reading integrated, coherent text.

Throughout the activities, the teacher and the student engage in conversations that lead the child into the use of supportive metacognitive strategies (e.g., rereading, lookback, inferring) within the context of reading. Situated instruction in comprehension monitoring, or contextual analysis, occurs as the child is engaged in the reading process. For example, the teacher may guide the student to use clues from an illustration, or to read to the end of the page to identify the meaning of an unknown word as the child is reading interesting stories at his or her instructional level (Taylor et al., 1995). Throughout the instruction, the child is asked what strategies were used to find the meaning of a word, or to solve a problem in the reading process. The teacher and the student discuss what strategies might be used, as well as how they might be applied to other reading materials in the classroom or at home (Spiegel, 1995).

Monitoring Student Progress

While most reading programs rely on specific skill assessment at predetermined intervals with annual standardized testing to determine a child's progress in reading, Reading Recovery emphasizes continual evaluation of a child's fluency and efficiency while he or she is engaged in the reading and writing process. The Reading Recovery teacher uses direct observations and daily recordings of specific skills and strategies, types of storybooks read, fluency, and comprehension. Daily charting of words read and written correctly, words missed, and words attempted provides the teacher and the student with immediate information regarding the effectiveness of instruction. The Observation Survey (Clay, 1979,

1985) is also used to determine categories in which specific instruction will be emphasized and to assist in the selection of reading materials.

Data recorded by the teacher help to determine instructional strategies, appropriateness of the reading materials selected, and the strengths or resources the child brings to the reading and writing process that can be used to establish the next goal. Spiegel (1995) referred to Reading Recovery as a program based on accelerated progress. Clay (1985) emphasized the use of proven reading strategies by good teachers and that the learning time is spent on teaching something the child needs to learn and is able to learn, and eliminates time spent on teaching "something the child doesn't need to learn" (p. 4). Effectiveness of instruction can be accomplished only if the student's progress is monitored and instruction adjusted in congruence with the child's reading behaviors.

Teacher–Student Interactions

A critical characteristic of the Reading Recovery process is collaboration between the teacher and the student (Spiegel, 1995). Good teachers, like good readers, have a wide range of instructional strategies that assist the child in developing fluency and efficiency. Good teachers communicate and collaborate with their students in identifying specific learning goals and relationships between the instructional activities and the instructional goals. Strassman (1992) interviewed students who were deaf regarding the purpose of their reading activity. The majority of the students' responses indicated little understanding of the purpose of the activity, its relationship to the reading task, or the goals of instruction. Similar findings have been reported with hearing students (Johnson, Allington, & Afflerbach, 1985).

Teacher–student interactions extend beyond the Reading Recovery sessions to include themes and topics that are current with the child's general program of study in the classroom. Spiegel (1995) provided a number of examples in which Reading Recovery teachers and their students extended and generalized strategies and practices learned in the tutorial sessions to the classroom and beyond. The general classroom teacher can be invited to participate in a Reading Recovery session, the two teachers may share a common space, or the classroom teacher may incorporate some of the strategies used by the Reading Recovery teacher in general classroom reading sessions. The principle of best practice is that the teachers and the child share common goals of instruction and communicate the ways and means to achieve those goals through modeling, role playing, questioning, and other interactive strategies that will influence the child's attitude toward reading, writing, and literacy proficiency.

Reading Recovery puts into practice established and proven principles of instructional design and reading. The general goal of the program is to integrate structural and visual cues and problem-solving strategies into a contextual format where meaning can be extracted and generalization can be practiced. Effectiveness of the Reading Recovery intervention program with hearing children has been generally impressive. Focused time on task appears to increase the rate of learning. Several studies reported that approximately two-thirds of the students who receive Reading Recovery intervention services during the first grade are able to read within the average range of their classmates over a sustained period of at least 3 years (Pinnell, 1989; Pinnell, Lyons, DeFord, Bryk, & Seltzer, 1994). While deaf and hard of hearing children have typically not been included in Reading Recovery, individual cases have been observed. Some local school districts have recruited highly skilled and experienced teachers of the deaf to receive year-long training through the Reading Recovery Trainer of Trainers model. Instructional adaptations for deaf and hard of hearing children included sound-symbol awareness through finger spelling and print, auditory awareness training based on the knowledge of print, sign and phonic finger spelling, and selection of reading stories that addressed the child's strengths in sound-symbol-sign awareness. Additional adaptations were made by monitoring the child's progress in general communication and literacy skills through direct observation, recording of reading and writing behaviors, and daily review of the running records of reading fluency.

Early Intervention in Reading

While Reading Recovery is considered one of the more effective reading intervention programs, it is costly and can be cumbersome. Short-term costs may be prohibitive in some schools, particularly during the training and implementation phases, when a one-to-one student–teacher ratio is required at half-hour intervals, 5 days a week. Pull-out practices used in the delivery of the program may create scheduling conflicts with field trips and other activities and may disturb the continuity of the classroom and create artificial barriers. Taylor, Short, Frye, and Shearer (1992) developed an alternative to the Reading Recovery program in which activities are provided in the regular classroom as part of the normal instructional day. This alternative program, Early Intervention in Reading, incorporates the best practices of instructional design for small groups of students.

The in-class reading intervention program focuses on the lower 20% of the children in the first-grade classroom and is delivered by the regular classroom teacher after receiving specialized training. Reading instruction is practiced in small group settings of four to seven children, minimally 3 days a week for approximately 20 minutes a day. The general progression of the intensified and specialized Early Intervention in Reading lessons begin with shortened stories of picture books, or summaries of the stories told through pictures, progressing to short stories of 40–60 words in level A, 60–90 words in level B, books with 50–150 words in level C, and books with 100–200 words that can be read independently by the students in level D. Each level extends over approximately an 8-week period, depending on the progression of the students.

Reading materials include a selected set of commercially available picture storybooks and short stories (e.g., *All By Myself* by Mercer Mayer, *Freight Train* by Donald Crews). The full text is initially read to the children and a shortened story prepared by the teacher in congruence with the students' reading skills. Some of the original storybooks may be read to the children with shortened stories read by the children. As the children progress, the original storybook may be read directly by the children. (A listing of selected stories used in the Early Intervention in Reading program can be found in Taylor et al., 1995, p. 150.)

The short stories are written on a chart, which is then used for reading by the teacher with the children. While reading the story, the teacher introduces or calls attention to selected sound-symbol relationships, uses of context clues, and other decoding strategies commensurate with the children's abilities. A short or shortened story is usually read and reread over a 3-day period. On the first day the children and the teacher select five words from the story to write. Words are recorded in sound boxes—that is, the children record one phoneme in each box provided on their papers, with help from the teacher as needed. The next two lessons include rereading the shortened stories and writing a sentence as a group about the story. The children record as many of the sound-letter associations as they are able, with additional spelling help and hints from the teacher. The children then reread the sentences they produced. Next, the stories are entered into a booklet where the children can illustrate them during free time. Teaching assistants, reading volunteers, or students from the upper grades provide assistance in working with individual students or with the other students in the class during the program.

An integral part of the Early Intervention in Reading program is the teacher's guidance in the development of phonemic awareness, decoding skills, and metacognitive strategies. The teacher consistently assists and encourages the students to make sense of the reading passage through the use of illustrations and cues within the passage. To ensure progress throughout the cycle, the teacher listens to the child read and reread familiar stories, recording reading behaviors at the end of the third day. The instructional goal is that the children will be reading the short story with a minimum of 92% accuracy by the end of the third day of instruction. If the goal is not met, the instructional strategies used, as well as the reading materials, must be reevaluated and changed.

Several studies are underway to evaluate the effectiveness of the Early Intervention in Reading program. Preliminary results indicate that many of the children who are members of the lowest group of emergent readers in the first grade demonstrate significant progress at the end of the first year and maintain that level of accomplishment in the second grade. Like the Reading Recovery program, Early Intervention in Reading relies on the implementation of best practices. The instructional design across programs provides the substance for successful reading experiences, including explicit and clearly stated instructional goals, intensive direct instruction, quality teaching practices, systematic monitoring of students' reading behaviors, a high frequency of opportunities for successful reading and writing experiences, and generalization of reading behaviors beyond the school into the home and the community. These practices are not limited to specific programs or a select group of students; rather, they can be incorporated into uniquely designed reading programs for children who are deaf or hard of hearing.

Shared Reading Project

Reading *to* children is a fundamental component in the development of literacy skills. The Shared Reading Project was developed by David Schleper (1996a) to assist parents and primary caregivers of deaf children in storytelling and book sharing through the use of American Sign Language. Schleper's design includes a wide range of book sharing strategies that have been identified through a number of studies of deaf and hearing parents reading to their children. The foundation for the project is based on Holdaway's (1979) *shared book experience* with preschool and young school-age hearing students, which incorporates the child's natural language with learning to read through adult reading models (Cooper, 1997). Principles of Holdaway's interactive approach include introducing print and meaning to children through reading and rereading stories and inviting them to participate as long as the story remains interesting and engaging. Concepts of print, phonemic awareness, and language are incorporated into the shared book experience by the model readers. Schleper (1996b) adapted the shared book experience procedures (see Cooper, 1997, pp. 177–178) for use with families and their young children who are deaf.

The pilot phase of the project was initiated in 1993 with a small group of families and was extended into a national program through Gallaudet University's Pre-College National Missions Programs (Schleper, 1996a). Shared Reading is supported through a network of trained tutors and readers. Parents and extended family members of young deaf children are invited to an introductory workshop where the ASL tutor/reader describes the components of emergent literacy and the goals of the program. Special accommodations (e.g.,

culturally diverse reading and stimulus materials, flexibility in scheduling, native-language interpreters) are made to include fathers, non–English-
speaking families, rural communities, and cultural and ethnic minorities.

Emergent literacy materials include a set of 12 "family book bags" that contain a storybook, a videotape of the story presented in ASL by a deaf adult, a
card that can be used as a bookmark with suggestions for reading to one's child,
and an activity guide for family use. Following the initial workshop, ASL
tutors/readers make weekly home visits during which individualized storybook
reading is conducted and family members practice their storybook signing/read-
ing communication skills. The tutors target specific reading strategy goals each
week and assist family members with any questions. The family book bag including the video and storybook remain in the child's home for 1 week and is
exchanged for another book bag by the ASL tutor weekly (Schleper, 1996b).

The Shared Reading program is designed to provide families with support
for emergent literacy practices before the child experiences significant delays or
frustrations in the reading process. Families are not only shown how to read a
storybook in ASL; they are also encouraged to use strategies that help the child
develop book knowledge, word knowledge, awareness of story structure, comprehension strategies such as using illustrations to gain information about the
story, and questioning strategies. Daily reading activities are encouraged, with
an emphasis on rereading stories that are interesting and fun for the child. The
instructional design includes time specifically set for daily reading, high levels of
positive child–parent interactions, and informal monitoring of parent and child
progress through parent–tutor journals. Research regarding the effects of the
Shared Reading program is in progress; however, teacher and family reports are
promising and positive.

In summary, emergent literacy programs are designed with the objective of
preventing reading difficulties and delays. Highly intensive, time-on-task models
of instruction delivered in small groups or one-to-one ratios are used to increase
the likelihood of success and prevent the long-term effects of reading failure at an
early age. Underlying common elements of instruction in each of the programs
reviewed include (a) direct instruction provided in connected and meaningful
contexts; (b) reading materials that are child-centered, that is, appropriate to the
child's emergent literacy skills and interests, and (c) teacher/parent and child
engaged in positive and successful reading experiences.

Technology and Reading

The field of education for children who are deaf or hard of hearing has had a
long and stellar history in the application of technology to the teaching and

learning process, particularly in the areas of language, reading, and writing. The application of systemic and scientifically based procedures has marked the history of deaf education with innovations such as programmed readers (e.g., PALS), linguistic reading programs (e.g., Merrill Linguistic Readers), basal reading programs (Reading Milestones, Reading Bridge), and computer-based language-reading-writing programs (e.g., PLATO). Electronic technologies such as mainframe computers, language master, filmstrips, overhead projectors, amplification systems, view masters, and captioned films containing carefully constructed and well-illustrated reading materials have passed through classrooms for deaf and hard of hearing children with the hope of resolving the discrepancies in reading and writing between deaf and hearing children. The 21st century holds a new set of computer-based technologies, tools, and instructional designs that build on the historical scaffold of literacy development with deaf and hard of hearing children. The availability of computer-based technology in communities, classrooms, and homes provides opportunities for both literacy growth and challenges for individuals who are deaf and hard of hearing. The following section provides a general overview of technology and literacy for deaf and hard of hearing learners, focusing on three instructional adaptations: (1) student-centered computer-enhanced instructional designs; (2) environmental computer-based adaptations, and (3) computer-based bridges.

Computer-Enhanced Instructional Designs

Several specialized programs have been developed as instructional tools addressing the language, reading, and writing needs of children who are deaf or hard of hearing. Nancy Fogel (1990) designed a computer-assisted instruction (CAI) program incorporating "direct instruction" principles into the interactive reading/language experience. She incorporated the graphic capabilities of computer technology and the visual modes of communication most familiar to deaf students through the use of animation, graphics, and text while maintaining "the instructional environment in which syntax, vocabulary, and figurative language are linguistically controlled and incrementally graduated in difficulty" (p. 2). Fogel demonstrated that use of visual and spatial computer-based designs to convey the meaning and lexical features of English is of particular benefit to children who are deaf or hard of hearing. Using an open format of CAI, Prinz and Nelson (1984) developed a program that allowed children to initiate their own communication through the selection of letters, words, or pictographs on an adapted keyboard. The children were able to construct sentences independently or sign/say the sentence to the teacher for input into the computer and read their statements in text and illustrations. The instructional design in both of these programs included features of high levels of interaction and feedback and graphics that were interesting, informative, and motivating to the students, thus providing opportunities for successful learning experiences.

In addition to specifically designed instructional programs, a wide range of authoring languages including interactive media such as Quick-Time, Authorware, and CAI open designs offer teachers and their students greater flexibility in developing personalized instructional reading and writing programs (King, 1997). Waldron and Rose (1996) developed the Graphic Communication Device (GCD), which is a child-friendly authoring tool that facilitates real time, simultaneous communication through reading and writing with options for graphics, animated signs, and pictographs. GCD software provides two-way distance communication using standard computer-phone setups.

Personal captioning technology has been used as a tool for literacy development in a number of classrooms using a variety of instructional strategies. Students are able to narrate story scripts, translate from ASL to English, create and solve problems, edit and retrieve through self-generated captioning (National Center for Accessible Media, 1997). Teachers in the TRIPOD program, Burbank, California, provided reading and writing instruction through short, commercially prepared ASL video stories that students viewed and for which they developed their own English-captioned scripts. After reviewing and editing the scripts with specific language objectives targeted for feedback, students prepared a captioned video at a computer workstation located in the classroom (Loeterman et al., 1997). Clarke School for the Deaf in Northampton, Massachusetts, established a Captioning Club for adolescents as an extracurricular activity in which members of the club selected the type of project they wanted to produce. The end result was a 4-minute video comedy, produced, directed, and creatively captioned by club members (National Center for Accessible Media, 1997).

While limited data are available regarding the benefits to students as captioners, teachers report that using captioning as a strategy for reading and composition can be an enriching, motivating, and productive experience; however, several issues must be factored into the process. The teacher and students should engage in discussion of prior knowledge about the topic and the video selected or created. Modeling composition and comprehension strategies are an integral part of the learning process. Captioning workstations should be easy to use, and classroom teachers should be competent users prior to introduction of the hardware to the students. Videos to be captioned should be kept short, with a 2-minute maximum, to reduce the labor-intensive process. Students may view the video several times so that the script can be discussed and formulated with continuity and story structure. The captioned text should be written with in-depth discussion on the selection of words, meanings, and relationships, as well as the social context of the content. The students can then prepare a draft of the captions in hard copy, review, edit, and revise with guidance and feedback from the teacher. Most important, the instructional objective must be clearly identified and implemented by the teacher and students (National Center for Accessible Media, 1997).

Environmental Computer-Based Adaptations

Computers provide a variety of communicative adaptations that have created new learning environments. The use of computer-based discourse systems has increased access to daily conversation and dialogue in classrooms for deaf students and in inclusive settings. Computer-based systems that facilitate visual communication have had a profound effect on the way language, reading, and writing experiences are provided to deaf and hard of hearing students. English National Form Instruction (ENFI), developed at Gallaudet University (Peyton & Baston, 1986), and the Daedalus Interchange are local area networks that support classroom communication through real-time written classroom interactions (Kern, 1995). Students participate in classroom communication through written discussion on personal computers networked to a teacher workstation. Each student can read, comment, and elaborate on all of the messages generated by others in the class. Marlatt (1996) used the ENFI system in a variety of activities, adapting the computer-based program to enhance instructional goals and students' needs. He reported that students showed a marked increase in composition skills and greater reading comprehension of conversational language as a result of their learning experiences through the ENFI system.

Discourse is a classroom-based technology that provides a system of group instruction in which each student has a wireless laptop computer networked to the teacher's desktop computer. The Discourse system provides options for visual-graphic displays, lesson management, individualized instruction, immediate student feedback, scoring, data management, and access to the Internet. Students and teachers are able to interact through signed or spoken language and standard English print simultaneously. Studies using the Discourse system with deaf, hard of hearing, and hearing students demonstrate dramatic increases in written expression, time-on-task behaviors, and reading skills (Robinson, 1998).

Network technologies, particularly the Internet, Web pages, and listservs, provide a wide range of options for information exchanges and interchanges that have a significant impact on written English and reading skills of students who are deaf or hard of hearing (Spiller, Heathly, Kenzen, & Rittenhouse,

1994). Newslines, virtual libraries, museums, and travelogues have been developed for deaf students by deaf students and other members of the deaf and hard of hearing communities (National Center for Accessible Media, 1996). Conferencing multimedia networks are being used to reduce isolation experienced by many high school and postsecondary students in general education settings. Through the use of video transmission, captioning, and voice, deaf and hard of hearing students interact with their instructors, peers, and deaf mentors across several locations and distances to increase specialized learning opportunities (Adkins, 1997).

Teachers and students have greater access to visual information, cultural diversity, events to develop and stimulate prior knowledge, and reading resources that change the mandate and dimensions of literacy. From virtual environments where students can reenact scenes from *Oliver Twist* to battery-operated toys such as Alpha Master, computers depend on good teachers who are able to provide learners with successful learning opportunities.

Computer-Based Bridges

A variety of environmental computer-based adaptations are available that enhance, as well as mandate, literacy fluency among deaf and hard of hearing individuals. For example, closed-captioned television positively influenced the reading comprehension and sight-word vocabulary of deaf adolescents (Koskinen, Wilson, & Jensema, 1986). Commercially available captioned videos are virtually books on tape for deaf, hard of hearing, and hearing readers. Technologies that offer greater access to information provide individuals with more information, resulting in opportunities for higher levels of literacy.

Real-time graphic display (RTGD) is a system in which spoken language is displayed in print almost simultaneously (Stuckless, 1981). As a stenographer records the spoken message phonetically, a computer converts the shorthand into standard print, displaying the message on a screen or monitor for audience viewing similar to the captioning seen on TV today. RTGD is used primarily in public forums, conferences, and selected classroom settings (Smith & Rittenhouse, 1990), as the cost of a stenographer plus the hardware can be prohibitive to most school districts. An alternative to RTGD is the low-cost, computer-assisted note-taking option, which is used primarily for taking notes in meetings, discussions, and classroom presentations (Vivan, 1991). Using a word-processing program and optional software for outlining, abbreviations, and graphics, a trained note taker can enter selected information, such as questions, and display the text in a convenient, real-time, and familiar format for the reader. Computer-based technologies such as television and commercial-movie captioning, TTYs, RTGD, and computer-assisted note taking allow deaf individuals to participate in common activities much as their hearing peers do. However, the bridge to literacy may be far more expansive than one could have imagined a decade ago.

Greater emphasis is being placed on the development of educational materials that have a "universal design"—that is, information is presented in a variety of modalities and formats to reach a wide range of learners. Printed educational materials are generally lacking in adaptability and flexibility. Teachers spend considerable amounts of time and effort adapting content and context to meet the needs of individual learners. Universal designs emphasize the use of digital media that allow teachers to select, edit, and reformat educational content (Council for Exceptional Children, 1998). For example, a digitized reading text with universal design allows the teacher to adapt the content to the learners' needs through the addition of illustrations, signed segments, dictionary references, or specific strategies or "hooks" such as lookback hints, repeated reading, or frames for questioning. While publishing and marketing obstacles need to be resolved, universally designed educational materials are available. Microsoft's SAMI provides graphics, captioning, word searches, and translation of text into spoken English and other languages. Texas School for the Deaf produced *Rosie's Walk* and *The Gift of the Magi* on CD-ROM with multiple language formats, including captions in standard English, ASL, and signed English; animation; music; and voice. In addition, the universal design allows students to click on an English word and see the sign equivalent, click on the graphic representation of an object and see the printed word, match English word phrases to ASL phrases, and select a variety of word games as supportive learning activities.

The continual evolution of educational technology provides greater opportunities for learning and literacy. Each of those opportunities is dependent on the application of effective instructional design principles and teachers who are able to link the student with the learning task. The opportunities for access to the information superhighway through services such as the World Wide Web provide students and teachers with resources, learning opportunities, and databases that are continually expanding (Foster & Quinn, 1996). The availability and accessability of these resources should have a profound effect on the literacy achievements of the next generation. Cultural, economic, and educational differences among deaf and hard of hearing learners need to be incorporated into instruction and computer-based technology to assure that all students have the opportunity for integrated curricular experiences and successful learning. Students who are deaf or hard of hearing will be consistently challenged by the redefinition of literacy and the demands that computer-based technology places on reading, composition, and information management.

Summary

Several instructional designs have been discussed in this chapter and are intended to give teachers some ideas about different ways instruction can be organized. Most instructional designs are not meant to be used alone but to be combined with other designs in whatever ways will be the most productive for students.

Scaffolding is a way to structure learning so that the teacher provides temporary supports that allow students to focus on fewer tasks at once. Keeping the demands within their range for learning allows students to experience success in those tasks and to build stepping stones so that they can eventually perform the whole task independently. Scaffolding is an instructional design that can be used in conjunction with almost any other instructional design the teacher wishes to use. For example, scaffolded learning experiences fit very appropriately into thematic instruction in an integrated curriculum design.

Thematic instruction within an integrated curriculum design provides students with a holistic approach to reading, writing, and the content areas. One of the major strengths of this approach is that students find it easier to understand the relationships between and among concepts and ideas and to connect those concepts and ideas learned in the classroom to their everyday lives. Content-area skills and information are not taught in separate periods as separate disciplines but are clustered around a common theme so that the overlap in the disciplines occurs naturally and students can more easily discern the interrelationships among the skills and concepts. Students assume a large part of the responsibility for their own learning—what they will learn, how they will learn it, and what varied paths of inquiry they will follow to extend their investigations. Through these activities students realize the need for and learn to use critical thinking skills—to move beyond learning information to application, analysis, synthesis, and evaluation of information. No longer are students reading to memorize information so that they can answer questions correctly; they themselves are formulating the questions that will lead them into continued inquiry and greater depths of learning.

Common characteristics among the three widely used early reading intervention programs that were reviewed—Reading Recovery, Early Intervention in Reading, and Shared Reading—include the principles of effective instruction—that is, time on task, individualized instructional strategies, monitoring student progress, and positive teacher/parent–child interactions. Early reading and writing practice in a highly motivating and accepting setting are critical to the development of a positive attitude toward literacy. Both the parent and the teacher have a critical role as models of the reading process and literacy. Deaf and hard of hearing students, like their hearing peers, need opportunities to be read to and to read. Early intervention programs provide systematic and somewhat scripted opportunities for storybook reading, writing, and the development of basic literacy skills to prevent reading delays or failure before they occur.

The systematic application of technology to the teaching and learning process is a critical component of quality instructional designs including scaffolded instruction, thematic units, and the integrated curriculum. Computer-based technology extends the boundaries of instructional design to provide optional avenues for interaction and learning. Instructional variations, such as having students do the captioning, enhance instructional design by allowing students opportunities for development and creativity, directing, editing, and production of products. Computer-based technologies can be used in a variety of educational settings to adapt instructional delivery to meet the needs of deaf and hard of hearing students. Using computer-based technology to promote literacy among students who are deaf or hard of hearing requires more than hardware, software, and a host of Web sites. Teachers must construct clearly stated learner objectives and apply carefully designed instructional strategies in a systematic manner to assure that each student has an opportunity to access information, to learn from the information, and to practice what has been learned.

P A R T

III

APPLICATIONS

CHAPTER

READING STRATEGIES

Preview

Understanding the reading process, how children learn to read, and how instruction occurs allows the teacher to plan the learning event and to modify instruction to fit the needs of the learner. A large repertoire of instructional techniques and an understanding of what each technique can do enable the teacher to select the most effective and efficient techniques for a particular learner and to apply different strategies when modifications are necessary. Brophy (1984) suggested that teachers often are reluctant to change their teaching techniques even when they are not working well because they lack readily available alternatives. Walker (1996) proposed that teachers resist changing their strategies because they lack knowledge about why one technique may be more effective in certain situations.

This chapter will provide descriptions of reading strategies, suggesting points at which they may be the most effective, although several may be used successfully in several parts of the reading event. The first section deals with strategies that are commonly used during *prereading activities*, such as strategies for motivating, activating prior knowledge, decoding, and preteaching vocabulary; the second section describes comprehension strategies or strategies to use *during reading*, including metacognitive strategies. Strategies that can be used during *postreading activities* are discussed last and include strategies for questioning, application, and elaborating. This chapter does not include an exhaustive list of strategies; rather, it includes a selected list of strategies that the authors have used or have seen used successfully with deaf and hard of hearing students.

Reading as a Part of the Language Arts

While this book focuses on reading, it is important to note that reading is only one component of the language arts, which also encompass writing, speaking/signing, and listening/receiving. In reading instruction teachers will want to include all aspects of the language arts, making connections among the various components. Children should frequently be engaged in reading, writing, speaking/signing, and listening/receiving activities in an integrated language arts curriculum that promotes active engagement in reading and writing with connections to real-world contexts. Olson and Homan (1993) suggested several common school activities that provide opportunities for the integration of the language arts, such as note taking (writing with listening/receiving or reading), summarizing (reading and writing), interpretation of reading using readers' theater (reading, writing, speaking/signing, and listening/receiving), and language experience stories (speaking/signing, listening/receiving, writing, and reading).

Rather than a "reading period," teachers should think of a language arts period and plan for the integration of all the components. As teachers become used to focusing on the concept of an integrated language arts, they will see how naturally these components blend to benefit the students. With deaf students the primary focus should be on reading and writing, as these two components are the major avenues for their exposure to the English language.

Instructional Models

In the late 1970s Durkin spent a great deal of time observing the teaching of reading in classrooms and concluded that teachers were spending very little time on actual instruction of reading strategies. Durkin found that while teachers gave workbook assignments and asked questions about text content, most of these exercises *tested* students' understanding of what they had read instead of teaching them *how to understand*. Consequently, much research during the 1980s was focused on discovering how to teach comprehension strategies to students.

Explicit Instruction Models

Explicit instruction, which involves four phases, was the name given to one widely researched model. The four phases in this model are (1) teacher modeling and explanation of a strategy; (2) guided practice, during which the teacher and students work through several examples of the strategy together using actual text, while the teacher gradually gives students more responsibility for task completion; (3) independent practice, in which students use the strategy on their own with teacher feedback; and (4) independent application of the strategy in real reading situations (Pearson & Dole, 1987). Taylor, Harris, and Pearson (1988) elaborated on the first phase of this model, *teacher modeling and explanation of a strategy*. During this phase, they suggested that the teacher: (a) explain *what* the strategy consists of, (b) explain *why* the strategy is important, (c) model *how* to perform the strategy, and (d) explain *when* to use the strategy in actual reading.

Examples of other research showing that comprehension can be taught explicitly were cited by Fielding and Pearson (1994). Their review of the research indicated that many strategies used for different purposes have been taught successfully, for example:

- using background knowledge to make inferences (Hansen & Pearson, 1983) or set purposes (Ogle, 1986);

- identifying the main idea (Baumann, 1984);

- identifying the sources of information needed to answer a question (Raphael & Pearson, 1985); and

- using the typical structure of stories (Fitzgerald & Spiegel, 1983) or expository texts (Armbruster, Anderson, & Ostertag, 1987) to help students understand what they are reading.

Fielding and Pearson (1994) maintained that because of the body of research conducted during the 1980s, teachers now have a much clearer understanding of what comprises quality instruction and how to make it part of a larger comprehension instructional program. They listed four areas for teachers to consider:

1. *Strategy authenticity*—Strategies taught to students should be like the ones used by successful readers. Instruction should focus on the flexible application of a strategy rather than a rigid sequence of steps.

2. *Demonstration*—Teachers should demonstrate how to apply each strategy successfully—what it is, how it is applied, and when and why it should be used. Teachers should also illustrate the processes they use by "thinking aloud" while they read.

3. *Guided practice*—Students and teachers should practice the strategy together, with the teacher giving feedback and gradually giving students more responsibility for performing the strategy and evaluating

their own performance. Guided practice is also a good time for students to share their reasoning processes—another activity especially important for less strategic readers.

4. *Text authenticity*—Students must be taught, reminded of, and given time to practice comprehension strategies while reading "real" texts—not just short passages taken out of context. This activity will increase the probability that students will apply these strategies in their independent reading.

Peer/Collaborative Learning Models

Another group of models that have proven to be effective in reading are those that provide opportunities for peer and collaborative learning. These models not only foster equity among students and a sense of community but also provide an avenue for students to gain access to the thinking processes of their peers. *Cooperative learning* (Johnson & Johnson, 1985) is one of the most widely researched peer learning models. A synthesis of this research was conducted by Fielding and Pearson (1994) and suggested that cooperative learning is most effective when certain conditions are present, for example, when students have a clear understanding of the goal, when students explain things to one another instead of only providing answers, when students understand that the success of the group depends on the satisfactory performance of each group member, and when group activities supplement teacher instruction. When used appropriately, cooperative learning has positive social and cognitive benefits for students of all abilities.

Another peer learning model that has been investigated is *reciprocal teaching*. In reciprocal teaching students take turns leading dialogues that involve summarizing, asking an important question about what was read, predicting information, and clarifying information. Reciprocal teaching seems to be the most effective when students, after initial instruction by the teacher, teach their peers how to participate in these dialogues (Palincsar, Brown, & Martin, 1987).

Numerous models of reading instruction are available for teachers to apply or modify and apply in their classrooms. It is important to note that applying one model does not preclude the use of other models. In fact, unless more than one model is used, children may end up with instruction that is deficient or lacking in some areas. As stated in earlier chapters, when planning instructional systems and designs, the teacher is encouraged to strive for a balanced approach; the same is true when planning strategies for the instruction of reading. Teachers are encouraged to know and apply multiple approaches that will lead to improvement in reading. They must have a full portfolio of instructional strategies in order to help students develop a full portfolio of reading strategies that will enable them to become successful readers.

Motivation Strategies

The first step in reading instruction, and a big part of preparing students to read, is motivating them. Whatever the task, it is more interesting and meaningful if they have a good reason for wanting to do it. Motivational activities should incite enthusiasm and eagerness to read the material. Sometimes the teacher will use activities that focus primarily on motivating the students; however, motivational activities frequently overlap with other kinds of prereading activities such as activating prior knowledge and preteaching concepts. In general, motivational activities will draw upon the interests and concerns of the students and will include student participation such as hands-on experiences and dramatization. These activities should be fun and aimed at getting the students interested and involved. They also should serve to direct students' thinking toward the themes, topics, and concepts of the text.

Teachers can use various strategies to encourage students to read, but they must keep in mind that ultimately motivation has to come from the learners themselves if they are to become independent readers outside of school. Motivational activities can contribute to students developing a desire to read by providing successful experiences in reading and by making reading personally meaningful and useful to the child.

Reading Aloud

"Read alouds" are frequently used by teachers to get students interested in reading books and may involve the teacher reading or a student (who has rehearsed) reading to the other students. Reading aloud can be used effectively at all levels. With deaf and hard of hearing children, there are several ways that read alouds can be handled. If the students are hard of hearing, the teacher may read and sign in a manually coded English (MCE) system simultaneously. If the students are deaf and receive ASL more accurately and efficiently than a MCE system, the teacher may read aloud while an aide or another teacher interprets the story in ASL. When reading aloud, the teacher usually pauses after selected passages for discussion and explanation that can focus the students' attention on the characterizations, plot development, use of language, and various other factors that present themselves in the text.

Reading aloud is a powerful activity for creating interest in a book. Frequently, students who do not usually enjoy reading will ask if they can have the book after the teacher has finished sharing it with the class. Other students may want to read books by the same author or books on the same topic, particularly if the teacher has such books displayed on a table and briefly discusses each one, highlighting points of interest. Parents and members of the deaf community can be invited to the classroom to share a book or a story.

Movies and Books

Many students are motivated to read a book after they have seen the movie. Sometimes they are motivated by movies they have seen at theaters or on television, and sometimes they are motivated by movies, particularly captioned films, that have been shown at school. Many movies are developed from books (many from quality books); however, marketing experts have realized that there are profits in products based on films, and now many books are developed from movies. While teachers may be concerned about the literary quality of books that grow from films and television movies or programs, children are highly motivated to read them, and this provides an opportunity to cultivate the reading habit and capitalize on reading instruction.

After students have seen the movie and read the book, they can participate in many activities that will help to develop their reading skills. These activities, which can be used at all levels, might include working individually, with a partner, or in small groups to accomplish such things as:

- describing a character;
- comparing the same character in the movie portrayal and the book portrayal;
- using a Venn diagram to show differences in the plot development of the movie and the book; and
- writing about or telling which version they enjoyed the most and why.

Keeping Charts and Journals

Many children are motivated to read when they are asked to keep visible evidence of the extent of their reading. For younger children, colorful, interesting charts can be provided to each student for them to record each book as they finish reading it. (For example, primary teachers may display large bookworms for each child on the wall, and as a book is read, the child can write the title in a segment of the worm.) With input and agreement from the students, teachers can establish goals for each child that, if met by the specified time, result in a class reward such as a pizza party or an ice-cream treat.

Older students can record the number of pages they read each day and graph the results at the end of the week or month. Another activity is journaling, in which students write a brief description or summary of each book they read, which can then be shared with the teacher, with a friend, or with the class.

Bookshares

Book sharing is a motivating activity in which students of all ages can participate, as well as teachers and other people in the school and community. In bookshares, a day is set in advance when a selected number of students and teachers will share with the audience a book they have read, giving a brief summary of the book, highlighting parts they found particularly enjoyable, exciting, scary, or interesting for one reason or another. They also tell why they liked the book and selected it to share with others. Students and teachers can invite other people in the school or community to come to school and share a book that they have read.

Reading to Younger Children

Another strategy that can be effective in motivating students to read is having them read aloud to younger children. Students who would not choose to sit down with a book and read for enjoyment or improvement may willingly practice reading a book so that they can read it effectively to a younger group of children. This strategy is particularly effective with deaf and hard of hearing students, whose independent reading level is frequently below age level, making it difficult to find books that they can read comfortably to practice their reading skills. They will often voluntarily read and then reread several times a book they are planning to read to a group of younger children. A variation of this strategy is pairing an older student with an elementary student for a "reading friend." Then, once a week or at some specified interval of time, the students have a "reading friend" period when the older student, the reading friend, reads a book to the younger student and the younger student reads to the reading friend.

Building and Activating Prior Knowledge

Having and using prior knowledge is an important part of the reading process. In fact, what is frequently labeled a comprehension problem may actually be a lack of prior knowledge, the failure to apply prior knowledge, or the failure to apply the appropriate prior knowledge. It is the teacher's responsibility to make sure that students have the necessary prior knowledge to understand the text that they are about to read. Prior knowledge of the content enables students to interpret ambiguous words and make inferences, predictions, and elaborations (Irwin & Baker, 1989). Building and activating prior knowledge are important prereading activities.

Many activities, some of which are not necessarily prereading activities, will develop prior knowledge. Vocabulary activities, many of which are presented during prereading, help to develop prior knowledge, and they are discussed later in this chapter. Irwin and Baker (1989, p. 49) suggested that before describing specific strategies, it may be helpful to note some general suggestions:

- Teachers should assess the extent of their students' prior knowledge before starting a reading selection.

- If it appears that the students already have the necessary knowledge, teachers should present activities for activating the appropriate prior knowledge. (Having prior knowledge does not guarantee that it will be applied appropriately for comprehension.)

- Before reading, teachers should ask questions that encourage students to connect the topic to their own experiences.

- Students, particularly young students, sometimes do not realize that it is permissible for them to use their own experiences to derive meaning from text. Therefore, in prereading discussions and activities, teachers should encourage them to do so.

- Teachers should consider firsthand and hands-on experiences for developing prior knowledge, including such activities as field trips, guest speakers, experiments, and films.

- Reading aloud to the students or having them read to themselves daily is a technique that develops background knowledge and exposes students to material and language.

- Teachers can provide related trade books, textbooks, and reference books and encourage students to do additional reading to build necessary prior knowledge. This technique can become a useful tool for students throughout their school and after-school careers.

Semantic Webs or Maps

Semantic webbing or mapping is a strategy that activates and builds on a student's prior knowledge (Heimlich & Pittelman, 1986); it is a strategy that is effective with students of all ages and with both narrative and expository texts. Semantic maps are diagrams that visually show the connections or the relations among subcategories of a topic. This strategy usually begins with a brainstorming session that encourages students to retrieve stored information and to see graphically the concepts they are retrieving. Students learn the meanings and uses of new words, see old words in a different perspective, and see the connections among words. Through discussion, the students can confirm and expand their own understandings of the concepts. According to Heimlich and Pittelman, they relate new concepts to their own background knowledge, thus promoting better comprehension. Semantic mapping is commonly used as a strategy for vocabulary development, for prereading and postreading, and as a study skill technique, as outlined below:

1. *Vocabulary development*

   a. Write the targeted vocabulary word in a circle in the middle of the board or chart paper.

   b. In a brainstorming session, encourage the students to think of as many words as they can that relate to the target word.

   c. As the students give their words, the teacher writes them all on the board.

   d. Next, the words must be categorized. The teacher may categorize the words and label each list with the appropriate category; or, depending on the level and skills of the students:

      • the students can categorize and label the categories;

      • the teacher can supply the category labels and the students list each word under the appropriate category; or

      • the teacher can list the words in the appropriate groupings and the students supply the category name.

   e. The teacher concludes the semantic mapping with a brief explanation of how the word relates to the story or selection, or the students are asked to predict how they think the word will connect to the story or selection. (See Figure 7.1 for an example of a semantic map.)

2. *Prereading and postreading* (to provide the teacher with an assessment of the students' prior knowledge on the topic)

    a. Follow the same steps as for vocabulary development, but, instead of using a vocabulary word in the middle circle of the web, write the topic of the reading selection.

    b. After reading the selection, the semantic map can be reviewed and discussed to emphasize the main ideas presented in the written material and to add new information that the students gained in their reading, putting them into the appropriate categories or adding new ones.

3. *Study skill technique*

    a. The semantic mapping strategy can be used as a study skill to guide the processing of textbook material.

    b. It can be used as an advance organizer.

    c. For some students, it can be an effective substitute for note taking and outlining. (Discussion on this technique can be found later in the chapter under "Study Strategies.")

Semantic Feature Analysis

Semantic feature analysis (SFA) is an effective strategy for demonstrating relationships among concepts within a category, as well as the uniqueness of each word (Pittelman, Heimlich, Berglund, & French, 1991). It is usually used with expository text. Through this procedure, students improve their vocabulary and categorization skills by building on their existing schemata and begin to refine and understand the nuances that make subtle differences in the ways words are used. Figure 7.2 shows an example of a semantic feature analysis grid. To create one, follow these steps:

    1. *Select a category.* SFAs can be constructed for most categories of words. With students new to this procedure, it is best to select categories that are concrete and familiar. The category word can be a vocabulary word or it may be one of the major topics of the story or selection. Write the category in the top left-hand box of the grid.

    2. *List words in the category.* List three or four words that name concepts or objects related to the category down the left side of the grid.

    3. *Add features.* Write three or four features (traits, characteristics, properties) of the category across the top of the grid. Ask the students to suggest additional features that at least one of the words in the category usually possesses, and add these to the row of features. Start with only a few features and allow students to add more later.

    4. *Determine feature possession.* Guide students through the matrix, asking them to decide if the word on the left of the grid has each of the features listed

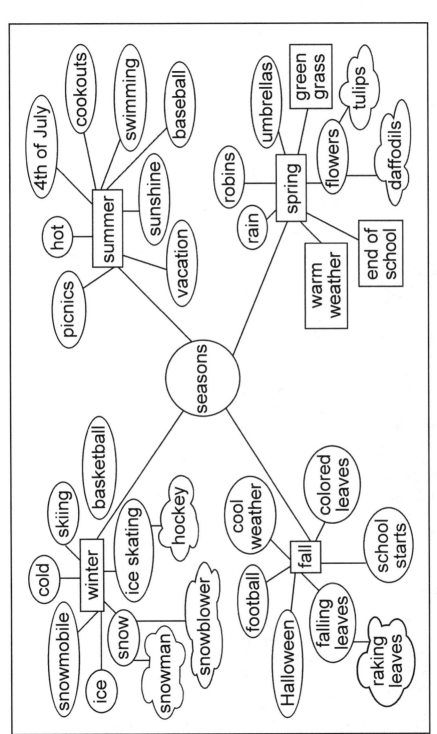

Figure 7.1. Semantic map for seasons.

across the top. If the students decide that it usually has a feature, put a plus (+) sign in the box; if it does not usually possess that feature, put a minus (−) sign in the box. If the students are unsure, put a question mark in the box. The question mark serves as a place holder, allowing discussion to continue while marking an area that will require investigation.

5. *Add more words and features.* Ask the students to add more words that fit the category and features that apply to those words. Add these to the grid or let the students add them.

6. *Complete the grid.* Direct the students to complete the grid either individually, with a learning partner, or in a small group. Suggest that they use reference books and other sources to find the answers for the boxes marked with question marks.

7. *Discuss the grid.* Have the students examine the completed grid carefully, noting the similarities and differences among the words. Ask them which words in the categories seem to be the most alike (share the most common features) and which ones seem to be the most different. Guide them in making generalizations as well as in noting the unique features of words.

The semantic features analysis strategy may be used as a technique to develop motivation, to develop vocabulary concepts, to develop and activate prior knowledge, and to summarize and review information at the end of a selection or unit. Discussion is an integral part of this procedure. As students examine and discuss the finished grid, they make judgments about the words. When first using this procedure, the teacher may have to demonstrate the process and show students how to analyze the words or concepts by features. Once the students are familiar with this technique, the teacher can serve as a facilitator, allowing the students to do most of the completion and analysis of the grid and eventually to take an active role in planning the grid and selecting the words and features to be compared. This strategy can be used with very young children but seems to be most effective when used with students who are 8 years old and older.

K-W-L

K-W-L is a strategy that can be used with any text but is probably most effective with expository text and with students who are at least 8 years old. Before starting the procedure, the teacher draws three columns on the board and labels the first one "What I **K**now," the second one "What I **W**ant to Know," and the third one "What I **L**earned" (see Figure 7.3). The procedure works as follows:

1. The teacher introduces the topic of the reading selection.

Sports	played with a ball	played with a round ball	players hit the ball	players kick the ball	players must run	players skate on ice	played with a puck	played with an oval ball	players tackle each other	players hit the ball with their heads	has a goal	has a goalie	has a net	a team sport
basketball	+	+	−	−	+	−	−	−	−	−	−	−	−	+
football	+	−	−	+	+	−	−	+	+	−	+	−	−	+
hockey	−	−	−	−	−	+	+	−	−	−	+	+	−	+
baseball	+	+	+	−	+	−	−	−	−	−	−	−	−	+
volleyball	+	+	+	−	−	−	−	−	−	−	−	−	+	+
soccer	+	+	−	+	+	−	−	−	−	+	+	+	−	+
tennis	+	+	+	−	+	−	−	−	−	−	−	−	+	−

Figure 7.2. Semantic feature analysis.

2. The students list in the first column what they already know about the topic.

3. Then they list in the second column what they want to know about the topic.

4. The students read, discuss, and study the assigned text.

5. When they are finished reading and discussing the text, they list in the third column what they learned.

6. A modification that teachers frequently use with this strategy is the addition of a fourth column ("What I Still Want To Know"), in which students list any topic that they wanted to learn but still did not know at the end of their study and any new line of inquiry that was triggered by their reading and discussion. With the addition of this modification, the strategy is usually referred to as K-W-L plus.

Card Arrangement

The *card arrangement* strategy is a simple technique designed to prepare students for reading narrative text by getting them to focus their thinking on the events in the story. Before the lesson the teacher selects the main events that occur in the story. The number of main events will depend on the ages and abilities of the students. For example, if the students are 7 years old and the story is *Goldilocks and the Three Bears,* the events selected by the teacher might be the following:

1. The three bears go for a walk in the woods.

2. Goldilocks goes into the three bears' house.

3. Goldilocks falls asleep on Baby Bear's bed.

4. The three bears find Goldilocks asleep on the bed.

5. Goldilocks is afraid and runs out of the house.

The teacher writes each main event on a card and then presents the cards to the students in mixed order. Teacher and students read and discuss the sentences, and the teacher asks the students to decide in what order they think the events will occur in the story and to arrange the cards accordingly. The children must agree on the order of events. After reading the story, the children compare their prediction of the order of events with the actual sequence in the story. This strategy can easily be adapted for older students.

What I know	What I want to know	What I learned	What I still want to learn

Figure 7.3. K-W-L plus chart.

Anticipation Guides

Anticipation guides can be used with students from elementary grades through high school. They are usually used with expository text but can also be used with some narrative texts. An anticipation guide is a series of statements to which each student must respond before reading the text. After the task is completed, they discuss their responses. The purpose of the anticipation guide is to activate prior knowledge and encourage students to think about what they will be reading.

The teacher determines the major concepts in the selection and writes those concepts in short, clear declarative sentences with a line in front of each statement. For example, the teacher may take major concepts from a selection on bats and arrange them in the following format:

Before reading the selection about bats, read the following statements and decide if they are true or false. Write a T (for true) and an F (for false) on the line before each statement.

_____ 1. Bats are birds.
_____ 2. Bats are very helpful because they eat many insects.
_____ 3. Bats are harmful because they suck blood from people.
_____ 4. Bats are mammals.
_____ 5. Bats are nocturnal.
_____ 6. Bats sleep upside down.

Discuss the students' responses before they read the selection, asking them to explain why they responded as they did. After reading the selection, have the students revisit their responses and compare their thoughts before and after reading the selection. To modify this activity, instead of having the students respond to the statements individually, the teacher can write the statements on an overhead transparency and have the students respond to and discuss them as a group.

Graphic Organizers

Graphic organizers are prereading activities that the teacher constructs to activate prior knowledge and to show students the connections that exist among the key concepts in a selection (expository text). This strategy can be used with students of all ages. Initially, graphic organizers are constructed by the teacher; once the students understand the process, they can work in cooperative groups and organize important concepts into their own graphic representations. Graphic organizers are used as follows:

1. The teacher analyzes the vocabulary of the selection and lists the vocabulary or concepts that are important for students to understand. The teacher may add relevant terms that the students already understand to help them relate what they know to the new material.

2. Using the terms from the list, the teacher constructs a graphic organizer (see Figure 7.4). This graphic organizer is not to show to the students but serves as a check for the teacher to verify that the words are connected in logical ways.

3. Put the students in groups of two or three and give each group the list of terms and a stack of 3 x 5 index cards.

4. The students write each word from the list on an index card. Then they work together to decide on a spatial arrangement of the cards that best shows the important relationships among the words.

5. The teacher may provide assistance as the students work. The students' arrangement may be different from the teacher's, but if they can satisfactorily explain the relationships among the terms, their arrangement should be accepted.

6. When the task is completed, the groups compare their graphic organizers and discuss the reasons for their arrangements.

7. After reading the text selection, the groups revisit their graphic organizers and decide if they should make any changes in them.

Student-Generated Questions

Teaching students to generate their own questions about material is an excellent way to motivate them and prepare them for reading. This strategy can be used effectively with both expository and narrative texts and with students at the upper elementary levels through high school.

Teachers can get students involved in asking questions by focusing their attention on a picture or illustration from the reading selection and asking what they would like to know about the picture. Have them ask questions that focus on the details in the picture or the overall message of the picture. Write, or have them write, the questions on the board or on a chart. Ask what else they want to know about the story or selection and record those questions. After reading the selection, read the questions they asked and discuss the answers.

Teachers can also get students involved in asking questions about material they will read by reading aloud or signing the first paragraph or two from a selection and then asking them what else they would like to know about the topic. The teacher can also ask them questions such as "What would you like to know about _____? (This may be the main character or a topic.) Having students generate their own questions about a story or a selection will arouse their interest and curiosity and give them a purpose for reading.

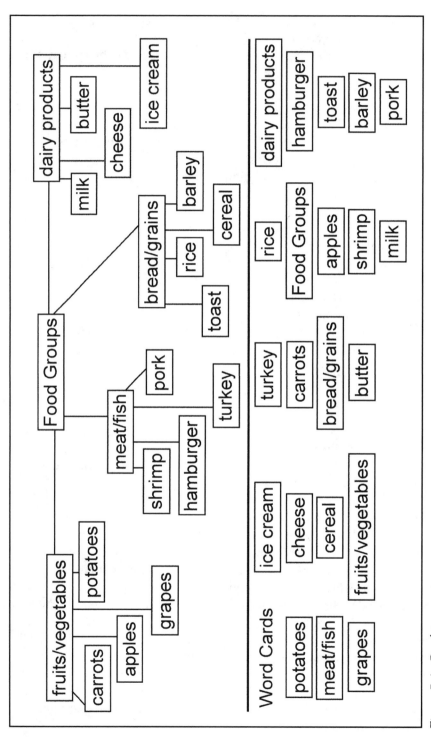

Figure 7.4. Graphic organizer.

Activating prior knowledge is an essential activity for preparing students for reading. It provides a frame of reference for the students that signals the connections they must make between the information they already have and the new information they will gain. Effective prereading strategies will help them recognize how the new material fits into their already existing conceptual frameworks or schemata.

Decoding Words

Decoding, or word recognition, is an important part of the reading process. In fact, Gough (1984) stated that word recognition is the foundation of the reading process. While the overall goal of reading is comprehension, the ability to recognize words is a prerequisite for achieving that goal. Skilled readers recognize words not only quickly but also automatically, which enables them to use more of their cognitive capacity for comprehension processes. Therefore, a goal for students is that they become automatic in word recognition so that they can think more about what they are reading.

This section will focus on some instructional strategies to develop students' decoding skills, or word recognition accuracy and fluency. These strategies are designed to develop the following:

- basic sight word knowledge
- use of context clues
- use of structural analysis

General Method for Teaching Basic Sight Words

McNinch (1981) developed a method for instructing low-achieving readers in sight words that includes teaching the word in both context and isolation. This strategy is effective with elementary students and with a few modifications could also be used with older students. It works as follows:

1. The teacher first explains what the students will learn, why they will learn it, and when they can use the strategy they learn.
2. The teacher presents the word to be learned in a sentence within the context of two or three other sentences. If possible, words in the sentences should be within the sight word vocabulary of the students or be words from their language experience stories. The sight word being taught should be highlighted.
3. The teacher points to the word and says or signs it.

4. The students read the sentences (silently first, then orally for hard of hearing students).

5. The teacher writes the word in isolation on the board.

6. The teacher asks the students questions about the word and gives them tasks to focus their attention. For example:

   a. What is the first letter?
   b. What is the last letter?
   c. How many letters are in the word?
   d. Spell the word.
   e. Trace the word and then write it without looking at the original word.

7. The students *practice* reading the word in sentences. (As much as possible, all other words should be sight words.)

8. The students practice reading the word in actual text (books, language experience stories, charts).

9. The teacher asks questions that require students to use the word to answer the questions. The teacher may also ask students to reread a sentence in the text containing the word.

10. The students engage in independent practice involving the word.

Practice Activities for Basic Sight Words

1. Have the students find additional examples of the target word in books or language experience stories, and try to read the sentences that contain the word. Students can chart the number of times they find each sight word.

2. Students who have sufficient hearing can read into a tape recorder the sight words they have been studying. The words should be written in isolation and in sentences on cards. The student reads the word, pauses, then reads the sentence. Afterward, the student can listen to what was recorded while looking at the cards and following along.

3. Students can play games using a number of the basic sight words they have been studying. Games such as concentration, checkers, and bingo can be developed and used for practicing sight words. Board games can be developed in which a player goes x number of spaces forward if he or she knows the sight word drawn from the stack. With games, it is important that the students be required to read (say or sign) the word, so it is not just a visual matching game.

4. Students can make flash cards of their sight words and practice them at least once a day, charting their number of correct responses after each trial.

Using Predictable Books for Sight-Word Development

Bridge, Winograd, and Haley (1983) developed a program for teaching basic sight words to beginning readers that makes use of predictable books and language experience stories. The pattern in predictable books provides good opportunities for students to practice reading high-frequency words. This procedure is effective with elementary children using narrative text:

1.   The teacher reads a predictable book to the children, then rereads it, encouraging them to join in as much as possible. The students take turns reading (saying or signing) the book with the teacher.

2. The next day the teacher reads the story again, focusing on particular sight words by leaving a blank for the word while reading or signing the book, stopping and pointing to the word, and asking the students to read it. Or, instead of showing the word, the teacher can ask the students to predict what word they think is next and then showing them the word to connect their prediction to print.

3. The teacher writes the story on a chart and the children practice reading the story without the aid of pictures. The students are given, in the appropriate order, individual word cards containing their sight words, which they read and place under the matching words on the chart.

4. On the third day, the students read or sign the story from the chart (together or individually). They are given their sight-word cards in random order and read and match them with the sight words in the chart story.

This procedure can also be used with language experience stories.

Context Clues

Although research suggests that less skilled readers rely on context more than good readers for help with word recognition, they use context less effectively than good readers. They self-correct fewer of their errors when they make word substitutions, and they make less use of semantic information on cloze passages (Taylor et al., 1988). These readers need to learn to monitor themselves for meaning as they are decoding and to self-correct substitutions that do not make sense in the context of their reading.

Many of the strategies used with hearing children involve taping their oral reading and having them listen to it to detect errors, or the teacher gives explicit instruction while the child is reading orally. Neither strategy is very effective with deaf or most hard of hearing students. Two strategies that can be used with deaf and hard of hearing children to help them develop their abilities to use *context clues* are cloze procedures (which are described later in this chapter under "Comprehension Strategies") and activities using incorrect word substitutions.

Incorrect Word Substitutions

This strategy can be used with students of all ages and with both narrative and expository text:

1. Using material appropriate for the student's age and reading level, the teacher presents a picture with a three- or four-line story or description of the picture in which at least one error occurs. (For older students, a picture may not be necessary.) For example, for a picture of a little boy walking in the rain, splashing through puddles:

> Luis walked in the rain.
> He did not wear his boats.
> He walked through puddles of snow.

2. The student identifies the incorrect word substitutions in the second and third lines and explains why the words are not correct. (This encourages students to think and talk about how they understand.)
3. Step 2 is repeated for each subsequent incorrect word substitution.

Contextual Processing

Walker (1996) described a strategy that is used to show students how to use context to figure out the meanings of new vocabulary words. This technique, *contextual processing*, can be used with students of all ages and with both narrative and expository text:

1. The teacher selects key vocabulary words to teach.
2. The teacher finds passages in the text in which context clues indicate the meaning of a key vocabulary word. If such text is not available, the teacher creates a three- to four-sentence paragraph in which context clues exist for the word.
3. The teacher writes the paragraph on the board, on a chart, or overhead.
4. The teacher reads or signs the paragraph to the students.
5. The students read the paragraph silently.
6. The teacher asks the students about the meaning of the key word. ("What does the paragraph tell you about the word _____?")
7. As students give their answers, they are asked to explain them.
8. The students write what they think the word means.
9. The teacher and students discuss the responses.
10. The teacher states the meaning of the word and exactly how that meaning can be derived from context.

11. The students think of similar situations or contexts in which they could use the word and write them down in a short paragraph. They should be encouraged to apply their own experiences when trying to think of these situations or contexts.

12. The students share the paragraphs applying the word to their own experiences.

Structural Analysis

Structural analysis is the process of identifying words by dividing them into morphemes or small meaningful units. Generally, in instruction on structural analysis, the teacher focuses on inflectional endings (usually verb endings) and affixes.

Inflectional Endings

This activity can be used with students who are 7 years old and older and with either narrative or expository text:

1. The teacher finds examples of words with the targeted inflectional ending (for example, verbs ending in *ed*) from language experience stories or other familiar reading materials and writes them on the board.

2. The teacher asks the students what the words have in common and what the ending has done to the verb's meaning.

3. The students write the root words in the list (without the ending).

4. The students add a few more verbs with the ending to the list on the board.

5. The teacher presents written sentences to the students in which one of the words from the list is deleted.

6. The students read the sentences and write the correct word from the list in the blank.

Modified Cloze Procedure

The teacher could also present a modified cloze procedure, in which blanks in the passage are followed by a word without the inflectional ending as well as the same word with the inflectional ending. Students would have to use context and be able to read both words to select the appropriate word for the blank. For example, *Tom* _____(*walk, walked*) *to school yesterday.*

Affixes

Knowing prefixes and suffixes enables students to recognize those word parts when attempting to decode unfamiliar words. For example, when confronted with the long word *undeniable*, they might have a better chance of identifying the word if they first recognize *un* as a prefix and *able* as a suffix, thus leaving the more easily recognized root word *deny* (*deni*). When meeting multisyllabic words, students should check to see if the words contain any prefixes or suffixes. If so, they should attend first to the root word, read it, and then reread it, adding the prefixes and suffixes.

Students, starting at the mid-elementary level, should receive explicit instruction in recognizing affixes; the following is a suggested procedure:

1. The teacher presents a root word and affix to the students, and they discuss how the word changed in meaning when the affix was added.

2. The teacher and students generate a list of other words containing the same affix and discuss the meaning of the root words and how it changed when the affix was added.

3. The students read the list independently and in pairs and review the meanings of the root words and the root words plus the affix.

4. The students fill in the blanks in written sentences with appropriate words from the list.

For additional practice, the students can play a concentration game that involves pairing root words and affixes. When they make a match, they must explain the meaning of the root word and the root word plus the affix before keeping the cards. Or the students can see how many words they can generate from a word wheel containing affixes and root words. When they find an appropriate match, they must explain the meanings.

The teacher and students should locate words containing prefixes and suffixes when reading and practice decoding these words by breaking off the prefixes and suffixes from the root word.

Automaticity

The ultimate goal for decoding is for the students to "crack the code" automatically so they can apply their cognitive energies (and the "space" in their working memories) toward comprehension. *Repeated reading* is an excellent technique for helping students achieve automaticity. It has been shown to facilitate automatic decoding among average readers and among special populations (Samuels et al., 1992) and lead to improved comprehension. Through repeated readings, students who have had a history of reading failure can experience the feeling of being able to read a selection successfully. The procedure for repeated reading is as follows:

1. The teacher chooses a short passage that is appropriate for the student.

2. The student reads and rereads this short passage until it can be read in about a minute.

3. Then the student moves on to the next short passage until all of the parts have been completed and the student can read the story fluently.

Teachers use repeated reading in several ways. One way is to chart reading accuracy and speed. Students at all levels can be taught to keep their own charts, which is usually motivating to students because they can see the progress they are making with each reading.

Young children, after instruction on a short reading story, can practice it by reading it to themselves several times. Then they select other people to whom they can read it. Children who do not read orally can read each page silently and then sign the passage to a partner.

Vocabulary

Several strategies for developing vocabulary word meanings are discussed else-where in this chapter (see discussions on semantic webs or maps, semantic fea-ture analysis, graphic organizers, cloze and modified cloze procedures, develop-ing sight-word vocabulary, predictable books, contextual processing, and Venn diagrams). All of these strategies are derived from schema theory and involve linking new words to the student's prior knowledge and personal experiences, exploring the meanings of new words and their relationships to other words and ideas, and connecting a word to the specific context in which the student will be encountering it in the reading passage. None of these strategies involves looking up a word in a dictionary and writing the meaning or having the stu-dent match a vocabulary word to its dictionary meaning. Such activities encour-age memorization of meanings, which is usually temporary, and do not foster conceptual development or the ability to store and retrieve the concept when appropriate.

Comprehension Strategies

Comprehension not only involves interacting with the text to construct mean-ing but also involves metacognitive processes in which students are aware of and have control over their comprehension (Taylor et al., 1988). Deaf and hard of hearing students frequently have difficulty comprehending what they read because they often do not actively read for meaning; instead, they focus on reading as a decoding process, devoting their attention to individual words. This strategy limits information processing to the word level and precludes information processing at the sentence, inter-sentence, and discourse levels. These students also frequently lack the metacognitive skills to monitor their comprehension; or, if they realize that they are not understanding, they often have inadequate fix-up or repair strategies to improve their comprehension. Many deaf and hard of hearing students think that because they can identify most of the words, they are reading; they are not understanding what the task of reading is or what it means to construct meaning—to comprehend.

The following strategies can be used to direct students' attention to text and to focus on gaining meaning. Several of the strategies serve dual purposes—to focus on gaining meaning and to develop metacognitive skills that will enable students to monitor their comprehension and apply fix-up strategies when they are needed.

Prediction Logs

Prediction logs encourage students to engage in active reading and to monitor their comprehension. This strategy is usually used with narrative text but can be used successfully with some expository texts. At points in the text designated by the teacher, the students write their predictions of what will happen and their reasons for the predictions. This strategy is effective with students at the upper elementary level through high school and consists of the following steps:

1. The teacher marks key points in the story at which the students will write predictions.
2. The students are given prediction log papers:

Name of story:	
Author:	
Prediction	**Reason for Prediction**
Part 1:	
Part 2:	
Part 3:	

3. After the students have completed the story and their predictions, they use their prediction logs as the basis for discussion.

4. With the teacher's guidance, they discuss how they constructed meaning through the story.

5. They discuss how their personal experiences influenced their understanding of the story.

6. They discuss predictions that were not confirmed and what they missed in reading that led them to the wrong conclusions.

7. Then the students write their reaction or their response to the story and the discussion.

Directed Reading-Thinking Activity (DR-TA)

The directed reading-thinking activity is a strategy that involves previewing, predicting, monitoring comprehension, and revising predictions. This strategy can be used with students at all levels and with either expository or narrative texts and is conducted as follows:

1. The teacher divides the reading material into segments appropriate for the students' reading level.

2. The teacher tells the students the purpose of the strategy they are using—to help them comprehend by previewing, predicting, and using their prior knowledge.

3. The students preview the material by looking at pictures and other graphic aids and reading titles and headings.

4. Based on their preview and their prior knowledge, the students predict the content of the selection.

5. The teacher writes their predictions on the board or chart.

6. Students read the section and stop at the point designated by the teacher.

7. They discuss whether their predictions were confirmed.

8. The teacher asks the students to support their ideas using the information in the text and to explain their reasoning.

9. The teacher then asks them to predict what will happen next and to explain why they think that.

10. Repeat steps 5–8.

11. The teacher and students discuss the story in relation to other stories, their personal experiences, and the author's purpose.

12. Teacher and students also discuss the strategies used to understand the story.

Question-Answer Relationships (QAR)

The question-answer relationships (QAR) strategy (Raphael, 1982) uses levels of questioning to encourage students to use different kinds of information in their reading to help them comprehend narrative text. It also aids in the development of inferring skills, as the students are taught to use information other than that which is directly stated. This strategy, which is usually effective with students in upper elementary through high school, focuses on four levels of questioning:

1. *Right there*—The response to this level of questioning requires *text-explicit* information, or information that is directly stated in the text.

2. *Think and search*—This response requires *text-implicit* information. The student must read carefully and then search different parts of the text to find information that fits together to answer the question.

3. *On my own*—This response is said to be *script-implicit* and requires the student to activate and apply appropriate prior knowledge as it relates to the text in order to answer the question.

4. *The author and me*—In this response the students need to think about what they know, what they have learned from the author, and how these pieces of information fit together.

The following lines provide examples of all four levels of questioning:

▶ Roberto was going to the store. He was thinking, "Bread, milk, and salsa." He put his hands in his pockets. "Oh, oh," he said. "I have to go back home."

(*Right there*) Where was Roberto going?

(*Think and search*) What kind of store was Roberto going to?

(*On my own*) How did Roberto feel?

(*Author and me*)   Why did Roberto have to go back home?

The teacher should explain to the students that they will be learning how to figure out where answers to questions come from and that this is important because answers come from different places. This information will help them improve their ability to answer questions during and after reading. When they are working on their own and are having difficulty answering questions, they should use the QAR categories to help them find the information. Below are suggested steps for this procedure:

1. The teacher finds or prepares several brief passages and one question from each of the QAR categories for each passage.

2. Using the first passage, the teacher explains each question category and how to use the text and/or their prior knowledge to find the answer.

3. The students are given the second passage with the questions, answers, and QAR labels. They are asked to explain the QAR labels for the questions and answers related to the passage.

4. Next, the students are given a passage with the questions and answers, and they have to provide the QAR labels and explain them.

5. Finally, students are given texts and questions and asked to answer the question and provide QAR labels and justifications.

Reciprocal Questioning (ReQuest)

ReQuest involves the students and teacher in silently reading portions of a text and then taking turns asking and answering questions. In this strategy, teachers serve as models for good questioning and answering by explaining how they arrived at the answers they give to the students' questions. As the students learn this procedure and become more skilled at asking and answering questions, teachers can let the students take over the teacher role. This strategy can be used with students who are 10 years old and older, and in a simplified form, it can be used with 8 and 9 year olds. This strategy is more effective with narrative text than with expository text.

First, the students must understand the rules for ReQuest:

1. The teacher and students read the first sentence silently.

2. Then they take turns asking questions about the sentence. The students ask questions first, and the teacher, with the book closed, must answer.

3. Then the students close their books, and the teacher asks questions.

4. The students may not answer with "I don't know." They must at least try to explain why they cannot answer.

5. If any question is not clear, then it must be rephrased or clarified.

6. The person who answers a question should be ready to justify the answer by referring to the book or explaining the background knowledge that was used.

Some teachers use one sentence at a time, particularly with students who are not familiar with this strategy or who have trouble comprehending what they read. However, text passages may vary in length, depending on the students' abilities. The following steps are suggested for this strategy:

1. The students and the teacher silently read the same segment of text.

2. The teacher closes the book and is questioned about the passage by the students.

3. Then the students close their books, and the teacher questions them about the material. The teacher should ask questions using all of the levels of QAR.

4. The students and teacher read the next segment of text and repeat steps 2 and 3.

5. When the students have processed enough information to make predictions about the remainder of the selection, the alternate questioning stops and the teacher begins to ask prediction questions such as, "What do you think the rest of the story/selection is about? Why do you think that?"

6. The students read the rest of the text silently.

7. The teacher facilitates a follow-up discussion of the material, starting with a comparison of students' predictions about what was read. Students select from their predictions those that might also have been logical to complete the text. The teacher should avoid labeling predictions as "right" or "wrong" but rather encourage the students to see that the text could have had several possible endings. For an additional activity, the students could rewrite the text using their own predictions.

Story Retelling

Story retelling is an easy strategy to use in the classroom and is particularly effective for deaf students because they can retell the story in ASL and not be hindered by having to write a summary of the story or responses to questions using English. Story retelling is particularly successful with elementary students but can be used with students of all ages. It works as follows:

1. After completion of the prereading activities, the teacher tells the students that they will be asked to retell the story when they have finished reading.

2. The teacher should inform the students if they are expected to include any specific information. They should also know that they will need to tell about the characters, setting, problem, main episodes, and resolution.

3. After reading, individual students are asked to retell the story as if telling it to a friend who does not know it.

4. The student tells the story, noting the important parts: story setting, characters, theme, plot, sequence, and resolution.

5. If the student is hesitant, the teacher may use prompts.

6. When the retelling is finished, the teacher asks questions about any important parts that were omitted, or the teacher can ask the student to reread important information that was omitted.

7. Retelling can also be adapted to small group or partner activities.

Cloze Instruction

Cloze instruction is a strategy that promotes comprehension and metacognitive skills by deleting target words from the text. The students must think about what word would make sense in the sentence and in the context of the whole story. It is a procedure that is used after the students have read the material, and it can be used with either narrative or expository text. This strategy, outlined below, can be effective with students 8 years old and older:

1. The teacher selects a text of 100–400 words, depending on the age and abilities of the students.
2. The teacher deletes the target words and inserts blanks. The target words may be nouns, verbs, or any other kinds of words that will challenge the students to think about meaning.
3. The student is instructed to read the entire passage before trying to fill in the blanks.
4. The student then goes back to the beginning of the passage and writes in the words that best fit the meaning of the sentence and the passage.
5. When the student is finished, the answers are reviewed to see if the student used the exact word that was deleted, a word similar in meaning, or a word that did not make sense.
6. The student reviews the choices made and discusses the strategies used to decide on the word choices. If the student chose any words that did not make sense, the teacher helps the student understand the strategies that could have been used to make a better selection.

Text Organization

Narrative and expository texts have different organizational patterns. Since knowledge of text structure facilitates comprehension, students need to learn about the organization of different texts. Narrative materials usually consist of a beginning, a middle, and an end and contain the following elements:

- *The beginning*—includes the setting (characters and places).

- *The middle*—includes the main character's problem, the plans made to solve the problem, and events in the story leading to the solution of the problem.

- *The end*—tells how the characters solved the problem and the reaction to the problem resolution.

Children usually understand narrative structure before they understand expository structure, probably because the latter can be organized in several different ways. The following list describes some of the ways expository text can be organized:

- *Temporal sequence*—describes or lists events in their order of occurrence.
- *Explanation*—explains such things as causes, effects, and enabling circumstances.
- *Comparison/contrast*—compares or contrasts two events or concepts.
- *Definition/example*—defines or gives examples.
- *Problem/solution*—explains the development of a problem and suggests solutions.
- *Process description*—describes the parts of a process.
- *Classification*—explains how concepts are classified.

Story Maps for Narrative Texts

This strategy is sometimes referred to as story grammar; it focuses on the sequence of events in a narrative text. It can be used with students at all levels. It can also be used as a scaffolding strategy to help students who have difficulty with story retelling. Story maps are used as follows:

1. The teacher makes a chart of the elements of narrative structure. Younger children may use a chart divided into only three parts labeled "beginning," "middle," and "end." For older students, divide the chart into segments labeled as shown below:

Setting
    Places
    Characters
Problem
Plan
    Event
    Event
Resolution
Reaction

2. The teacher prepares questions from the story to lead the students through the story map.

3. The teacher discusses the organization of the story and explains the story map.

4. The students read the story.

5. The teacher uses the prepared questions to guide the students as they fill in the story map together.

6. The teacher and students compare this story with other story maps they have made.

Pattern Guides for Expository Texts

Many different kinds of pattern guides can be used to help students get a sense of how expository material is organized, thus aiding in their comprehension. The following pattern guides are only a few examples.

Time Lines (pattern guides for history—chronological order of events)

1. The teacher gives the students a time line and tells them that using the time line will help them see the sequence of events.

2. As the students read the chapter, they fill in the events on the time line. Page numbers are given for additional help.

/		/		/	
1939 (p.232)		1940 (p. 234)		1944 (p. 245)	1945 (p. 250)

Comparison Charts (pattern guides for science—compare/contrast organization)

1. The teacher gives the students the compare/contrast chart like the one below and asks them to fill it out as they read the chapter. This task can be done individually or with a partner.

Compare the Body Systems of a Chicken and a Human

	Chicken	Human
Respiratory		
Digestive		
Reproductive		

2. After the students have read and completed the chart, the teacher leads a discussion using the following questions:

    a. Which system in a chicken and a human is the most alike?
    b. Tell how they are the same.
    c. Which system is the most different?
    d. Tell how it is different.
    e. Why do you think the systems are different?

Cause-and-Effect Charts (pattern guides for social studies)

As the students (upper elementary and above) read a chapter, they look for the cause-and-effect relationships listed in the following chart. Their assignment is to complete the cause-and-effect statements by filling in the blanks with the appropriate information.

Cause	Effect
1. The people who settled Jamestown did not know how to farm, fish, or take care of themselves.	Within a year, half had died of starvation, disease, and Indian attacks.
2. Powhatan captured John Smith and wanted to kill him. Pocahontas pleaded for his life.	_____ _____ _____
3. _____ _____	The Indians begin to bring corn and turkeys to the English settlers.
4. Smith announced that anyone who did not work would not eat.	_____ _____
5. The colonists began to cultivate tobacco.	_____ _____
6. _____ _____	The colonists began to work harder and harder.

After reading the chapter, the teacher and students, the students in small groups, or the students in pairs discuss the responses on their charts.

Critical Reading and Metacognitive Strategies

Critical reading is one of the ultimate goals of reading. When readers have developed that skill, they are well on their way to becoming independent thinkers. Critical reading allows the reader to analyze situations, make comparisons, and determine fact from opinion and propaganda. Critical readers realize that just because something is in print does not mean that it is true. Critical readers can read newspapers, magazines, and messages on the Internet and judge for themselves the credibility of the statements. Considering the media deluge in today's society, critical reading skills are very important.

Venn Diagram

A Venn diagram strategy is another technique that can be used to encourage students to compare and contrast two objects or entities. This procedure can be used with either expository text or narrative text and is effective with students at all levels. It works as follows:

1. The teacher writes the two target words (e.g., butterflies and moths) on the board.
2. The students list as many characteristics as they can under each word. This step may be done with the entire class, in small groups, or in pairs.
3. The teacher or a student draws the Venn diagram (two overlapping circles) on the board (see Figure 7.5.).
4. The students determine which characteristics butterflies and moths have in common and write them in the overlapping part of the two circles.
5. Then they write the unique characteristics of each in the parts of the circles that do not overlap.
6. The teacher and students discuss the diagram, and the students can then write a short paper comparing and contrasting the two insects.

If this strategy is used before a reading selection to build and activate prior knowledge, the teacher and students would perform steps 1 and 2 before reading the text. After reading the text, the students could add to their list of characteristics and then continue with steps 3 through 6.

With narrative text, this strategy is usually used after reading. Then the students may be asked to compare and contrast two characters, events, or places from the story. This strategy is particularly effective for comparing two different stories that the children have read or that the teacher has read to them (see Figure 7.6) or for comparing two different genres.

Fact or Opinion

Fact or opinion exercises encourage students to read critically and evaluate the truth in what they are reading. This strategy can be used with either expository

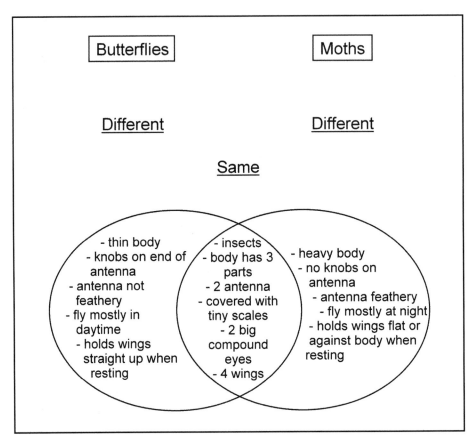

Figure 7.5. Venn diagram.

or narrative texts and with students about 9 years old and older. It works as follows:

1. The teacher explains the difference between fact and opinion and gives examples.

2. Starting with the examples, the teacher asks the students what clues are in the text that can alert the reader to whether it is a fact or an opinion.

3. After listing the clues from the examples, the teacher and students can elaborate on other clues from their own experiences.

4. The teacher and students discuss why it is important to distinguish fact from opinion.

5. On an overhead transparency, the teacher can show the students a list of statements that they are to evaluate as fact or opinion. If the statement is fact,

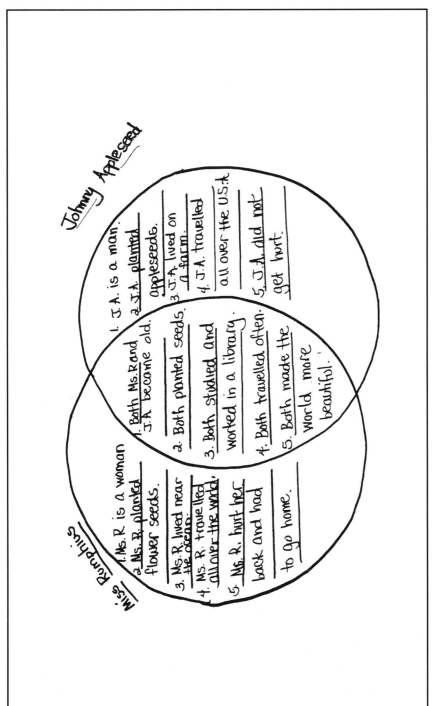

Figure 7.6. Venn diagram developed by 8-year-old deaf students to compare two stories.

the students must indicate next to that statement where they could find information to verify the it (e.g., encyclopedias, dictionaries, textbooks, newspapers). They may also be asked to write their proof by the statement.

6. The students can do the first three or four together as a group.

7. The teacher asks the students to circle the clues in each statement.

8. The students may complete the rest of the statements independently, in small groups, or in pairs.

9. For a supplement to this activity, the teacher might copy paragraphs out of the students' textbooks, then have the students work in pairs to underline opinion statements in red and factual statements in blue.

10. After completing the task, the students should discuss their responses.

The following is an example of a fact or opinion exercise for middle school students.

FACT OR OPINION?

Directions: During or after reading the chapter, label each of the statements below as fact (F) or opinion (O) on the line to the left. If a statement is a fact, write your proof in the column to the right. Underline the clues in the statement that helped you make your decision.

	Statement	Proof
_____	1. Washington Irving lived from 1783 to 1859.	
_____	2. Irving wrote "The Legend of Sleepy Hollow."	
_____	3. His stories are like snapshots that capture life in Dutch New York.	
_____	4. Some scholars say that American literature began with Irving.	
_____	5. Irving became a lawyer when he was 23, and he also worked in his family's knife factory.	

Comprehension Rating

Many readers who are deaf and hard of hearing do not have well-developed metacognitive skills and do not monitor their comprehension as they read. They continue reading and are not aware of whether they do or do not understand what they are reading. In addition, they frequently do not have adequate fix-up or repair strategies for improving their comprehension when they do realize that they are not understanding the text. Comprehension rating is a four-step strategy that can be effective in improving comprehension monitoring skills. This procedure can help students focus their attention on meaning, evaluate their comprehension while reading, and develop repair strategies to improve their comprehension (Taylor et al., 1988). Comprehension rating can be used with both narrative and expository texts and with students who are 10 years old and older.

Step 1

Using cloze passages, the teacher shows the students that they do not have to read every word in a passage to understand the meaning and discusses some repair strategies they can use when they do not understand, such as rereading or reading ahead to see if the meaning is revealed in the next two or three sentences. The teacher also demonstrates comprehension monitoring while reading aloud to the students—for example, "I understand this paragraph, so I'll read on" or "This paragraph doesn't make sense; I'd better reread it."

Step 2

1. This step focuses attention on meaning during silent reading and involves comprehension rating tasks. The students are given single sentences to read and rate for comprehension. Some sentences make sense; some sentences do not make sense because they contain nonsense words (*The frake was very noisy*), and some sentences do not make sense because of faulty logic (*Susie laughed and laughed because she fell down*). Working in small groups or independently, the students rate their comprehension of the sentences, using a plus (+) for sentences they understand and a minus (−) for sentences they do not understand.

2. When they are finished, they discuss the reasons for their ratings.

3. When they are successful at rating sentences, students are given paragraphs to read and rate for comprehension. Some paragraphs make sense; some do not make sense because of faulty logic, inserted sentences that are out of context, or ideas that are nonsensical (*The car had a flat steering wheel*). The students can work in small groups or individually and rate the paragraphs in the same manner as they did the sentences.

4. When they are finished, they discuss the reasons for their ratings.

Step 3

1. In this step, the students move to a three-point comprehension rating task and use "real text." The students may work individually or in small groups and rate sentences, paragraphs, and then longer text using three ratings:

a. I understand well. (I have a clear picture in my head and could explain it to someone else.)

b. I understand a little. (I have an incomplete picture in my head and could not explain this to someone else.)

c. I don't understand.

2. The teacher and students share their ratings and discuss their reasons.

Step 4

1. When students show competence in the first three steps (knowing when they do not understand), attention should be directed to learning fix-up strategies. Taylor, Harris, and Pearson (1988) suggested that students be taught fix-up strategies at the word level and at the idea level. The teacher presents mini-lessons focusing on each strategy so that the students can begin to apply them. Taylor et al. listed the following strategies (pp. 204–205):

a. Word-level fix-up strategies

- Read around the word—maybe the word can be skipped and you can still understand or figure it out from context clues.

- Use context clues for help in decoding or predicting what a word means.

- Look for structural clues within words.

- Sound out words.

- Use a dictionary.

- Ask for help.

b. Idea-level fix-up strategies

- Read on to make it clearer.

- Reread carefully to make it clearer.

- Look again at the title, pictures, headings, and graphics.

- Ask yourself questions.

- Put ideas into your own words as you go along.

- Picture the ideas in your head while you read.

- Relate ideas to your personal experiences.

- Ask someone to clarify things.

2. Students are given a list of these fix-up strategies. Each strategy is modeled by the teacher and practiced by the students. Then the students are asked to use the strategies when they experience comprehension difficulties during actual reading.

3. The students are asked to make notes or mark places in the text where they used fix-up strategies, and later explain to the teacher which strategies they used. If a student cannot do this independently, the teacher works with him or her individually, giving guidance about which fix-up strategy would work best.

Study Strategies

It is apparent that most strategies that have been discussed in this chapter serve dual or multiple purposes; such is the case with many study strategies, which also can be used for developing or activating prior knowledge, presenting vocabulary, and teaching comprehension skills. In addition to the study strategies presented in this section, other sections contain such strategies as: semantic webs or maps, semantic feature analysis, K-W-L and K-W-L plus, anticipation guides, graphic organizers, QAR, student-generated questions, prediction logs, DR-TA, cloze procedures, time lines, comparison charts, cause-and-effect charts, Venn diagrams, and fact or opinion charts.

Summarizing

To summarize text—that is, to reduce text to its main points—students must be able to recognize and analyze text structure. If they are not familiar with the organization of expository and narrative text, they will find it difficult to identify the important information they will need for their summary (Vacca & Vacca, 1996). Good summarizers write in their own words, maintain the author's point of view, and follow the sequence of ideas as presented in the text.

Kintsch and van Dijk (1978) developed some basic rules for summarization from analyzing how adults summarize effectively. While their rules have been modified and adapted for use in various classrooms, the procedures, which are listed below, remain essentially the same. This strategy is effective with middle school and high school students using either expository or narrative text.

1. Students must learn to delete unnecessary details.

2. Students should learn to collapse lists. For example, if the text lists crops that are grown in a certain area as corn, potatoes, onions, tomatoes, and beans, the student could summarize that as "food-producing crops."

3. Students should identify and use topic sentences, which are frequently found at the beginning or end of a paragraph. If a topic sentence is not explicitly stated, then students must create their own topic sentences, which is probably the most difficult task that students must do in this procedure.

4. Students must integrate the information. After they have written the topic sentences and other important information from paragraphs in the text, they must rewrite that information, which is usually choppy and stilted, into text that is fluent and cohesive.

5. Students must polish the summary. This step is similar to the revision step in the writing process; other students read and respond to the summary. The writer then incorporates the suggestions and ideas of classmates to produce a fluent and meaningful summary.

Summarizing is not an easy task for most students, and it seems to be especially difficult for deaf and hard of hearing students. Most teachers find it beneficial to demonstrate these steps for the students several times before asking them to summarize on their own. When demonstrating, teachers should think out loud so the students understand the processes that are occurring. After several demonstrations, guided practice is important to help the students learn to summarize and to maintain their self-confidence. Working with partners or in small groups can also be helpful.

The PREP System for Study

To effectively use this strategy, students should have some knowledge of how narrative and expository texts are organized. PREP (Schmelzer, Christen, & Browning, 1980) stands for:

- **P**review the selection.
- **R**ead the selection.
- **E**xamine by asking and answering questions.
- **P**rompt yourself with memory aids.

This strategy can be used with students in all grades, although for very young children it is usually modified by using only the first two steps initially and adding the last two steps when the students (usually 9 or 10 year olds) can handle the activities successfully. PREP is frequently applied to expository text but also can be used effectively with narrative text.

1. *Preview*. Students will have to be taught how to preview a text selection. The teacher should tell the students that they need to preview the selection to

find out what the major concepts are and to set a purpose for reading. In previewing, the students read the title; look at pictures, graphs, and charts; read the introduction or the opening paragraph; read the headings and subheadings; and read the last paragraph or the summary. The teacher and students discuss what the students learned during their preview. Then the students brainstorm topics that they want to know about the major concepts, which the teacher records on the board or chart as questions.

2. *Read.* After setting their purpose in the preview step, the students read the selection. With younger students, teachers can follow the DR-TA strategy for this section. Older students should read and take notes as a means of recording, reviewing, and retaining information. One kind of note taking, a summary sheet, uses a paper divided into two columns. The left column is the *recall column,* in which the teacher or students record general headings or subheadings. The students write the actual notes in the right column. The notes should be brief; the students should not copy word for word from the text, and they should use abbreviations whenever possible. After completing their reading and note taking, the students should be given time to study their notes (rereading them, covering the notes, trying to remember the important points without looking, rereading again if necessary).

3. *Examine.* In this step, the children develop questions about the selection either during or after reading. Initially, the teacher should demonstrate and guide their question development, withdrawing support as the students become able to ask their questions independently. After the questions are written, individual students can lead the group discussion by asking the questions they have written.

4. *Prompt.* This step is designed to help students remember what they have read. At the end of each section for which there is a heading, the students stop reading, turn their books over, and try to remember the important things they have read. This procedure can be a group activity until the children learn how to do it and can perform it by themselves.

SQ3R

SQ3R is a strategy for studying expository text that can be used with middle school and high school students. The procedure includes five steps (**s**urvey, **q**uestion, **r**ead, **r**ecite, and **r**eview) and is designed to help students monitor their own comprehension and learning.

1. The teacher introduces the content-area text.

2. The teacher begins the *survey* step by explaining to the students how to *skim* the entire selection to get a general idea of the information contained

within the selection. The teacher directs the students to use headings and sub-headings as key information in understanding the overall framework.

3. After the text is surveyed, the students develop *questions* that they think will be answered in the selection. The teacher provides guidance, helping the students to focus on the headings and subheadings to form questions for each section.

4. The students *read* the first text section, keeping in mind the questions they developed for that section. After reading each section, students proceed to the next step.

5. The students *recite* answers to the questions they developed for each section after it is read. Students should refer to the text only when necessary and try to answer the questions using their own words. This step can be done with the whole class or with small groups.

6. The three steps question, read, and recite are repeated for each section.

7. After the complete selection is read, students *review* their questions and answers for the entire text.

Readers' Workshop

Readers' workshop is a procedure that is usually associated with the whole language approach and manages reading instruction through the use of trade books and reading materials other than basals. However, readers' workshop can also be used effectively in a balanced reading program. The framework for this approach to reading is constructed around five important elements: time, choice, response, community, and structure (Atwell, 1987; Hagerty, 1992; Hansen, 1987).

Time

In a readers' workshop approach, students are given a large block of *time* each day to spend reading. They are encouraged to browse in the classroom library, the school library, or the public library (usually on weekly field trips) and select books that interest them and that they want to read.

Choice

Choice is considered to be a critical element and one of the major contributors to establishing motivation to read. Frequently, younger students do not know how to make appropriate choices when selecting books, and teachers are encouraged to help them develop this ability. Hagerty (1992) claimed that learning how to make appropriate choices is a process that improves over time as students have the opportunity to practice. Most of the time students are allowed to make their own choices of books they want to read; the exception to this is when the teacher wants the whole class to read the same book because it is connected to the current instructional theme or to a content-area unit.

Response

Response in readers' workshop refers to the time allowed periodically throughout the reading of a book and after the book is finished for the student to react to the book in some way. Readers may discuss their books with each other in peer conferences, responding to their own book as well as books the others have read, or readers may share reactions to their books in conference with the teacher or with the whole class. Response can also take the form of writing, drama, or art.

Community

A sense of *community* is established through readers' workshop as students actively support each other as readers, work cooperatively to help each other learn, and treat all readers with respect. When the classroom functions as a community, everyone is a learner and a teacher and everyone's contributions are important.

Structure

Although readers' workshop may be considered by some to be an unstructured procedure, it actually has a *structure* and a management system that are recognized by the students and that provide comfortable parameters for them. The casual observer might think that readers' workshop is a time when students just sit around and read; however, on closer observation, the observer will see that the teacher provides an instruction time, models good reading strategies for students to use, and provides them with ample amounts of time to practice those strategies with reading materials that they select themselves. Hagerty (1992) suggested that the structure of readers' workshop should include three elements: (1) a mini-lesson, (2) an activity time, and (3) a share session. Reutzel and Cooter (1991) added a fourth element, which they labeled "state-of-the-class." The length of time for the workshop period will vary depending on the ages of the students; it may last from 30 minutes in a kindergarten classroom to an hour or more with older students.

Mini-lessons

A *mini-lesson* is exactly that—a short lesson that lasts 5 to 10 minutes. If it is going to be longer, teachers should inform students so they will know what to expect. During a mini-lesson, the teacher teaches only one topic about reading. Topics for mini-lessons are usually based on: (a) a need that the teacher has observed during the time the students were reading, sharing, or responding; (b) teacher-selected skills taken from the scope and sequence charts of a basal series; and (c) prereading activities to assist students with new books they choose to read in their literature response groups (Reutzel & Cooter, 1991). The mini-lesson may include a small group of students or all of the students, but it should include only those students who need instruction or review on the selected topic.

Atwell (1987) categorized mini-lessons into three different kinds, depending on their focus. A mini-lesson that focuses on *procedure* might model for students how to give a book talk, how to respond to a peer's book share, or how to evaluate one's own reading. A lesson on *literary elements* might target character development, theme, or setting and why a particular component is important to story structure. A mini-lesson on *strategies and skills* might focus on using context clues, how to monitor comprehension, or story maps. An important point to remember is that the mini-lesson should help students connect and apply what they have learned to their own reading.

State-of-the-Class

State-of-the-class is an activity that requires approximately 3 to 5 minutes and is a period during which the students inform the teacher and each other of their responsibilities and progress in readers' workshop. Reutzel and Cooter (1991) suggested that the teacher keep a chart of a large grid posted in the room. Each student, with the teacher's help and guidance, records her or his daily responsibility—such as "select new book," "confer with teacher," "write response in journal"—and checks it off when completed, thus enabling the teacher to review individual progress and keep track of what each student is doing.

Activity Time

The *activity time* portion of readers' workshop can last about 30 to 40 minutes and includes time for the students to read independently or with a partner, confer with the teacher or with each other, and respond to their reading with writing, drama, or art (Hagerty, 1992). Students can make various kinds of written responses to their reading; several of these are discussed in Chapter 8.

Share Sessions

Share sessions can occur with a small or large group and usually last about 15 to 20 minutes. This time provides a framework for constructing meaning through active participation with other readers and gives students the opportunity to learn about themselves and each other as readers and writers. Share sessions also provide a forum in which students can express what they have learned, give and receive positive feedback, and engage in emotional interpretations of their reading. This time is also important for teachers, as it provides an opportunity for them to observe and evaluate student reaction and note strategies that individual students are using as they read. While the share sessions are primarily for students, teachers can also participate when appropriate by sharing what they have learned from their reading or helping students to make connections or apply specific knowledge or strategies to their reading.

Readers' workshop is a natural approach that fosters in children an enjoyment of books and reading. Students frequently look forward to being able to respond to their reading in some way and to sharing what they have read with others. Cordeiro (1992) suggested that readers' workshop sustains students' belief in themselves—that they are readers and that they know how to proceed through the workshop process.

Readers' Theater

Readers' theater, an activity in which students assume roles in reading or signing portions of a text, can be used effectively with narratives and poetry and has even been done successfully with expository materials (Young & Vardell, 1993). This strategy encourages students to become actively engaged in searching for the meaning of text as they use their voices or signs to interpret the text for an audience, which might be their classmates or another class or a TV camera so that they can enjoy their own performances. The "actors" present the text using their voices or signs in expressive ways to convey the meaning of the text, reading or signing fast or slowly, loudly or softly (in a large or small signing space), and highlighting certain words and phrases by the reading or signing rate and emphasis on important parts of the text (Hoyt, 1992).

Readers' theater gives students a purpose for reading, writing, and sharing their learning. Dixon, Davies, and Politano (1996) maintained that it benefits students by increasing their skills as readers and writers and expands their ability to represent what they learn. Readers' theater motivates students by making the concepts in content areas come alive and encourages learners to shift from passive to active involvement in their learning. Readers' theater also instills poise, confidence, and power as students work together toward shared goals (Dixon et al., 1996).

The Process

Readers' theater is easy to use in the classroom. It involves two or more students reading a script (not memorizing it) as a character, a storyteller, or a narrator. One student may read different parts and change character by changing voice or signing style. It does not necessarily use scenery, makeup, or props, thus requiring the audience members to listen and watch carefully and use their imaginations to picture the scenes.

Dixon, Davies, and Politano (1996, pp. 10–11) described the process for preparing and performing readers' theater:

1. The teacher and students choose a script. The script can be a prepared script, the students can adapt a text selection, or they can write a new script.
2. The teacher works with the students to establish roles (director, narrator, characters).
3. The students read the script several times to determine how they will interpret the meaning.
4. The students practice until all are satisfied and comfortable with their interpretations.
5. The students perform.

When students perform, they are reading their scripts, not reciting from memory, which initially appears to present a problem for readers who sign and cannot easily hold a script while they are interpreting the text. This problem is easily solved by using music stands to hold the scripts or projecting them using an overhead projector.

Script Writing

Readers' theater is very flexible and provides opportunities for students to learn a wide array of skills in an active, engaged manner. It certainly encourages students to read for meaning so they can interpret the text for others. It is also an effective strategy to use to connect content areas to reading and writing and to make the study of history, science, and math become interesting and exciting. For example, at the end of a unit on desert plants, the teacher and students could prepare a readers' theater script as a closing event for their study, using a process described by Dixon and his colleagues (1996, p. 54):

1. The teacher and students create a web of the major concepts they studied in the unit.

2. The students categorize the ideas into major groups.

3. The students and teacher choose a script structure.

4. The students write the script.

5. The students practice and present their readers' theater script to the audience.

For example, after studying a unit on desert plants, the students might decide they want to share their information in the form of readers' theater with another class. The students themselves write the script, part of which might look like this:

READER 1: Hot sun beating down on the earth.
READER 2: No rain, no water.
READER 3: What do you see on the desert?
READER 2: A huge plant!
READER 4: With arms that stick out and up and down!
READER 3: What is that plant?
READER 1: A saguaro!
READER 4: A giant saguaro cactus with white, waxy flowers on top.

The script would continue with more information about the saguaro and other plants that the students had studied in their unit.

Readers' theater is a technique that is not used every day in the classroom. It should be used occasionally so that students continue to enjoy it and do not lose interest. All students do not have to participate as writers and actors for every readers' theater production—some may become the audience. After reading selections or units that teachers think might be well suited to readers' theater, teachers can ask students if they would like to produce a performance. Those students who want to write, script (put an existing story into the format of a play), produce, and perform can do so while the other students participate in different activities.

Summary

Teachers are encouraged to think about reading as one component of language arts and to provide learning experiences for their students integrating all of the aspects of reading, writing, speaking/signing, and listening/receiving. The strategies described in this chapter provide for a combination of all or most of these components in their implementation. Teachers are encouraged to use explicit instruction most of the time when teaching reading strategies to students, rather than implicit instruction, which requires students to do a great deal of inferring to understand the what, how, why, and when of strategies they can use. Many deaf and hard of hearing students do not yet have well-developed inferring skills and usually do not acquire much information about strategies they can use through implicit instruction.

Several reading strategies were described in this chapter that are effective with deaf and hard of hearing children; however, it is important to note that not all strategies are equally effective with all children. Some students may benefit from one strategy but, because of particular learning styles, may not benefit from another, while the opposite may be true for other students. For this reason, teachers are encouraged to develop a large repertoire of instructional strategies so that they may serve all students equally well. Another argument for using a variety of strategies is to make the learning activities interesting for the students. It does not take long for students to become bored when they are asked to go through the same old routines again and again.

Finally, for each strategy described in this chapter, attention was focused on the purpose, the appropriate kind of text, and the recommended student ages. Many strategies can be used for different purposes; however, the major point is that the teacher should determine the purpose before selecting strategies. Several of the strategies can be used with both narrative and expository text, but some are appropriate for one or the other, and teachers should make sure they match the strategy to the text structure. Student ages or levels have been recommended for each strategy, but, remembering that all children develop and learn at different rates, the teacher remains the final, and best, judge of which strategies are in the appropriate instructional range for each student.

Working with students to develop their ability to read is one of the most fun, exciting, and rewarding experiences a teacher can have. Knowing and using a wide array of instructional strategies effectively can insure that the students share their teacher's enthusiasm for reading experiences. Reading is, after all, the foundation of all their content-area learning, as well as an activity to be enjoyed and cherished for the rest of their lives.

CHAPTER

WRITING AND SPELLING

Preview

Many years have elapsed since educators believed reading and writing to be two separate disciplines that should be taught in two separate periods. Traditionally, the writing period was viewed predominantly as a time to develop penmanship rather than composition skills. The prevailing belief is that reading and writing are similar processes and should be integrated in classroom instruction. This chapter starts with a brief review of the research on written language development of deaf children and then considers the reading-writing connection from the perspectives of information processing, naturalist and social-constructivist theorists, and implications for instruction. The next section elaborates on those implications by applying them to classroom practices. A prominent approach to writing currently used in classrooms is the writing process, which is described, as well as ways to integrate writing activities across the curriculum. The last section looks at spelling, its role in reading and writing, and some recommended classroom practices for the development of spelling skills in students.

Written Language and Deaf Children

Reading and written language abilities have frequently been used as indicators of English-language development in deaf and hard of hearing children, with most of the studies using the scores and products of hearing children as sources for comparison. Not surprisingly, deaf children were found to have notable delays and differences in their development of written language forms (Heider & Heider, 1940; Kretschmer & Kretschmer, 1986; Quigley, Wilbur, Power, Montanelli, & Steinkamp, 1976). The results of these studies indicated that deaf children tend to use greater numbers of basic syntactic structures, including nouns, verbs, and determiners, and demonstrate less frequent use of adverbs, auxiliaries, conjunctions, and complex structures than hearing children. Yoshinaga (1983) noted that semantic complexity appears to peak in hearing children at 13 years of age and in deaf children at about 12 years of age. However, she found that some deaf children demonstrated continued growth in complex semantic units across the age range of 10 to 18 years. Ewoldt (1985) and Quigley and Paul (1989) both noted that the research on writing and deaf children has focused mostly on the product rather than the process of writing. Ewoldt claims that a process-oriented approach to writing would reduce the stilted and immature characteristics of written language produced by deaf children.

Paul (1990) stated that it is not surprising that research on the written language development of deaf students reflects the same low levels of achievement as the research on their reading abilities. Similar to their experience in reading, most deaf students are struggling with trying to learn low-level (e.g., mechanical skills) and high-level (e.g., content and organization) skills at the same time. Paul also noted that the abilities to read and write are similar in that they involve similar processes and are both affected by a primary language form to which most deaf children do not have access in their early, formative years.

The Reading-Writing Connection

Reading and writing have many commonalities. Both are social activities, and they frequently share the same purpose, structure, and process. By teaching reading and writing together, the ultimate purpose of communication can be more clearly realized. Readers are communicating with an author and are influenced by the author's words and intentions. Writers write with the idea of communicating with readers—of influencing or informing them. Good writing considers who the readers might be and attempts to communicate appropriately (Flower & Hayes, 1981). These notions of authorship and audience can be developed fully only when students have opportunities to experience the perspectives of both reading and writing and the connections between them.

The Information-Processing Perspective

Information-processing theory has been the framework for developing several models of both reading and writing processes (de Beaugrande, 1982; Hayes & Flower, 1980; LaBerge & Samuels, 1974; Stanovich, 1980). In a literature review, McCarthey and Raphael (1992, p. 4) determined that these models were guided by three basic assumptions: (1) reading and writing consist of a number of subprocesses used to perform specialized tasks; (2) readers and writers have limited capacity for attention so that trade-offs occur across the subprocesses; and (3) competence in reading and writing is determined by the degree of attention needed to operate subprocesses; thus, the less memory needed, the more efficient the operation.

Flower and Hayes (1981) described the subprocesses in writing as consisting of three recursive phases: (1) planning, in which writers set goals and make plans; (2) translating, in which writers change their ideas into written form; and (3) reviewing, in which writers check their plans and ideas. Beck (1985) concluded that readers operate at several levels, such as word recognition, understanding and using syntactic structures, accessing background knowledge, and operating with fluency as they read. Writers also operate at several levels, such as planning and organizing their ideas, making decisions about relevant and redundant information, and monitoring their plans as they draft and revise written material (Raphael & Englert, 1989). The results of research indicate that readers and writers must handle several subprocesses at the same time, and the manner in which they do this is influenced by the amount of attention needed to perform a task and by how effective the reader or writer is in shifting attention to the processes most useful for the task at hand.

The concept of automaticity (LaBerge & Samuels, 1974) applies to writing in much the same way it applies to reading. Initially, specific subprocesses, such as decoding in reading or handwriting and spelling during composition, require so much cognitive attention that the higher-level processes, such as metacognitive strategies, cannot be employed. However, when the reader/writer reaches automaticity in the specific subprocesses (e.g., when he or she has conquered handwriting and has developed a larger spelling vocabulary), new routines can be learned (Carr, Brown, Vavrus, & Evans, 1990). Some of the subprocesses do not become automatic—for example, comprehension and planning always require some conscious attention—but the more subprocesses that do become automatic, the more attention the reader or writer has left to apply to more cognitively demanding activities in reading and writing.

In their investigations, Shanahan (1984) and Shanahan and Lomax (1986) found reading and writing to be interactive processes, particularly in terms of their components. One component that is shared by new readers and writers is sound-symbol relationships. Young students' ability to use phonic rules in decoding correlates with their ability to spell words when writing. However, the emphasis shifts as children mature, and such knowledge plays a secondary role to the knowledge of vocabulary, story structure, and comprehension strategies in older students.

Stotsky (1983) reviewed the literature examining reading-writing connections and found that, in general, better writers tend to be better readers, and that better readers tend to produce more syntactically mature writing than less able readers. Wittrock (1983) concluded that writing experiences influence reading comprehension and that students improved in comprehension of text when they wrote paragraph summaries after their reading. He also found that comprehension of text improved when students wrote responses linking their own experiences to what they had read. Several studies suggested that reading and writing abilities benefit from knowledge of text structure, particularly that of expository text (Armbruster, Anderson, & Ostertag, 1987; Raphael & Kirschner, 1985), and Duin and Graves (1987) found that knowledge of word meanings is an important factor in comprehension and can improve the quality of writing.

Researchers investigating the role of information processing in reading and writing have compiled evidence to indicate that these two processes have a strong relationship. Their work has also helped educators to understand the processes in terms of their complexities, their components, and the knowledge base of skilled readers and writers.

The Naturalist Perspective

The naturalist perspective of learning draws on the work of Piaget (1926) and Chomsky (1965) and focuses on children's innate cognitive structures and their innate predisposition toward the development of language. The whole language approach embraces this perspective, believing that children's abilities to learn reading and writing will unfold in the appropriate environment because reading and writing are based on the acquisition of oral language and share many of the same characteristics. Because of this premise, it is difficult to apply this perspective to deaf children who are still struggling to acquire a language base. One of the shared characteristics of reading and writing is that they develop naturally (Goodman, 1986). Thus, formal instruction in the development of specific skills is usually avoided in favor of allowing children to learn to read and write by being actively involved in real reading and writing.

This perspective is founded on three premises (McCarthey & Raphael, 1992): (1) thinking resembles natural, universal structures; (2) the child actively constructs knowledge; and (3) reading and writing develop through stages. The first premise draws on Piaget's research, especially his explanations of the two cognitive structures, assimilation and accommodation, using these structures to explain how young children assimilate new knowledge in existing schemata or change existing schemata to fit what they encounter in the world. Piaget's work suggested that these two structures are universal and that they emerge from and transform previous stages. The second condition also is derived from Piagetian theory and suggests that learning occurs when children are actively involved in constructing their own meanings and when they have firsthand experiences that provide opportunities for them to map language onto already existing cognitive structures. The third premise, also Piagetian in nature, holds that children's internal structures progress through universal stages and mature and change as children interact with other people and with their environment. Therefore, proponents of this perspective believe that children must actively engage in real reading and writing activities and have many opportunities to interact with print.

The research of Graves and Calkins defines many of the instructional parameters that are derived from this perspective. For example, Graves and Hansen (1983) found that children's development in writing was related to their drawings, that students rehearsed before writing, and that interaction with peers facilitated their learning. Calkins (1983) found that children improved in text revision when they had opportunities for continual writing and talking about their writing.

This perspective provides additional information for teachers by suggesting the kind of environment that is necessary for children to acquire the knowledge bases identified by information-processing theorists (McCarthey & Raphael, 1992). However, Florio-Ruane and Lensmire (1989) suggested that learning to become an effective writer encompasses even more than what is defined by the information-processing and the naturalist perspectives. They maintained that mature writers have also acquired beliefs, values, and attitudes about themselves and their world. The social-constructivist perspective addresses this aspect of a writer's development.

The Social-Constructivist Perspective

The social-constructivist view of learning conceptualizes knowledge as a social artifact that is consensually formed through social interaction (Bruffee, 1986). A social-constructivist theory of learning is predicated on three assumptions: (1) knowledge is constructed through the individual's interaction with the sociocultural environment; (2) higher mental functions, including reading and writing, are social and cultural in nature; and (3) knowledgeable members of a culture can help others learn.

Much of the research in this field of thought focuses on the role of culture in learning. The relationship between literacy practices in schools and the value of literacy within communities are important aspects of the role of culture. Heath's studies (1982) of the preschool environments of children in upper and lower socioeconomic levels strongly indicated the advantages of children in homes where the literacy experiences closely matched those of the school. These children were more successful in school because they had already learned the patterns of literacy behavior such as responding to questions, labeling and grouping items, linking text characters to real-life events, and listening quietly to stories read by others. In contrast, those children from families whose culture did not place the same emphasis on literacy behaviors were not as successful in school.

The social-constructivist theory accounts for variations among cultures in language practices and in the ways children learn to read and write in different settings. It emphasizes the need for educators to be sensitive to the values and practices of different cultures and to realize and understand that all children will not enter school at the same stage of readiness to begin to learn to read and write. Children who are deaf and hard of hearing frequently are similar in their literacy behaviors to the second group of students, albeit for different reasons. Their parents may place a great deal of importance on literacy and literacy behaviors in the home; however, because parents and child frequently do not share an accurate and comfortable communication environment, the child cannot take advantage of the literacy experiences provided.

Implications for Instruction

The information gained from studies of different learning models suggests several instructional practices that should be effective with students. The practices derived from the information-processing model are different in nature and more structured than those derived from the naturalist and social-constructivist models; however, all three approaches can be effective with students and fit into a balanced approach to reading and writing. Some of the more significant practices gleaned from the research are as follows:

1. Children should engage in meaningful practice to develop automaticity in some of the lower-level skills (decoding, handwriting, spelling) so that they can give more attention to performing the higher-level skills (comprehension, planning).

2. Children should learn and practice prediction skills since predicting is important in reading (as discussed previously).

3. Journal writing is encouraged so that students can explore topics of interest.

4. Writers should have many opportunities to write and to revise their writing.

5. Readers and writers should be given many opportunities for interactions in which their teacher and peers can respond to their reading and writing.

6. Readers and writers should be allowed periods of sustained silent reading and writing, as well as time for sharing their reading and writing.

7. Students should have clear objectives that can be formulated through predicting and brainstorming.

8. Students should be presented with problems that will encourage them to work together on a project that will increase literacy learning.

9. Teachers should model metacognitive strategies in reading and writing by "thinking aloud."

10. Teachers should model reading and writing strategies and assist students in gradually gaining control of the processes so that they can become independent in their reading and writing activities.

Instructional Approaches in Writing

Instructional practices in writing have changed tremendously over the past 20 years due to the new information that has been made available to teachers through the research derived from the three theoretical perspectives discussed. No one perspective provides an adequate explanation of the processes of reading and writing, and so, again, teachers are encouraged to present a balanced approach, drawing from all of the research and its implications and tailoring their applications of instructional practices to fit the needs of the students.

The Traditional Approach

More than 20 years ago teachers did not have the advantage of the information derived from research that today's teachers have. They probably taught writing in the same manner that writing was taught to them and engaged in what was commonly called the traditional way of teaching writing.

The traditional approach to the teaching of writing was actually quite simple. Writing was almost a synchronized performance, in that the students were to start writing at the same time and finish at the same time—usually within the writing period. The teacher gave the students a writing assignment, telling them what form their writing was to take—for example, a social letter, a thank you note, or a narrative—and frequently gave them a topic, such as their summer vacations or their most exciting experiences. Then the students wrote. When they completed their writing, they gave their papers to the teacher, who took them home and, with a red pen, made corrections, usually for grammar. The next day the teacher returned the papers, and the students had to rewrite them, incorporating all of the teacher's corrections. Clearly, this approach focused solely on the product; how the children learned was not considered.

Unfortunately, this approach persists in some classrooms today but, happily, not in many. If the traditional approach to the teaching of writing is analyzed, it quickly becomes apparent that very little teaching actually occurs. It is not surprising that employers and university instructors have complained for many years that the high school graduates they were receiving were poor writers. It was time for a change. The theoretical perspectives that have been cited earlier in this chapter have provided hypotheses about how children learn to write; the instructional implications have been actualized in many classrooms and will, hopefully, result in better writers.

The Process Writing Approach

The way writing is taught in classrooms today is vastly different from the traditional approach to writing. Instead of assigning topics and expecting all the students to be doing the same thing at the same time, teachers now guide their students through the writing process from the initial step of helping them determine what they will write about to the eventual "publication" of their work. In the writing process, teachers do not expect students to have a finished product after their first draft—even experienced authors cannot accomplish that feat! Instead, teachers help children discover what they want to say and teach them ways to use grammar and to make word choices that will make their writing clearer and more interesting for an audience (Weaver, 1994). Teachers using the writing process, like traditional teachers, are concerned about the *product*; however, unlike teachers in the traditional approach to writing, they are equally or perhaps even more concerned about the *process* of writing.

The writing process contains several elements through which children progress at their own rates. These elements are not steps occurring in a linear fashion; rather, they are recursive, and children move back and forth between and among the components. The elements of the writing process include the following:

1. prewriting
2. composing

3. revising
4. editing
5. publishing
6. skill instruction
7. conferencing

Prewriting

Prewriting is central to the process of writing for any writer. The activities during this phase are anything that prepares the students for writing. It is during prewriting that students select a topic, determine the audience, explore different aspects of the topic, and research possibilities for elaboration of the topic if necessary. During this time writers also begin to organize their writing, sometimes mentally and sometimes with the help of graphic organizers such as semantic maps, outlines, and story maps. They also rehearse, practicing different ways to express their thoughts. Rehearsing may be an individual activity, with writers mentally thinking through how they will express their thoughts, or it may be a partner or a small group activity in which the writers discuss some of their thoughts and revise and clarify them through peer interaction.

Composing

When students have finished their preparation, they begin the actual writing. At this point, some teachers who are initiating the writing process approach in their classrooms may begin to feel uncomfortable because all of the students will not be prepared to write at the same time. The time and activities needed for preparation may be different for each student, which means that all of the students will not be doing the same thing at the same time. Some may still be in the prewriting stage—selecting topics, exploring, and organizing—when others are starting to write their first draft. It is probably safe to say that from this time on in the writing process, the classroom will be a very busy place, with students doing different activities and progressing through the different phases at their own pace. During this composition phase, writing the first draft, students are encouraged to focus on their ideas (the content) and get them down on paper. They are encouraged *not* to focus on grammar, sentence structure, and spelling (the mechanics of writing) at this time. Becoming too concerned about the mechanics of writing during the first-draft stage can cause students to lose their focus on the content and may result in compositions that are stilted and uninteresting.

Revising

When students have finished their first drafts, they participate in a conference on their writing. This conference may be held with a writing partner, with a small group of peers, or with the teacher. With a writing partner or with a small group of peers, the students share and respond to each other's writings. After reading a classmate's first draft, a student should respond in a positive way, noting such characteristics as points of interest and good word choices but also asking questions about sections that were not clear or pieces of information that were left out. No student or teacher should write on another student's paper. Writers have ownership of their writing, and, usually, they are the only ones to make marks on the paper. After the conference, the student thinks about the contributions of peers and the teacher, organizes these new ideas, and begins revising the first draft. During revision, the student is "revisiting" some of the prewriting activities and is composing again, thus illustrating the recursive nature of these steps. Another example of how these steps or elements are recursive occurs after the revision of the first draft is completed. The writer seeks a partner, and again they engage in reading and responding to each other's compositions. When the writers are satisfied with the *content* of their work, they begin editing.

Editing

During editing, students focus mostly on the mechanics of writing; however, they do not focus on all the mechanics of writing simultaneously. They focus only on those elements that are within their skill level. For example, young students who are just beginning to write may edit only for capital letters at the beginning of sentences and periods or question marks at the end, while an older student may focus on all punctuation as well as subject-verb agreement throughout the composition. Monitoring the skills that each student needs to work on can be a difficult task for teachers. For this reason many teachers keep a checklist of skills that have not yet been attained but are within the appropriate range for each student and check them off as the student demonstrates knowledge and application of each skill. This skills checklist is frequently kept in the student's portfolio so the student is aware of progress made.

Publishing

In the writing process publishing is viewed as the dissemination of a piece of writing to an audience who will read and react to the content. Not every piece of writing is published; when students write every day, they may decide not to publish some of their work. They put any unpublished writing into their working portfolios. Sometime in the future, they may decide to review that particular composition, polish it up, and prepare it for publication.

Publication can take many forms. It may be informal sharing with a classmate, the teacher, or a small group of peers. Writing can also be shared with another class or with other people in the school environment such as the principal, secretary, or custodian. Posting finished work on the bulletin board or in the hall for people to read is another way to share writing. Sometimes writing is published in school or class newspapers, magazines, or literary journals. Many students enjoy making books of their finished work to take home to share with their families or to put into the classroom or school library to share with other students. Some pieces will go into their showcase portfolios, which will be shared later with friends and families and will also be used as one tool for evaluating the students' progress in their development of writing skills.

An activity that is very popular in many schools, particularly in elementary departments, is Young Authors' Day. Periodically, during the school year, the students celebrate their writing. One school celebrates Young Authors' Day every month in an assembly of the elementary department. The teachers and students select an "author of the month" from each class, and at the celebration, each teacher briefly tells about the writing activities in their classroom that month, and each author of the month reads and displays a selected piece of writing. The other students then react to the writing by making positive comments about it. A great deal of praise and applause occurs, making the students very proud to be authors.

Skill Instruction

Specific skill instruction occurs during mini-lessons as well as during conferences. However, informal skill instruction occurs daily. When children are writing, teachers should also be writing, working with small groups of students in skill instruction, or circulating around the classroom, being available to answer questions and to give guidance and informal instruction as needed by individual students. The teacher conducts mini-lessons daily (5–10 minutes) with small groups of students or with the entire class if all need work on the same skill. While observing the students, the teacher makes note of skills instruction needed, and during a mini-lesson the teacher presents instruction on one skill only that the students need at that time. If different skills are needed by different students, the teacher may conduct two or three mini-lessons with different small groups while the other children are writing.

Conferencing

Conferencing is an important part of the writing process and involves much more than skill instruction; however, usually the skill instruction that occurs is not on the mechanics of writing but on the content. A common way to start a conference is for the student to read a piece of writing to the teacher, who then responds with comments or questions. Again, the comments are always phrased in a positive and supportive manner; for example, the teacher might say, "I really enjoyed your description of the car race, but I'm not sure what happened to the car that was in the lead. Can you explain that?" After the student explains, the teacher suggests adding the additional information to the writing to make it clearer for the readers.

In addition to responding to the student's writing, the teacher might ask questions such as "Did you have trouble with any part?" or "What was the hardest part for you to write and why?" The teacher and student discuss the strong characteristics of the writing and decide on skills that the student needs to improve, which then become topics for the next mini-lesson and a focus for the student in revision and editing. Current interests of the student and future topics for writing are discussed and guidance given for the next writing piece the student undertakes.

The Writing Workshop

The writing workshop is a way of organizing the writing process approach in the classroom—all of the components of the writing process are components of the writing workshop. Calkins (1994) stated that children need to have a predictable time in the schedule for writing and a predictable structure to the order of events so that they can anticipate and plan for it. They are more comfortable when they know what to expect.

The framework of the writing workshop consists of mini-lessons, work time, state-of-the-class reports, conferencing, share sessions, and the publication celebration. Calkins suggested that *mini-lessons* can occur either at the beginning of the workshop or at the end. If mini-lessons are positioned at the end, the first module of the workshop is *work time*. During this module, the students engage in all of the activities related to their writing: prewriting, drafting, responding, revising, rewriting, and editing. *State-of-the-class* reports and *conferencing* make up the next module. After that module, Calkins (1994) has suggested an activity she calls *share sessions*. In this activity, the students gather in a circle, taking turns in the "author's chair" to read their drafts and get comments and suggestions, or they talk about the writing process itself, discussing what they did, how they did it, their feelings, and the problems they had. The last event of the writing workshop is the *publication celebration*.

The actual order in which teachers construct their daily writing workshops may vary and depends on where the students are in the process. The writing workshop "modules" are flexible and can be arranged in a variety of ways to meet the needs of young writers.

Writing Activities in the Classroom

When writing is confined to one period during the school day, children frequently do not generalize to reading and content areas the knowledge and skills they learn and use during the writing period. In addition, to become fluent and effective writers, children must practice their writing just as they must practice their reading to become fluent and effective readers. Therefore, writing—and reading—should be integrated across the curriculum. This section will describe journaling strategies that the authors have observed or experienced using with deaf and hard of hearing students to incorporate writing into reading and all content areas.

Many different kinds of journals can be used with students, but regardless of the kind of journaling that occurs, the purpose is the same: journals provide a variety of opportunities for students to build reading-writing-thinking relationships (Bromley, 1993). Young children can be encouraged to draw pictures in their journals and talk or sign about them, since talking and signing are precursors to writing. The teacher can write what the children say or sign next to the pictures in their journals. If the children are signing ASL, the teacher would write the communication in English, explaining that the text contains the same thoughts but in a different language. Older students can be encouraged to write their thoughts, ideas, and opinions on topics they choose or in response to their reading, or they can write summaries to help them synthesize their learning in science, social studies, and math.

Mayher and Lester (1983) wrote that in order to grow as readers, children must learn to use their own knowledge, experiences, and emotions to construct personal meaning and develop a sense of text ownership. Students who choose what to write about and how to write it feel that they have control over their own work (Rupert & Brueggeman, 1986; Staton, 1988). Researchers have shown that journals encourage understanding, imagining, speculating, questioning, and the shaping of ideas (Atwell, 1987; Fulwiler, 1982; Mayher, Lester, & Pradl, 1983). Clearly, using journals in the classroom can serve many purposes and benefit students in a variety of areas.

Reading Response Journal

Atwell (1987) believed that using dialogue journals in reading would encourage sustained reflection. She speculated that students' written responses to books would show more reflection than their discussions, that writing would give them time to consider their responses, and that by having the time to think about their thinking, students would gain more insight into what they had read.

Students do not automatically begin writing response journals. They must be prepared, and they must be given some time to understand the process and understand exactly what is expected of them. Teachers should explain that using a response journal is similar to writing letters back and forth—except that it is focused on one topic, responses to their reading—and that a journal is a place to share their ideas, express their feelings, and ask questions (Wollman-Bonilla, 1989). Wollman-Bonilla suggested that teachers provide some initial guidance by first modeling this approach. She recommended that teachers share their own written responses to a book the students have recently completed, pointing out that the focus is on writing down ideas rather than on neatness or spelling. Teachers should suggest a variety of possibilities for the content of students' responses, such as those in the following list suggested by Wollman-Bonella (1991, p. 22):

1. What you liked and disliked and why.
2. What you wish had happened.
3. What you wish the author had included.
4. Your opinion of the characters.
5. Your opinion of the illustrations, tables, and figures.
6. What the text reminded you of.
7. What you felt as you read.
8. What you noticed about how you read.
9. Questions you have after reading.

Students may write either as they are reading or after reading, and they should be allowed to refer to the text to reconsider sections, solve disputes, and figure out how the book evoked ideas and feelings. It is very important that students understand that there is no "right answer" and that their opinions, whatever they might be, are valid.

Teachers should also make sure that the students understand that a reading response is not the same as retelling a story, which is a recounting of the plot. Teachers can explain that students will be writing about their personal reactions to the book, not a summary of the story. Finally, teachers should let the students know that they will respond to what is written in the journals, not by grading or evaluating, but by discussing what was written, encouraging the writers, and leading them to deeper thinking and understanding.

A common question that teachers have when considering the initiation of response journals in their classrooms is "How will I ever find the time to respond to each student's journal?" Teachers of deaf and hard of hearing students have an advantage that their colleagues who teach hearing students do not have—small class sizes, which makes responding more manageable. Although students should read independently daily, they may not be required to write responses every day; perhaps two times a week is sufficient. On other days they might meet for discussion of their reading in an individual conference, with a small group, or with the whole class. Initially, replying to students' response journals will take longer than after teachers are used to the process. After a while, it will become less time consuming, and teachers will find that reading their students' journals provides them with greater insight into how the students read and think. In addition, teachers who have used response journals indicate that writing replies to response journals does not take any more time than preparing and grading worksheets.

The *way* teachers reply to students' response journals is very important. It is essential that students do not feel that they are being criticized, that they are not embarrassed or put on the defensive. Teachers must first gain the trust of their students and show that they are sincerely interested in what the students think. Initially, even though they may not agree, teachers should validate the students' ideas rather than challenge their views. Later, after trust is gained, teachers can begin to introduce different perspectives to challenge their thinking. Wollman-Bonilla (1991) stated that when teachers establish an appreciation for their students' ideas, the students become more comfortable with exploring their responses and different perspectives.

Teachers' replies to text should help students develop their reading abilities and improve their comprehension. To accomplish these goals, Wollman-Bonilla (1991, p. 35) suggested that teachers might use their replies to:

- share their own ideas and responses;
- provide information;
- develop students' awareness of literary techniques;
- develop students' awareness of reading strategies;
- model elaboration; and
- challenge students to think in new ways.

Keeping reading response journals should be beneficial and fun for both students and teachers. The written feedback provided by teachers will help students learn about reading, about literature, and about writing to learn.

Dialogue Journals

Dialogue journals are similar to reading response journals except that the topic does not have to be a response to reading; it can be a topic that either the student or the teacher chooses. Dialogue journals are interactive, cumulative, self-initiated, and functional (Bromley, 1993). They are interactive in that they allow teachers and students to exchange information about personal preferences and opinions. They are cumulative in that they are an ongoing collection of communication exchanges—like an extended conversation, which is not always possible in a busy classroom. Dialogue journals are self-initiated, as teachers and students choose what they write about and can respond to an entry or ignore it and move on to another topic. Finally, they are functional in that teachers and students are using writing for a real purpose—communication.

Dialogue journals have many benefits. One benefit is that students have opportunities to learn by taking part in a nonthreatening activity. Another advantage is that through their replies teachers can provide informal writing instruction, as well as accurate models for students to imitate. In addition, students have opportunities to develop fluency through practice and to build motivation and confidence in their writing abilities. Another very important benefit is that they provide a natural environment for students to connect reading, writing, and thinking.

Before starting dialogue journals, teachers might have their students begin by keeping a personal journal, in which they write about topics of their choice. After they become accustomed to writing in journals, teachers can introduce them to dialogue journals, starting by saying that they would like to have a written conversation with each student in his or her journal. Students and teachers should decide on a specific time and day or days for journal writing; it should occur frequently, but not so frequently that it becomes a burden for either teachers or students. As stated earlier, keeping dialogue journals is much like writing short letters back and forth, with the writing being mostly social in nature.

Buddy Journals

Buddy journals are a variation of the dialogue journal, in which students write back and forth to each other. It is a natural way to read and write, providing a purpose and a personally meaningful context as students interact socially (Bromley, 1993). Buddy journals connect reading and writing, as students have to read to be able to respond to their buddies' written communication.

Students create their own topics and can write about anything they want that is appropriate. The teacher does not evaluate or grade the buddy journals; they serve the students' purposes rather than those of the teacher. In their writing, students ask and answer questions, share experiences and feelings, discuss ideas, and develop relationships with one another.

Character Journals

Character journals are journals in which a student assumes the personality of a character in a book and writes entries about life and feelings from the character's perspective. This kind of journal may be used when the student is reading a story or a book, or when the teacher is reading a chapter book to the class. After the story or a section of the book, students write extenuations of the reading in their character journals. For example, they would elaborate on how a character felt when a certain event occurred, what a character thought about other people in the story, or how a character changed during the course of the book. Character journals provide opportunities for the student to look at people and situations from a different perspective, which fosters comprehension, problem solving, and learning in general.

Learning Logs

The learning log strategy is easy to implement and is particularly effective when used regularly. Students keep ongoing records in their own language about what they are learning (Vacca & Linek, 1992). Generally, students keep learning logs in their content-area classes. During the last 5 to 10 minutes of a class, students write in their logs, summarizing the lesson, reacting to class activities and discussions, asking questions, linking new knowledge with prior knowledge, reflecting on what they have learned, and identifying problems they are having in understanding the material presented. The teacher can read and reply to the learning logs, answering questions or directing the student to resources that will give the needed information; or students can share their learning logs in pairs or small groups or with the whole class, helping each other answer questions and solve problems that are raised.

Knowing that they will be writing in learning logs at the end of a period, at certain times throughout the day, or at the end of the school day encourages students to attend during class and provides them with opportunities to take time to think about what they have learned. Writing a summary of what they have learned reinforces and clarifies concepts, helps them to realize what they did not understand, and gives them the opportunity to formulate questions to guide further study.

Only a few kinds of journals have been described in this chapter. A wide variety of journals can be used in classrooms to encourage students to write and to become comfortable with their writing. Journal writing may not be easy to initiate with deaf and hard of hearing students because writing is not usually their favorite activity. However, if teachers start slowly and give students the time and support they need to learn the process and to understand what is expected of them, they will find that journal writing not only provides many good learning experiences for their students but also provides many benefits for teachers. Journaling provides teachers with another way to communicate with their students, an insight into their students' reading and thinking processes, and a way to learn more about their students as individuals.

Learning from Writing

Langer and Applebee (1987) conducted a series of studies from which they draw some general conclusions about the role of writing in learning. They found that the more content is manipulated, the more likely it is to be understood and remembered. The results of their investigations indicated that any kind of written response to reading leads to better comprehension and retention than reading without writing. However, the effects of writing on learning seem to be specific in that the information and ideas remembered are those that students express in writing. Thus, if students focus their writing on the important concepts, they will benefit more from the writing activity than if they focus on the insignificant information. Unfortunately, Langer and Applebee did not find that the process of writing, in which students are thinking about what they read and selecting what to write, leads to a review and reconceptualization of *all* of the text.

In their review of research on writing, Vacca and Linek (1992) concluded that different types of writing assignments result in different patterns of thinking and learning. Langer and Applebee's studies resulted in similar findings: Different writing tasks influenced the kind of learning that took place. The writing tasks of note taking, answering comprehension questions, and summarizing led the students to focus their attention across the text as a whole, resulting in somewhat superficial manipulation of the material. Analytic writing tasks resulted in a more narrow focus on a specific body of information, resulting in better comprehension of a smaller body of information. This kind of writing task would be more appropriate when the emphasis is on concepts and specific relationships among concepts in the text rather than retention of a larger body of facts. Therefore, writing seems to be a very productive technique that teachers can use to orchestrate the kinds of cognitive engagement that leads to content-area learning (Langer & Applebee, 1987).

A final interesting conclusion drawn from this series of studies is that if content is familiar and relationships are well understood by the readers, a writing response probably has no major effect on comprehension and retention. Thus, if students are highly effective readers, simply reading the text may be all that is needed to ensure comprehension.

Spelling

Spelling is important for two relatively diverse reasons. Graves (1994, p. 255) suggested that "spelling, probably more than any other aspect in the school curriculum, is used to mark social status." Adults seem to rank spelling as being almost as important as reading and mathematics and sometimes seem to rank spelling skill above the ability to write. Indeed, when reading a student's composition, teachers may overlook the quality of the writing because of the interruptions caused by misspelled words. However, spelling is important because children who are learning to write words using invented or constructive spellings are establishing attitudes toward words and writing. They will learn while developing their spelling and writing skills that it is not enough for the writer to know what the text says; it is important for a reader to be able to understand the message as well.

An interdependent relationship exists among reading, writing, and spelling skills. These skills contribute to each other's development when they are integrated in the curriculum (Ehri, 1989). When writing, learners are attending to the sounds in words and to the letters that represent those sounds. They develop expectations about how spelling might be structured and become interested in how the general spelling system works. When learners read, they are exposed to the conventional spellings of words, which reinforce for them the correct option of many spelling possibilities. Ehri (1989) maintained that reading "provides the input learners need to store the correct spellings of specific words in memory and also to figure out how the system works." Thus, writing creates an interest in spelling, and the alphabetic structure of print and reading directs writers toward the conventional forms.

The literature on how children develop spelling skills pertains to hearing children, and all of it emphasizes the development of letter-to-sound correspondence and how children "construct" spellings by sounding out the word and by representing the sounds they hear in oral language. K. Goodman (1992) suggested that the develop of spelling is a constructive process in which children invent the spelling system just as they invent other language systems. This holistic perspective, the development of language control through use, maintains that children learn spelling without direct instruction if they read and write. Milz (1982) and Y. Goodman and Wilde (1985) studied the evolution of children's writing and demonstrated the development over time of conventional spelling skills that children achieved without explicit instruction.

The fact that learning to spell appears to be quite dependent on phonemic reception and understanding presents a perplexing educational dilemma for teachers of children who do not hear or who do not hear accurately the sounds of English language. This section will describe the stages of spelling development for hearing children, the components of a spelling program, and the adaptations that can be made for students who are deaf and hard of hearing.

The Stages of Spelling Development

Most hearing children progress through five identifiable stages in their development of spelling skills: (1) prephonemic spelling, (2) early phonemic spelling, (3) letter-name spelling, (4) transitional spelling, and (5) conventional spelling (Temple, Nathan, Temple, & Burris, 1993).

Prephonemic Spelling

In prephonemic spelling, children use symbols (letter strings) from the alphabet to represent words, but they have not yet discovered that the letters they use represent the speech sounds or phonemes in words. Their letter strings look like writing, but they have not attempted to represent sounds in any systematic way. Children at this stage have not yet learned to read, but they appear to know something about written language. They know how letters are formed and that they are supposed to represent words.

Early Phonemic Spelling

In early phonemic spelling, children use letters to represent sounds in words but provide only a partial mapping of all the sounds in a word (Schirmer, 1994). They have discovered the phonetic principle and know basically how spelling works; however, they write down only one or two of the sounds in any given word.

Letter-Name Spelling

The difference between the letter-name spelling stage and the early phonemic spelling stage appears to be a matter of degree. Children gradually represent more and more phonemes with letters until they are using letters to map all of the sounds in a word. Children choose the letters they use on the basis of the similarity between the sound of the letter-names and the respective phonemes.

Spelling during this stage is sometimes called "invented" or "constructive" spelling because some letter choices differ from the conventional spelling; however, choices are usually systematic and perceptually correct (Hoffman & McCully, 1984). As children have more experiences with print through reading, they begin to see differences in their way of spelling and conventional spelling. Consequently, they begin to change their spelling, leading them into the next stage.

Transitional Spelling

In the transitional stage, children move from reliance on sounds to represent words to using many of the features of standard spelling. They frequently misspell words with irregular spelling, usually writing the word the way it sounds (e.g., *cud* for *could*, *mite* for *might*). Transitional spellers are readers. They will continue to develop correct spelling patterns through continued reading, writing, and attention to how words are put together.

Conventional Spelling

In the conventional spelling stage, children are using traditional orthography and are doing so usually by the end of second grade. However, as they continue to develop more complex vocabularies, they will be challenged to develop more sophisticated spelling strategies, such as relationships of word families (*photograph, photography; separate, separation*). If they do not develop strategies beyond those they learned in second grade, their spelling will look plausible but unlearned (Temple et al., 1993). To enable children to continue to progress toward mature spelling, teachers must cultivate their curiosity; teachers should point out and discuss patterns and oddities in word spellings and encourage the use of dictionaries so that their students will continue in their development of spelling skills.

The description of these stages suggests that children learn spelling through discovery; however, most children will not learn to spell by discovery alone. Memorization is also involved in learning to spell. Most deaf and many hard of hearing children will not learn to spell through discovery but must rely heavily on memorization, letter patterns, and word families. Deaf, hard of hearing, and hearing children need guidance in discovering spelling patterns and will need to have words presented in groups reinforced by discussions of spelling patterns. All children need to be encouraged and taught to memorize the correct spellings of many words (Temple et al., 1993). Only when they have a large store of correctly spelled words in mind will they be able to infer correct spelling patterns.

Components of a Spelling Program

Many sources are available that describe components of spelling programs that focus on the letter-sound correspondences in words and sounding out words to identify the appropriate letter representations. Because these components are not useful or are of limited use for deaf and hard of hearing students, this section will describe components of spelling programs that do not rely on the student's ability to hear.

Hillerich (1985, p. 165) described four components that teachers should provide in a successful spelling program: (1) using a good word list, (2) introducing words with a pretest and immediate correction by the student, (3) teaching pupils how to study a word for spelling, and (4) having students keep a record of progress to measure their success. Two additional activities, using a dictionary and frequent writing, enhance the spelling program.

Using a Good Word List

Children need to know how to read and spell certain common words. Lederer (1991) identified 11 words as constituting 25% of all words used in spoken language. Those 11 words are as follows:

I	is	the	a	in
to	and	it	you	of
that				

Clay (1993) identified those 11 and 14 more words that are important for children to learn because they are used frequently in writing. The additional 14 words are the following:

am	come	see	we	at
on	look	this	like	me
my	here	up	go	

These words are not easy for children to learn because they convey very little meaning and therefore do not lend themselves to imagery. Children generally must be taught these words in the context of reading and writing.

Graves (1994) suggested that teachers rely heavily on word lists for study and weekly tests. Fry, Fountoukidis, and Polk (1985) have developed high-frequency word lists in which the first 25 words make up about a third of all printed material and the first 100 make up about half of all written material. Unquestionably, students must learn to recognize these words automatically and also to spell them correctly. In addition, Graves suggested that the weekly tests include two words that each student selects because she or he continues to misspell them and three words that each student selects because the student wants to use them in future writing. For the test, the teacher dictates the words from the high-frequency list, using them in sentences, and then directs the students to write their two "demon" words and the three words they wish to use in their writing. Graves claims that this approach to spelling is effective if students keep the three lists—high-frequency words, demon words, and personal words—in their writing folders.

Introducing Words with a Pretest and Immediate Correction

The words selected for correct spelling words should be administered as a pretest before students have the opportunity to see them. After the pretest, the students should immediately correct the words and, in this way, discover the words that need to be studied. In correcting their own tests, they discover where they made mistakes in each misspelled word. Hillerich (1985) suggested using a pretest sheet, a lined page consisting of three columns. The first column contains the list of new spelling words; the students write the words during the pretest in the middle column; and the third column is for writing corrections. The pretest sheet is given to students with the first column folded over so that they cannot see the new words. During the pretest, the teacher says a word, uses it in a sentence, then says the word again. This step generally causes problems when sign language is being used because many words that appear on high-frequency lists do not have a sign but are finger spelled. Teachers with students who are deaf or hard of hearing have yet to devise a satisfactory way to resolve this problem. After the pretest has been administered, students fold open the first column and correct their misspellings, writing the correct spelling of the word in the third column. That column then becomes their study list.

Teaching Students How To Study Spelling Words

The study method for spelling words consists of four steps:

   1. The student looks at the word and says it. (Students who do not use speech can sign or finger spell the word.)
   2. The students close their eyes and spell (or finger spell) the word, then

check to see if they spelled it correctly. If not, they repeat the step until the spelling is correct.

3. The students cover the word and write it. They check to see if they are correct and, if not, repeat the step until they write the word correctly.

4. The students repeat step 3 three more times.

The study method emphasizes memorization. Hillerich (1985) maintained that visual memory is important for good spelling, and that correct spelling is a visual memory, kinesthetic operation.

In addition to the pretest, teachers should also administer a check test after the students have had a day or two to study, to determine how the study is going. On a different day, the mastery test should be administered.

Having Students Keep a Record of Progress

Keeping a record of their own spelling progress provides students with a sense of accomplishment. To coincide with this spelling program, students should develop a bar graph to record the number of words they spelled correctly on the pretest, the check test, and the mastery test. The bars can be made in different colors and will, hopefully, point out the increase in number of words spelled correctly as a result of study.

In addition to word lists and spelling tests, Hillerich (1985) and Graves (1994) encouraged the use of two other approaches to ensure an effective spelling program. One is teaching students how to use a dictionary to help with spelling, and the other is frequent writing.

Using a Dictionary for Spelling Help

The first question usually asked by students when directed to use a dictionary for spelling help is "How can I find a word if I don't know how to spell it?" Teachers of hearing children usually begin by asking the student to sound out the word to determine the initial letter or the letters in the first syllable. Lacking that avenue, teachers of deaf students need to work with their children to develop the ability to make "educated guesses." Many deaf students can use visual memory and lipreading to figure out the first letter of a word and then, at least, begin their search in the right section of the dictionary.

In addition, during reading, writing, and spelling activities in the classroom, teachers should always be looking for ways to develop letter and spelling awareness in their students. For example, if a word encountered in reading has an unusual spelling, such as pneumonia, the teacher should point out the oddities. Calling attention to various letter combinations will not ensure that the students learn the spelling of the word, but should help them remember enough about the word to find it in the dictionary. Discussing root words will also help with dictionary searches; students may not know how to spell *comparable* but could find *compare* in the dictionary. Providing daily practice will help children become familiar with dictionaries and enable them to increase their skills in using them. Teachers might select two or three words from different content areas each day to use in dictionary searches. Initially, teachers should demonstrate efficient ways to find a word (for example, using the guide words), give students guided practice, and then allow them to work independently, with partners, or in small groups.

Frequent Writing

Frequent writing is necessary to develop good spellers; in fact, good spelling skills are needed only for writing. Students can read effectively without being able to spell words accurately; however, in writing, inaccurately spelled words reflect negatively on the writer's abilities.

Having students learn to spell words from high-frequency lists is a memorization task, and if those words are not used frequently, students will soon forget them. When writing, students will need to use the high-frequency words often, and frequent writing will give them opportunities to practice those words so that they will become automatic and increase writing fluency.

Summary

Students who are deaf and hard of hearing generally have difficulty in learning-to-write activities and tend to give up or rush through their writing, giving little thought to what they are composing and focusing only on finishing the task.

Traditional writing approaches were generally quite deflating for deaf and hard of hearing students. They labored over getting a few words down on paper only to have that paper returned covered with red marks. Whether or not deaf and hard of hearing students will become better writers through the use of the writing process is not known; what is apparent is that the writing process approach is much more positive and supportive and seems to produce far fewer frustrations in students. In the writing process approach, students are given more instruction in how to prepare for writing, how to write, and how to reflect on writing. Students are not on their own but can consult with the teacher or with peers to get suggestions for improving, and then have the opportunity to continue revising until they are satisfied.

In writing, as in reading, becoming good requires practice. Journaling is one way for students to get practice in writing and to gain many other beneficial learning experiences such as practice in reading, learning to elaborate, and thinking in new ways by considering other perspectives. There are many kinds of journals teachers can use in their classrooms for different purposes. The three potential problem areas in initiating journal writing that teachers will need to attend to are motivating students for a writing activity; helping them understand the process, which is nonthreatening; and devising a management system for journal writing and replies.

For many years, most teachers have believed that writing contributes to learning and can lead to students' rethinking, revising, and reformulating what they know. However, few studies have investigated *when* students learn from writing, *what kinds of* learning result from engagement in different writing experiences, or *how* writing can be used to help students understand and remember the material read (Langer & Applebee, 1987). Some of the studies that have focused on how writing fosters learning have indicated that almost any kind of writing activity leads to better learning than when students read without writing. Different kinds of writing activities lead students to focus on different kinds of information and to think about that information in different ways. In short, there is a strong indication that writing does assist learning.

Spelling is a skill that is needed only for writing; however, that in no way diminishes its importance. Writers are frequently judged on first impressions of their writing, and, if a first impression is based on a written note with several misspellings, the reader is likely to decide that the writer is not an educated person. Deaf students' contacts with hearing people in everyday activities frequently require note writing for communication. A note that is well written with correctly spelled words will create a more positive first impression than a note with words inaccurately spelled. Therefore, spelling programs are very necessary for developing important life skills in students with hearing losses.

CHAPTER

Content-Area Reading

Preview

While most students will enter school with a schema for storybook reading, few students will have conceptual experiences with expository text. The transition from reading narrative and literature to reading expository text requires changes in expectations and purpose, while fundamentals such as decoding, word knowledge, and syntactic and semantic skills remain the same. Content-based textbooks, information resources including computer-based Web sites, and reference materials such as encyclopedias and dictionaries are not designed for learning to read and generally assume that the reader has basic skills in reading and language.

The demand for content literacy increases as a child progresses through the school years into adulthood, while instruction in reading decreases, with only minimal attention given to the unique aspects of informational reading. Expository reading instruction creates a paradigm shift from learning about reading to learning about subject matter through reading and includes a host of conceptually based processes including descriptions, classifications, and explanations developed with the expressed purpose of providing new information to the reader.

This chapter reviews variables that influence content-based reading and writing and describes strategies that can be used to develop comprehension skills in content areas. While the techniques reviewed represent "best practice," they are not considered the only methods of developing efficient content comprehension skills. Principles and practices introduced in earlier chapters establish a foundation that applies to all reading experiences. Strategies such as skimming and scanning, using study guides, and self-questioning are techniques that are most applicable to informational and content reading and are cross-referenced with literature-based practices.

Text Materials

The transition from learning to read to the process of reading to learn can be challenging to a young reader, particularly if the informational text is topically foreign. In the report *Becoming a Nation of Readers* (Anderson, Hiebert, Scott, & Wilkinson, 1985) the transition to content-area textbooks was identified as a child's most likely first experience with frustrations in reading. Rentel, Matchim, and Zutell (1979) proposed that if new learning is to occur through reading text-based information, the reader must already have fundamental knowledge of the concepts and content presented in the readings. For example, a science lesson focusing on the biological functions of the heart requires conceptual understanding of biological systems including muscles, bones, skin, and blood prior to reading to learn more about the heart. Without substantive content knowledge, students experience frustration in attempting to extract meaning from the reading process. While content-based textbooks are designed to provide new information, acquiring the concept of the heart as a muscular pump, for example, can be achieved only if the student is prepared for the concepts and content of the text.

The complexity of syntax, semantics, word knowledge, and word identification skills differs considerably when reading narratives and expository texts. These differences are of serious concern to teachers of deaf and hard of hearing students (King & Quigley, 1985). Differences occur because content-area reading often requires specific concept vocabulary knowledge and definition, while word knowledge in literature may not be as critical to comprehension of the passage. A second distinction is that the vocabulary in literature-based readings may include new terms for already known concepts (e.g., *couple* means "two" or "join"). In content-based text, the instructional goal may include the learning of concepts and the labeling of parts, such as skin, muscles, and bones, as new terms and new concepts. The third differential in word knowledge is the high probability of semantic relatedness among words such as *heart, valve, aorta,* and *ventricles,* whereas narratives and literature-based texts are less likely to use strings of semantically related vocabulary (Armbruster & Nagy, 1992).

Few content-related texts are available for use with students who are deaf or hard of hearing. In fact, many school administrators, parents, and teachers do not feel there is a need for specialized texts. A common practice among programs serving deaf and hard of hearing children is to adopt textbooks used in general education as the basis for curricula in social studies, geography, science, mathematics, and language arts (King, 1983; Takemori & Snyder, 1972; Wathum-Ocama, 1987). When asked to describe their opinions of textbooks available, teachers reported that instructional materials (e.g., textbooks, encyclopedias) incorporated a wide range of concepts with insufficient organization (Anderson & Armbruster, 1984a; Tyson & Woodward, 1989) and were written at a level that was linguistically and semantically too complex for the intended reader (Chall & Conrad, 1990; Wathum-Ocama, 1987). A common practice reported by the teachers was to tell students about a topic or to read the text to the students. Some teachers resorted to the textbook as a topical guideline and relied primarily on activities and lecture as the sources for learning. The net result is that students who are deaf rarely experience reading informational texts and have few opportunities to learn how to learn through reading (Armbruster, 1991). The demand for more appropriately constructed and "readable" content-based texts is outweighed by factors such as economics and demand in the marketplace (Elliot & Woodward, 1990).

Readability

The idea of selecting textbooks that match the reading efficiency of students has received considerable attention for more than a century. Identifying texts that are "readable" or accessible to the reader is one of the many important tasks that determine effective teaching practices. In the broadest sense, readability is a measure of the relationship between the reader and the usefulness of the text in "reading to learn." In an effort to identify text difficulty, several evaluative systems referred to as *readability formulas* have been developed to facilitate the process (Fry, 1990; King & Quigley, 1985; Vacca, Vacca, & Gove, 1995). Estimating readability levels of content-based text materials has focused on the structure and levels of difficulty as indicated through sentence, word, syllable, and letter frequency counts as primary indicators of text difficulty. The unit of measure used to indicate text difficulty is typically expressed as a "grade level," indicating the reading achievement level a student should demonstrate to make an appropriate match. However, reading achievement scores that are obtained on standardized tests are not equivalent or highly correlated with readability measures. The usefulness of readability "scores" is to assist teachers and programs in the comparative evaluation of texts and to provide a developmentally linear guide for developers of instructional materials in their selection of vocabulary and use of linguistic structures.

Fry's Readability Graph (1968, 1990) is the most frequently referenced formula in programs and studies with deaf children (LaSasso, 1978). The Fry grade-level score reflects the level of difficulty in two dimensions: (1) the average number of sentences in a selected 100-word sample passage; and (2) the average number of syllables in the sample passage (Vacca, Vacca, & Gove, 1995). Another type of readability measure is the Syntactic Complexity Formula (Botel & Granowsky, 1972), which yields a score reflecting the complexity of syntactic structures used within the text. Frequency of occurrence and points ranging from zero to three are awarded to specific syntactic structures, based on their complexity level. The score is the average number of points per sentence and can be used to evaluate, compare, and prepare text materials (Dawkins, 1975). Streng, Kretschmer, and Kretschmer (1978) modified the Syntactic Complexity Formula for use with deaf and hard of hearing children, as illustrated in Figure 9.1. However, the majority of teachers of deaf and hard of hearing children do not use readability formulas to determine text difficulty (LaSasso, 1987).

Estimating text difficulty through the use of readability measures provides only a crude assessment of text characteristics with no acceptable assumptions for making a match between the reader and the text (Vacca, Vacca, & Gove, 1995). Readability measures reflect a limited set of variables usually based on linear dimensions such as word count or syntax difficulty. No single measure of text difficulty can account for the complex set of variables within and between the text and the reader. True readability measures are provided only by the ability of the reader to gain meaning from the text. Nelson (1978) recommends that

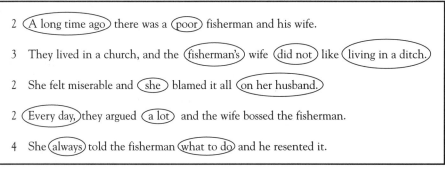

Figure 9.1. Application of adapted Syntactic Complexity Formula. Streng et al. (1978) computed a total score by awarding points for each syntactic structure used. The more complex structures received a greater number of points. The current formula is based on Streng's but modifies it to provide one point for gerunds in object position (rule 22-A) and three points for clauses in object position (rule 35-A). *Note.* Adapted from *Reading and Deafness* (p. 182), by C. King and S. P. Quigley, 1985, San Diego, CA: College-Hill. Story from *Reading Milestones* (level 8, book 5), edited by S. Quigley and C. King, 1984, Austin, TX: PRO-ED, Inc. Reprinted with permission.

content-based texts need to be accessible to the students, and that readability formulas provide inadequate data to determine a student-text match. Functional readability measures require explicit instruction that occurs prior to, during, and after reading informational materials. Students should be prepared to read and learn from the text and from other informational resources and should be guided through the reading process.

Selection of Content-Based Textbooks

The selection of content-related textbooks is not only a challenge to the teacher of deaf and hard of hearing students, it is often described as an impossible task. While a number of linguistically controlled content-based materials were developed specifically for deaf students during the 1970s and 1980s (see King & Quigley, 1985, pp. 166–168), the majority of those materials are out of print or out of date. Specialized content materials have been criticized as being "condescending" to deaf children and too restrictive in scope and sequence (Lane, 1992). In addition, the emphasis on national education standards and the focus of IDEA to include deaf and hard of hearing children in the general education curriculum has discouraged the use of specially designed content-based texts. With few exceptions (see Table 9.1) content materials currently available for deaf and hard of hearing individuals tend to be informational rather than instructional—that is, the materials are not designed to convey a progression of information (King & Quigley, 1985). These informational documents, such as tax guides, computer and Internet user guides, and health care pamphlets, are prepared with the goal of accessibility for deaf adults through the use of controlled linguistic features; these documents are not intended to be instructional tools.

The process of selecting content-based texts and instructional materials includes numerous factors and characteristics that have become increasingly complex with the advent of computer-based and Internet-related resources. Guidelines and checklists available in general introductory texts and professional journals can be used to create a customized set of evaluative criteria that best meets the needs of teachers and students, as well as the curriculum and subject matter (see Beck & McKeown, 1991; Vacca, Vacca, & Gove, 1995). Vacca, Vacca, and Gove (1995) recommend three general factors that need to be considered in analyzing textbook characteristics:

- How difficult is the text to understand?
- How usable is the text?
- How interesting is the text? (pp. 413–415)

Table 9.1

Content-Based Texts Designed for Deaf and Hard of Hearing Students

Author	Title	Content	Grade Level
P. Cunningham & J. Doblmeier	*Botany: The Science of Plants*	Science	High School
J. Kearney	*Loans and Credits*	Mathematics	High School
S. Gillespie	*Map Skills*	Social Studies	Elementary
K. Semanchik	*Music and You*	Science	High School
N. Lederman	*The Science of Sound*	Science	High School
J. Lattyak & S. Dedrick	*Time Concepts*	Mathematics	Elementary
E. Foster	*Time is Now*	Mathematics	Elementary
E. Foster	*Counting Money*	Mathematics	Elementary
M. McGlothlin	*Understanding Math Story Problems*	Mathematics	Elementary

The challenge in matching content-based textbooks, resources, and readers who are deaf and hard of hearing is magnified by the assumptions teachers are required to make regarding word knowledge, transitions between first and second languages, experiences, prior knowledge, linguistic links, and readability levels. Assessment protocols for readability and text accessibility are described in Chapter 10.

Literature

Traditional content-based, textbook-based instruction has received considerable criticism from observers and researchers alike (Guzzetti, Kowalinski, & McGowan, 1992). Critics have noted that textbooks present too many concepts with lists of facts compressed into broad presentations with few opportunities for students to "personalize" the content and concepts of the text. A number of studies have demonstrated that textbooks coupled with worksheet tasks and lecture-recitation sessions are insufficient and ineffective resources for learning (Brozo & Tomlinson, 1986). The alternative has been to supplement content-based textbooks with literature that provides a setting or schema and greater depth and richness of resources related to new concepts. Anders and Guzzetti (1996) identified six reasons for using literature across the curriculum:

1. Literature can accommodate for those students who have difficulty reading textbooks;

2. Literature can motivate those students who find the textbooks boring;

3. Literature can provide a background for concepts in textbooks;

4. Literature can be used as a supplement to the textbook;

5. Literature can provide relevancy to the students' lives; and

6. Literature increases the students' interest in the content area (pp. 112–118).

Developing a literature-based instructional approach to content begins with identifying the most salient concepts to be learned. Structures such as thematic units and integrated learning paradigms generally follow the instructional designs and strategies described in Chapters 6 and 7. Strategies described in this chapter can be applied to literature-based reading as well as content-based texts and instructional materials. While the inclusion of literature as a supplement to informational or content reading has grown exponentially in the past decade, literature as an alternative to textbooks is inadvisable. The demand for fluency and efficiency with informational text is a critical skill in society and the workplace. If students are to reach their full potential as literate adults, explicit instruction and practice with a well-orchestrated and complete curriculum plan in the use of content-based informational materials are required.

Expository Comprehension

Reading is a complex process that includes skills too numerous to address within a book such as this. Expository comprehension adds to the complexity of reading through the explicit goal of obtaining new content-based information from the text. Teachers are challenged by how to teach reading to learn while the students are in the process of learning to become more efficient readers. Research over the past three decades focusing on content reading processes has verified that the strategies used in the reading of content-based textbooks across academic areas (e.g., social studies, mathematics) are fundamentally similar to the processes used in reading narratives, literature, and storybooks. Guzzetti (1982) concluded from her research with elementary school students, comparing literature and content-based reading, that "it is not the content of the material in and of itself that affects the ability of any type of reader to reconstruct meaning. Rather, it is the reader's prior knowledge and interest in content material that influences comprehension" (Anders & Guzzetti, 1996, p. 10). In this section, selected strategies and techniques for use with students who are deaf or hard of hearing are presented to assist teachers in designing instructional programs that promote student comprehension of content-based materials, including prereading, during reading, and postreading activities.

Prereading Activities

Prereading activities connect the student to the informational text and assist them in establishing "anchor points" for what they already know and what they are about to learn (Cooper, 1997). Graves, Watts, and Graves (1994) summarized the seven objectives of prereading activities as: (1) to motivate and set up purposes of reading; (2) to activate background knowledge; (3) to build text-specific knowledge; (4) to teach vocabulary and concepts; (5) to relate the readings to students' lives; (6) to help focus the reading process; and (7) to suggest strategies (p. 140). Prereading activities serve multiple functions in preparing students to engage with content-related text. While these activities are not distinctively different from activities used with narrative text, they may play a more critical role in activating students' prior knowledge, that is, in helping them to recall information they already know, and in the introduction of new concepts. The teacher's role in prereading preparation is critical to the successful comprehension of informational text. Prereading strategies reviewed in Chapters 6 and 7 can also be applied to expository reading. Additional strategies follow.

Previewing

Previewing strategies may include activities such as predicting, questioning, reviewing text materials, and a host of other events that prepare and motivate the student to learn through reading. Previewing may also include specific instruction in the use of reading strategies such as lookback, self-questioning, and preparation for the use of study skills. Each of the activities selected should provide a link between the instructional goals and objectives, the reader, and the informational text to be read.

Prequestions assist students in focusing on the purpose and theme of the reading assignment and the processes used to acquire specific information from the context that is critical to understanding the subject. They are designed by the teacher to activate prior knowledge and to emphasize those aspects of the text that are important. Students can participate in the prequestioning process as a means of identifying their special interests and activating their knowledge of concepts related to the topic. For example, prior to reading about the skeletal system, a fourth-grade teacher displayed a model of a skeleton and several x-rays, photos, and models of skeletal parts in the science corner. The teacher then asked the students to describe the displays and prepared a set of questions: "What would we be like if we didn't have a skeleton? How many bones do you think you have in your body? Do you have more bones now than you had when you were born? How has your skeleton changed as you have gotten older? What makes your skeleton change? What would you do if you broke a bone?" After some discussion, the students generated questions about broken bones, nutrition, and other known concepts. Next, the teacher told the students why she had the skeleton on display and what they were going to learn through reading.

Another prequestioning activity includes predicting and hypothesizing. Predicting events and outcomes as a prereading activity assists the students in bridging the text and the purpose for reading with their own expectations. For example, prior to reading about volcanoes, students recorded their predictions on a computer disk—how it feels to be close to an erupting volcano, its appearance, and its environmental effects. One student chose to illustrate his predictions about places where volcanoes are located on the world map, while another illustrated the process of a volcano erupting. The students' predictions and hypotheses were then saved for review, comparison, and discussion during reading and postreading sessions.

Previewing also includes preteaching of concepts and vocabulary required for comprehension of the text. Graves, Watts, and Graves (1994) emphasized the need for "teaching students to read words that are in their oral and/or signed vocabulary, teaching words and signs that are new labels for known concepts, and teaching words and signs that represent new and potentially difficult concepts" (p. 142). Scientific terms such as *magma*, *lava*, and *geologist* should be represented through finger spelling and print for bilingual students, while conceptual discussions and definitions can be conveyed in the reader's first language. Selected strategies for teaching vocabulary are provided in Chapter 7.

Skimming and Scanning

Skimming is an intensive previewing process that provides readers with an overview and insight into the main ideas and concepts of the text. It is a skill that assists readers in establishing a schematic reference for content and important ideas. Using the skimming strategy, students quickly read items such as key words, phrases, and sentences to get the main idea of a passage (Mercer & Mercer, 1998). Coupled with prereading questions and an overview of the content of the text, skimming can be highly motivating in preparation for making predictions and developing hypotheses about the concepts and content to be read. Students in the lower elementary grades can be introduced to skimming through explicit instruction and modeling by the teacher. Vacca et al. (1995) suggested that students be given an entire passage and told to read the passage in no more than 2 minutes. They should be encouraged to move quickly through each page so they get to the end before the two minutes have passed. The students are then asked to tell or write down what they remember. Discuss with the students what they recall from skimming the text and how they used key words and text organization to help them skim. An alternative skimming procedure recommended by Mercer and Mercer (1998) includes the following steps:

1. Read the title and headings (dark print) as they appear.

2. Read the introduction (i.e., a few paragraphs at the beginning of a chapter or article).

3. Read the first sentence of each subsequent paragraph. In textbooks, the first sentence usually contains the main idea of the paragraph.

4. Read the captions of pictures and study any illustrations in the chapter.

5. Read the conclusion or chapter summary (p. 553).

Discuss with the students why skimming is a helpful strategy and how it can assist them in their daily reading. Have them identify when skimming is useful in locating important facts. Illustrate times when it is inappropriate to use skimming and ask the students to generate their own examples of skimming applications. While discussing the skimming procedure, ask the students if they noticed other aspects of the text that helped them make meaning of the words on the page. Model for the students how skimming can be useful as a prereading activity, particularly when they are searching for specific information from resources and reference materials.

Scanning is a variation of skimming, with the goal of locating specific information within a text. While students are required to read quickly through a text, they are required to retain specific information and to anticipate how that information might appear. Activities that may be useful in developing scanning skills include locating key words in the dictionary, identifying the time or place of events published in the newspaper, and responding to factual questions within a short passage. Mercer and Mercer (1998) developed a five-step scanning system for use with students:

1. Remember the specific questions to be answered.

2. Estimate in what form the answer will appear (i.e., word, name, number, graphic, date).

3. Use the expected form of the answer as a clue for locating it.

4. Look for clues by moving the eyes quickly over the page. When a section that appears to contain the answer is found, read it more carefully.

5. Find the answer, record it, and stop reading.

Skimming and scanning are useful strategies for students to become acquainted with the content of texts they are about to read, to locate specific information quickly, and to review resources for future readings. Skimming and scanning are particularly beneficial when using content-based resources through the Internet and Web pages. Locating specific links and pages and identifying headings and subheadings requires the user to skim and scan large numbers of screens for access entry points and information desired.

Advanced Organizers

An advanced organizer is "any effort by a teacher to prepare students conceptually for incoming information by hooking the major concepts of the new information to the concepts already possessed by the learners" (Swaby, 1983, p. 76). Organizers are packaged in a variety of activities, illustrations, discussions, and written presentations. Chapter 7 illustrates a number of graphic organizers that are used as part of the literature-based reading and comprehension process. Advanced organizers occur as a prereading activity with the objective of bridging what the students know with new information presented in the text.

Advanced organizers should emphasize important concepts and ideas presented in the content-based text. It is important to focus on the key concepts and to reduce extraneous information within the organizer. Regardless of the form that the advanced organizers are given (e.g., illustrations, discussions, analogies), they should be carefully prepared to incorporate students' culture, experiences, and knowledge with ideas presented in the text. Personalizing the organizer and using real-life experiences builds stronger connections between the students and their readiness for reading to learn (Vacca et al., 1995).

Visual advanced organizers were developed by Diane Joseph (1989) as prereading activities for science-based text materials with elementary school children who were deaf. Static organizers use simple illustrations with labels for key concepts in the text. Dynamic organizers incorporate semantic mapping and relational graphic displays to illustrate more dynamic concepts (see Figure 9.2). While both types of organizers helped to prepare students for text comprehension, a critical component in facilitating the links between the organizer and the text was the teacher. While organizers such as pictures, discussions, models, illustrations, and video displays are intended to prepare the student for

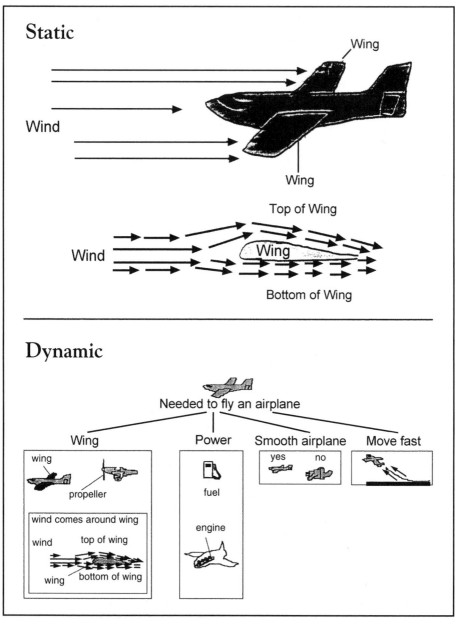

Figure 9.2. Static and dynamic organizers. *Note.* From *The Effects of Visual Structural Overviews and Advanced Organizers on Deaf Students' Reading Comprehension,* by D. Joseph, 1989, unpublished doctoral dissertation, University of Minnesota, Minneapolis. Reprinted with permission.

contextual reading, the bridge between the prereading activities and the text must be carefully constructed by the teacher. Well-prepared questions and discussion connecting the student's experiences and knowledge base with the information presented in the organizer provide the foundation for passage into the content-based text. Without bridging organizers and other prereading activities, students may have difficulty or fail to apply their prior knowledge to the text, thus preventing the construction of meaning.

Additional Strategies

Strategies that may be taught prior to reading expository text include studying the organizational and typographical aids such as chapter titles, subheadings, and bold and italicized print. Teachers can illustrate the organizational structure that is created through headings and subheadings, drawing analogies to the process of note taking and outlining. Students may be asked why they think the author used elements such as headings and bold print. The process of reading to the end of a paragraph or section and pausing to think about what was learned and how much was understood is an important strategy for students to acquire and could be modeled by the teacher. The teacher should discuss with students the importance of understanding key words in the title and subheadings and what resources are available both within the content of the text and through alternative references such as cooperative-learning group discussions, dictionaries, encyclopedias, computer-based software, and Internet resource displays. Another strategy that may be included in prereading activities is the study of illustrations, diagrams, and graphs contained within the text (Graves, Watts, & Graves, 1994). Teachers may elect to practice with the students activities such as skimming through the reading selection and reviewing visual information to make predictions and draw hypotheses about the text. Vacca et al. (1995) provided a list of text-related previewing strategies that can be used as a guide and practiced with students until they are able to guide themselves:

- Read the title, converting it into a question.
- Read the introduction, summary, and study questions, stating the main points.
- Read the heads and subheads; then convert them to questions.
- Read any highlighted print.
- Study visual materials; what do pictures, maps, and such tell about a chapter's content? (pp. 432–433)

Reading Activities

Effective content-based reading requires that students be adequately prepared for the concepts and content to be read and be able to engage in reading with a purpose and a sense of control of the text. During-reading strategies are used to assist students in reading for meaning, reading to learn new information, and monitoring their own comprehension of the text. The strategies described in this section are focused on content-based texts designed to develop good readers. These strategies can be effective only if students are prepared to read the text and the text is accessible to the students. Effectiveness of each of the strategies discussed here and in previous chapters can be modeled for students with specific skills and communication avenues that will be helpful in guiding them through the process of reading expository text.

Study Guides

Study guides can be developed to support and direct students during informational reading and to assist readers in independently identifying important points (Armbruster, Anderson, & Ostertag, 1989; Wood, Lapp, & Flood, 1992). They may be designed to incorporate a broad range of comprehension strategies and may be adapted to meet the individual needs of students as they progress through the reading materials. Study guides used with early elementary students have two or three fundamental questions and may include illustrations and graphics as supporting information. As students become more proficient and independent in the use of study guides with informational text, the complexity of the design can be enhanced to provide greater support in content-related topics (see Wood et al., 1992).

An increasing number of study guides that are commonly related to specific reading assignments and projects are available on Web sites for use with secondary and postsecondary students. Computer-based study guides can be linked to teacher-developed and Internet dictionaries and other resources that assist the student in content-related comprehension and concept development. Study guides may incorporate literature-based readings as well, extending and integrating textbook data with narrative information.

The primary objectives for the use of study guides are to develop: "(1) skills and strategies necessary for effective reading, and (2) an understanding of a significant segment of a content area" (Wood et al., 1992, p. 5). Cooper (1997) developed a set of guidelines for the design and construction of study guides that can easily be applied to reading practices with deaf and hard of hearing students:

- Determine your purpose.

- Decide on the amount of support you want to provide.

- When putting the study guide together, follow the flow of the chapter. Since the activities and questions should help students actively construct meaning, it is important to focus on ideas in the order they appear.

- Include opportunities for students to write.

- Incorporate opportunities for students to make predictions about and monitor their reading.

- Provide questions and activities that bring out key concepts or main ideas.

- Include activities and questions on all study guides that require students to think about and make use of what they have read.

- Provide activities and questions that will pull together or summarize the text. (pp. 440–447)

Features that can be incorporated into study guides include illustrated or graphic sidebars that help students with word knowledge and text structure, and highlighted clues that explicitly guide students in strategies such as repeated reading, lookback, and self-questioning. Computer-based study guides may be linked to ASL or Cued Speech video dictionaries and supportive video displays that assist students in the comprehension of concepts within the text. Study guides provide a concise and focused perspective of the reading materials.

Anticipation guides are a type of study guide consisting of statements for students to consider as part of the prereading, reading and postreading activities (Vacca et al., 1995; Wood, Lapp, & Flood, 1992). Anticipation guides evolved from the early works of Herber (1970) and his interests in reading guides. Some examples are given in Chapter 7. Various types of guides have been developed for use in content-area reading, including Prediction Guides (Nichola, 1983) and the Extended Anticipation Guide (Duffelmeyer, Baum, & Merkley, 1987). Anticipation guides are developed by the teacher and used with the explicit purpose of preparing students for content-area reading.

The teacher prepares the anticipation guide statements and introduces the guide as a prereading, during-reading, and postreading activity. For example, in preparation for reading a science text about spiders, a teacher prepared an anticipation guide for the students. The students were told to mark the statements they agreed with and be prepared to give at least two reasons that they agreed or disagreed with the following statements (Quigley, Paul, McAnally, Rose, & Payne, 1991):

- Spiders can be found in almost any place in the world.

- Most spiders have eight eyes, but they cannot see very well. They are near-sighted.

- Female spiders live longer than male spiders.

- Most spiders are friendly to humans and are important to the environment.

- Spiders' enemies are other spiders and animals that catch small creatures, such as frogs, toads, and birds.

- Spiders can live only in warm climates.

- Male spiders live longer than female spiders.

Following a discussion in which students presented their choices and hypotheses on why they agreed or disagreed, the students read the passage about spiders as an independent assignment. The next day, during the postreading activities, the students reviewed their anticipation guides and revisited their responses based on the information learned through reading. The anticipation guides used in the prereading activities functioned as an advance organizer, as well as a tool for the teacher to identify students' prior knowledge and preparation for the content concepts. During reading, the anticipation guides provided students with references for important facts and findings. Postreading activities included locating information in the text that supported student responses on the anticipation guide.

Effective use of techniques such as the anticipation guide or other study guides mandates the active involvement of students in discussion and analysis of the content-related statements. For those students who are not active participants in the process, the checklist becomes a routine activity of comprehension assessment with little value as a comprehension strategy (Wood et al., 1992) or a technique for reading to learn.

Self-Questioning on Main Ideas

Taylor et al. (1995) reviewed the self-questioning-on-main-ideas study strategy used with middle and secondary school students, focusing on the comprehension of expository text. The technique teaches the students how to identify the main idea in each paragraph using key questioning elements of what, why, how, and when. Once the main idea is identified, the students are taught to develop a question and the answer to the question using the main idea. The first element guides the reader to ask and answer *what* is the topic and main idea of the paragraph. The second element focuses on *why* comprehension of the reading material is an important component of the reading process. The third element models *how* the self-questioning strategy is used. Taylor et al. (1995) described this element in the following manner:

First, the teacher demonstrates how to identify the main ideas for paragraphs, then decides on one or two words that state the topic of the paragraph. Next, a main idea sentence about the topic of the paragraph is generated. The teacher provides several examples of possible main idea sentences for a particular paragraph as well as several inappropriate main idea sentences. Then the students are shown how to generate and answer a question about the main idea and are provided with several examples of possible questions that could have been generated for a particular paragraph. Several inappropriate questions are also discussed. (p. 246)

The final element is *when* students should use the self-questioning strategy. Generally, students are encouraged to use the technique when reading informative text that is difficult to comprehend. Modeling and guided self-questioning practice should be provided by the teacher until the student is able to demonstrate independent skills in generating questions.

Ellis and Lenz (1997) developed a pneumonic tool for use in self-questioning on main ideas. The acronym FIST may be displayed on the student's desk or a bookmark as a reminder to use the strategy while reading.

- First sentence in the paragraph is read.
- Indicate a question using the information in the first sentence.
- Search for the answer to the question.
- Tie the answer to the question in your own words.

The self-questioning-on-main-ideas strategy was initially used with secondary low-achieving students (Andre & Anderson, 1978–79) and later applied to middle school readers (Davey & McBride, 1986). While no known studies are available regarding the effectiveness of self-questioning on main ideas with deaf or hard of hearing students, Strassman (1997) observed instruction in general self-questioning strategies and noted that the strategy was beneficial in reading comprehension with middle school students who were deaf.

Reciprocal Teaching

Reciprocal teaching is a procedure developed and investigated by Palincsar and Brown (1984). It was designed to teach students how to approach and apply strategies to content-based text. The emphasis is placed on students developing independence in the selection and use of reading strategies that will help them construct meaning from the text. It extends the practice of simply teaching students how to use comprehension strategies to developing students as strategic users and thinkers. With more than 40 specific strategies to select from, teachers need to be flexible and acutely aware of the specific strengths and needs each student brings to the reading task (Palincsar, 1986; Wittrock, 1983). In addition, reciprocal teaching is highly dependent on the teacher's ability to interact with students as a model for reading comprehension using four specific activities or strategies as the structure for each lesson:

1. *Summarizing*—identifying and paraphrasing the main idea of the text.

2. *Question generating*—self-questioning about the type of information that is generally tapped on tests of comprehension and recall.

3. *Clarifying*—discerning when there has been a breakdown in comprehension and taking the necessary action to restore meaning (e.g., reading ahead, rereading, asking for assistance).

4. *Predicting*—hypothesizing what the structure and content of the text suggest will be presented next. (Palincsar, 1986, p. 119)

The reciprocal teaching process begins with a daily practice in which the teacher models and provides instruction in the four comprehension strategies while reading a selected text with the students. For example, the teacher introduces the title of the reading passage and then engages in a dialogue with the students, making predictions about what they might expect to read. While recording predictions, the teacher encourages the students to use what they already know about the topic coupled with information from the title to shape their hypotheses. The next step is silent reading with the students, followed by a question generation session about the text. In this phase, the teacher models questions about the content, with the students responding, and discusses the topic using the self-questioning strategy. The third step is the teacher's summary of the reading and a discussion, with the students elaborating on the summary with their own comments. The fourth step is a transition from the summary into clarifications about the text. In this phase, the teacher models a variety of strategies that students can use to remedy any breakdown in comprehension.

The "reciprocal" component of instruction occurs as the teacher and students practice the four-step process daily, with the teacher gradually relinquishing the teaching to the students. As the students progress in their familiarity with the process, the teacher transfers the modeling role and decision-making responsibilities to the students. As the students assume the teaching role, the classroom teacher becomes the coach and mentor, introducing additional strategies, providing feedback and support, and guiding students in making choices on how and what strategies can be used to increase comprehension.

While reciprocal teaching has had a positive impact in teaching students how to study and how to learn from content-based text, the process requires that teachers be particularly skilled in leading discussions, engaging students in the process, and retreating when appropriate. The classroom teacher must determine how much, when, and what type of support each student needs. Reciprocal teaching requires practice and preparation. Hermann (1988) emphasized the need for teachers to be well prepared for the implementation of reciprocal teaching. He recommended that text segments be carefully selected to accommodate the four-step comprehension activities, and that questions and predictions be prepared for each passage. It is important for the teacher to anticipate, particularly in the initial instruction phase, that students will not be familiar with making predictions or with questioning strategies. Hermann also suggested underlining main ideas and summary sentences and noting words that may be particularly challenging to the reader to assist students as they assume the teaching role.

Additional Strategies

A variety of strategies are used by individuals during the process of reading as ways and means of making the text meaningful and memorable. Underlining the main idea or key words, outlining, note taking, and using graphic organizers are just a few of literally dozens of techniques that can be used to enhance the study skills and comprehension of content-based literature. Ellis and Lenz (1997) developed two cognitive activities for note taking and study skills. The first is CAN DO, which is designed for acquiring and recalling content information:

- Create a list of items to be learned.
- Ask yourself if the list is complete.
- Note the main ideas and details using a free diagram.
- Describe each component and how it relates to others.
- Overlearn main parts, then supporting details.

RIDER is another pneumonic tool introduced by Ellis and Lenz (1987), which uses visual imagery strategies in which students are guided to develop visual representation of concepts and ideas of the text and to progressively modify those images as they read the next statement. Imagery has had a positive effect on reading comprehension with elementary and secondary school readers (Gambrell & Bales, 1986). Students are instructed to picture in their mind what they read in the first sentence (e.g., *Have you ever folded a piece of paper and sailed it across the room?*). The students are then asked to tell what they remember about the sentence. Teacher–student discussions help to develop an image for information not recalled. Then students read the next sentence (e.g., *You can discover how a plane stays in the air from the gliding piece of paper.*) and add to or change their image of events based on new information (Taylor et al. , 1995). The steps of RIDER are as follows:

- **R**ead the sentence.

- **I**magine. Mentally make a picture or an image.

- **D**escribe how the new image is different from the one for the last sentence.

- **E**valuate the image to make sure it is complete.

- **R**epeat the steps to RIDE as you read the next sentence (Ellis & Lenz, 1997).

Studies reviewing the effectiveness of strategies such as these have concluded that their effectiveness is highly dependent on the ability of the reader to implement techniques as a bridge to the content and concepts to be learned (Anderson & Armbruster, 1984b). In Chapter 6 and 7 of this book several other strategies are discussed that may be used during reading, including summarizing, the PREP system for study, and the SQ3R techniques.

Postreading Activities

Postreading activities are a critical component in the expository reading process and are considered as part of the whole planning process. In addition to providing reinforcement and clarification in making meaning of the text, postreading activities provide students with opportunities to extend what they have learned from the text to sharing their opinions about what they read and applying that information to their own lives. Strategies introduced in the prereading phase, such as making predictions and hypothesizing and developing prior knowledge maps and lists, are effective only when postreading activities are activated.

Postreading discussions may be teacher directed or take place in student-centered groups such as "cooperative learning" or "buzz" group. Discussion skills such as watching and listening to other students, respecting opinions, providing constructive feedback, and participating and leading discussions require explicit instructional plans and must be explicitly modeled within the classroom. Alvermann, Dillion, and O'Brien, (1987) pointed out that discussions and the students' ability to gain information from discussion groups do not "just happen."

In addition to discussion sessions during postreading activities, writing and retelling are equally important strategies for comprehension and help students reconstruct schemata with the addition of new information. Application and practice through writing, retelling, and activities such as dramatics and "doing something" (e.g., baking, building, making) with the new knowledge are all considered invaluable to the comprehension of content-based text.

Writing About Content

Writing about content areas is as important to the development of literacy as reading literature, particularly when the emphasis is placed on process-oriented writing (Anders & Guzzetti, 1996). The process of writing about content provides students with an opportunity to formulate ideas about the text and personalize the concepts through their own words and style of expression. Content-based writing is not only a valuable tool for recall and study skills, it is also an important literacy skill for independent living and learning. Content-based or informational writing is "real-world writing." Recording events, making grocery lists and notes, requesting information, and participating in subject-centered listservs are just a few examples of the need for expository writing.

Early "writing" about content topics may include sequencing or illustrating pictures related to information read with the students, such as a selection explaining how a seed grows into a tree. As writing skills develop, students may include content writing through visual mapping, classification tables, and report writing. Ruddell (1963) suggested that content teachers establish a writing routine with their students in which journals or logs can be shared, with the teacher incorporating expository writing. Inclusive in the process are reporting of facts, observations, cause-effect events, and relational comments in which students are able to relate new concepts learned to what they already know.

Wilson (1996) developed an "expert" postreading writing activity with secondary-level students who were deaf. As part of the social studies curriculum, students selected topics of special interest. Working in small groups, they studied an interest area in depth, conducting a search for literature-based and reference information. Using their notes, discussions, and resources, they developed a computer-based expert system that could be used by other students, introducing concepts and information related to their topic of study. The format of the expert system required students to plan, compose, and edit brief informational paragraphs, question-and-answer items, and alternative mappings and feedback forms. All the students who participated in the development of the expert systems had greater recall of the subject matter than students who did not engage in writing as a postreading activity.

Cudd and Roberts (1989) used a variety of paragraph frames that gave readers a reference for organizing information and writing about it. A summary of different types of paragraph frames with examples of "word frames" is provided in Table 9.2.

Such additional writing strategies as prediction logs, reciprocal questioning (ReQuest), story maps, time lines, and comparison and cause-effect charts (discussed in Chapter 7) are systematic procedures that help readers organize information and understand content.

Writing about content begins with teacher modeling and guided practice. Content teachers should be encouraged to write to their students and with their students about content-related topics. Report writing, observations, newspaper reporting, and providing directions are all part of the content-based writing process, in which students are engaged in informational writing. Students should also be encouraged to use writing about what they read as a strategy for recall and remembering and for communication (Taylor et al., 1995).

Armbruster (1991) made six recommendations for increasing comprehension and fluency in writing content-based text that are highly applicable for use with students who are deaf or hard of hearing. The first recommendation supports an integrated literature-based and content-based text approach in which concepts learned can be applied to new knowledge across disciplines. The second recommendation is to encourage students at all levels to engage in reading and writing informational materials for real-world applications. The third area emphasizes the use of scaffolding instruction, in which modeling and guided

Table 9.2
Paragraph Frames

Type	Definition	Word Frames
Sequential	Sequence of events	First . . . Next . . . Finally . . .
Enumeration	Begins with the main idea and includes other important ideas that are not sequenced	Summary statement For example . . . In addition . . . In conclusion . . .
Reaction	Responds to what was read	Summary statement Before I read this, I knew . . . I learned that . . . An interesting thing was . . . I want to learn about . . .
Compare	Tells how two or more things are similar	. . . are similar in several ways . . . First . . ., second . . ., finally . . .
Contrast	Tells how two or more things are different	. . . differ in many ways . . . first . . ., second . . ., finally . . .

Note. Adapted from Reading Difficulties: Instruction and Assessment (2nd ed.) (pp. 247–248), by B. Taylor, L. A. Harris, P. D. Pearson, and G. Garcia, 1995, New York: McGraw-Hill. Copyright 1995 by McGraw-Hill. Adapted with permission.

reading of texts and informational resources demonstrate and support the development of strategic readers who are able to read and study independently. The fourth recommendation focuses on the need for explicit and modeled instruction in prereading, during-reading, and after-reading strategies to enable students to manage their own reading activities, build connections between what they know and what they have learned, and use the reading-writing connection to increase comprehension. The fifth area encourages the use of collaborative learning activities between teacher and student and among students. The final suggestion focuses on the quality of teacher training to assure that teachers are prepared to implement the five recommendations.

Summary

This chapter has focused on reading to learn, with specific emphasis on strategies and techniques that can be used with deaf and hard of hearing students in content-based instruction. While little differences exist in the processes of learning to read and reading to learn, expository reading and writing are distinctive in purpose and function. In contrast to that of novels and storybooks, expository comprehension is highly dependent upon the reader's interest, motivation, and prior knowledge of the content and concepts. Specific demands are placed on word knowledge, facility with linguistic structures, and organizational skills. While there is a general movement away from teaching deaf and hard of hearing students how to read as they progress through the elementary grades, explicit instruction in the use of strategies in learning through reading should be carefully orchestrated into the reading process across the curriculum and throughout the student's educational experiences. Prereading activities such as the introduction of advance organizers, previewing, skimming, and scanning can assist students in developing a familiarity with and referent for the content to be read. Outlines, study guides, and anticipation guides assist students in focusing on relevant concepts and opportunities to integrate the reading and writing processes as tools for learning. Strategies such as self-questioning, lookback, group discussions, note taking, visual imagery, and summarizing contribute to efficiency and proficiency in reading to learn.

While the availability of content-based texts designed specifically for use with students who are deaf or hard of hearing has declined dramatically in the past decade, selection of content-based texts and instructional materials should be made on the basis of their accessibility, interest, and relevance to the needs and goals established with the student. While available textbooks have generally underserved students who are deaf or hard of hearing, access to resources such as Web pages, the Internet, virtual museums, videos, newspapers, and magazines can enhance concept development, reading comprehension, and expository writing opportunities. Unfortunately, there is a dearth of research available on content reading and strategies that are most effective with students who are deaf or hard of hearing. The strategies for prereading, during-reading, and postreading activities reviewed in this chapter and previous chapters are only as effective as the teacher who provides the instruction.

CHAPTER

ASSESSMENT

Preview

Assessment is a broad term that is frequently applied to acts of testing, measurement, and evaluation of products, portfolios, and self reports. Tests may be classified as standardized, norm-referenced, and criterion-referenced, while use of the broader term *assessment* is generally divided into categories of formal and informal. Classroom assessment of reading and writing is complex and cannot be simply quantified onto a continuum. It is an "interpretive process" (International Reading Association & National Council of Teachers of English, 1994, p. 11) that is influenced by diverse relationships including cultural backgrounds, experiences, abilities, and items and tools used. Teachers are often faced with the dilemma of engaging in the process of assessment in response to multiple needs expressed by parents, students, administrators, and political officials.

Assessment of reading and writing abilities of deaf and hard of hearing students has focused primarily on tests that have been designed and standardized for hearing students (Bradley-Johnson & Evans, 1991). It is important to understand the principles and relationships of assessment and instruction and to be able to select or design procedures that will assist in identifying and demonstrating the reading processes used by deaf students. Mesick (1988) emphasized the need for "appropriateness, meaningfulness and usefulness" (p. 35) of the information gleaned from assessment and the inferences drawn from the data as an integral part of instructional planning and evaluation. This chapter provides an overview of assessment and testing, emphasizing issues that are particularly relevant to the education of deaf and hard of hearing students.

Purpose of Assessment

Selection of measurement tools and application of data acquired from the assessment process are primarily dependent on the purpose. Kavale (1979) cautioned that if the purpose of assessment is unknown, "the best test to use is none" (p. 9). Generally, assessments are conducted to determine students' abilities and instructional needs, as well as the effectiveness of instruction, and to monitor students' progress. The International Reading Association and the National Council of Teachers of English (IRA & NCTE, 1994) developed 10 fundamental standards for the assessment of reading and writing (see Table 10.1). A review of those standards emphasizes the need for the purpose to be student-centered and clearly articulated with instruction. The usefulness of assessments and their results depends on the interaction of: (a) the knowledge, skills, and goals of the assessor; (b) the tools used to gather information; (c) the characteristics of the individual assessed; and (d) the knowledge, product, or

Table 10.1
IRA & NCTE Standards for the Assessment of Reading and Writing

1. The interests of the student are paramount in assessment.
2. The primary purpose of assessment is to improve teaching and learning.
3. Assessment must reflect and allow for critical inquiry into curriculum and instruction.
4. Assessments must recognize and reflect the intellectually and socially complex nature of reading and writing and the important roles of school, home, and society in literacy development.
5. Assessment must be fair and equitable.
6. The consequences of an assessment procedure are the first, and most important, consideration in establishing the validity of the assessment.
7. The teacher is the most important agent of assessment.
8. The assessment process should involve multiple perspectives and sources of data.
9. Assessment must be based in the school community.
10. All members of the educational community—students, parents, teachers, administrators, policy makers, and the public—must have a voice in the development, interpretation, and reporting of assessment.

Note. From *Standards for the Assessment of Reading and Writing* (pp. 13–38), by the International Reading Association and National Council of Teachers of English, 1994, Newark, DE: Author. Copyright 1994 by the International Reading Association. Reprinted with permission.

process that is assessed. Taylor et al. (1995) referred to the fact that in an ideal educational world, the purpose of assessment would be indistinguishable from the relationships between a student's development of literacy and instruction. For all practical purposes, teachers should be able to gather information about a student's reading and writing abilities and apply that information to instructional growth within daily routines.

Student Performance and Instructional Needs

The single most important focus of assessment is the student. Assessments help to identify what students already know, what they need to know, and what they are learning (Cooper, 1997). Assessments focused on student performance should identify the literacy strategies that the student is using and evaluate the effectiveness of instruction and whether it should be changed or adapted to foster more efficient growth. Teachers of students who are deaf and hard of hearing are consistently confronted with the dilemma of attempting to define the most appropriate curricular and instructional goals. Assessment provides the foundation for curricular adaptations, instructional planning, and student progress.

Assessment of literacy among deaf and hard of hearing students has traditionally used standardized testing of reading achievement and linguistic analysis of writing samples for the purpose of group comparisons, grade equivalencies, and research. Teachers have relied on a variety of informal observational data, as well as their experience and personal knowledge of literacy development to determine the direction for instruction. Concern about low reading achievement levels among deaf children has led to an increased emphasis and need for accountability systems in the teaching of reading and writing. Teachers of deaf and hard of hearing children have become increasingly sensitive and aware of assessment protocols and the dearth of research on informative assessment practices.

King and Quigley (1985) identified six areas in which the performance of deaf students is influenced by assessment tasks. These areas include (1) the parameters surrounding the assessment task; (2) the type of task; (3) the format of the task; (4) the type of information assessed; (5) the reader-based variables; and (6) the text-based variables. While research on each of these variables is limited (see King & Quigley, 1985, pp. 216–238), special consideration should be given to tasks that have been identified as affecting deaf and hard of hearing students' literacy and assessment outcomes. A summary of recommendations related to these areas includes the following:

Assessment Protocol

- Knowledge of and practice with test-taking strategies should be provided.
- Explicit instruction in the use of lookback strategies should be included in the curriculum.
- Silent reading of text should precede oral or sign reading.

Type of Task

- Recognition tasks tend to yield higher scores than recall tasks.
- Instruction should be provided in the problem-solving strategies used in recognition and recall tasks.

Type of Information

- Explicit and implicit questioning strategies should be introduced at all levels of reading comprehension.
- Practice in making predictions should be provided using prior knowledge and information in the text.

Reader-Based Variables

- All assessment strategies should be reviewed to eliminate economic and culturally based variables.
- The teacher/assessor should determine that the reader has appropriate prior knowledge.
- Common proficiency in language should be evident between the reader and the person(s) conducting and interpreting the assessment data.

Text-Based Variables

- Directions should be provided that are clearly understood and in the language of the reader.
- Reading materials and assessments should be selected that are within the linguistic and instructional level of the reader.

The framework for assessing deaf and hard of hearing children is influenced by a number of variables, particularly the assessor's communication match with the student and the assessor's ability to be acutely aware of the skills the student brings to the reading task. For example, teachers are challenged by students whose oral productions may not be sufficiently precise to determine miscues in the analysis of reading fluency. Students with English as a second language require instruction in the use of strategies for making a transition from their first language to their second language. In addition, students who are deaf and are members of other cultural groups may bring a third language as a significant variable into the testing and assessment process. These issues and other general issues such as language, experience, economics, placement, and family support impact on the selection and systems used to assess a deaf or hard of hearing student's literacy skills and on the applicability of the results.

Instructional Accountability

Accountability has become a significant issue in the education of deaf and hard of hearing children. Assessment data resulting from national studies as well as local research efforts have implicitly defined the conditions of accountability within programs for students with hearing loss (Allen, 1986; Andrews, Winograd, & DeVille, 1994; Davey & LaSasso, 1985; Holt, 1994; Strassman, 1997) and explicitly attributed the inadequate English literacy among deaf children to the ineffectiveness of instructional strategies (Paul, 1996; Strassman, 1997). The reauthorization of the Individuals with Disabilities Education Act (IDEA) has placed a new emphasis on accountability by mandating student goals and indicators to determine the effectiveness of instruction. This mandate focuses on the inclusion of students who are deaf or hard of hearing in district and state testing practices and general education performance standards. Specifically, IDEA (Sec. 612 (a) (17) (B)) mandates that deaf and hard of hearing children participate in state and local district/school assessments. State and local educational agencies must make the results of assessments public through the reporting of group performance levels and the number of deaf and hard of hearing children participating in regular and alternative assessments. Section 614 (d) of IDEA requires that the IEP include specifications regarding modifications made to accommodate the needs of the student. If a child does not participate in the general education reading and writing assessments, the IEP must include a statement regarding why it was not appropriate and what alternative form of assessment will be used to determine student progress. While accountability statements within IDEA provide general guidelines, the responsibility for monitoring students' progress is placed on educators who are providing direct instruction and services to children who are deaf or hard of hearing.

Performance Standards

The emphasis on national performance standards and on state and national tests has gained momentum not only within IDEA, but also within political, social, and economic circles surrounding schools. School districts failing to meet predetermined literacy levels are being threatened with "take over" by state agencies. Test results of local school programs, including residential and day school programs for deaf and hard of hearing students, are made available to the public for the purpose of accountability and comparison.

Performance standards are neither new nor innovative. Perhaps the earliest recorded performance standard was developed by Jacobo Rodriguez Pereira (1715–90), who established learner objectives for each deaf student in his tutelage. Upon a student's achievement of the objective, Pereira received a fee for demonstrating accountability in his teaching (Bender, 1960). Similar practices of payment for instructional outcomes occurred throughout England and France during the 19th century. Schools have experienced a variety of movements driven by testing and assessments, such as "outcome-based education," "statements of competency," "learner objectives" (Tyler, 1949), and "mastery of learning" (Nelson, 1998). Current practices focus on "basic standards" of literacy that specify skills, scores, or more general descriptions of performance that students must achieve prior to graduation. For example, the State of California included the following as part of the language arts standard for graduation:

> Students will analyze the philosophical arguments presented in literary works, determining whether the author's position has contributed to the quality of the work and the believability of the character. (Jago, 1998, p. 685)

Standards for achievement and the means for assessing the degree to which students meet those standards vary considerably within and between local and national programs. Norm-referenced tests such as the *Iowa Test of Basic Skills* and the *Stanford Achievement Test* are commonly used as indicators of achievement in some schools, while other schools have developed tests or performance criteria for portfolios that display products of students' literacy skills. For example, the State of Minnesota provides a "basic standards" test in reading, mathematics, and written composition that students must pass to graduate. In addition, "high standards" have been identified and students are assessed through performance measures to determine if they achieve those standards (Minnesota Department of Children, Families and Learning, 1997). Figure 10.1 illustrates a sample of a performance measure for reading.

In accordance with IDEA, achievement tests are given to *all* students following state and local guidelines, with the option of accommodations or modifications for those students with IEPs. Tindal, Heath, Hollenbeck, Almond and Harniss (1998) studied the effects of two accommodation conditions on statewide achievement tests. In the first condition, half of the mathematics word

---

A *student shall demonstrate comprehension of literal meaning by:*

Reading, listening, and viewing nonfiction and fiction selection to:

- identify main ideas and support details;

- retell main events or ideas in sequence through oral reading and retelling;

- pronounce new words using phonics through oral reading and retelling;

- demonstrate techniques of improving and expanding vocabulary through a vocabulary log;

- demonstrate age-appropriate reading rate through oral reading and retelling;

- interpret figurative language through fiction and nonfiction journals;

- make predictions based on information in the selection through fiction and non-fiction journals; and

- compare and contrast settings, ideas, or actions through fiction and nonfiction journals.

Figure 10.1. Sample of a performance measure for profile of learning standards. *Note.* From *Profile of Learning Standards,* by Minnesota Department of Children, Families and Learning, 1998, St. Paul, MN: Office of Graduation Standards.

problems were given under the standard paper-and-pencil testing practices, and the remainder of the problems were read orally to the students. Performance scores of fourth-grade special education students were significantly better when the problems were read to the students. No significant effects were found for the second accommodation, in which students were allowed to mark their responses directly in the test booklet rather than transferring their responses to an answer sheet. While no research has been conducted regarding accommodations for deaf and hard of hearing students, current practices include the presentation of directions through sign language, use of cued speech interpretation for auditory-oral assessments, ASL translation of math word problems, extended time, and small group administration. Examples of modifications include lowering the minimum score for "passing" the student and selection of an alternative test (e.g., *Test of Syntactic Ability, Test of Written Language*).

Accommodations and modifications must be carefully considered and integrated into the assessment of student achievement levels (Tindal et al., 1998). While state guidelines vary regarding the notation and impact of achievement testing, the results of including or excluding accommodations can have a significant impact on a student's future. Postsecondary opportunities, including college admission, apprenticeships, and job training, are increasingly connected to state assurances of "mastery of learning" and "basic skill competencies."

Formal Assessments

Formal assessments such as norm-referenced and criterion-referenced tests are measures that provide statistically based systems for comparisons. Formal assessments are generally used in response to social and political concerns, as well as parental request, for making comparisons between groups of students. They are also used to determine placement of students, to monitor student progress, and to provide accountability. Taylor et al. (1995) suggested that these types of tests tend to emphasize what students are unable to do or not do rather than identifying strengths of the student on which the teacher can build. The relationship between formal assessments and instruction is often illusive.

Norm-Referenced Assessments

Norm-referenced tests "provide a way of describing student performance relative to the performance of other students who took the same test" (Graves, Watts, & Graves, 1994, p. 194). Scores may be reported as percentile ranks, which indicate the relative position of each student compared with individuals included in the norm group. For example, if Johnny's reading achievement score is at the 75th percentile, 25% of the individuals in the norm sample received higher scores and 74% received lower scores than Johnny.

Scores on norm-referenced assessments such as the *Stanford Achievement Test* are frequently reported as grade-equivalent scores. These scores are difficult to interpret and may be misleading, particularly to students and their parents, because students are frequently tested "out of level," that is, given test forms intended for younger students. The grade-equivalent score compares a student's performance with the average grade level of students in the norm sample who received the same score on the test. For example, if 10-year-old Anna received a grade-equivalent score of 5.8 on a "level 3" reading comprehension test, her score on the test would have been the same as that of average students in the sample who were in the eighth month of the fifth grade. Grade equivalency scores are not related to readability levels assigned to instructional materials; they are also not equivalent across reading tests (Schreiner, 1979). In addition, few reading and writing tests include deaf and hard of hearing students in the norm-referenced sample.

Standardized Assessments

Most norm-referenced tests are standardized—that is, procedures for administration, scoring, and data interpretation are clearly specified and must be followed to interpret the test results. Generally, standardized reading achievement tests include subtests in areas such as word recognition, word knowledge, comprehension, and composition. Standardized reading tests are used primarily to determine the overall reading performance of a group of students or an individual student compared to a norm sample using standard scores. Subtests on a standardized reading test may be used to identify areas of strength and weakness and provide the teacher with general information that may suggest further assessment or observation. Standardized test scores may also be used to assess students' progress through the comparison of scores over time. Taylor et al. (1995) noted that the majority of formal norm-referenced, standardized reading tests are designed for the average student and cautioned educators regarding the use of such tests with students who have difficulty reading:

> Pupils at the extremes (high or low) are not measured as accurately by tests that are designed for a particular grade level. . . . The bulk of the items on such tests are geared to the level being tested. . . . The result for low-achieving pupils is failure to measure what they do know. (p. 342)

When a test is standardized, any changes in the administration, response, or scoring protocols invalidate the results of the test. For example, the *Peabody Picture Vocabulary Test* (PPVT) is a norm-referenced standardized test that measures an individual's ability to match a picture with a vocabulary word presented orally. Adapting the PPVT by presenting the test items through sign language, finger spelling, cued speech, or print changes the standards of the test and invalidates the test results. Decisions that are made on the basis of invalid test data are unfair to the student and inappropriate for instruction.

Few literacy tests have been standardized with deaf or hard of hearing students. The most widely used achievement test for deaf and hard of hearing students in the United States is the *Stanford Achievement Test–Hearing Impaired*. The SAT–HI has the same subtests as the SAT for hearing individuals; however, components of the subtests have been reorganized into a different subset of test batteries to parallel the development of reading patterns in deaf children. Hotto and Schildroth (1982) provided a set of "dos and don'ts" that are applicable to the use of most norm-referenced and standardized tests with deaf and hard of hearing students:

- To diagnose specific strengths and weaknesses in a skill area, use raw scores.

- To examine a student's growth over one or more academic years, use scaled scores.

- To compare the performance of hearing-impaired students with that of hearing students, use *grade-equivalent scores*. (Do not compare scores across test levels.)

- To compare a hearing-impaired student to a large representative group of hearing-impaired students, use *percentile ranks*.

- Do not view a numerical score as a way to pinpoint ability. Each score represents a range within which a student is performing in a given subject area.

- Do not average subtest scores and expect the overall average to describe a student's achievement. (p. 19)

While standardized tests are widely used, careful consideration must be given to their administration and interpretation. Attention should be given to the selection of standardized assessments that are "culturally and economically inclusive"—that is, items should not exclude the students being tested. For example, while preparing to administer a standardized reading achievement test to urban students with limited economic resources, the teacher, Ms. Gardner, found that the comprehension subtest included three short passages with topics on camping, planning a vacation, and animals in the woods. Prior to administering the test, Ms. Gardner questioned the students about their background knowledge and experiences, asking questions such as: Who has seen animals in the woods? When should we begin to plan a vacation? and How can we prepare for our camping trip? Of the 30 students, only 3 had been on a vacation, and none had experience with or prior knowledge of outdoor camping or animals in the woods. This example illustrates the importance of carefully examining standardized test content. Teachers and school administrators must decide if the test results will provide information needed to make good instructional decisions regarding students and programs.

Diagnostic Assessments

Diagnostic assessments are designed to identify a student's ability to complete or perform a specific task and are usually used to identify skills in the reading process that need to be developed. A variety of standardized diagnostic tests are commercially available (e.g., *Diagnostic Reading Scales, Stanford Diagnostic Reading Test, Woodcock Reading Mastery Tests*) (see Miller, 1986). These tests are generally used once the teacher has identified a student's strengths and weaknesses through either standardized achievement tests or reading survey tests. Standardized diagnostic reading tests are designed to serve those students whose reading performance is below that of their peers. The tests provide a variety of formats for administration, scoring, and evaluation; however, no tests are known to have been standardized for use with deaf or hard of hearing students.

Diagnostic assessments approach reading development from a bottom-up perspective; that is, the reading process is identified through a set of discrete subskills, including competencies in phonics, structural analysis, word knowledge, reading rate, literal comprehension, and inferential comprehension (Watts, Graves, & Graves, 1994). Unlike norm-referenced tests, standardized diagnostic tests do not compare one student to a norm group; rather, the focus is on a set of skills or tasks the student is expected to master. While some test formats may be different from the instructional format, selection of a diagnostic test should be based on its relevancy to the reading process, production of meaningful data, and usefulness in determining instructional goals and strategies for reading and writing.

The following set of questions was initially proposed by Ramsey (1967) and has been adapted to assist teachers in selecting the most appropriate diagnostic assessment tool for their instructional plans:

1. Does the test assess a reading skill or ability in the most natural manner, that is, as the skill would be used in any reading situation?

2. Does the test provide real opportunities for the student to respond and minimize the opportunities for guessing correctly?

3. Does an item assess a specific skill rather than a broad spectrum of abilities?

4. Does the response provide the teacher with opportunities to observe the performance a student is using in a specific reading skill?

5. Does the assessment of comprehension reflect the student's understanding of the text, or is it a measure of other factors such as culture or linguistic fluency?

Diagnostic assessments may be more inclusive than single testing units that are typically isolated from instruction. A teacher may elect to use diagnostic teaching where instruction and diagnosis of reading difficulties are a seamless process. Walker (1996) provided the example of diagnostic teaching in which the instructional goal is focused on the three-step strategy of making predictions, reading to find specific or more information, and summarizing. For example, Alex was engaged in reading about tornadoes and high winds that had hit the area, and summarizing what he had read, his teacher noted that he was unable to sequence events within the story. A diagnostic assessment led to a change in his instructional goals, whereby the teacher introduced a visual story map and provided direct instruction and practice in sequencing events. Walker emphasized that the diagnostic assessment and teaching process should use authentic materials and real literacy activities as part of instruction and have a direct impact on the student's reading and writing abilities.

The use of diagnostic tests and assessment protocols places considerable emphasis on teachers' observation skills and their knowledge of the reading process and complementary instructional strategies. Teachers of students who are deaf or hard of hearing must know the student's language level, be able to comprehend and use the student's communication system, and have an extensive knowledge base in the development of literacy skills, including word knowledge, decoding, and reading comprehension.

Criterion-Referenced Assessments

Criterion-referenced assessments (CRAs) include lists of items or skills that students should be able to do if they have mastered the skill or concept being tested. In contrast to standardized norm-referenced assessments, criterion-referenced assessments identify what a student can do on a particular task. For example: *The student will be able to add the prefixes dis- and un- to base words that are in the third-grade reading basal series with 80% accuracy.* The score of a CRA is related to an "absolute standard," that is, the achievements or mastery a student has accomplished in relationship to the tasks or objectives completed. CRAs are related to diagnostic reading tests and may be used in tandem with them. While diagnostic assessments tend to identify strengths and weaknesses, CRAs emphasize the accomplishment or mastery of specific skills. Both assessment procedures focus on a bottom-up approach to the reading process.

A general concern regarding the use of CRAs is the emphasis placed on a sequence or set of skills that tend to be isolated from the general process of reading. Because reading is a complex process, mastery of specific isolated skills, such as syllabification or the addition of prefixes, may be too far removed from the context of reading (Kavale, 1979). However, CRAs can be useful in developing instructional objectives that promote reading fluency and comprehension. Criterion-assessment tools may be developed for a specific curricula, to be used in classrooms where authentic reading materials are part of the routine progress-monitoring system.

Informal Assessments

Informal assessments are the most frequent method of evaluating instructional effectiveness and students' abilities, progress, and processes used. King and Quigley (1985) divided informal assessment into two categories. The first category includes informal protocols such as the cloze procedure, informal reading inventories (IRIs), and reading miscue inventories (RMIs). The second type focuses on unobtrusive measures and dynamic assessments that are continuous and interwoven into instruction (p. 187). Informal assessments such as checklists, retelling, and anecdotal or running records allow the teacher to construct or select a tool for each student that is instructionally informative and directly related to reading and writing objectives (Taylor et al., 1995). Assessments integrated with instruction allow for frequent and direct measures that guide the teacher's decisions regarding the efficacy of specific strategies in literacy instruction.

Observations and Anecdotal Records

Teachers use a wide range of anecdotal records, such as video and audio records, running records, cumulative product folders, daily notes, and paper-and-pencil tests. Anecdotal records and observations are maintained throughout the academic year and assist in determining the direction of instruction. A critical component of using observations and anecdotal records for assessment is the teacher's clear understanding of what is being observed, as well as the goal of the observation. In addition, there must be a systematic method and a habitual practice of recording observations. Relying on mental notes can become a common practice, particularly when faced with time constraints; however, consistent and regularly recorded observations and notes are the only reliable means of maintaining anecdotal records. Computer-based technologies provide teachers with a variety of formats for reminders and note-keeping systems that are efficient and effective means for maintaining observational data.

The purpose of observations may be sufficiently broad to include such things as the types of reading materials the student selects spontaneously and identification of time spent in independent reading, or it may be specific to word recognition strategies or the vocabulary relationships between English words and ASL vocabulary. A variety of observation checklists are available in professional journals and magazines, in literacy textbooks, and at Web sites.

Cloze Procedures

The cloze procedure has been used as an assessment in reading comprehension in a variety of studies with deaf and hard of hearing children and as a means of determining text difficulty (LaSasso, 1978; Moores, 1987). The format commonly used in the cloze procedure is the open format—that is, the student is required to fill in missing words from a paragraph or short passage. Studies of the cloze procedure have suggested a variety of strengths and weaknesses in its usefulness as a classroom-based assessment of reading. While the test is easy to administer, students have expressed considerable frustration with the difficulty of the task (Pikulski & Pikulski, 1977). Teachers have had difficulty scoring responses that are syntactically and synonymously correct but poorly matched semantically. Concern regarding the focus on sentence comprehension rather than text comprehension by cloze critics has been commonly addressed through assessment construction in which knowledge of the passage is required to complete the cloze response. While the cloze procedure has been highly correlated with reading abilities among both deaf and hearing students, it has also reflected the student's writing skills and facility with language (LaSasso, 1980; Parker, Hasbrouck & Tindal, 1989). Subsequently, a modified format of the cloze procedure has been investigated as a valid means of classroom-based reading assessment. The modified system is referred to as the maze procedure.

In the maze assessment procedure, the student selects one word from a multiple-choice set of responses. The typical maze includes two distracters and the correct response in a three-choice set. One of the distracters is semantically similar to the correct response, while the other is syntactically similar, as illustrated in Figure 10.2. In addition, it is recommended that students be given the opportunity to read the complete passage silently prior to the administration of the maze. The passages selected may be commercially or teacher prepared and directly related to the curriculum and text materials used in the classroom. Commercially prepared passages are generally graduated in difficulty following norms established for hearing students, which are not transferable to deaf or hard of hearing students (Reynolds, 1986). Passage length may range from 100 to 120 words for younger students, while standardized passages (e.g., in *Degree of Reading Power* [DRP]) for more advanced students may contain 300 to 400 words. Parker, Hasbrouck, and Tindal (1989) suggested that passages should be "long enough for internal coherence, but short enough for efficient administration" (p. 231). Deletion of words may be syntactically specific (e.g., nouns and verbs), or it may follow a pattern such as deletion of every seventh word. The process of scoring the maze can provide teachers with critical information regarding the student's comprehension and linguistic skills through careful inspection of the responses. A comprehensive review of research regarding the

---

The ice-cream cone originated in 1904 at the St. Louis World's Fair. Some people (ate, say, frozen) that the cone was invented (what, yesterday, when) an ice-cream vendor (ran out of, run up, found) paper dishes. He looked (at, up, around) for another way to feed the large crowds of people who were waiting for a dish of ice cream.

Figure 10.2. The maze procedure.

construction, reliability, and validity of the maze as a classroom-based assessment tool has been published by Parker, Hasbrouck and Tindal (1989).

While the maze has been used extensively as a curriculum-based measurement (CBM), only one study is available regarding its use with deaf and hard of hearing students. Reynolds (1986) used the DRP, a modified cloze test or maze, with deaf college students as a means of assessing reading comprehension. Results of the study suggested general validity in the assessment of reading comprehension with deaf students. While more research is needed, the maze can provide teachers with a direct measure of reading comprehension that is instructionally related to the curriculum.

Story Retell Procedures

Story retell is a relatively new and natural process of assessing a student's comprehension of text. While retelling of stories can be observed as a routine activity in daily instruction, its use as an informal measure of comprehension for students who are deaf or hard of hearing has only recently received attention in the literature. Andrews, Winograd, and DeVille (1994) used story retelling scores to determine the effectiveness of ASL summary as an instructional strategy in reading comprehension with 11- and 12-year-old students who were deaf. The story retelling assessment process was administered individually and recorded on video for scoring. After reading a story in print, the students were given the direction "Tell me everything you remember about the story." Standard prompts were given as needed: "Tell me more about (the main character)"; "What else do you remember?" "Is there anything else you wanted to say?" Finally, a question related to this specific study was asked: "What lesson did you learn from that story for yourself?" (pp. 380–381). Scoring procedures included the ratio of pausal units used by the students compared to the number of pausal units—breaks that occur naturally in the presentation of ideas—in the printed passage. A value score of 3 was given to pausal units that closely matched a paraphrase of the text, a 2 was assigned to matches that approximated the context, and a 1 for pausal units that were far from the paraphrased text. The quantitative assessment in this retelling process provided a raw score indicating the number of pausal units retold by the student and a relatively "weighted" score referring to the accuracy of the pausal units.

Story retelling may be used with very young children, as well as older students with emerging reading skills, as an assessment of the child's ability to follow a story being read or told in sign language or cued speech. Students can retell the story orally, through sign language, or in writing. Teachers can use the information gained through retellings to determine students' abilities to organize information and to recall what they have heard or seen. Modified guidelines for story retelling recommended by Morrow (1989) and Cooper (1997) include the following:

1. *Selecting the text*—Determine your purpose for using story retelling as an assessment tool. If the results of the assessment will be used for comparisons over time, select stories that are equivalent, that is, narratives that are approximately at the same reading level or informational texts with the same difficulty levels.

2. *Preparing the text*—Prior to presenting the text to the students, identify the pausal units or idea units that will be used as the measurement units. With story narratives, identify the setting, place, time, characters, problem, actions, or events that lead to the outcome. For informational texts, identify the theme, main ideas, and supporting information. List the units of measure on a sheet of paper.

3. *Reading and retelling the text*—Have the students read the text silently, or, prior to the students' silent reading, read the story to the students orally, with cued speech, or in ASL. Immediately following the reading, ask a student to retell the story or the text. Prompt the student with "Tell me more . . ." and "Keep going, you're doing a nice job. . . ." As the student is retelling the passage, check off the ideas or units that you prepared earlier. After the student finishes, ask questions about any specific components of the reading that were omitted.

4. *Summarizing and evaluating retellings*—Scoring summary sheets may be used to quantify results (see Morrow, 1989); points may be assigned to each component identified on the prepared recording sheet, or ratios may be calculated as described above by Andrews et al. (1994). Specific notations should be recorded on the scoring sheet regarding observations that may be relevant to instructional planning for such areas as sequencing skills, elaboration, creative components, and exceptions.

Use of story retelling data over time is dependent on consistency in administration, scoring, and equivalency among readings. If measurement of student progress and the effects of instruction is the primary purpose of the assessment, student retelling scenarios may be video recorded to facilitate consistency in scoring protocol and procedures.

Informal Reading Inventories

Informal reading inventories (IRIs) are the most prevalent reading assessments in classrooms with hearing pupils (Harris & Lalik, 1987), and they are prominent in many educational settings with deaf and hard of hearing students. IRIs may be teacher developed or commercially prepared with explicit scoring criteria. Most IRIs consist of a collection of short stories or expository passages prepared with varying levels of reading difficulty. Students may read the passages orally and answer comprehension questions or the students may read the passages silently and retell what they read through sign language or oral report, responding to comprehension questions. IRIs can be useful in gathering data regarding reading fluency, comprehension, and ability to make a transition from standard English to sign language. IRIs can also be used to determine whether the reading materials selected are appropriate for students and within the instructional level of readability.

A teacher-constructed IRI can be developed following the guidelines by Graves, Watts, and Graves (1994) and adapted for use with deaf or hard of hearing students:

1. Select two passages (100–125 words for beginning readers and 200–250 words for higher levels) from a book that you are considering using with the student. The passages should be representative of the book in sentence length, vocabulary, and prior knowledge required.

2. Introduce the passage to the student by saying/signing something such as, "I'm going to have you read this paragraph about tornadoes to me. Then I'd like you to tell me what you read about."

3. Ask the student to designate her or his preferred mode for reading, for example, oral English, oral English plus cued speech, signed English, or translating to ASL. If the student selects oral English, oral English plus cued speech, or signed English, proceed to the next step. If the student chooses ASL, have the student read the passage silently before reading it aloud to provide an opportunity to organize concepts and adapt printed English statements into ASL concepts.

4. As the student is reading, follow along with a duplicate copy. Circle the words that the student has difficulty with or omits during reading, noting in the margins any substitutions of one word for another. In addition, note any significant behaviors exhibited by the reader, such as lack of expression during reading, finger pointing, holding the text close to the eyes.

For those students translating the passage into ASL, circle the words or phrases that were semantically incorrect, noting incorrect signs or substitutions for the word or concept intended and omission of phrases or concepts. Indicate words that are deliberately finger spelled (with the exception of proper nouns).

5. After the passage has been read, check comprehension by asking the student to retell what he read. Initially, ask the student to respond without looking back at the passage. However, the student may need to look back to give a satisfactory retelling. Characterize the retelling with simple descriptions such as "complete, coherent, and shows good understanding," "somewhat sketchy but showing basic understanding," or "sketchy and not showing much

understanding." Ask a question or two, perhaps an inferential question and an application question, and record the student's responses. Notes should indicate whether the student needed to look back to retell the passage.

6. Repeat the process with the second passage to check and confirm your observations from the first passage (Graves, Watts, & Graves, 1994, p. 197).

Data obtained from the IRI can be used to determine (a) the reader's comprehension and interpretation of the text; (b) the reader's ability to use text-based and reader-based strategies to extract meaning; (c) the effects of the reader's word and syntactic knowledge on text comprehension; and (d) the reader's ability to relate different codes (e.g., ASL) and modes of communication (e.g., cued speech, signed English) to print. Through IRIs, the teacher has the opportunity to identify patterns of reading behaviors that either support or detract from reading fluency and comprehension, as well as the general effect of reading instruction. *Reading Recovery* (Clay, 1993) uses a running record assessment similar to an IRI to determine instructional objectives and effectiveness (Pinnell, Fried, & Estice, 1990).

Miscue analysis, or reading miscue inventories (RMIs), are similar to IRIs in purpose and function. However, miscue inventories provide a more detailed inventory and systematic analysis of the reader's responses to the text. For the purpose of assessing reading abilities with deaf children IRIs and RMIs have had limited use. Ewoldt (1982) recommended the use of miscue analysis with deaf children as an observational tool for determining patterns of oral reading behavior. Ensor and Koller (1997) used miscue analysis as an evaluation measure while studying the effects of repeated reading. In their study, total communication (sign plus speech) was used as part of the reading process and in the miscue analysis. Procedures followed were similar to those described above. Acceptable miscues included self-corrections and substitutions that were a semantic match. Unacceptable miscues included "the wrong sign for the word intended, omission of words and any substitutions for words that were syntactically or semantically incorrect" (Ensor & Koller, 1997, p. 66).

Procedures for calculating the quantitative data for a miscue analysis with deaf and hard of hearing readers are particularly challenging. Ensor and Koller (1997) calculated two scores using the miscue analysis procedure. The first score was the number of words read correctly divided by the number of total words in the story to determine the students' word recognition scores. The second score was the number of words read correctly with acceptable miscues divided by the total number of words in the story to provide a quantitative measure of overall reading accuracy as an indication of reading comprehension. It should be noted that although deaf and hard of hearing students may not recognize every word;

they may be able to comprehend the meaning and have a good understanding of the text.

Curriculum-Based Measures

Curriculum-based measurement (CBM) is an informal, systematic, direct measurement designed to assess students' progress within the curriculum. CBM was designed by Stanley Deno at the University of Minnesota and is an increasingly critical complement to norm-referenced assessment protocols and effective instruction (Bradley-Johnson & Evans, 1991). CBM was developed using five specific criteria in response to the real-world needs of teachers and students. These criteria included (1) assessments that are connected to the students' curricula; (2) assessments that are easy to administer and completed quickly to permit frequent use; (3) assessments that are economical and efficient to develop, produce, and use; (4) assessments that are available in multiple forms and formats; and (5) assessments that are sensitive to changes in the students' academic behaviors and achievements over short time periods (Marston, 1989). These fundamental characteristics have resulted in procedures that are task oriented, with direct repeated measurements of students' abilities, and integrated with curriculum and instruction. Measurements are visually displayed using a graphic format to assist the teacher and students in quickly identifying progress, maintenance, or regression in reading and writing. In addition, the graphically displayed measures can be used to establish learner goals through projected trend lines.

Teacher-developed assessments focus on what students have been learning, and mark progress through weekly measurements. While CBM is an informal assessment tool, several procedures have been standardized to establish technical adequacy—that is, validity and reliability—in making comparisons among students and when comparing a student's performance across time (Deno, 1989).

While no known research has been conducted to standardize CBM procedures with deaf and hard of hearing students, many teachers have implemented CBM with their students as a means of monitoring reading and writing progress (Meredith & Walgren, 1998). CBM procedures used with deaf students include weekly assessments using the modified cloze or maze procedures, number of words read orally or signed in 2 to 3 minute timed samples, story retelling, and correct word sequences in writing. Scores are recorded weekly on a graph where the teacher and the student can visually inspect student progress within the curriculum. Consistent use of the same procedures for administration and scoring can assist the teacher in determining the effectiveness of instruction as it occurs (Bradley-Johnson & Evans, 1991).

Reading Levels

Informal reading assessments are frequently used to identify the match between the materials to be read and the reading level of the student. As discussed earlier, some standardized achievement scores can be converted into "grade-level" scores to describe a relationship between the performance of a student and that of a norm-sample of average readers in a specified grade placement. The grade-level score has no direct relationship to the reading level assigned to graded reading materials, nor does it provide information on the instructional needs of the students. The use of informal reading inventories in the classroom is one way teachers can determine if the selected text materials are appropriate for use with students. The scheme for determining the match between student and materials includes three general reading performance levels, with characteristics that define each level:

- *Independent level*—The student is able to read a selected passage from the text with fluency, retell a short selection taken from the text, and appropriately respond to applied and inferential questions about the selection read.

- *Instructional level*—The student is able to read a selected passage from the text with some difficulty and may need some help with vocabulary from the teacher. The student is able to retell the selection taken from the text but needs to look back and reread portions of the text to provide an accurate report. The student responds to some of the inferential and applied questions but demonstrates some difficulty in providing clear and appropriate responses.

- *Frustration Level*—The student's attempt to read the selected passage is labored, with significant pauses and corrections and an error rate of more than 10% of the words in the text. The student retells only a few segments of the text, with trials for looking back and rereading, or inaccurately retells the content of the text. The student does not respond appropriately to applied and inferential questions (Graves, Watts, & Graves, 1994).

While determining reading levels is a gross measure, an informal estimate of readability is a useful tool in determining the instructional match between the reading materials and the student. Direct assessment between the text to be read and the reader provides the best estimate of readability. Students are strongly influenced by their prior knowledge and social and cultural experiences that may influence the readability of any given text. For example, Mason, a fourth-grade student who is deaf, was exceptionally interested in agriculture and farm machinery. While his SAT scores indicated a 2.3-grade reading equivalency, his readability level in a 10th-grade agricultural text was at the instructional level. In fact, Mason often helped the teacher with some of the technical terms!

Providing independent reading-level materials gives students an opportunity to read on their own and to conduct investigations, and motivates students to enjoy reading without a struggle. For example, Charlie, a 5-year-old child who is deaf, was caught sneaking his *Reading Milestones* reader into bed and reading under the covers. His mother complained that she had an ample supply of wonderful children's books but Charlie chose to spend his time reading books she found boring. When asked, Charlie said that he took the books from school because he was "a good reader with the books." Charlie's independent reading level is the goal of reading instruction.

The instructional level is best defined by Vygotsky's (1978) *zone of proximal development*—that is, the text is within the range of the student's abilities at the most challenging level. Taylor et al. (1995) described material at the instructional level as being "material that is just beyond the student's grasp; material that is scaffolded properly will lead to growth" (p. 138). Texts and materials to be used in the classroom settings should generally be at the instructional level, where students are able to comprehend the theme and concepts in the text and have word recognition skills at approximately the 90% level. At this level, the teacher is able to provide sufficient support during the reading process, while students increase their abilities to read independently. Texts that are determined to be at the frustration level for a student are inappropriate for use as an instructional tool or for free-time reading. Texts at the independent reading level are most appropriate for independent study, as resource materials and for recreational reading.

Informal reading inventories may be used to determine readability levels of text materials. Procedures for developing an IRI using materials common to the classroom are described earlier in this chapter. In attempting to determine the instructional level, it is advisable to begin with text that is approximately 2 to 3 years below the students' grade level. If the material is too difficult, text from lower levels should be used.

Authentic Assessment

Authentic assessment is included as a separate topic in this chapter for the purpose of definition, although examples of authentic assessments are interwoven throughout each of the subtopics. Assessments including processes or products that are original works of the student are referred to as *authentic assessments*. It is a generic term that has been refined from labels such as "holistic assessment," "performance-based assessment" and "product-based assessment" (Hart, 1994). Authentic assessments such as portfolios, story retellings, journals, oral or signed readings, compositions, letters, and e-mail exchanges are just a few examples of product-oriented methods. Process methods may include observations of students' daily work, checklists, student self-evaluations, developmental checklists, and interviews with students and family members. Unlike formal tests, authentic assessments are not segregated from instruction and are considered part of the informal assessment process. Hart identified the benefits of authentic assessments as having greater instructional relevance than norm-referenced standardized tests. Authentic assessments may be more closely aligned to students' strengths, experiences, and cultural characteristics, with student involvement as the centerpiece of the process. Portfolio assessment is currently the most popular form of authentic assessment and is discussed in the following section.

Portfolios: Introduction and Purpose

Many definitions and descriptions of portfolios exist in the literature, each definition seemingly shaped by the individuals using them. DeFina (1992) observed that portfolios are singularly flexible tools whose parameters allow enough variability to expand their definition to meet a variety of student needs. Hart (1994) offered a general definition, stating that portfolios are containers that hold evidence of a student's skills, ideas, interests, and accomplishments. However, regardless of the forms portfolios might take, they should be more than collections of papers; portfolios should reflect thoughtfully organized bodies of work. Paulson and Paulson (1991) offered a definition of portfolios as:

> a purposeful, integrated collection of student work showing student effort, progress, or achievement in one or more areas. The collection is guided by performance standards and includes evidence of students' self-reflection and participation in setting the focus, selecting contents, and judging merit. (p. 295)

Portfolios can be used for both instruction and assessment and are one of the most popular methods of authentic assessment currently used in classrooms. Danielson and Abrutyn (1997, p. v) listed four purposes for portfolios:

1. to engage students in learning content;
2. to help students learn the skills of reflection and self-evaluation;

3. to document student learning in areas that do not lend themselves to traditional assessment; and

4. to facilitate communication with parents.

A fifth purpose is added by Hart (1994), who stated that portfolios enable students and teachers to become partners in the assessment process.

Portfolios can be used to accomplish many educational goals; therefore, teachers who are implementing portfolios in their classroom need to define their purposes and the outcomes they want to achieve. Defining purposes and outcomes will help teachers make decisions about the kinds of portfolios to use and how to organize them. Ryan (1994, p. 9) listed the following questions for teachers to consider:

1. Should the portfolio be a collection of work or a sample of best work?
2. Will only finished products be included in the portfolio?
3. Will the portfolio be given to the next teacher?
4. Who will select what goes into the portfolio?
5. Who will have access to the portfolio?
6. How will students be involved?

If teachers want the portfolio to provide information on the acquisition and application of skills, they will want to look at the *products* of student learning. If they are looking for information for diagnosis and improvement of student strengths and needs, they will want to look at the *process* of student performance (Ryan, 1994). When teachers have made decisions about purposes and outcomes of portfolios, they can make decisions about the kinds of portfolios and the process they will use.

Portfolio Evaluation and Standardized Testing

Because teachers will want to use multiple approaches to assessment in their classrooms, they need to know what different assessment procedures will accomplish so they can make good decisions in selecting assessment formats and processes. Portfolio assessment accomplishes different purposes than standardized testing does. For example, while tests provide indications of students' achievement at a particular point in time, portfolios document learning over a period of time. Portfolios represent a range of students' reading and writing, while testing provides a "snapshot" of students' work. Portfolio assessment represents a collaborative approach, in which students participate with teachers and others to check their progress and set ongoing learning goals; testing provides few opportunities for collaboration, since tests are usually machine scored or scored by teachers. Finally, portfolios address improvement, effort, and achievement, while testing addresses achievement only (Tierney, Carter, & Desai, 1991).

Portfolio assessment has particular advantages for deaf and hard of hearing students. It provides a convenient and efficient means of documentation of improvement over time and allows the students, teachers, and parents to see progress that is being made. It is usually more positive, since it focuses on improvement rather than achievement in terms of a grade equivalent or a numerical score, which often is depressing for all those concerned. It is difficult to find standardized tests that are appropriate and nondiscriminatory for deaf and hard of hearing students, although that is not to say that standardized tests should not be administered. Many states and school districts require that all students take standardized tests so that a measure of overall effectiveness of state and district programs and curricula is obtained. When deaf and hard of hearing students are mainstreamed, it is sometimes beneficial to have a measure comparing them to hearing peers to get an indication of how they will fare in regular classrooms. In general, most standardized tests are frustrating for this population because of the English-language factor and deflating because frequently when older students take the screening test, they qualify for a test level intended for much younger children. In addition, the results are questionable because it is difficult to "tease out" the variable of English language from the variables of knowledge and application.

Types of Portfolios

Frequently, teachers and students keep several kinds of portfolios, each one serving different purposes. It is important for teachers to have clear goals, to understand why they want to use portfolios, and to know who the intended audience might be. When they know these things, they will be able to select the portfolios appropriate for their purposes.

The three major kinds of portfolios are working portfolios, display or showcase portfolios, and assessment portfolios. Each of these appears to have distinct characteristics; however, they tend to overlap in practice (Danielson & Abrutyn, 1997).

Working Portfolios

A working portfolio is a collection of work in progress and completed work. It serves as a storage unit until various pieces are moved to the showcase portfolio or the assessment portfolio or until the student takes them home. The pieces in the working portfolio show evidence of the student's strengths and needs, which prompt discussions between teacher and student on progress toward learning objectives and directions for future instruction.

The primary audience for the working portfolio is the student, although the teacher is also involved when they engage in discussions on progress. The student's role is to work on the pieces in the portfolio and to reflect on the quality of the work, thus becoming more reflective and self-directed. However, with young children, teachers play a primary role as they teach the children how to think about their work. Parents can also be an audience for the working portfolio if the portfolio is used in parent conferences or in Individualized Education Plan (IEP) meetings. The opportunity to look through the working portfolio and see improvement occurring can be particularly helpful for parents of a deaf or hard of hearing child who find it difficult to accept their child's present skill levels or do not have a realistic picture of the progress their child is making.

Working portfolios usually focus on a specific area, such as reading and writing or one of the content areas. The pieces included relate to the objectives of that unit and document the student's progress toward achieving the objectives. The working portfolio should have a large collection of work in order to have enough evidence to determine achievement. Periodically, or at the end of the learning unit, some of the pieces may be transferred to the assessment portfolio to document achievement of the objectives or to the showcase portfolio, which is a collection of the child's best works and will be displayed during celebrations and conferences and at any other opportunity the child might have to "show off" learning achievement. When students move a piece of work to a different portfolio, they must give reasons for their selection, thus causing them to reflect on their work and self-evaluate.

Showcase Portfolios

The showcase portfolio is a collection of the student's best work. Keeping showcase portfolios is very rewarding and a source of pride for students. It is, indeed, exciting to see the pride and self-confidence students exhibit as they display their best work and interpret its meaning.

The major purpose of the showcase portfolio is to demonstrate the highest level of achievement attained by the student (Danielson & Abrutyn, 1997). This portfolio may be maintained from year to year to document growth over time. The student is the major audience for the portfolio, along with any other individual with whom the student chooses to share it. Other audiences may include a future teacher, who will learn a great deal about the student from studying these works.

Assessment Portfolios

The assessment portfolio serves the primary function of documenting what a student has learned. Students select the work that goes into this portfolio and must explain how each piece reflects their mastery of a curriculum objective. Assessment portfolios may span any period of time and may be used to demonstrate mastery in any or all of the curriculum areas. The audiences for assessment portfolios are teachers, who monitor learning achievement; parents, who also monitor the learning achievement; school administrators, who monitor program effectiveness; and the students themselves, who monitor their own achievement.

Components of a Portfolio

The components of a portfolio will depend on the kind of portfolio. The important factor is that the teacher and students determine from the beginning what will be included. A review of the literature indicated general agreement that some student-selected, some teacher-selected, and some collaboratively selected materials should be included (Abruscato, 1993; Ballard, 1992; Cooper & Brown, 1992; Johns, 1992; Simmons & Resnick, 1993). It is not possible to list the components of each kind of portfolio. The following list gives examples of the work that might be included. No two portfolios will contain exactly the same materials (Clemmons, Laase, Cooper, Areglado, & Dill, 1993):

1. *Baseline samples*—At the beginning of the year, samples of work representing each component selected should serve as a baseline for comparison of work throughout the year.

2. *Reading-response journal entries*—Reading responses encourage students to think critically about what they read, to construct meaning from text, and to connect reading, writing, and thinking. They provide important information for assessing the student's comprehension. Reading responses are kept together in a separate binder or folder, and at specified intervals, the student can copy a journal entry and insert it in the portfolio.

3. *Learning log entries*—Learning logs contain responses students make to topics of study in various content areas. This kind of writing gives students opportunities to interact with content material and encourages them to think about what they are learning. As with reading-response journal entries, a copy of a learning log can be added to the portfolio at designated times.

4. *Writing samples*—A writing sample is an original piece of writing that shows the writing process. Sometimes students include a first draft, on which revisions have been made, along with the finished product; and sometimes they

include only the finished product, depending on the decision made when the teacher and students decided on the components of their portfolios.

5. *Videotape recordings*—Videotapes offer a unique way of recording some of the students' activities. Videotapes may be made of the students performing readers' theater, participating in literature response groups, sharing projects, or reading to younger students, for example.

6. *Text samples*—A copy of a page or two from books that students have read may be included in the portfolio. Text samples document the types and levels of texts the students are reading. When students select these pages for their portfolios, they should write their reasons.

7. *Lists of books read*—The students can keep records of books read in and out of school, noting the title, author, and illustrator of each book. They may want to record other kinds of information as well, such as number of pages read, genre, and date when they finished reading the book. This information can be graphed at the end of the year to show progress.

8. *Records of portfolio conferences*—During portfolio conferences, teachers and students discuss the portfolio and note the students' goals and accomplishments. If the present goals have been attained, the students set new goals for themselves. Teachers take notes during the conferences, which are then added to the portfolio.

Many other kinds of student work may be included in the portfolio, but teachers and students should take care not to include so much that the portfolio becomes unwieldy and difficult to use and assess. Teachers and students may decide to maintain more than one working portfolio—for example, one for reading and writing and another one for the content areas—or one for each content area. A major advantage of portfolios is that they are flexible and can be used in almost any way to meet the needs of each student.

Portfolio Assessment

The definitions of portfolio assessment range from the simple to the complex. A review of the literature completed by Gillespie, Ford, Gillespie, and Leavell (1996) revealed that most educators agreed that it is a formative assessment; it is multidimensional, and it provides teachers with a comprehensive picture of a student's abilities and literacy development (Harlin, Lipa, & Phelps, 1992; Valeri-Gold, Olson, & Deming, 1991–92).

Advantages of Portfolio Assessment

The information drawn from the literature review indicated that portfolio assessment offers many advantages to students and teachers, as well as parents.

Many of the advantages have been discussed previously but will be listed again as they pertain to the different groups.

Students. The major advantage of portfolio assessment is that it allows students to participate actively with teachers in the evaluation process (Gillespie et al., 1996). Other perceived advantages of portfolio assessment included the following:

1. Portfolios allow students to reflect on their progress and their areas of need as readers and writers over time (Ballard, 1992; Bell, 1992; Cooper & Brown, 1992; Van Horn & Guaraldi, 1994).

2. Portfolios facilitate the students' understanding of the reading, writing, and thinking connection (Ballard, 1992; Ford, 1993).

3. Portfolios help to create a cooperative climate among students through peer collaboration (Ballard, 1992; Cooper & Brown, 1992; Ford, 1993).

4. Portfolios provide opportunities for students to assume responsibility for their own learning and to become more independent (Ballard, 1992; Johns, 1992; Moje, Brozo, & Haas, 1994; Van Horn & Brown, 1993).

5. Portfolios contribute to the development of self-esteem and more positive attitudes toward reading and writing (Bell, 1992; Biggs, 1990; Van Horn & Guaraldi, 1994).

Teachers. Portfolio assessment appears to provide benefits to teachers, also. The perceived advantages of portfolio assessment for teachers included the following:

1. Portfolios provide teachers with a more meaningful picture of student growth (Biggs, 1990; Harlin et al., 1992; Van Horn & Guaraldi, 1994).

2. Portfolios generate data that may be useful in instructional decision making (Farr, 1991; Ford, 1993; Van Horn & Brown, 1993).

3. Portfolios allow for the integration of assessment and instruction (Biggs, 1990; Farr, 1990; Valeri-Gold et al., 1991–92; Van Horn & Guaraldi, 1994).

4. Portfolios provide a rich base for student-teacher conferences (Calfee & Perfumo, 1993; Farr, 1990; Johns, 1992).

Parents. Parents also benefit from portfolio assessment. The perceived advantages include the following:

1. Portfolios demonstrate children's knowledge and competence, as well as their growth over time (Cooper & Brown 1992; Harlin et al., 1992; Johns, 1992; Wolf, 1993).

2. Portfolios provide tangible evidence for facilitating communication among students, teachers, and parents (Calfee & Perfumo, 1993; Farr, 1991).

Disadvantages of Portfolio Assessment

Portfolio assessment has some disadvantages that cannot be ignored by educators and that will need to be addressed in the future before this approach to assessment can gain credibility beyond the testimonial level. One of the greatest weaknesses of portfolio assessment is the increased workload for the teacher (Christian, 1993; Johns, 1992; Wolf, 1993). Additional disadvantages have also been identified, as follows:

1. Portfolios may decrease instructional time by requiring too much class time for such management tasks as making decisions about selections and completing documentation (Christian, 1993; Wolf, 1993).

2. Teachers may neglect some of the critical elements in this approach by not holding enough conferences, not allowing students to make choices in selecting materials for inclusion, not trying to show students the connection between instruction and assessment, not providing continuous feedback, and providing too much teacher direction (Cooper & Brown, 1992; Ford, 1993).

3. The grading of portfolios is controversial (Christian, 1993; Johns, 1992; MacGinitie, 1993).

4. Portfolios require a high level of inservice for teachers to understand the procedures of data gathering and interpreting (Abruscato, 1993; Simmons & Resnick, 1993).

5. Portfolio assessment may encourage teachers to think that one assessment fits all and use portfolios to the exclusion of other assessment procedures (Farr, 1991; Johns, 1992; Paulson, & Paulson, 1991).

6. The reliability and validity of the data collected, as well as the standardization of portfolio content, have not been determined and remain controversial (Farr, 1990; Maeroff, 1991).

While portfolio assessment has many advantages that are very appealing to educators, the significant disadvantages have yet to be resolved. In addition, if teachers do not maintain the integrity of the intent of this process, many of the advantages will disappear. For example, one critical element is that students are to reflect on the development of their strengths and their areas of need as readers and writers over time; however, if teachers do not encourage students to do self-assessment and do not model the process and guide them through it as they are learning, this important advantage of portfolios will not develop. Without the element of self-reflection, portfolio assessment cannot exist and the portfolio becomes just a notebook full of papers (Gillespie et al., 1996). Students' accepting responsibility for their own learning is another important aspect of this approach, but it is doubtful that students will be able to do this without guidance from teachers. For portfolios to become effective means of assessment, students must be taught how to develop portfolios, how to take responsibility for their own learning, and how to evaluate their own performance (Ford, 1993; Paulson, & Paulson, 1991; Wolf, 1991).

In summary, portfolio assessment appears to be promising, but it has not yet reached full development. Consequently, it should be used cautiously and in conjunction with other kinds of assessments. Farr (1991) noted that four different groups of people need to know how students are progressing—students, parents, teachers, and school administrators. He suggested that any single assessment procedure would not provide the information needed by each of the four audiences.

Writing Assessments

Assessments of written expression follow formats similar to those established for reading—that is, standardized, norm-referenced, diagnostic, and criterion-referenced assessments are commercially available. Like reading, writing is a complex process that cannot easily be reflected in a unidimensional score or described on a linear scale. Incorporated into the assessment system are multidimensional perspectives of the writing process, the product, and the purpose for which the process and the product were developed (Isaacson, 1996; Luckner & Isaacson, 1990). While several discrete skills such as punctuation, capitalization, number of words and the use of specific grammatical structures can be quantitatively measured, the assessment of a student's ability to communicate through writing is a qualitative measure that includes the reader's judgment of effectiveness. Informal assessments are more closely related to the instructional process and can be productively included in the planning and evaluation schemata. However, formal writing assessments provide objective, consistent, and comparative data.

Formal Writing Assessments

Norm-referenced standardized tests generally focus on specific areas of writing, including word choice, the mechanics of writing, and the general coherence of the writing sample. The *Written Language Syntax Test* (WLST) (Berry, 1981) is the only known formal assessment of written language that was designed specifically for use with deaf and hard of hearing students or that includes a sample of deaf students in the norm sample. The WLST is designed for use with students ranging from approximately 10 to 17 years of age. It consists of three writing tasks or levels and a screening test that guides the assessor in deciding which of the three levels of the test are most appropriate for a particular student. In the first task, students are given a picture and a set of words and directed to write a statement or a declarative sentence about the picture using the words provided. The second task mirrors the first; however, students are directed to write a question. In the last task, students are given a picture and directed to write a story about the picture. Scoring is based on the number of grammatically correct sentences produced by the students. Scoring is also matched with a set of performance objectives for writing that provide the teacher with information that can be used in instructional planning and evaluation (Berry, 1981; Bradley-Johnson & Evans, 1991).

Yarger (1996) reviewed the use of the *Test of Written Language–Third Edition* (TOWL–3) (Hammill & Larsen, 1996) with deaf and hard of hearing students. The TOWL–3 consists of two formats; the first is a set of controlled stimuli requiring student responses, and the second is a spontaneous subtest similar to the WLST in which students are given a picture and directed to write a story about it. A protocol for prompting the students in planning and organizing their story is provided in the administration manual. Yarger identified four possible limitations that should be considered when using the TOWL–3 with deaf or hard of hearing students. The first is that the pictures used as stimuli in the spontaneous writing sample may not be similar to the prior knowledge or cultural experiences of the child. The ability of a child to tell a story or compose a selection regarding a somewhat unknown topic would not provide a substantive assessment of the child's abilities. The second limitation concerns the delivery of instructions to the students. Students who elect to speech-read the directions may miss information, while delivery of the oral directions through sign language invalidated the test. The third area of concern is the assessment of discrete skills in isolation. Student performance may be enhanced through the use of context, whereas determining correct grammar in isolated sentences may be particularly challenging for some students. The fourth area is the protocol used in scoring the spelling test. Yarger's review found that no credit was given for invented spellings when students attempted to use words a level higher than their peers. While Yarger identified these limitations in discussion of the TOWL–3, they can be applied to most standardized writing assessments.

Informal Writing Assessments

Most informal assessments are based on authentic writing samples produced by students. The stimuli used to evoke a particular sample or set of samples vary depending on the purpose of the assessment and evaluation protocol. The approach may be a holistic or analytical process, as determined by the purpose and the procedures used by the evaluator. The *holistic* perspective views writing in its entirety (Cooper, 1997). Each component is interdependent, is considered to influence other skills or components, and is scored using a single overall rating based on a rubric. The *analytical* process evaluates a variety of characteristics of the writing sample; each components is evaluated and scored as a distinct unit.

Informal writing assessments may be subdivided into five categories for evaluation: fluency, syntax, structure, vocabulary, and content. *Fluency* is commonly defined as the number of words written (Isaacson, 1988). The average sentence length is determined by counting the total number of words written and dividing by the total number of sentences. Cartwright (1988) reported that the average 8 year old produces a mean-length sentence of approximately eight words and the length of sentences increased by one word per year.

Syntax refers to the grammatical structures and rules used in constructing sentences. While the majority of informal assessments quantify the number of structural errors produced in the writing sample (Mercer & Mercer, 1998; Stuckless & Marks, 1966), scoring of weaknesses provides limited instructional data. Syntax competencies can be assessed both quantitatively and qualitatively by recording the number and type of sentences attempted and correctly constructed including simple, compound, and complex patterns. Teacher-constructed checklists document students' spontaneous patterns of production and are used to demonstrate progress as well as to profile strengths and instructional goals. Commonly used protocols with students who are deaf or hard of hearing focus on the production of basic sentence patterns, the extension and expansion of basic patterns, and the use of transformations that create more complex sentences (Powers & Wilgus, 1983; Quigley & Paul, 1984; Yoshinaga-Itano & Snyder, 1985).

Structure includes syntax and other conventions and mechanical aspects of written products such as punctuation, capitalization, and format (e.g., business letter, informal note, technical paper). Spelling and handwriting conventions may be assumed within the assessment of structure, as well. Checklists can be developed in tandem with syntax profiles, in which students are given credit for the appropriate use of conventions such as periods, commas, colons, quotation marks, apostrophes, and capitalization of proper nouns. The increasing availability of computer-based software to perform syntax and structure analysis is greatly reducing the time required of teachers to conduct analytical assessments. In addition, grammar, language, and word-check programs can be incorporated into instruction with deaf and hard of hearing learners and used as self-assessment tools.

Correct word sequence (CWS) is a system of syntactical and structural assessment developed by Videen, Deno and Marston (1982). CWS was designed as an efficient and informative measurement that allows teachers to regularly monitor student progress. A CWS is defined as two adjacent, correctly spelled words that are acceptable in standard English—that is, the word sequence is syntactically and semantically correct and appropriate to the context. After reading the student's work, the teacher places a "caret" (^)between every two correct words in a sequence. Typically, the beginning and the end of the sentence are not included as part of the word sequence (Parker, Hasbrouck, & Tindal, 1989); however, mechanical aspects such as punctuation and capitalization may be incorporated into CWS scoring. Figure 10.3 illustrates the use of CWS with a writing sample produced by a 10-year-old student who is deaf. Weekly measures of CWS are recorded graphically and used by the student and teacher to monitor progress in the syntax and structure of written language.

Quantitative and qualitative measures of *vocabulary* or word use are reflected in the number and variety of words used appropriately in the written passage. The Type Token Ratio (TTR) is a quantitative measure of the number of different words used in relation to the total number of words used in the

---

Tree House

They^sat^on^the^treehouse. They^saw^many^birds^and^brids^

watched^the^boys^sat^on^the^treehouse

They^eat^some sandwich^and The^birds^went^to^eat sandwich^too

They^like Live^in treehouse. The^birds beside^the^boys.

Then^they was^ice. Same ice^is chill can't^move.

They^thought bride^is^pretty some^ugly^birds.

The^end.

(39 out of a possible 50 CWS)

Figure 10.3. Sample of correct word sentences (CWS) scoring procedure.

passage. A high ratio is an indication of a diversity of words selected; however, the TTR does not account for the semantic or pragmatic value of the vocabulary. Using a variety of words is referred to as word maturity. Deno, Mirkin, and Marston (1982) quantified vocabulary maturity as the number of words used in a written product that do not appear on the Dolch Word List (Dolch, 1955, 1960). Isaacson (1996, p. 194) referred to the measure of word maturity as a comparison between use of overused, repetitive words and use of new, mature words.

Assessment of content is one of the more challenging aspects in the evaluation of writing skills. *Content* reflects the ideas, organization, and accuracy of the written product (Cartwright, 1960) and reflects the student's abilities with fluency, syntax, structure, and vocabulary. Isaacson (1988) extended the definition of content to include the intended purpose and audience. Content is significantly influenced by the expectations of the reader and the culture, experiences, and language fluency of the writer. While a variety of rubrics and holistic measures have been used in the evaluation of content, instruction is dependent on specific characteristics or measures that can lead to both qualitative and quantitative achievement in written context. In his scale for the evaluation of factual paragraphs, Isaacson (1996, p. 191) incorporated a set of eight questions that guide the teacher in assessment as well as instruction:

- Does the first sentence tell the topic?
- Are all the other sentences about the topic?
- Do the sentences tell about facts, not opinions?
- Are the facts accurate?
- Is the amount of information sufficient?
- Is the information presented in logical order?
- Is the most important information or main idea first?

Each of the categories described as part of an informal writing assessment contributes to information regarding a student's strengths and needs. Analytical data can be used to ensure student progress and to establish instructional priorities within specific skill areas. Holistic assessment provides an overall impression of the student's ability to use written expression that is functional, intelligible, and conventional. No single measure reflects the general patterns of writing, including analytical characteristics, semantics, written discourse, and pragmatics (Musselman & Szanto, 1998). Teachers of children who are deaf and hard of hearing are becoming increasingly aware of the need for integrative assessment and instructional practices that include authentic measures, processes, and products to insure literacy growth.

Rubrics

Rubrics are used for grading the general quality of a writing sample through the process of assigning some evaluative score or level to the writing sample. Outlines or topical headings and subheadings used to guide the evaluation process are referred to as *rubrics*. While rubrics were initially used as categories for holistic scoring, they have been designated as analytical categories, somewhat similar to criterion-referenced assessments in which skills are matched to state and national performance statements (Bratcher, 1994).

Using rubrics as an approach to holistic scoring assumes that all aspects of writing are interdependent and therefore influence each other. The holistic assessment approach is usually applied to instructional writing, while other forms of informal assessment may be used with spontaneously developed writing samples or literature-based writing responses (Cooper, 1997, p. 553). An example of rubrics as a holistic scoring system is given in Table 10.2.

Bratcher (1994) illustrated a variety of rubrics used in evaluation protocols to monitor students' progress, determine class placements, and compare students within a group. Rubrics can range from the holistic approach, yielding a single score, to the rubrics of a highly analytical sequence in which writing is divided into component parts. In that case, each part or rubric is assigned a score, indicating the quality of that component. Rubrics may be developed by the teacher using skill-based systems of analysis or criterion-referenced evaluations in which points are assigned to individual skills such as punctuation, verb tense, process used in prewriting, sequence of ideas, and perspective. Two rubrics have been used and validated for use with deaf and hard of hearing students for evaluating authentic writing samples: the *NTID Writing Test* (Albertini et al., 1986) and the *Six-Trait Analytical Scale* (Spandel & Stiggins, 1990).

The *NTID Writing Test* follows a rubic format similar to that described in Table 10.2. A study was conducted with deaf college students to investigate the validity of the rubric as an evaluation tool for placement of postsecondary students in English-language classes. The *TOEFL Test of Written English* (Educational Testing Service, 1992) was used as the comparative or criterion for concurrent validity. The results of the study indicated that the *NTID Writing Test* was a valid assessment of postsecondary students who were deaf or hard of hearing and could be used effectively to determine placement in graduated English classes (Albertini, Bochner, Dowaliby, & Henderson, 1997).

The use of the *Six-Trait Analytical Scale* (Spandel & Stiggins, 1990) was evaluated in a longitudinal study conducted by Heefner and Shaw (1996) at the Kansas School for the Deaf. The children participating in the study ranged from

Table 10.2
Rubric for Holistic Scoring Procedure

0   *Responses that cannot be evaluated*

The composition is not related to the topic; is not readable because it is wholly illegible or incoherent; is written largely in a language other than English; contains an insufficient amount of writing to evaluate; is nonexistent.

1   *A very inadequate response score*

The composition is not related to the assigned topic; is very difficult to follow, lacks a coherent focus; is disorganized; contains errors in sentence formation, word usage, and mechanics that are frequent enough to detract from the overall quality of the composition.

2   *A less than adequate response score*

The composition is related to the assigned topic; is somewhat focused; lacks a beginning, a middle, or an end; presents obstacles for the reader in moving from idea to idea; contains errors in sentence formation, word use, and mechanics that are frequent enough to detract from the overall quality of the composition.

3   *An adequate response, passing score*

The composition is related to the assigned topic; has a central idea that is clearly expressed; has some supporting details and sufficient development; has a beginning, a middle, and an end; presents minor obstacles for the reader in moving from idea to idea; has errors in sentence formation, word use, and mechanics that do not substantially detract from the overall quality of the composition.

4   *A more than adequate response score*

The composition is related to the assigned topic; has a central idea that is clearly expressed; is well developed with supporting details; has a beginning, a middle, and an end; demonstrates control of language that enhances the overall quality of the response; may have errors in sentence formation, word use, and mechanics that do not detract from the overall quality of the composition.

Note. From *Minnesota Basic Standards Test of Written Composition,* by the Minnesota Department of Children, Families, and Learning, 1997, St. Paul, MN: Author.

8 through 21 years of age. Authentic writing samples were elicited through the use of wordless storybooks that were projected for class viewing and story prompts. The picture stories were viewed two or three times, followed by brief motivation questions asked by the teacher. The students were then directed to write about the pictures and were given as much time as needed to complete the assignment, with one opportunity to revise and rewrite. The writing products were scored by three trained raters using the rubric provided in the test, which

assigned individual scores for ideas, organization, voice, word choice, sentence fluency, and conventions. The results of the study indicated that the scale was a valid and reliable measure of student growth in writing and produced data that was helpful to teachers in instructional planning and evaluation (Heefner & Shaw, 1996).

The advantage of using rubrics as a grading or evaluative procedure is that "they communicate the teacher's grading guidelines to the student. . . . They also communicate a clear message to the writer about what the evaluator thinks is successful and what he or she thinks needs more work"(Bratcher, 1994, p. 44). The disadvantage is that the evaluator must become very familiar with the definitions and the process and must practice for consistency in scoring.

Summary

Assessment is an ongoing process that is highly interpretive and intricately interwoven into instruction and evaluation. Specific attention must be given to the purpose for the assessment and the characteristics and needs of the learner. Few formal assessment tools are appropriate for use with students who are deaf or hard of hearing. Variables that must be considered as an integral part of the assessment process, in addition to the preemptive characteristics of culture and economics, include (a) the purpose of assessment and how the data will be interpreted; (b) the student's familiarity with test taking and assessment strategies; (c) the student's prior knowledge of the content and purpose of the assessment; (d) the communication match between the student and the assessor; and (e) the match between the type of tasks and the purpose of the assessment. Generally, teachers of deaf and hard of hearing learners must rely on informal tests and measurements such as anecdotal and running records, and authentic measures including story retell, CBM, and portfolio assessments.

Portfolios are used for four major purposes in classrooms: (1) to engage students in learning, (2) to facilitate the development of skills in reflection and self-evaluation, (3) to document student learning, and (4) to draw parents into a partnership with schools. Teachers and students generally maintain three major kinds of portfolios, beginning with *working portfolio*, from which selected completed works are transferred to either the *showcase portfolio* or the *assessment portfolio*. Portfolio assessment shows a great deal of promise; however, there are significant obstacles to overcome, such as the issues of reliability and validity. Most educators support the use of a multiple assessment approach, which includes both traditional assessment (standardized tests) and alternative assessment (portfolio assessment and performances assessment). This approach would add to the paper-and-pencil test opportunities for students to demonstrate their knowledge and competencies in authentic settings (Gillespie et al., 1996). Using a multiple approach to assessment would enable teachers to assess student progress through assessments that encourage student thinking as well as application of skills.

Effective educators use data gleaned from portfolios and other assessment processes to determine the direction for instruction as well as to monitor student progress. Assessment provides a basis for the articulation of instruction within the domain of reading and writing, as well as across content areas, including the identification of readability and functional literacy levels. A balanced and integrated approach incorporating analytical and holistic perspectives of reading and writing ensure that quantitative and qualitative dimensions will be considered. Progress monitoring through formal and informal assessment strategies such as CBM, portfolio assessments, and teacher-developed records ensures that students receive instruction that is appropriate to their needs and will foster literacy growth.

References

Abruscato, J. (1993). Early results and tentative implications from the Vermont portfolio project. *Phi Delta Kappan, 74*, 474–477.

Ackerman, D. B. (1989). Intellectual and practical criteria for successful curriculum integration. In H. H. Jacobs (Ed.), *Interdisciplinary curriculum: Design and implementation* (pp. 25–37). Alexandria, VA: Association for Supervision and Curriculum Development.

Adams, M. J. (1990). *Beginning to read: Thinking and learning about print.* Cambridge, MA: MIT Press.

Adkins, T. (1997, Winter). Using distance-learning technology with students who are deaf or hard of hearing. *Educational Audiology Association Newsletter*, 22–23.

Ahlgren, I. (1992, Spring). S-languages and W-languages from the learner's perspective. *Sign Post: Journal of the International Sign Language Research Association*, 13–17.

Ahlgren, I. (1994). Sign language as the first language. In I. Ahlgren & K. Hyltenstam (Eds.), *Bilingualism in deaf education: Proceedings of the International Conference on Bilingualism in Deaf Education, Stockholm, Sweden: Vol. 27. International Studies on Sign Language and Communication of the Deaf.* Hamburg, Germany: Signum-Verlag.

Akamatsu, C. T. (1988). Instruction in the text structure: Metacognitive strategy instruction for literacy development in deaf students. *ACEHI/ACEDA, 14*, 13–32.

Akamatsu, C. T., & Andrews, J. F. (1993). It takes two to be literate: Literacy interactions between parent and child. *Sign Language Studies, 81*, 333–360.

Albertini, J. (1993). Critical literacy, whole language, and the teaching of writing to deaf students: Who should dictate to whom? *TESOL Quarterly, 27*, 60–73.

Albertini, J., Bochner, J. H., Cuneo, C., Hunt, L., Nielson, R., Seago, L., & Shannon, N. B. (1986). Development of a writing test for deaf college students. *Teaching English to Deaf and Second-Language Students, 4*(2), 5–11.

Albertini, J., Bochner, J. H., Dowaliby, F., & Henderson, J. B. (1997). Valid assessment of writing and access to academic discourse. *Journal of Deaf Studies and Deaf Education, 2*(2), 71–77.

Albertini, J., & Shannon, N. (1996). Kitchen notes, "The grapevine," and other writing in childhood. *Journal of Deaf Studies and Deaf Education, 1*(1), 64–73.

Allen, T. (1986). Patterns of academic achievement among hearing impaired students, 1974 and 1983. In A. Schildorth & M. Karachmer (Eds.), *Deaf children in America* (pp. 161–206). San Diego, CA: College-Hill Press.

Allen, V. (1994). Selecting materials for the reading instruction of ESL children. In K. Spangenberg-Urbschat & R. Pritchard (Eds.), *Kids come in all languages: Reading instruction for ESL students* (pp. 108–131). Newark, DE: International Reading Association.

Allington, R., Guice, S., Michelson, N., Baker, K., & Li, S. (1996). Literature-based curricula in high-poverty schools. In M. F. Graves, P. van den Broek, & B. M. Taylor (Eds.), *The first R: Every child's right to read* (pp. 73–96). New York: Teachers College Press and International Reading Association.

Alvermann, D. E., & Boothby, P. R. (1982). Text differences: Children's perceptions at the transition stage in reading. *Reading Teacher, 36*(3), 298–302.

Alvermann, D. E., Dillion, D. R., & O'Brien, D. G. (1987). *Using discussion to promote reading comprehension.* Newark, DE: International Reading Association.

Ammon, P. (1985). Helping children learn to write in ESL: Some observations and hypotheses. In S. W. Freedman (Ed.), *The acquisition of written language: Response and revision* (pp. 65–84). Norwood, NJ: Ablex.

Anders, P. L., & Guzzetti, B. J. (1996). *Literacy instruction in the content areas.* Fort Worth, TX: Harcourt Brace College Publishers.

Anderson, R. C. (1977). The notion of schemata and the educational enterprise. In R. C. Anderson, R. J. Spiro, & W. E. Montague (Eds.), *Schooling and the acquisition of knowledge.* Hillsdale, NJ: Erlbaum.

Anderson, R. C. (1981). *A proposal to continue a center for the study of reading* (Tech. Proposal, 4 vols.). Urbana: University of Illinois, Center for the Study of Reading.

Anderson, R. C. (1996). Research foundations to support wide reading. In V. Greaney (Ed.), *Promoting reading: Views on making reading materials accessible to increase literacy levels* (pp. 55–77). Newark, DE: International Reading Association.

Anderson, R. C., & Freebody, P. (1981). Vocabulary knowledge. In J. T. Guthrie (Ed.), *Comprehension and teaching: Reading perspectives.* Newark, DE: International Reading Association.

Anderson, R. C., & Freebody, P. (1985). Vocabulary knowledge. In H. Singer & R. Ruddell (Eds.), *Theoretical models and processes of reading* (pp. 343–371). Newark, DE: International Reading Association.

Anderson, R. C., Hiebert, E., Scott, J., & Wilkinson, I. (1985). *Becoming a nation of readers: The report of the commission on reading.* Washington, DC: National Institute of Education and Center for the Study of Reading.

Anderson, T. H., & Armbruster, B. B. (1984a). Content area textbooks. In R. C. Anderson, J. Osborn, & R. J. Tierney (Eds.), *Learning to read in American schools* (pp. 193–226). Hillsdale, NJ: Erlbaum.

Anderson, T. H., & Armbruster, B. B. (1984b). Studying. In P. D. Pearson (Ed.), *Handbook of reading research* (pp. 657–678). New York: Longman.

Andre, M. E. D. A., & Anderson, T. H. (1978–79). The development and evaluation of a self-questioning study technique. *Reading Research Quarterly, 14,* 605–623.

Andrews, J. F., & Mason, J. M. (1984). *How do young deaf children learn to read? A proposed model of deaf children's emergent reading behaviors.* (Technical Report No. 329). Urbana-Champaign: University of Illinois.

Andrews, J. F., & Mason, J. M. (1991). Strategy usage among deaf and hearing readers. *Exceptional Children, 57,* 536–545.

Andrews, J. F., Winograd, P., & DeVille, G. (1994). Deaf children reading fables: Using ASL summaries to improve reading comprehension. *American Annals of the Deaf, 139*(3), 378–386.

Anthony, R. J., Johnson, T. D., Mickelson, N. I., & Preece, A. (1991). *Evaluating literacy: A perspective for change.* Portsmouth, NH: Heinemann.

Applebee, A. N. (1991). Environments for language teaching and learning: Contemporary issues and future directions. In J. Flood, J. M. Jensen, D. Lapp, & J. R. Squire (Eds.), *Handbook of research on teaching the English language arts.* New York: Macmillan.

Armbruster, B. B. (1991, May 5). *Content and reading instruction.* Paper presented at the Conference on Reading Research, Las Vegas, Nevada.

Armbruster, B. B., Anderson, T. H., & Ostertag, J. (1987). Does text structure/summarization instruction facilitate learning from expository text? *Reading Research Quarterly, 22,* 331–346.

Armbruster, B. B., Anderson, T. H., & Ostertag, J. (1989). Teaching text structure to teach reading and writing. *Reading Teacher, 43,* 130–137.

Armbruster, B. B., & Nagy, W. E. (1992). Vocabulary in content areas. *Reading Teacher, 45*(7), 550–551.

Artley, S. A. (1965). *Student responses to classroom instruction* (Research Series No. 109). Ann Arbor: Michigan State University, College of Education.

Aschbacher, P. R. (1991). Humanitas: A thematic curriculum. *Educational Leadership, 49*(2), 16–19.

Atwell, N. (1987). *In the middle: Writing, reading and learning with adolescents.* Upper Montclair, NJ: Boynton/Cook.

Au, K. H. (1993). *Literacy instruction in multicultural settings.* Fort Worth, TX: Harcourt Brace Jovanovich.

Au, K. H., & Mason, J. M. (1983). Cultural congruence in classroom participation structures: Achieving a balance of rights. *Discourse Processes, 6,* 145–167.

Babbidge Committee Report. (1965). *Education of the deaf in the United States.* Report of the advisory committee on the education of the deaf. Washington, DC: U.S. Government Printing Office.

Baker, L., & Brown, A. L. (1984). Metacognitive skills and reading. In P.D. Pearson (Ed.), *Handbook of reading research* (pp. 353–394). New York: Longman.

Ballard, L. (1992). Portfolios and self-assessment. *English Journal, 81,* 46–48.

Barnes, D. (1976). *From communication to curriculum.* New York: Penguin Books.

Barton, D., & Ivanic, R. (Eds.). (1991). *Writing in the community.* Newbury Park, CA: Sage.

Baumann, J. F. (1984). Effectiveness of a direct instruction paradigm for teaching main idea comprehension. *Reading Research Quarterly, 22,* 93–108.

Beane, J. A. (1990). *A middle school curriculum: From rhetoric to reality.* Columbus, OH: National Middle School Association.

Beane, J. A. (1991). The middle school: The natural home of integrated curriculum. *Educational Leadership, 49,* 9–13.

Beane, J. A. (1993). Problems and possibilities for an integrative curriculum. *Middle School Journal, 24,* 18–23.

Bebko, J. M., Lacasse, M. A., Turk, H., & Oyen, A. (1991). Recall performance on a central-incidental memory task by profoundly deaf children. *American Annals of the Deaf, 137,* 271–277.

Beck, I. L. (1985). Five problems with children's comprehension in the primary grades. In J. Osborn, P. T. Wilson, & R. C. Anderson (Eds.), *Reading education: Foundations for a literate America* (pp. 239–253). Lexington, MA: Lexington Books.

Beck, I. L., & McKeown, M. G. (1991). Social studies texts are hard to understand: Mediating some of the difficulties. *Language Arts, 68*(6), 482–490.

Beck, I. L., McKeown, M. G., & Omanson, R. C. (1987). The effects and uses of diverse vocabulary instructional techniques. In M. G. McKeown & M. E. Curtis (Eds.), *The nature of vocabulary acquisition.* Hillsdale, NJ: Erlbaum.

Beck, I. L., Omanson, R. C., & McKeown, M. G. (1982). An instructional redesign of reading lessons: Effects on comprehension. *Reading Research Quarterly, 17,* 462–481.

Bell, S. (1992). Portfolio evaluation and Paulo Freire's *Pedagogy of the oppressed:* A descriptive analysis. *Teaching English in a Two-Year College, 19,* 95–96.

Bench, R. (1992). *Communication skills in the hearing impaired.* San Diego, CA: Whurr.

Bender, R. E. (1960). *The conquest of deafness*. Cleveland, OH: Press of Western Reserve University.

Bernhardt, E. (1993). *Reading development in a second language: Theoretic, empirical & classroom perspectives*. Norwood, NJ: Ablex.

Berry, S. R. (1981). *Written Language Syntax Test*. Washington, DC: Gallaudet University Press.

Betts, E. (1946). *Foundations of reading*. New York: American Book.

Biggs, S. A. (1990). Secondary perspectives: Portfolios illuminate the path for dynamic, interactive readers. *Journal of Reading, 33,* 644–647.

Bjorck-Akesson, E., & Granlund, M. (1995). Family involvement in assessment and intervention: Perceptions of professions and parents in Sweden. *Exceptional Children, 61*(6), 520–535.

Blair, F. (1957). A study of the visual memory of deaf and hearing children. *American Annals of the Deaf, 102,* 254–263.

Bloom, B. S. (1956). *Taxonomy of educational objectives: The classification of educational goals. Handbook 1: Cognitive domain*. New York: David MacKay.

Botel, M., & Granowsky, A. (1972). A formula for measuring syntactic complexity: A directional effect. *Elementary English, 49,* 513 –516.

Bowe, F. (Ed.). (1988). *Toward equality: Education of the deaf*. Commission on Education of the Deaf, Report to Congress and the President. Washington, DC: U.S. Government Printing Office.

Bowe, F. (1991). *Approaching equality: Education of the deaf*. Silver Spring, MD: T. J. Publishers.

Braden, J. (1994). *Deafness, deprivation, and IQ*. New York: Plenum Press.

Bradley-Johnson, S., & Evans, L. D. (1991). *Psychological assessment of hearing-impaired students: Infancy through high school*. Austin, TX: PRO-ED.

Bratcher, S. (1994). *Evaluating children's writing: A handbook of communication choices for classroom teachers*. New York: St. Martin's.

Brewer, W. (1975). Memory for ideas: Synonym substitution. *Memory and Cognition, 3,* 458–464.

Bridge, C., Winograd, P., & Haley, D. (1983). Using predictable materials vs. preprimers to teach beginning sight words. *Reading Teacher, 36,* 884–891.

Bromley, K. (1993). *Journaling: Engagements in reading, writing, and thinking*. New York: Scholastic.

Brooks, J., & Brooks, M. (1993). *In search of understanding: The case for constructivist classrooms*. Alexandria, VA: Association for Supervision and Curriculum Development.

Brophy, J. (1984). The teacher as thinker: Implementing instruction. In G. Duffy, L. Roehler, & J. Mason (Eds.). *Comprehension instruction: Perspectives and suggestions* (pp. 71–92). New York: Longman.

Brown, A. L. (1992). Design experiments: Theoretical and methodological challenges in creating complex interventions in classroom settings. *Journal of Learning Sciences, 2,* 141–178.

Brown, M. W. (1975). *Goodnight moon*. New York: Scholastic.

Brown, P. M., & Brewer, L. C. (1996). Cognitive processes of deaf and hearing skilled and less skilled readers. *Journal of Deaf Studies and Deaf Education, 1*(4), 263–270.

Brozo, W. G., & Tomlinson, C. M. (1986). Literature: The key to lively content courses. *Reading Teacher, 40,* 288–293.

Bruer, J. T. (1994). *Schools for thought*. Cambridge, MA: MIT Press.

Bruffee, K. A. (1986). Social construction, language, and the authority of knowledge: A bibliographic essay. *College English, 48,* 773–790.

Bruner, J. (1986). *Actual minds, possible worlds*. Cambridge, MA: Harvard University Press.

Buell, E. (1934). Reading for the deaf. *American Annals of the Deaf, 60,* 1–5.

Byrd, T. (1997, Fall). Telling tales in ASL. *Preview, 22–23.*

Calfee, R. C., & Perfumo, P. (1993). Student portfolios: Opportunities for a revolution in assessment. *Journal of Reading, 36,* 532–537.

Calkins, L. (1980). When children want to punctuate: Basic skills belong in context. *Language Arts, 57,* 567–573.

Calkins, L. (1983). *Lessons from a child.* Portsmouth, NH: Heinemann.

Calkins, L. (1994). *The art of teaching writing.* Portsmouth, NH: Heinemann.

Campbell, R. (1991). Speech in the head? Rhyme skill, reading and immediate memory in the deaf. In D. Reisberg (Ed.), *Auditory imagery* (pp. 73–93). Hillsdale, NJ: Erlbaum.

Campione, J. (1981, April). *Learning, academic achievement, and instruction.* Paper presented at the second annual Conference on Reading Research of the Center for the Study of Reading, New Orleans, LA.

Carr, T. H., Brown, T. L., Vavrus, L. G., & Evans, M. (1990). Cognitive skills maps and cognitive skill profiles: Componential analysis of individual differences in children's reading ability. In T. H. Carr & B. A. Levy (Eds.), *Reading and its development: Component skills approaches.* San Diego, CA: Academic.

Carrell, P., Devine, J., & Eskey, D. (1988). *Interactive approaches to second language reading.* New York: Cambridge University Press.

Carroll, D. (1986). *Psychology of language.* Monterey, CA: Brooks/Cole.

Carson, J. (1990). Reading-writing connections: Toward a description for second language learners. In B. Kroll (Ed.), *Second language writing: Research insights for the classroom* (pp. 88–101). New York: Cambridge University Press.

Carson, J., Carrell, P., Silberstein, S., Kroll, B., & Kuehn, P. (1990). Reading-writing relationships in first and second language. *TESOL Quarterly, 24,* 245–266.

Carver, R. J. (1990, June). *The challenge: Access, literacy and the deaf child.* Plenary address at the 12th Biennial Convention of American Society of Deaf Children, Vancouver, British Columbia.

Carver, R. J. (1990, November). *The hidden agenda of literacy in deafness: A Hobson's choice?* Paper presented at the Jones Memorial Lecture in Deafness, University of Alberta, Edmonton, Alberta.

Center for Assessment and Demographic Studies (CADS). (1991). *Stanford achievement test, 8th edition: Hearing-impaired norms booklet.* Washington, DC: Center for Assessment and Demographic Studies, Gallaudet Research Institute, Gallaudet University.

Chall, J. S., & Conrad, S. S. (1990). Textbooks and challenge: The influence of educational research. In D. L. Elliott & A. Woodward (Eds.), *Textbooks and schooling in the United States* (pp. 42–55). Chicago: National Sociey for the Study of Education.

Chall, J. S., Jacobs, V., & Baldwin, L. (1990). *The reading crisis: Why poor children fall behind.* Cambridge, MA: Harvard University Press.

Chamot, A., & O'Malley, J. (1986). *A cognitive academic language learning approach: An ESL content-based curriculum.* Rosslyn, VA: National Clearinghouse for Bilingual Education.

Chamot, A., & O'Malley, J. (1994). *The CALLA handbook: How to implement the cognitive academic language learning approach.* Reading, MA: Addison-Wesley.

Chomsky, N. (1965). *Aspects of a theory of syntax.* Cambridge, MA: MIT Press.

Chomsky, N. (1968). *Language and mind.* New York: Harcourt, Brace & World.

Christian, B. (1993). Freshman composition portfolios in a small college. *Teaching English in a Two-Year College, 20,* 289–297.

Clark, E. V. (1973), What's in a word? On the child's acquisition of semantics in his first language. In T. E. Moore (Ed.), *Cognitive development and the acquisition of language*. New York: Academic.

Clark, H. H., & Clark, E. V. (1977). *Psychology and language: An introduction to psycholinguistics*. New York: Harcourt Brace Jovanovich.

Clark, S. N., & Clark, D. C. (1992). Interdisciplinary teaming programs: Organization, rationale, and implementation. In S. Clark & D. Clark (Eds.), *Schools in the middle: A decade of growth and change*. Reston, VA: National Association of Secondary School Principals.

Clark, S. N., & Clark, D. C. (1994). *Restructuring the middle level school: Implications for school leaders*. Albany, NY: State University of New York Press.

Clark, S. N., & Clark, D. C. (1995). *The middle level principal's role in implementing interdisciplinary curriculum*. Reston, VA: National Association of Secondary School Principals.

Clay, M. M. (1967). The reading behavior of five year old children: A research report. *New Zealand Journal of Educational Studies, 2*, 11–31.

Clay, M. M. (1979, 1985). *The early detection of reading difficulties*. Exeter, NH: Heinemann.

Clay, M. M. (1993). *Reading recovery: A guide for teachers in training*. Portsmouth, NH: Heinemann.

Clemmons, J., Laase, L., Cooper, D., Areglado, N., & Dill, M. (1993). *Portfolios in the classroom: A teacher's sourcebook*. New York: Scholastic.

The College Board. (1983). *Degrees of reading power. PA series*. New York: College Entrance Examination Board.

Commission on Education of the Deaf. (1988). *Toward equality: Education of the deaf, a report to the President and the Congress of the United States*. Washington, DC: U.S. Government Printing Office.

Conrad, R. (1970). Short-term memory processes in the deaf. *British Journal of Psychology, 61*, 179–195.

Conrad, R. (1979). *The deaf school child*. London: Harper & Row.

Conway, D. F. (1990, December). Semantic relationships in the word meanings of hearing-impaired children. *Volta Review*, 339–349.

Cooper, J. D. (1997). *Literacy: Helping children construct meaning* (3rd ed.). Boston: Houghton Mifflin.

Cooper, W., & Brown, B. J. (1992). Using portfolios to empower student writers. *English Journal, 81*, 40–45.

Cordeiro, P. (1992). *Whole learning: Whole language and content in the upper elementary grades*. Katonah, NY: Richard C. Owen.

Corson, H. (1973). *Comparing deaf children of oral parents and deaf parents using manual communication with deaf children of hearing parents on academic, social and communication functioning*. Unpublished dissertation, University of Cincinnati, Ohio.

Council for Exceptional Children. (1998). The revolution in educational materials. *Today, 4*(6), 1–15.

Crafton, L. K. (1991). *Whole language: Getting started . . . moving forward*. Katonah, NY: Richard C. Owen.

Crews, D. (1978). *Freight train*. New York: Scholastic.

Cromer, R. (1976). The cognitive hypothesis of language acquisition and its implications for child language deficiency. In D. Morehead & A. Morehead (Eds.), *Normal and deficient child language* (pp. 283–333). Baltimore: University Park Press.

Cudd, E. T., & Roberts, L. (1989). Using writing to enhance content area learning in the primary grades. *Reading Teacher, 42*, 392–404.

Cummins, J. (1981). The role of primary language development in promoting educational success for language minority students. In California State Department of Education (Ed.), *Schooling and language minority students: A theoretical framework* (pp. 3–49). Los Angeles: California State University, Evaluation, Dissemination, and Assessment Center.

Cummins, J. (1991). Language development and academic learning. In L. M. Malave & G. Duquette (Eds.), *Language, culture and cognition*. Philadelphia: Multilingual Matters.

Cunningham, A. E. (1990). Explicit versus implicit instruction in phonemic awareness. *Journal of Experimental Child Psychology, 50*, 429–444.

Czarnecki, E., Rosko, D., & Fine, E. (1998). How to call up notetaking skills. *Teaching Exceptional Children, 30*(6), 14–19.

Daneman, M., Nemeth, S., Stainton, M., & Huelsmann, K. (1995). Working memory as a predictor of reading achievement in orally educated hearing-impaired children. *Volta Review, 97*, 225–241.

Danielson, C., & Abrutyn, L. (1997). *An introduction to using portfolios in the classroom*. Alexandria, VA: Association for Supervision and Curriculum Development.

Davey, B. (1987). Post passage questions: Task and reader effects on comprehension and metacomprehension processes. *Journal of Reading Behavior, 19*, 261–283.

Davey, B., & King, S. (1990). Acquisition of word meanings from context by deaf readers. *American Annals of the Deaf, 135*(3), 227–234.

Davey, B., & LaSasso, C. (1983). An examination of hearing-impaired readers' test-taking abilities on reinspection tasks. *Volta Review, 85*, 279–284.

Davey, B., & LaSasso, C. (1985, January). Relations of cognitive style to assessment components of reading comprehension for hearing-impaired adolescents. *Volta Review*, 17–27.

Davey, B., & McBride, S. (1986). Effect of question generation training on reading comprehension. *Journal of Educational Psychology, 78*, 256–262.

Davis, F. B. (1944). Fundamental factors of comprehension in reading. *Psychometrika, 9*, 185–197.

Dawkins, J. (1975). *Syntax and readability*. Newark, DE: International Reading Association.

de Beaugrande, R. (1982). Psychology and composition: Past, present, and future. In M. Nystrand (Ed.), *What writers know: The language, process, and structure of written discourse* (pp. 211–267). San Diego, CA: Academic.

DeFina, A. (1992). *Portfolio assessment: Getting started*. New York: Scholastic.

Deno, S. L. (1989). Curriculum-based measurement and special education services: A fundamental and direct relationship. In M. R. Shinn (Ed.), *Curriculum-based measurement: Assessing special children* (pp. 1–17). New York: Guilford Press.

Deno, S. L., Mirkin, P. L., & Marston, D. B. (1982). Valid measurement procedures for continuous evaluation of written expression. *Exceptional Children, 48*, 368–371.

deVilliers, P., & Pomerantz, S. (1992). Hearing-impaired students learning new words from written context. *Applied Psycholinguistics, 13*, 409–431.

Diehl, W. A., & Mikulecky, L. (1980). The nature of reading at work. *Journal of Reading, 24*, 221–234.

DiStefano, P., & Valencia, S. (1980). The effect of syntactic maturity on comprehension of graded reading passages. *Journal of Educational Research, 73*, 247–251.

Dixon, N., Davies, A., & Politano, C. (1996). *Learning with readers theatre: Building connections*. Winnipeg, Canada: Peguis.

Doblmeier, J. (1981). *Environmental science*. Washington, DC: Gallaudet College, Outreach Programs.

Dodd, B. (1980). The spelling abilities of profoundly pre-lingually deaf children. In U. Frith (Ed.), *Cognitive processes in spelling* (pp. 423–440). New York: Academic Press.

Dodd, B. (1987). Lipreading, phonological coding and deafness. In B. Dodd & R. Campbell (Eds.), *Hearing by eye: The psychology of lip-reading* (pp. 163–175). Hillsdale, NJ: Erlbaum.

Dolch, E. W. (1955). *Methods in reading*. Champaign, IL: Garrard.

Dolch, E. W. (1960). *Better spelling*. Champaign, IL: Garrard.

Dolman, D. (1992). Some concerns about using whole language approaches with deaf children. *American Annals of the Deaf, 137,* 278–282.

Dressler, C. (1997). Sign of the times. *Education Bulletin: Harvard Graduate School of Education, 41*(2), 4–7.

Duffelmeyer, F. A., Baum, D. D., & Merkley, D. J. (1987). Maximizing reader-text confrontation with an extended anticipation guide. *Journal of Reading, 31,* 146–150.

Duin, A. H., & Graves, M. F. (1987). Intensive vocabulary instruction as a prewriting technique. *Reading Research Quarterly, 22,* 311–330.

Durkin, D. (1966). *Children who read early.* New York: Teachers College Press.

Durkin, D. (1978–79). What classroom observations reveal about reading comprehension instruction. *Reading Research Quarterly, 14,* 481–538.

Durkin, D. (1986). Reading methodology textbooks: Are they helping teachers teach comprehension? *Reading Teacher, 39,* 410–417.

Durkin, D. (1989). *Teaching them to read* (5th ed.). Needham Heights, MA: Allyn & Bacon.

Eastman, P. D. (1960). *Are you my mother?* New York: Beginner Books.

Edelsky, C. (1982). Writing in a bilingual program. *TESOL Quarterly, 16,* 211–228.

Edelsky, C., Altwerger, B., & Flores, B. (1991). *Whole language: What's the difference?* Portsmouth, NH: Heinemann.

Edelsky, C., & Harman, S. (1988). One more critique of reading tests—with two differences. *English Education, 20,* 157–171.

Educational Testing Service. (1992). *TOEFL Test of Written English* (3rd ed.). Princeton, NJ: Author.

Ehri, L. C. (1989). Movement into word reading and spelling: How spelling contributes to reading. In J. M. Mason (Ed.), *Reading and writing connections* (pp. 65–81). Needham Heights, MA: Allyn & Bacon.

Elliot, D. L., & Woodward, A. (1990). Textbooks, curriculum and school improvement. In D. L. Elliot & A. Woodward (Eds.), *Textbooks and schooling in the United States* (pp. 222–232). Chicago: National Society for the Study of Education.

Ellis, E. S., & Lenz, B. K. (1997). A component analysis of effective learning strategies for LD students. *Learning Disabilities Focus, 2,* 94–107.

Engberg-Pedersen, E. (1993). *Space in Danish Sign Language: The semantics and morphosyntax of the use of space in a visual language.* Hamburg, Germany: Signum-Verlag.

Englert, C. S., Raphael, T. E., Anderson, L. M., & Fear, K. L. (1988). Students' metacognitive knowledge about how to write informational texts. *Learning Disability Quarterly, 11,* 18–46.

Enright, D. S., & McCloskey, M. L. (1988). *Integrating English: Developing English language and literacy in the multilingual classroom.* Reading, MA: Addison-Wesley.

Ensor II, A. D., & Koller, J. R. (1997). The effects of the method of repeated readings in the reading rate and word recognition accuracy of deaf adolescents. *Journal of Deaf Studies and Deaf Education, 2*(2), 61–70.

Erickson, M. (1987). Deaf readers reading beyond the literal. *American Annals of the Deaf, 132,* 291–293.

Erting, C. (1992). Partnerships for change: Creating new possible worlds for deaf children and their families. In *Bilingual considerations in the education of deaf students: ASL and English.* Washington, DC: Gallaudet University, College for Continuing Education.

Erting, C. (1994). *Deafness, communication, social identity: Ethnography in a preschool for deaf children.* Burtonsville, MD: Linstok.

Ewoldt, C. (1981). A psycholinguistic description of selected deaf children reading in sign language. *Reading Research Quarterly, 17,* 58–89.

Ewoldt, C. (1982). Diagnostic approaches and procedures and the reading process. In R.E. Kretschmer (Ed.), *Reading and the hearing-impaired individual* [Special issue]. *Volta Review, 84,* 83–94.

Ewoldt, C. (1985a). A descriptive study of the developing literacy of young hearing-impaired children. *Volta Review, 87,* 109–126.

Ewoldt, C. (1985b). What does "reading" mean? *Perspectives for Teachers of the Hearing Impaired, 4,* 10–13.

Ewoldt, C. (1990). The early literacy development of deaf children. In D. Moores & K. Meadow-Orlans (Eds.), *Educational and developmental aspects of deafness.* Washington, DC: Gallaudet University Press.

Ewoldt, C., Israelite, N., & Dodds, R. (1991). The ability of deaf students to understand text: A comparison of the perceptions of teachers and students. *American Annals of the Deaf, 137,* 351–361.

Farr, R. (1990). Trends: Reading, setting directions for language arts portfolios. *Educational Leadership, 48,* 103.

Farr, R. (1991). The assessment puzzle. *Educational Leadership, 49,* 95.

Fielding, L. G., & Pearson, P. D. (1994, February). Reading comprehension: What works. *Educational Leadership, 51,* 62–68.

Fielding, L. G., Wilson, P. D., & Anderson, R. C. (1986). A new focus on free reading: The role of trade books in reading instruction. In T. E. Raphael (Ed.), *The context of school-based literacy,* (pp. 149–160). New York: Random House.

Firth, U. (1985). Beneath the surface of developmental dyslexia. In K. E. Patterson, K. C. Marshall, & M. Coltheart (Eds.), *Surface dyslexia: Neuropsychological and cognitive studies of phonological reading.* Hillsdale, NJ: Erlbaum.

Fischler, I. (1983). Contextual constraints and comprehension of written sentences by deaf college students. *American Annals of the Deaf, 128,* 418–424.

Fisher, C. W., & Hiebert, E. H. (1990). Characteristics of tasks in two approaches to literacy instruction. *Elementary School Journal, 91,* 3–18.

Fitzgerald, J., & Spiegel, D. (1983). Enhancing children's reading comprehension through instruction in narrative structure. *Journal of Reading Behavior, 15,* 1–17.

Fleury, P. (1979, 1982). *Controlled language science series.* Beaverton, OR: Dormac.

Flood, J., & Lapp, D. (1986). Types of texts: The match between what students read in basals and what they encounter in tests. *Reading Research Quarterly, 21,* 284–297.

Florio-Ruane, S., & Lensmire, T. (1989). The role of instruction in learning to write. In J. Brophy (Ed.), *Advances in research on teaching: Vol. 1. Teaching for meaningful understanding and self-regulated learning.* Greenwich, CT: JAI Press.

Flower, L., & Hayes, J. (1981). Plans that guide the composing process. In C. H. Frederiksen & J. Dominic (Eds.), *Writing: The nature, development, and teaching of written communication* (pp. 39–58). Hillsdale, NJ: Erlbaum.

Fogel, N. S. (1990, April). *A computer approach to teaching English syntax to deaf students.* Paper presented at the Annual Meeting of the American Educational Research Association, Boston, MA.

Forbes, E. (1971). *Johnny Tremain.* New York: Dell.

Ford, M. (1993). The process and promise of portfolio assessment in teacher education programs: Impact on students' knowledge, beliefs, and practices. In T. Rasinski & N. Padak (Eds.), *Inquiries in literacy learning and instruction* (pp. 145–152). Kent, OH: College Reading Association.

Foster, K., & Quinn, G. (1996). Untangling the World Wide Web. *TECH-NJ, 7*(1), 1–10.

Fox, S. (1991). Metacognitive strategies in a college world literature class. *American Annals of the Deaf, 139,* 506–511.

Fractor, J. S., Woodruff, M., Martinez, M., & Teale, W. (1993). Let's not miss opportunities to promote voluntary reading: Classroom libraries in the elementary school. *Reading Teacher, 46,* 476–485.

Freebody, P., & Byrne, B. (1988). Word-reading strategies in elementary school children: Relation to comprehension, reading time, and phonemic awareness. *Reading Research Quarterly, 23*(4), 441–453.

Fruchter, A., Wilbur, R., & Fraser, B. (1984). Comprehension of idioms by hearing-impaired students. *Volta Review, 86,* 7–18.

Fry, E. (1990). A readability formula for short passages. *Journal of Reading, 33*(8), 594–597.

Fry, E., Fountoukidis, D., & Polk, J. (1985). *The new reading teacher's book of lists.* Englewood Cliffs, NJ: Prentice-Hall.

Fulwiler, T. (1982). The personal connection: Journal writing across the curriculum. In T. Fulwiler & A. Young (Eds.), *Language connections: Writing and reading across the curriculum* (pp. 15–31). Urbana, IL: National Council of Teachers of English.

Furth, H. (1966). *Thinking without language.* New York: Free Press.

Furth, H. (1971). Education for thinking. *Journal of Rehabilitation of the Deaf, 5*(1), 7–17.

Furth, H. (1973). *Deafness and learning: A psychosocial approach.* Belmont, CA: Wadsworth.

Galdone, P. (1973). *Three billy goats gruff.* New York: The Seabury Press.

Gambrell, J., & Bales, R. J. (1986). Mental imagery and the comprehension-monitoring performance of fourth- and fifth-grade poor readers. *Reading Research Quarterly, 21,* 454–464.

Gamoran, A., & Nystrand, M. (1992). Taking students seriously. In F. M. Newman (Ed.), *Student engagement and achievement in American secondary schools* (pp. 40–61). New York: Teachers College Press.

Garrison, W., Long, G., & Dowaliby F. (1997). Working memory capacity and comprehension processes in deaf readers. *Journal of Deaf Studies and Deaf Education, 2*(2), 78–92.

Geers, A., & Moog, J. (1989, February/March). Factors predictive of the development of literacy in profoundly hearing-impaired adolescents. *Volta Review,* 69–86.

Gergen, K. J. (1985). The social constructionist movement in modern psychology. *American Psychologist, 40,* 266–275.

Gersten, R., Keating, T., & Irvin, L. K. (1995). The burden of proof: Validity as improvement of instructional practice. *Exceptional Children, 61*(6), 510–519.

Gibbs, K. W. (1989). Individual differences in cognitive skills related to reading ability in the deaf. *American Annals of the Deaf, 134,* 214–218.

Giddings, L. R. (1992). Literature-based reading instruction: An analysis. *Reading Research and Instruction, 31,* 18–30.

Gillespie, C. S., Ford, K. L., Gillespie, R. D., & Leavell, A. G. (1996). Portfolio assessment: Some questions, some answers, some recommendations. *Journal of Adolescent & Adult Literacy, 39,* 480–491.

Gillespie, C. W., & Twardosz, S. (1996). Survey of literacy environments and practices in residences at schools for the deaf. *American Annals of the Deaf, 141,* 224–229.

Gillespie, C. W., & Twardosz, S. (1997). A group storybook-reading intervention with children at a residential school for the deaf. *American Annals of the Deaf, 142,* 320–332.

Giorcelli, L. (1982). *The comprehension of some aspects of figurative language by deaf and hearing subjects.* Unpublished doctoral dissertation, University of Illinois, Urbana.

Goodman, K. (1970). Reading: A psycholinguistic guessing game. In H. Singer & R. Ruddell (Eds.), *Theoretical models and processes of reading* (pp. 259–272). Newark, DE: International Reading Association.

Goodman, K. (1984). Unity in reading. In A. Purves & O. Niles (Eds.), *Becoming readers in a complex society*. The 83rd Yearbook of the National Society of the Study of Education: Part I (pp. 79–114). Chicago: University of Chicago Press.

Goodman, K. (1986). *What's whole about whole language?* Portsmouth, NH: Heinemann.

Goodman, K. (1989). Whole-language research: Foundations and development. *Elementary School Journal, 90,* 207–222.

Goodman, K. (1992). Whole language research: Foundations and development. In S. J. Samuels and A. E. Farstrup (Eds.), *What research has to say about reading instruction* (pp. 46–69). Newark, DE: International Reading Association.

Goodman, K., & Gollasch, F. (1980). Word omissions: Deliberate and non-deliberate. *Reading Research Quarterly, 16,* 6–31.

Goodman, K., & Goodman, Y. (1978). *Reading of American children whose language is a stable rural dialect of English or a language other than English* (Final Report No. C-003-0087). Washington, DC: National Institute of Education.

Goodman, K., Goodman, Y., & Flores, B. (1979). *Reading in a bilingual classroom.* Rosslyn, VA: National Clearinghouse for Bilingual Education.

Goodman, Y., & Wilde, W. (1985). *Writing development: Third and fourth grade O'odham (Papago) students* (Occasional Paper No. 14). Tucson, AZ: Program in Language and Literacy, University of Arizona.

Gormley, K., & Franzen, A. M. (1978) . Why the deaf can't read: Comments on asking the wrong questions. *American Annals of the Deaf, 123,* 11–32.

Gough, P. (1972). One second of reading. In J. Kavanaugh & I. Mattingly (Eds.), *Language by ear and by eye: The relationships between speech and reading* (pp. 331–358). Cambridge, MA: MIT Press.

Gough, P. (1984). Word recognition. In P. D. Pearson (Ed.), *Handbook of reading research* (Vol. 1) (pp. 225–253). White Plains, NY: Longman.

Gough, P. (1985). One second of reading. In H. Singer & R. Ruddell (Eds.), *Theoretical models and processes of reading* (3rd ed.) (pp. 661–686). Newark, DE: International Reading Association.

Grabe, W. (1991). Current developments in second language reading research. *TESOL Quarterly, 25*(3), 375–406.

Graves, D. (1994). *A fresh look at writing.* Portsmouth, NH: Heinemann.

Graves, D., & Hansen, J. (1983). The author's chair. *Language Arts, 60,* 176–183.

Graves, M. F. (1996). The continuing quest toward literacy for all children. In M. F. Graves, P. van den Broek, & B. M. Taylor (Eds.), *The first R: Every child's right to read* (pp. ix–xix). New York: Teachers College Press and International Reading Association.

Graves, M. F., & Graves, B. (1994). *Scaffolding reading experiences.* Norwood, MA: Christopher-Gorden.

Graves, M. F., Watts, S., & Graves, B. (1994). *Essentials of classroom teaching: Elementary reading.* Needham Heights, MA: Allyn & Bacon.

Green, F. (1986). Listening to children read: The emphatic process. *Reading Teacher, 39,* 536–543.

Greenberg, M., & Kusche, C. (1989). Cognitive, personal, and social development of deaf children and adolescents. In M. Wang, M. Reynolds, & H. Walberg (Eds.), *The handbook of special education: Research and practice* (Vol. 3) (pp. 95–129). Oxford, England: Pergamon.

Griffith, P. L., & Ripich, D. N. (1988). Story structure recall in hearing impaired, learning disabled, and nondisabled children. *American Annals of the Deaf, 133*(1), 43–50.

Groht, M. (1958). *Natural language for deaf children*. Washington, DC: Alexander Graham Bell Association for the Deaf.

Gunderson, L., & Shapiro, J. (1987). Some findings on whole language instruction. *Reading-Canada-Lecture, 5*(1), 22–26.

Guthrie, J. T., & McCann, A. D. (1997). Characteristics of classrooms that promote motivations and strategies for learning. In J. T. Guthrie & A. Wigfield (Eds.), *Reading engagement: Motivating readers through integrated instruction* (pp. 128–148). Newark, DE: International Reading Association.

Guthrie, J. T., & Seifert, M. (1983). Profiles of reading activity in a community. *Journal of Reading, 26*, 498–508.

Guzzetti, B. J. (1982). A psycholinguistic analysis of the reading strategies of high, average, and low ability readers across selected content areas. *Dissertation Abstracts International, 43*(4), 1026-A (University Microfilms No. DA 8211081).

Guzzetti, B. J., Kowalinski, B. J., & McGowan, T. (1992). Using a literature-based approach to teaching social studies. *Journal of Reading, 36*, 114–122.

Hagerty, P. (1992). *Readers' workshop: Real reading*. Richmond Hill, Ontario: Scholastic Canada.

Hakuta, K. (1990). *Bilingualism and bilingual education: A research perspective. Occasional Papers in Bilingual Education*. Washington, DC: National Clearinghouse for Bilingual Education.

Halliday, M. A. K., & Hasan, R. (1976). *Cohesion in English*. London: Longman.

Hammill, D., & Larsen, S. (1996). *Test of Written Language* (3rd ed.). Austin, TX: PRO-ED.

Hansen, B. (1990). Trend in the progress toward bilingual education for deaf children in Denmark. In S. Prillwitz & T. Vollhaber (Eds.), *Sign language research and application* (pp. 51–64). Hamburg, Germany: Signum-Verlag.

Hansen, J. (1981). An inferential comprehension strategy for use with primary children. *Reading Teacher, 34*, 665–669.

Hansen, J. (1987). *When writers read*. Portsmouth, NH: Heinemann.

Hansen, J., & Pearson, P. D. (1983). An instructional study: Improving the inferential comprehension of fourth grade good and poor readers. *Journal of Educational Psychology, 75*, 821–829.

Hanson, V. (1985). Cognitive processing in reading: Where deaf readers succeed and where they have difficulty. In D. Martin (Ed.), *Cognition, education, and deafness: Directions for research and instruction* (pp. 108–110). Washington, DC: Gallaudet University Press.

Hanson, V. (1989). Phonology and reading: Evidence from profoundly deaf readers. In D. Shankweiler & I. Liberman (Eds.), *Phonology and reading disability: Solving the reading puzzle* (pp. 69–89). Ann Arbor: University of Michigan Press.

Hanson, V. (1990). Recall of order information by deaf signers: Phonetic coding in temporal order recall. *Memory and Cognition, 18*, 604–610.

Hanson, V., & Bellugi, U. (1982). On the role of sign order and morphological structure in memory for American Sign Language. *Journal of Verbal Learning and Verbal Behavior, 21*, 621–633.

Hanson, V., & Fowler, C. (1987). Phonological coding in word reading: Evidence from hearing and deaf readers. *Memory and Cognition, 15*, 199–207.

Hanson, V., Goodell, E. W., & Perfetti, C. A. (1991). Tongue-twister effects in the silent reading of hearing and deaf college students. *Journal of Memory and Language, 30*, 319–330.

Harlin, R., Lipa, S., & Phelps, S. (1992). Portfolio assessment: Interpretations and implications for classroom teachers and reading teachers. In N. Padak, T. Rasinski, & J. Logan (Eds.), *Literacy research and practice: Foundations for the year 2000* (pp. 203–208). Kent, OH: College Reading Association.

Harris, L., & Lalick, R. (1987). Teachers' use of informal reading inventories: An example of school constraints. *Reading Teacher, 40,* 624–630.

Harris, M., & Beech, J. R. (1998). Implicit phonological awareness and early reading development in prelingually deaf children. *Journal of Deaf Studies and Deaf Education, 3*(3), 205–217.

Hart, B. O. (1975). Learning to read begins at birth. *Volta Review, 76,* 168–172.

Hart, D. (1994). *Authentic assessment: A handbook for educators.* Menlo Park, CA: Addison-Wesley.

Hatcher, C., & Robbins, N. (1978). *The development of reading skills in hearing impaired children.* Cedar Falls, IA: University of Northern Iowa (ERIC Document Reproduction Service Number ED 16790).

Hawisher, G. E., & Selfe, C. L. (1989). *Critical perspectives on computers and composition instruction.* New York: Teachers College Press, Columbia University.

Haydon, D. M. (1996). Carrying meaning in written language: Some considerations for teachers and their classes. *Volta Review, 98*(1), 147–168.

Hayes, J. R., & Flower, L. S. (1980). Identifying the organization of writing processes. In L. W. Gregg & E. R. Steinberg (Eds.), *Cognitive processes in writing* (pp. 3–30). Hillsdale, NJ: Erlbaum.

Hayes, P., & Arnold, P. (1992). Is hearing impaired children's reading delayed or different? *Journal of Research in Reading, 15,* 104–116.

Hazelwood, D., & Pollard, G. (1996). New horizons in technology and deaf education. *TELA Themes, 2,* 3–4.

Heath, S. B. (1980). Functions and uses of literacy. *Journal of Communication, 30,* 123–133.

Heath, S. B. (1982). What no bedtime story means: Narrative skills at home and at school. *Language in Society, 11,* 49–75.

Heath, S. B. (1983). *Ways with words: Language, work and life in communities and classrooms.* New York: Cambridge University Press.

Heefner, D. L., & Shaw, P. C. (1996). Assessing the written narratives of deaf students using the six-trait analytical scale. *Volta Review, 98*(1), 147–168.

Hefferman, H. (1960). Significance of kindergarten education. *Childhood Education, 36,* 313–319.

Heider, F., & Heider, B. (1940). A comparison of sentence structures of deaf and hearing children. *Psychological Monographs, 52,* 42–103.

Heiling, K. (1993, November). *A psychologist's perspective.* Presentation at the Conference on Education of Deaf Children with Cochlear Implants: A New Challenge for the Teacher, Luxembourg.

Heimlich, J. E., & Pittelman, S. D. (1986). *Semantic mapping: Classroom applications.* Newark, DE: International Reading Association, Reading Aids Series.

Herber, H. L. (1970). *Teaching reading in content areas.* Englewood Cliffs, NJ: Prentice-Hall.

Hermann, B. A. (1988). Two approaches for helping poor readers become more strategic. *Reading Research Quarterly, 42,* 24–28.

Hiebert, E. H. (1996). Creating and sustaining a love of literature . . . and the ability to read it. In M. F. Graves, P. van den Broek, & B. M. Taylor (Eds.), *The first R: Every child's right to read* (pp. 15–36). New York: Teachers College Press and International Reading Association.

Highlights of the National Literacy Act of 1991, Public Law 102–73. (1991). Washington, DC: Southport Institute for Policy Analysis.

Hillerich, R. L. (1985). *Teaching children to write, K–8: A complete guide to developing writing skills.* Englewood Cliffs, NJ: Prentice-Hall.

Hinchley, J., & Levy, B. A. (1988). Developmental and individual differences in reading comprehension. *Cognition and Instruction, 51,* 3–47.

Hirsch, Jr., E. D. (1988). *Cultural literacy: What every American needs to know*. New York: Vantage Books.

Hoffman, J. M., Roser, N. L., & Battle, J. (1993). Reading aloud in classrooms: From the modal to a "model." *Reading Teacher, 46*, 496–505.

Hoffman, S., & McCully, B. (1984). Oral language functions in transaction with children's writing. *Language Arts, 61*, 41–50.

Holdaway, D. (1979). *The foundations of literacy*. Portsmouth, NH: Heinemann.

Holland, M. (1967). Billy had a system. In B. Martin, Jr. (Ed.), *Sounds of mystery* (pp. 52–63). New York: Holt, Rinehart, & Winston.

Holt, J. (1994). Classroom attributes and achievement scores for deaf and hard of hearing students. *American Annals of the Deaf, 139*, 430–437.

Hornberger, N. H. (1989). Continua of biliteracy. *Review of Educational Research, 59*, 271–296.

Hotto, S., & Schildroth, A. (1982, November). The Stanford Achievement Tests: A special edition for hearing-impaired students. *Perspectives*, 18–19.

Hoyt, L. (1992). Many ways of knowing: Using drama, oral interactions, and the visual arts to enhance reading comprehension. *Reading Teacher, 45*, 580–584.

Hudelson, S. (1981). *Learning to read in different languages*. Washington, DC: Center for Applied Linguistics.

Hudelson, S. (1984). "Kan yu ret an rayt en ingles": Children become literate in English as a second language. *TESOL Quarterly, 18*, 221–238.

Hudelson, S. (1986). ESL children's writing: What we've learned, what we're learning. In P. Rigg & D. Enright (Eds.), *Children and ESL: Integrating perspectives* (pp. 23–54). Washington, DC: Teachers of English to Speakers of Other Languages.

International Reading Association and National Council of Teachers of English. (1994). *Standards for the assessment of reading and writing*. Newark, DE: Author.

Iran-Nejad, A., Ortony, A., & Rittenhouse, R. (1981). The comprehension of metaphorical uses of English by deaf children. *Journal of Speech and Hearing Research, 24*, 124–130.

Irwin, J. W., & Baker, I. (1989). *Promoting active reading comprehension strategies: A resource book for teachers*. Englewood Cliffs, NJ: Prentice-Hall.

Irwin, J. W., & Davis, C. A. (1990). Assessing readability: The checklist approach. *Journal of Reading, 24*, 124–130.

Isaacson, S. L. (1988). Assessing the writing product: Qualitative and quantitative measures. *Exceptional Children, 56*(6), 528–534.

Isaacson, S. L. (1996). Simple ways to assess deaf or hard of hearing students' writing skills. *Volta Review, 98*(1), 183–200.

Israelite, N. (1988). On readability formulas: A critical analysis for teachers of the deaf. *American Annals of the Deaf, 133*, 14–17.

Israelite, N., Ewoldt, C., & Hoffmeister, R. (1992). *Bilingual-bicultural education for deaf and hard-of-hearing students*. Toronto, Ontario: MGS Publications Services.

Jackson, D. W., Paul, P. V., & Smith, J. C. (1997). Prior knowledge and reading comprehension ability of deaf adolescents. *Journal of Deaf Studies and Deaf Education, 2*(3), 172–184.

Jacobs, H. H. (1989). *Interdisciplinary curriculum: Design and implementation*. Alexandria, VA: Association for Supervision and Curriculum Development.

Jacobs, H. H. (1991). Planning for curriculum integration. *Educational Leadership, 49*(2), 27–28.

Jago, C. (1998). A teacher's adventures in standards land. *Phi Delta Kappan, 79*(9), 685.

Jenkins, J. J. (1976). Four points to remember: A tetrahedral model of memory experiments. In L. S. Cermak & F. I. M. Craik (Eds.), *Levels of processing in human memory*. Hillsdale, NJ: Erlbaum.

Johns, J. (1992). How professionals view portfolio assessment. *Reading Research and Instruction, 32,* 1–10.

Johnson, D., & Johnson, R. (1985). The internal dynamics of cooperative learning groups. In R. Slavin, S. Sharon, S. Kagan, R. Hertz-Lazarowitz, C. Webb, & R. Schmuck (Eds.), *Learning to cooperate, cooperating to learn*. New York: Plenum.

Johnson, D. D., Toms-Bronowski, S., & Pittelman, S. D. (1982). Vocabulary development. *Volta Review, 84,* 11–24.

Johnson, D. W., Johnson, R. T., & Holubec, E. J. (1990). *Circles of learning: Cooperation in the classroom* (3rd ed.). Edina, MN: Interaction Book Company.

Johnson, P. (1981). Effects on reading comprehension of language complexity and cultural background knowledge. *TESOL Quarterly, 16,* 503–516.

Johnson, P. H., Allington, R. L., & Afflerbach, P. (1985). The congruence of classroom and remedial reading instruction. *Elementary School Journal, 85,* 465–477.

Johnson, R. E., Liddell, S. K., & Erting, C. J. (1989). *Unlocking the curriculum: Principles for achieving access in deaf education*. Gallaudet Research Institute Working Paper 89-3. Washington, DC: Gallaudet University.

Johnston, P. (1981). *Background knowledge, reading comprehension and test bias*. Unpublished doctoral dissertation, University of Illinois, Urbana-Champaign.

Johnston, P., & Pearson, P. D. (1982). *Prior knowledge, connectivity, and the assessment of reading comprehension*. Urbana-Champaign: University of Illinois, Center for the Study of Reading.

Jones, B., Palincsar, A., Ogle, D., & Carr, E. (1987). *Strategic teaching and learning: Cognitive instruction in the content areas*. Alexandria, VA: Association for Supervision and Curriculum Development.

Joseph, D. (1989). *The effects of visual structural overviews and advanced organizers on deaf students' reading comprehension*. Unpublished doctoral dissertation, University of Minnesota, Minneapolis.

Juel, C. (1988). Learning to read and write: A longitudinal study of 54 children from the first through the fourth grades. *Journal of Educational Psychology, 89,* 437–447.

Just, M., & Carpenter, P. (1987). *The psychology of reading and language comprehension*. Boston: Allyn & Bacon.

Karmiloff-Smith, A. (1979). *A functional approach to child language: A study of determiners and reference*. New York: Cambridge University Press.

Kaufman, A. S., & Kaufman, N. L. (1983). *K*ABC Kaufman assessment battery for children: Interpretive manual*. Circle Pines, MN: American Guidance Services.

Kavale, K. (1979). Selecting and evaluating reading tests. In R. Schreiner (Ed.), *Reading test and teachers: A practical guide* (pp. 9–34). Newark, DE: International Reading Association.

Kearney, J. (1981). *Loans and credits*. Washington, DC: University Gallaudet Outreach Programs.

Kelly, L. P. (1993). Recall of English function words and inflections by skilled and average readers. *American Annals of the Deaf, 138*(3), 288–296.

Kelly, L. P. (1995). Processing of bottom-up and top-down information by skilled and average deaf readers and implications for whole language instruction. *Exceptional Children, 61,* 318–334.

Kelly, L. P. (1996). The interaction of syntactic competence and vocabulary during reading by deaf students. *Journal of Deaf Studies and Deaf Education, 1*(1), 75–90.

Kern, R. G. (1995). Restructuring classroom interaction with networked computers: Effects on quantity and characteristics of language production. *Modern Language Journal, 79*(4), 457–476.

King, C. M. (1983). *Survey of language methods and materials used with hearing-impaired students in the United States*. Paper presented at the Convention of the Association of Canadian Educators of the Hearing Impaired, Convention of the American Instructors for the Deaf, and the Convention of Executives for American Schools for the Deaf, Winnipeg, Canada.

King, C. M. (1997, March). *Learning with globally accessible, interactive media materials*. Keynote presentation at the International Conference on Computer-Assisted Instruction (ICCI), Taipei, Taiwan.

King, C. M., & Quigley, S. (1985). *Reading and deafness*. Austin, TX: PRO-ED.

Kintsch, W., & van Dijk, T. (1978). Toward a model of text comprehension and production. *Psychological Review, 85*, 363–394.

Klima, E., & Bellugi, U. (1979). *The signs of language*. Cambridge, MA: Harvard University Press.

Koskinen, P. S., Wilson, R. M., & Jensema, C. J. (1986). Using closed-captioned television in teaching and reading to deaf students. *American Annals of the Deaf, 131*(1), 43–47.

Kozol, J. (1985). *Illiterate America*. New York: Anchor Press.

Kretschmer, R. E. (1982). Reading and the hearing-impaired individual: Summation and application. In R. E. Kretschmer (Ed.), Reading and the hearing-impaired individual. *Volta Review, 84*(5), 107–122.

Kretschmer, Jr., R. R., & Kretschmer, L. W. (1986). Language in perspective. In D. M. Luterman (Ed.), *Deafness in perspective* (pp. 131–166). San Diego, CA: College-Hill.

Krinsky, G. G. (1990). The feeling of knowing in deaf adolescents. *American Annals of the Deaf, 135*, 389–395.

Kuntze, M. (1993). Developing students' literacy skills in ASL. *Post Milan ASL & English literacy: Issues, trends, and research*. Conference Proceedings. Washington, DC: Gallaudet University.

LaBerge, D., & Samuels, S. J. (1974). Toward a theory of automatic information processing in reading. *Cognitive Psychology, 6*, 293–323.

LaBerge, D., & Samuels, S. J. (1976). Toward a theory of automatic information processing in reading. In H. Singer & R. Ruddell (Eds.), *Theoretical models and processes of reading*. Newark, DE: International Reading Association.

Lane, H. (1990). Bilingual education for ASL-using children. In M. Garretson (Ed.), Eyes, hands, voices: Communication issues among deaf people. *A Deaf American Monograph, 40*(1,2,3,4), 79–85.

Lane, H. (1992). *The mask of benevolence: Disabling the deaf community*. New York: Knopf.

Lane, H., Hoffmeister, R., & Bahan, B. (1996). *A journey into the deaf-world*. San Diego, CA: Dawn Sign Press.

Langer, J. A., & Applebee, A. N. (1987). *How writing shapes thinking: A study of teaching and learning*. NCTE Research Report No. 22. Urbana, IL: National Council of Teachers of English.

Lartz, M. N., & Lestina, L. J. (1995). Strategies deaf mothers use when reading to their young deaf or hard of hearing children. *American Annals of the Deaf, 140*, 358–362.

LaSasso, C. (1978). National survey of materials and procedures used to teach reading to hearing impaired children. *American Annals of the Deaf, 123*, 22–30.

LaSasso, C. (1980). The validity and reliability of the cloze procedure as a measure of readability for prelingually, profoundly deaf students. *American Annals of the Deaf, 125*, 559–563.

LaSasso, C. (1985). Visual matching test-taking strategies used by deaf readers. *Journal of Speech and Hearing Research, 28*, 2–7.

LaSasso, C. (1986). A comparison of visual matching test taking strategies of comparably aged normal-hearing and hearing-impaired subjects with comparable reading levels. *Volta Review, 88,* 231–241.

LaSasso, C., & Davey, B. (1983, October–November). An examination of hearing-impaired readers' test-taking abilities on reinspection tasks. *Volta Review,* 279–284.

LaSasso, C., & Davey, B. (1987). The relationship between lexical knowledge and reading comprehension for prelingually, profoundly hearing-impaired students. *Volta Review,* 89(4), 211–220.

LaSasso, C., & Mobley, R. (1997). *Results of a national survey of reading instruction for deaf students.* Monograph of Collected Papers from the 23rd Annual Conference, The Association of College Educators—Deaf and Hard of Hearing, Santa Fe, NM.

Law, B., & Eckes, M. (1990). *More than just surviving: ESL for every classroom teacher.* Winnipeg, Manitoba: Peguis.

Lederer, R. (1991). *The miracle of language.* New York: Pocket Books.

Lessow-Hurley, J. (1990). *The foundation of dual language instruction.* White Plains, NY: Longman.

Levine, E. (1976). Psycho-cultural determinants in personality development. *Volta Review, 78,* 258–267.

Leybaert, J. (1993). Reading in the deaf: The roles of phonological codes. In M. Marschark & M. D. Clark (Eds.), *Psychological perspectives on deafness.* Hillsdale, NJ: Erlbaum.

Leybaert, J., & Charlier, B. (1996). Visual speech in the head: The effect of cued-speech on rhyming, remembering and spelling. *Journal of Deaf Studies and Deaf Education,* 1(4), 234–248.

Liben, L. (1979). Free-recall by deaf and hearing children: Semantic clustering in trained and untrained groups. *Journal of Experimental Child Psychology, 27,* 105–119.

Lichtenstein, E. (1984). Deaf working memory processes and English language skills. In D. Martin (Ed.), *International symposium on cognition, education, and deafness: Working papers* (Vol. 2) (pp. 331–360). Washington, DC: Gallaudet University Press.

Limbrick, E., McNaughton, S., & Clay, M. (1992). Time engaged in reading: A critical factor in reading achievement. *American Annals of the Deaf, 137,* 309–314.

Limbrick, L. (1991). The reading development of deaf children: Critical factors associated with success. *Teaching English to Deaf and Second Language Students, 9,* 4–9.

Livingston, S. (1997). *Rethinking the education of deaf students: Theory and practice from a teacher's perspective.* Portsmouth, NH: Heinemann.

Loeterman, M., Kelly, R. R., Morse, A. B., Murphy, C., Rubin, A., Parasnis, I., & Samar, V. (1997). Students as captioners: Approaches to writing and language development, Part 2. *TELA Themes,* 5(3), 3–6.

Luckner, J. J., & Isaacson, S. (1990). A method of assessing the written language of hearing-impaired students. *Journal of Communication Disorders, 23,* 219–233.

Lyon, R. (1997, May). Politics burying knowledge of effective strategies. *Special Education Report,* 9–10.

MacGinitie, W. (1993). Some limits of assessment. *Journal of Reading, 36,* 556–560.

Maeroff, G. (1991). Assessing alternative assessment. *Phi Delta Kappan, 73,* 272–281.

Mahshie, S. (1995). *Educating deaf children bilingually.* Washington, DC: Pre-College Programs, Gallaudet University.

Malstrom, J. (1977). *Understanding language: A primer for language arts teachers.* New York: St. Martin's.

Mandler, J., & Johnson, N. (1977). Remembrance of things parsed: Story structure and recall. *Cognitive Psychology, 9,* 111–151.

Manning, G., & Manning, D. (Eds.). (1989). *Whole language: Beliefs and practices, K–8.* Washington, DC: National Education Association.

Marlatt, E. A. (1996). ENFI: An approach to teaching writing through computers. *American Annals of the Deaf, 141*(3), 240–244.

Marrow, L. M. (1989). Using story retelling to develop comprehension. In K. D. Muth (Ed.), *Children's comprehension of text: Research into practice* (pp. 37–58). Newark, DE: International Reading Association.

Marschark, M. (1993). *Psychological development of deaf children.* New York: Oxford Press.

Marston, D. B. (1989). A curriculum-based measurement approach to assessing academic performance: What is it and why do it. In M. R. Shinn (Ed.), *Curriculum-based measurement: Assessing special children* (pp. 18–78). New York: Guilford Press.

Marston, D. B., & Deno, L. S. (1981). *The reliability of simple, direct measures of written expression.* (Research Report No. 50). Minneapolis: University of Minnesota, Institute for Research on Learning Disabilities.

Martin, B., Jr. (1967). *Cowboy and his paraphernalia: Sounds of a young hunter.* New York: Holt, Rinehart & Winston.

Martin, B., Jr. (1992). *Brown bear, brown bear, what do you see?* New York: Henry Holt and Company.

Martin, D. (1985). *Cognition, education, and deafness: Directions for research and instruction.* Washington, DC: Gallaudet University Press.

Mason, J. (Ed.). (1989). *Reading and writing connections.* Needham Heights, MA: Allyn & Bacon.

Mason, J., & Au, K. H. (1986). *Reading instruction for today.* Glenview, IL: Scott, Foresman.

Mason, J. A., & Au, K. H. (1990). *Reading instruction for today* (2nd ed.). New York: HarperCollins.

Mather, S. A. (1989). Visually oriented teaching strategies with deaf preschool children. In C. Lucas (Ed.), *The sociolinguistics of the deaf community* (pp. 165–187). New York: Academic.

Mather, S. A. (1990). Home and classroom communication. In D. Moores & K. Meadow-Orlans (Eds.), *Educational and developmental aspects of deafness.* Washington, DC: Gallaudet University Press.

Mattingly, I. (1984). Reading, linguistic awareness, and language acquisition. In J. Downing & R. Valtin (Eds.), *Language awareness and learning to read* (pp. 9–26). New York: Springer Verlag.

Maxwell, M. (1984). A deaf child's natural development of literacy. *Sign Language Studies, 44,* 191–224.

Maxwell, M. (1985). Some functions and uses of literacy in the deaf community. *Language in Society, 14,* 205–221.

Maxwell, M. (1986). Beginning reading and deaf children. *American Annals of the Deaf, 131,* 14–20.

Maxwell, M. M., & Doyle, J. (1996). Language codes and sense-making among deaf school children. *Journal of Deaf Studies and Deaf Education, 1*(2), 122–136.

Mayer, C., & Wells, G. (1996). Can the linguistic interdependence theory support a bilingual-bicultural model of literacy education for deaf students? *Journal of Deaf Studies and Deaf Education, 1,* 93–107.

Mayher, J., & Lester, N. (1983). Putting learning first in writing to learn. *Language Arts, 60,* 717–722.

Mayher, J., Lester, N., & Pradl, G. (1983). *Learning to write/writing to learn.* Upper Montclair, NJ: Boynton/Cook.

McAnally, P. L., Rose, S., & Quigley, S. P. (1994). *Language learning practices with deaf children* (2nd ed.). Austin, TX: PRO-ED.

McCallum, R. D. (1988). Don't throw the basals out with the bath water. *Reading Teacher, 42,* 204–208.

McCarr, D. (1973). Individualized reading for junior and senior high school students. *American Annals of the Deaf, 118,* 488–495.

McCarthey, S. J., & Raphael, T. E. (1992). Alternative research perspectives. In J. W. Irwin & M. A. Doyle (Eds.), *Reading/writing connections: Learning from research.* Newark, DE: International Reading Association.

McGill-Franzen, A., & Gormley, K. (1980). The influence of context on deaf readers' understanding of passive sentences. *American Annals of the Deaf, 125,* 937–942.

McLaren, P. (1988). Culture or canon? Critical pedagogy and the politics of literacy. *Harvard Educational Review, 58,* 213–234.

McNinch, G. H. (1981). A method for teaching sight words to disabled readers. *Reading Teacher, 35,* 269–272.

Meadow, K. (1968). Early manual communication in relation to the deaf child's intellectual, social, and communicative functioning. *American Annals of the Deaf, 113,* 29–41.

Meadow-Orlans, K. P. (1997). Effects of mother and infant hearing status on interactions at twelve and eighteen months. *Journal of Deaf Studies and Deaf Education, 2*(1), 26–35.

Meadow-Orlans, K. P., & Steinberg, A. G. (1993). Effects of infant hearing loss and maternal support on mother-infant interactions at eighteen months. *Journal of Applied Developmental Psychology, 14,* 407–426.

Meek, M. (1983). *Achieving literacy.* London: Routledge & Kegan.

Menyuk, P. (1988). *Language development: Knowledge and use.* Glenview, IL: Scott, Foresman.

Mercer, C. D., & Mercer, A. R. (1998). *Teaching students with learning problems* (5th ed.). Upper Saddle River, NJ: Prentice-Hall.

Meredith, S., & Walgren, M. (1998). *Performance assessment and intervention: The problem solving model for deaf and hard of hearing students* (2nd rev.). Minneapolis, MN: Ann Sullivan Communication Center for the Deaf and Hard of Hearing, Minneapolis, Public Schools. (Technical Report).

Merrill, M. D., & Tennyson, R. D. (1987). *Teaching concepts: An instructional design guide.* Englewood Cliffs, NJ: Educational Technology Publications.

Messick, S. (1988). The once and future issues of validity: Assessing the meaning and consequences of measurement. In H. Wainer & H. S. Braun (Eds.), *Test validity* (pp. 33–45). Hillsdale, NJ: Erlbaum.

Metsala, J. L. (1997). Effective primary-grades literacy instruction = balanced literacy instruction. *Reading Teacher, 50,* 518–521.

Meyer, M. (1983). *All by myself.* Racine, WI: Western.

Miller, J., Chapman, R., & Bedrisian, J. (1977). *Defining developmentally disabled subjects for research: The relationships between etiology, cognitive development, language and communicative performance.* Paper presented at the Second Annual Boston University Conference on Language Development, Boston, MA.

Miller, W. H. (1986). *Reading diagnosis kit* (3rd ed.). West Nyack, NY: Center for Applied Research in Education.

Millett, N. C. (1986). *Teaching the writing process: A guide for teachers and supervisors.* Boston: Houghton Mifflin.

Milz, V. (1982). *Young children write: The beginnings* (Occasional Paper No. 5). Tucson: Program in Language and Literacy, University of Arizona.

Minnesota Department of Children, Families and Learning. (1997). *Manual for the implementation of state of Minnesota graduation standards.* St. Paul, MN: Author.

Minnesota Department of Children, Families and Learning. (1998). *Graduation standards resource book.* Faribault, MN: Minnesota State Academy for the Deaf.

Moje, E., Brozo, W., & Haas, J. (1994). Portfolios in a high school classroom: Challenges to change. *Reading Research and Instruction, 33,* 275–292.

Moores, D. (1992). What do we know and when do we know it? In M. Walworth, D. Moores, & T. J. O'Rourke (Eds.), *A free hand: Enfranchising the education of deaf children.* Silver Spring, MD: T. J. Publishers.

Moores, D. F. (1987). *Factors predictive of literacy in deaf adolescents with deaf parents. Factors predictive of literacy in deaf adolescents in total communication programs.* (Final report to NIH-NINCDS No. 83-19). Washington, DC: Center for Studies in Education and Human Development, Gallaudet University.

Moores, D. F. (1996). *Educating the deaf: Psychology, principles and practices* (4th ed.). Boston: Houghton Mifflin.

Morris P. J., II, & Tchudi, S. (1996). *The new literacy: Moving beyond the 3Rs.* San Francisco: Jossey-Bass.

Morrow, L. M. (1989). Using story telling to develop comprehension. In K. D. Muth (Ed.), *Children's comprehension of text: Research into practice* (pp. 37–58). Newark, DE: International Reading Association.

Mullis, I. V. S., Campbell, J. R., & Farstrup, A. E. (1993). *NAEP 1992 reading report card for the nation and the states.* Washington, DC: U.S. Department of Education.

Musselman, C., & Szanto, G. (1998). The written language of deaf adolescents: Patterns of performance. *Journal of Deaf Studies and Deaf Education, 3*(3), 217–230.

Myklebust, H. (1964). *The psychology of deafness* (2nd ed.). New York: Grune & Stratton.

Nagy, W. E., & Herman, P. A. (1987). Breadth and depth of vocabulary knowledge: Implications for acquisition and instruction. In M. G. McKeown & H. E. Curtis (Eds.), *The nature of vocabulary acquisition.* Hillsdale, NJ: Erlbaum.

National Center for Accessible Media. (1996). *Success stories.* Boston: WGBH Educational Foundation.

National Center for Accessible Media. (1997). *Writing with video: An idea book for captioning in the classroom.* Boston: WGBH Educational Foundation.

National Literacy Act of 1991. (1991). Washington, DC: U.S. Government Printing Office.

Neilsen, B. (1991). *Use of the OS-400 reading test.* (Working paper). Copenhagen, Denmark: Kastelsvej School.

Nelson, J. (1978). Readability: Some cautions for the content area teacher. *Journal of Reading, 21,* 620–625.

Nelson, K. E., & Camarata, S. M. (1997). Improving English literacy and speech-acquisition learning conditions for children with severe to profound hearing impairments. *Volta Review, 98,* 17–41.

Nelson, W. W. (1998). The naked truth about school reform in Minnesota. *Phi Delta Kappan, 79*(9), 679–684.

Newman, J. M., & Church, S. M. (1990). Myths of whole language. *Reading Teacher, 44,* 20–26.

Nichola, J. N. (1983). Using prediction to increase content area interest and understanding. *Journal of Reading, 27,* 225–228.

Norden, K., Tvingstedt, A-L., & Heiling, K. (1989). *A longitudinal study of deaf children.* (Occasional paper). Malmo, Sweden: Lund University Department of Educational Research.

Nover, S. M. (1995). Politics and language: American Sign Language and English in deaf education. In C. Lucas (Ed.), *Sociolinguistics in deaf communities* (pp. 109–163). Washington, DC: Gallaudet University Press.

Nurss, J., & Hough, R. (1992). Teaching adults to read. In J. Samuel, & A. Farstrup (Eds.), *What research has to say about reading instruction* (2nd ed.). Newark, DE: International Reading Association.

Ogle, D. (1986). K-W-L: A teaching model that develops active reading of expository text. *Reading Teacher, 39,* 564–570.

Olsen, H. (1984). *Skills for living.* Washington, DC: Gallaudet University Outreach Programs.

Olson, M. W., & Homan, S. P. (Eds.). (1993). *Teacher to teacher: Strategies for the elementary classroom*. Newark, DE: International Reading Association.

Padden, C. (1984, April). *Literacy in deaf families*. Paper presented at the Ethnography and Education Research Forum, Philadelphia, PA.

Padden, C., & Ramsey, C. (1993). Deaf culture and literacy. *American Annals of the Deaf, 13*, 96–99.

Palincsar, A. (1986). Metacognitive strategy instruction. *Exceptional Children, 53*, 115–124.

Palincsar, A., & Brown, A. L. (1984). Reciprocal teaching of comprehension-fostering and comprehension-monitoring activities. *Cognition and Instruction, 1*, 117–175.

Palincsar, A., & Brown, A. L. (1986). Interactive teaching to promote independent learning from text. *Reading Teacher, 39*, 771–777.

Palincsar, A., Brown, A. L., & Martin, S. M. (1987). Peer interaction in reading comprehension instruction. *Educational Psychologist, 22*, 231–253.

Paris, S., Lipson, M., & Wixson, K. (1983). Becoming a strategic reader. *Contemporary Educational Psychology, 8*, 293–316.

Parker, R., Hasbrouck, J., & Tindal, G. (1989a). *Combining informal teacher judgement and objective test scores to make cross-classroom reading group placements* (Research Report No. 4). Eugene: University of Oregon.

Parker, R., Hasbrouck, J., & Tindal, G. (1989b). The maze as a classroom-based reading measure: Construction methods, reliability, and validity. *Journal of Special Education, 26*(2), 195–218.

Parnell, D. R. (1987). *The little red hen*. Auburn, ME: Ladybird Books.

Patberg, J., Dewitz, P., & Samuels, S. J. (1981). The effect of context on the size of the perceptual unit used in word recognition. *Journal of Reading Behavior, 13*, 33–48.

Paul, P. (1984). *The comprehension of multimeaning words from selected frequency levels by deaf and hearing subjects*. Unpublished doctoral dissertation, University of Illinois, Urbana-Champaign.

Paul, P. (1990). Using ASL to teach English literacy skills. *The Deaf American, 40*(1–4), 107–113.

Paul, P. (1992). The use of ASL in teaching reading and writing to deaf students: An interactive theoretical perspective. In *Bilingual considerations in the education of deaf students: ASL and English (Conference Proceedings)*. Washington, DC: Gallaudet University.

Paul, P. (1993). Deafness and English text-based literacy. *American Annals of the Deaf, 138*, 72–75.

Paul, P. (1996a). First- and second-language English literacy. *Volta Review, 98*, 5–16.

Paul, P. (1996b). Reading vocabulary knowledge and deafness. *Journal of Deaf Studies and Deaf Education, 1*(1), 3–15.

Paul, P., & Gustafson, G. (1991). Hearing-impaired students' comprehension of high frequency multiple-meaning words. *Remedial and Special Education, 12*(4), 52–62.

Paul, P., & O'Rourke, J. (1988). Multimeaning words and reading comprehension: Implications for special education students. *Remedial and Special Education, 9*(3), 42–52.

Paul, P., & Quigley, S. (1990). *Education and deafness*. White Plains, NY: Longman.

Paul, P., & Quigley, S. (1994). *Language and deafness* (2nd ed.). San Diego, CA: Singular.

Paulson, P. R., & Paulson, F. L. (1991). Portfolios: Stories of knowing. In P. Dreyer (Ed.), *Knowing: The power of stories* (pp. 294–303). Claremont, CA: Claremont Reading Conference.

Pearson, P. D. (1982). *Asking questions about stories*. Needham, MA: Ginn.

Pearson, P. D. (1996). Reclaiming the center. In M. F. Graves, P. van den Broek, & B. M. Taylor (Eds.), *The first R: Every child's right to read* (pp. 259–274). New York: Teachers College Press and International Reading Association.

Pearson, P. D., & Dole, J. A. (1987). Explicit comprehension instruction: A review of research and a new conceptualization of instruction. *Elementary School Journal, 88*(2), 151–165.

Pearson, P. D., & Fielding, L. (1991). Comprehension instruction. In R. Barr, M. Kamil, P. Mosenthal, & P. D. Pearson (Eds.), *Handbook of reading research* (Vol. 2). New York: Longman.

Pearson, P. D., & Johnson, D. (1978). *Teaching reading comprehension.* New York: Holt, Rinehart & Winston.

Pearson, P. D., & Spiro, R. (1980). Toward a theory of comprehension instruction. *Topics in Language Disorders, 1,* 71–88.

Pease, D., Gleason, J. B., & Pan, B. (1987). Gaining meaning: Semantic development. In J. B. Gleason (Ed.), *The development of language* (2nd ed.) (pp. 101–134). Columbus, OH: Merrill.

Peregoy, S., & Boyle, O. (1990). Kindergartners write! Emergent literacy of Mexican American children in a two-way Spanish immersion program. *Journal of the Association of Mexican American Educators,* 6–18.

Peregoy, S., & Boyle, O. (1991). Second language oral proficiency characteristics of low, intermediate, and high second language readers. *Hispanic Journal of Behavioral Sciences, 13*(1), 35–47.

Peregoy, S., & Boyle, O. (1993). *Reading, writing, and learning in ESL: A resource book for K–8 teachers.* White Plains, NY: Longman.

Perkins, D. (1986). *Knowledge as design.* Hillsdale, NJ: Erlbaum.

Perkins, D. (1991). Educating for insight. *Educational Leadership, 49*(2), 4–8.

Perkins, D. (1992). *Smart schools: From training memories to educating minds.* New York: Free Press.

Petitto, L. A., & Marentette, P. F. (1991). Babbling in the manual mode: Evidence for the ontogeny of language. *Science, 251,* 1493–1496.

Peyton, J. K., & Baston, T. (1986). Computer networking: Making connections between speech and writing. *ERIC Clearinghouse on Languages and Linguistics News Bulletin, 10,* 1–6.

Piaget, J. (1926). *The language and thought of the child.* Orlando, FL: Harcourt Brace Jovanovich.

Piaget, J. (1952). *The origins of intelligence in children* (2nd ed.). New York: International University Press.

Pikulski, J. J., & Pikulski, E. C. (1977). Cloze, Maze, and teacher judgement. *Reading Teacher, 30,* 766–770.

Pinhas, J. (1991). Constructive processing in skilled deaf and hearing readers. In D. Martin (Ed.), *Advances in cognition, education, and deafness* (pp. 296–301). Washington, DC: Gallaudet University.

Pinnell, G. S. (1989). Reading Recovery: Helping at-risk children learn to read. *Elementary School Journal, 90,* 159–189.

Pinnell, G. S., Fried, M. D., & Estice, R. M. (1990). Reading Recovery: Learning how to make a difference. *Reading Teacher, 43,* 282–295.

Pinnell, G. S., Lyons, C. A., DeFord, D. E., Bryk, A. S., & Seltzer, M. (1994). Comparing instructional models for literacy education of high-risk first graders. *Reading Research Quarterly, 29,* 9–38.

Pintner, R. (1918). The measurement of language ability and language progress of deaf children. *Volta Review, 20,* 755–764.

Pittelman, S. D., Heimlich, J. E., Berglund, R. L., & French, M. P. (1991). *Semantic features analysis: Classroom applications.* Newark, DE: International Reading Association.

Powers, A., & Wilgus, S. (1983). Linguistic complexity in the written language of deaf children. *Volta Review, 85,* 201–210.

Pressley, M. (1988, June). *Overview of cognitive and metacognitive theories as they relate to special education populations and findings of pertinent intervention research.* Paper presented at Publishers' Workshop, Washington, DC. (Available from Information Center for Special Education Media and Materials, LINC Resources, Inc., Columbus, OH.)

Pressley, M., & Rankin, J. (1994). More about whole language methods of reading instruction for students at risk for early reading failure. *Learning Disabilities Research & Practice, 9*, 156–167.

Pressley, M., Rankin, J., & Yokoi, L. (1996). A survey of instructional practices of outstanding primary-level literacy teachers. *Elementary School Journal, 96*, 363–384.

Prinz, P., & Nelson, K. E. (1984). Reading is fun: With a keyboard, a hat, and an alligator. *Perspectives,* 2–4.

Prinz, P., & Strong, M. (1995, July). *The interrelationship among cognition, sign language, and literacy.* Paper presented at the 18th International Congress on Education of the Deaf, Tel-Aviv, Israel.

Pritchard, R. (1990). The effects of cultural schemata in reading processing strategies. *Reading Research Quarterly, 25*, 273–295.

Quigley, B. A. (1990). This immense evil: The history of literacy education as a social policy. In T. Valentine (Ed.), *Beyond rhetoric: Fundamental issues in adult literacy education.* Athens: University of Georgia, Department of Adult Education.

Quigley, B. A. (1997). *Rethinking literacy education: The critical need for practice-based change.* San Francisco: Jossey-Bass.

Quigley, S., & Frisina, R. (1961). *Institutionalization and psychoeducational development of deaf children.* (CEC Research Monograph). Washington, DC: Council on Exceptional Children.

Quigley, S., & Kretschmer, R. E. (1982). *The education of deaf children: Issues, theory, and practice.* Baltimore: University Park Press.

Quigley, S., McAnally, P., King, C., & Rose, S. (1991). *Reading milestones: Teacher's Guide.* Austin, TX: PRO-ED.

Quigley, S., & Paul, P. (1984). *Language and deafness.* San Diego, CA: College-Hill.

Quigley, S., & Paul, P. (1989). English language development. In M. Wang, M. Reynolds, & H. Walberg (Eds.), *The handbook of special education: Research and practice* (Vol. 3, pp. 3–21). Oxford, England: Pergamon.

Quigley, S., & Paul, P. (1990). *Language and deafness.* San Diego, CA: Singular.

Quigley, S., Paul, P., McAnally, P., Rose, S., & Payne, J. (1991). *Reading bridge: Patterns.* Austin, TX: PRO-ED.

Quigley, S., Power, D., & Steinkamp, M. (1977). The language structure of deaf children. *Volta Review, 79*, 73–84.

Quigley, S., Wilbur, R., & Montanelli, D. (1974). Question formation in the language of deaf students. *Journal of Speech and Hearing Research, 17*, 699–713.

Quigley, S., Wilbur, R., Power, D., Montanelli, D., & Steinkamp, M. (1976). *Syntactic structures in the language of deaf children.* Urbana-Champaign: University of Illinois, Institute for Child Behavior and Development.

Ramsey, W. (1967). The values and limitations of diagnostic reading tests for evaluation in the classroom. In T. C. Barrett (Ed.), *The evaluation of children's reading achievement* (pp. 65–78). Newark, DE: International Reading Association.

Raphael, J., & Englert, C. (1989). Integrating reading and writing instruction. In P. Winograd, K. K. Wixson, & M. Y. Lipson (Eds.), *Improving basal reader instruction* (pp. 231–255). New York: Teachers College Press.

Raphael, T., & Kirschner, B. M. (1985). *The effects of instruction in compare/contrast text structure on sixth-grade students' reading comprehension writing products.* (Research Series No. 161). East Lansing: Michigan State University, Institute for Research on Teaching.

Raphael, T., & Pearson, P. D. (1985). Increasing students' awareness of sources of information for answering questions. *American Educational Research Journal, 22,* 217–236.

Raskin, E. (1968). *Spectacles.* New York: Aladdin Books.

Rentel, V. M., Matchim, J., & Zutell, J. (1979). *Basic teaching principles and methods: Reading.* Unpublished technical manual, Ohio State University, Columbus.

Resnick, L. B. (1987). *Education and learning to think.* Washington, DC: National Academy Press.

Reutzel, D. R., & Cooter, R. B., Jr. (1991). Organizing for effective instruction: The reading workshop. *Reading Teacher, 44,* 548–554.

Reynolds, H., & Booher, H. (1980). The effects of pictorial and verbal instructional materials on the operational performance of deaf subjects. *Journal of Special Education, 14,* 175–187.

Reynolds, H. N. (1986, December). Performance of deaf college students on a criterion-referenced modified cloze test of reading comprehension. *American Annals of the Deaf,* 361–364.

Rhodes, L., & Shanklin, N. (1993). *Windows into literacy: Assessing learners, K–8.* Portsmouth, NH: Heinemann.

Rigg, P. (1986). Reading in ESL: Learning from kids. In P. Rigg & D. Enright (Eds.), *Children and ESL: Integrating perspectives* (pp. 55–92). Washington, DC: Teachers of English to Speakers of Other Languages.

Rigg, P. (1990). Using the language experience approach with ESL adults. *TESL Talk, 29,* 188–200.

Robbins, N., & Hatcher, C. (1981). The effects of syntax on the reading comprehension of hearing-impaired children. *Volta Review, 83,* 105–115.

Robinson, S. (1998, June). *The reading and writing connection through the DISCOURSE educational communication system.* (Technical Report: DISCOURSE Project Summary.) Minneapolis: University of Minnesota.

Rodda, M., Cumming, C., & Fewer, D. (1993). Memory, learning and language: Implications for deaf education. In M. Marschark & M. D. Clark (Eds.), *Psychological perspectives on deafness.* Hillsdale, NJ: Erlbaum.

Rodda, M., & Grove, C. (1987). *Language, cognition, and deafness.* Hillsdale, NJ: Erlbaum.

Rose, S. (1997). *Looking for literacy: Challenges in the field of education with deaf and hard of hearing children.* (Department of Educational Psychology, Special Education Programs, Technical Report). Minneapolis: University of Minnesota.

Rosenblatt, L. (1978). *The reader, the text, the poem: The transactional theory of the literary work.* Carbondale, IL: Southern Illinois Press.

Rosenblatt, L. (1989). Writing and reading: The transactional theory. In J. Mason (Ed.), *Reading and writing connections* (pp. 153–176). Needham Heights, MA: Allyn & Bacon.

Rottenberg, C. J., & Searfoss, L. W. (1991). Becoming literate in a preschool class: Literacy development of hearing impaired children. *Journal of Reading Behavior, 24,* 463–479.

Routman, R. (1997). Back to the basics of whole language. *Educational Leadership, 54,* 70–74.

Ruddell, R. B. (1963). The effect of the similarity of oral and written patterns of language structure on reading comprehension. *Elementary English, 42,* 403–410.

Rumelhart, D. (1977). Toward an interactive model of reading. In S. Dornic (Ed.), *Attention and performance VI* (pp. 573–603). New York: Academic Press.

Rumelhart, D. (1980). Schemata: The building blocks of cognition. In R. J. Spiro, B. C. Bruce, & W. F. Brewer (Eds.), *Theoretical issues in reading comprehension*. Hillsdale, NJ: Erlbaum.

Rupert, P. R., & Brueggeman, M. A. (1986). Reading journals: Making the language connection in college. *Journal of Reading, 30*, 26–33.

Ryan, C. D. (1994). *Authentic assessment*. Westminster, CA: Teacher Created Materials.

Ryan, E. B. (1981). Identifying and remediating failures in reading comprehension: Toward an instructional approach for poor comprehenders. In T. G. Waller & G. E. MacKinnon (Eds.), *Advances in reading research* (Vol. 2) (pp. 223–261). New York: Academic Press.

Sachs, J. (1967). Recognition memory for syntactic and semantic aspects of connected discourse. *Perception and Psychophysics, 2*, 437–442.

Samuels, S. J. (1988). Decoding and automaticity. *Reading Teacher, 41*, 756–760.

Samuels, S. J., Miller, N., & Eisenberg, P. (1979). Practice effects on the unit of word recognition. *Journal of Educational Psychology, 71*, 514–520.

Samuels, S. J., Schermer, N., & Reinking, D. (1992). Reading fluency: Techniques for making decoding automatic. In J. Samuels & A. Farstrup (Eds.), *What research has to say about reading instruction*. Newark, DE: International Reading Association.

Sarachan-Deily, A. B. (1985). Written narratives of deaf and hearing students: Story recall and inferences. *Journal of Speech and Hearing Research, 28*, 151–159.

Satchwell, S. E. (1993). Does teaching reading strategies to deaf children increase their reading levels? *ACEHI/ACEDA, 19*, 38–48.

Schick, B., & Gale, E. (1995). Preschool deaf and hard of hearing students' interactions during ASL and English storytelling. *American Annals of the Deaf, 140*, 363–370.

Schirmer, B. R. (1994). *Language and literacy in children who are deaf*. New York: Macmillan.

Schirmer, B. R. (1995). Mental imagery and the reading comprehension of deaf children. *Reading Research and Instruction, 34*, 177–188.

Schirmer, B. R., & Woolsey, M. L. (1997). Effect of teacher questioning on the reading comprehension of deaf children. *Journal of Deaf Studies and Deaf Education, 2*, 47–56.

Schleper, D. (1996a, Fall). Shared reading, shared success. *Preview, Pre-College Programs*, 1–5. Washington, DC: Gallaudet University.

Schleper, D. (1996b). *Wholistic structures of teaching deaf children reading and writing*. Keynote presentation at the State Conference for Teachers of the Deaf and Hard of Hearing, St. Paul, MN.

Schleper, D. (1996c). Write that one down! Using anecdotal records to inform our teaching. *Volta Review, 98*(1), 201–210.

Schleper, D. (1997). *Reading to deaf children: Learning from deaf adults*. Washington, DC: Gallaudet University, Pre-College National Mission Programs.

Schleper, D., & Farmer, M. (1991). *An interdisciplinary approach to applying recent research in literacy in the education of hearing impaired learning disabled students*. Washington, DC: U.S. Department of Education, U.S. Printing Office (Grant No. R11780077).

Schleper, D., & Paradis, S. J. (1990). Learning logs for math: Thinking through writing. *Perspectives in Education and Deafness, 9*, 14–17.

Schmelzer, R. V., Christen, W. L., & Browning, W. G. (1980). *Reading and study skills: Book one*. Rehoboth, MA: Twin Oaks.

Schreiner, R. (1979). Testing and reading: A plan for evaluation. In R. Schreiner (Ed.), *Reading tests and teachers: A practical guide* (pp. 1–8). Newark, DE: International Reading Association.

Searfoss, L. W., & Readence, J. E. (1989). *Helping children learn to read* (2nd ed.). Englewood Cliffs, NJ: Prentice-Hall.

Serwatka, T. S., Hesson, D., & Graham, M. (1984, February–March). The effect of indirect intervention on the improvement of hearing-impaired students' reading scores. *Volta Review, 81–88.*

Shanahan, T. (1984). The nature of the reading-writing relation: An exploratory multivariate analysis. *Journal of Educational Psychology, 76,* 466–477.

Shanahan, T. (Ed.). (1990). *Reading and writing together: New perspectives for the classroom.* Norwood, MA: Christopher Gordon.

Shanahan, T., & Lomax, R. (1986). An analysis and comparison of theoretical models of the reading-writing relationship. *Journal of Educational Psychology, 78,* 116–123.

Shanahan, T., Robinson, B., & Schneider, M. (1995). Avoiding some of the pitfalls of thematic units. *Reading Teacher, 48,* 718–719.

Shapiro, J. (1990). Research perspectives on whole-language. In V. Froese (Ed.), *Whole-language: Practice and theory.* Needham Heights, MA: Allyn & Bacon.

Short, K. G., & Burke, C. L. (1991). *Creating curriculum: Teachers and students as a community of learners.* Portsmouth, NH: Heinemann.

Sikora, D. M., & Plapinger, D. S. (1997). The role of informal parent and teacher assessment in diagnosing learning disabilities. *Volta Review, 98,* 19–29.

Simmons, W., & Resnick, L. (1993). Assessment as the catalyst of school reform. *Educational Leadership, 50,* 11–15.

Siple, P. (1978). Linguistic and psychological properties of American Sign Language. In P. Siple (Ed.), *Understanding language through sign language research* (pp. 3–23), New York: Academic Press.

Slater, B. (1981). *History—economics—political science.* Beaverton, OR: Dormac.

Slavin, R. E. (1987). *Cooperative learning: Student teams* (2nd ed.). Washington, DC: National Education Association.

Smith, F. (1975). The role of prediction in reading. *Elementary English, 52,* 305–311.

Smith, F. (1983). Reading like a writer. *Language Arts, 60,* 558–567.

Smith, F. (1988). *Understanding reading* (4th ed.). New York: Holt, Rinehart & Winston.

Smith, F. (1992). Learning to read: The never-ending debate. *Phi Delta Kappan, 73,* 432–441.

Smith, K. (1990). Entertaining a text: A reciprocal process. In K. Short & C. Pierce (Eds.), *Talking about books* (pp. 17–31). Portsmouth, NH: Heinemann.

Smith, S. B., & Rittenhouse, R. K. (1990). Real-time graphic display: Technology for mainstreaming. *Perspectives, 9,* 2–5.

Smith, S. L., Carey, R. F., & Harste, J. C. (1982). The contexts of reading. In A. Berger & H. A. Robinson (Eds.), *Secondary school reading: What research reveals for classroom practice.* Urbana, IL: National Conference on Research in English and ERIC Clearing House on Reading and Communication.

Spandel, V., & Stiggens, R. (1990). *Creating writers: Linking assessment and writing instruction.* New York: Longman.

Spencer, E., Bodner-Johnson, B., & Gutfreund, M. (1992). Interacting with infants with a hearing loss: What can we learn from mothers who are deaf? *Journal of Early Intervention, 16*(1), 64–78.

Spiegel, D. L. (1995). A comparison of traditional remedial programs and Reading Recovery: Guidelines for success for all programs. *Reading Teacher, 49,* 86–96.

Spiller, D., Heathly, A., Kenzen, M., & Rittenhouse, R. (1994). Making connections: Students, technology, and learning. *Perspectives in Education and Deafness, 12*(4), 6–9.

Spiro, R. (1977). Remembering information from text: Theoretical and empirical issues concerning the "State of Schema" reconstruction hypothesis. In R. Anderson, R. Spiro, & W. Montague (Eds.), *Schooling and the acquisition of knowledge* (pp. 137–165). Hillsdale, NJ: Erlbaum.

Stahl, S. A., McKenna, M. C., & Pagnucco, J. R. (1993). *The effects of whole language instruction: An update and a reappraisal.* Paper presented at the National Reading Conference, Charleston, SC.

Stahl, S. A., & Miller, P. D. (1989). Whole language and language experience approaches for beginning reading: A quantitative research synthesis. *Review of Educational Research, 59,* 87–116.

Stanovich, K. E. (1980). Toward an interactive-compensatory model of individual differences in the development of reading fluency. *Reading Research Quarterly, 16,* 32–71.

Stanovich, K. E. (1986). Matthew effects in reading: Some consequences of individual differences in the acquisition of literacy. *Reading Research Quarterly, 21,* 360–407.

Staton, J. (1988). An introduction to dialogue journal communication. In J. Staton, R. W. Shuy, J. K. Peyton, & L. Reed (Eds.), *Dialogue journal communication: Classroom linguistic, social and cognitive views* (pp. 1–32). Norwood, NJ: Ablex.

Stauffer, R. G. (1969). *Directed reading maturity as a cognitive process.* New York: Harper & Row.

Stein, N., & Glenn, C. (1979). An analysis in story comprehension in elementary school children. In R. Freedle (Ed.), *New directions in discourse processing.* Norwood, NJ: Ablex.

Stephens, D. (1991). *Research on whole language: Support for a new curriculum.* Katonah, NY: Richard C. Owen.

Sternberg, R. J. (1987). Most vocabulary is learned from context. In M. G. McKeown & M. E. Curtis (Eds.), *The nature of vocabulary acquisition* (pp. 89–105). Hillsdale, NJ: Erlbaum.

Stotsky, S. (1983). Research on reading/writing relationships: A synthesis and suggested directions. *Language Arts, 60,* 627–643.

Strassman, B. K. (1992). Deaf adolescents' metacognitive knowledge about school related reading. *American Annals of the Deaf, 137,* 326–330.

Strassman, B. K. (1997). Metacognition and reading in children who are deaf: A review of research. *Journal of Deaf Studies and Deaf Education, 2*(3), 140–149.

Strassman, B. K., Kretschmer, R. E., & Bilsky, L. H. (1987). The instantiation of general terms by deaf adolescents/adults. *Journal of Communication Disorders, 20,* 1–13.

Streng, A., Kretschmer, R. R., & Kretschmer, L. (1978). *Language, learning, and deafness: Theory, application, and classroom management.* New York: Grune & Stratton.

Strong, M. (1995). A review of bilingual/bicultural programs for deaf children in North America. *American Annals of the Deaf, 140*(2), 84–94.

Strong, M., & Prinz, P. (1997). A study of the relationship between American Sign Language and English literacy. *Journal of Deaf Studies and Deaf Education, 2,* 37–46.

Stuckless, E. R. (1981). Real-time transliteration of speech into print for hearing-impaired students in regular classrooms. *Volta Review, 83,* 326–330.

Stuckless, E. R., & Birch, J. (1966). The influence of early manual communication on the linguistic development of deaf children. *American Annals of the Deaf, 106,* 436–480.

Stuckless, E. R., & Marks, C. (1966). *Assessment of the written language of deaf students.* Pittsburgh, PA: University of Pittsburgh, School of Education.

Sullivan, J. (1978). Comparing strategies of good and poor comprehenders. *Journal of Reading, 21,* 710–715.

Sulzby, E. (1985). Children's emergent reading of favorite storybooks: A developmental study. *Reading Research Quarterly, 20,* 458–481.

Sulzby, E. (1988). Assessment of emergent literacy: Storybook reading. *Reading Teacher, 44,* 498–500.

Sulzby, E. (1989). Assessment of writing and of children's language while writing. In L. Morrow & J. Smith (Eds.), *The role of assessment and measurement in early literacy instruction* (pp. 83–209). Englewood Cliffs, NJ: Prentice-Hall.

Supalla, T. (1990). Serial verbs of motion in ASL. In S.D. Fischer & P. Siple (Eds.), *Theoretical issues in sign language research: Vol. 1. Linguistics* (pp. 127–152). Chicago: University of Chicago Press.

Svartholm, K. (1994). Second language learning in the deaf. In I. Ahlgren & K. Hyltenstam (Eds.), *Bilingualism in deaf education: Proceedings of the International Conference on Bilingualism in Deaf Education, Stockholm, Sweden.* International Studies on Sign Language & Communication of the Deaf, Vol. 27. Hamburg, Germany: Signum Press.

Swaby, B. (1983). *Teaching and learning reading.* Boston: Little, Brown.

Swartz, S. L., & Klein, A. F. (1996). *Reading Recovery: An overview.* San Francisco: San Francisco Unified School District.

Takemori, W., & Snyder, J. (1972). Materials and techniques used in teaching language to deaf children. *American Annals of the Deaf, 122,* 475–479.

Taylor, B. M., & Beach, R. W. (1984). The effects of text structure on middle-grade students' comprehension and production of expository text. *Reading Research Quarterly, 19,* 134–146.

Taylor, B. M., Frye, B. J., & Maruyama, G. (1990). Time spent reading and reading growth. *American Educational Research Journal, 27,* 351–362.

Taylor, B. M., Harris, L. A., & Pearson, P. D. (1988). *Reading difficulties: Instruction and assessment.* New York: Random House.

Taylor, B. M., Harris, L. A., Pearson, P. D., & Garcia, G. (1995). *Reading difficulties: Instruction and assessment* (2nd ed.). New York: McGraw-Hill.

Taylor, B. M., Short, R. A., Frye, B. J., & Shearer, B. A. (1992). Classroom teachers prevent reading failure among low-achieving first-grade students. *Reading Teacher, 45,* 592–597.

Taylor, D. (1983). *Family literacy: Young children learning to read and write.* Exeter, NH: Heinemann.

Taylor, D., & Dorsey-Gaines, C. (1988). *Growing up literate.* Portsmouth, NH: Heinemann.

Teale, W. E. (1986). The beginnings of reading and writing: Written language development during the preschool and kindergarten years. In M. R. Simpson (Ed.), *The pursuit of literacy: Early reading and writing* (pp. 1–29). Dubuque, IA: Kendall/Hunt.

Teale, W. E., & Sulzby, E. (Eds.). (1986). *Emergent literacy: Writing and reading.* Norwood, NJ: Ablex.

Temple, C., Nathan, R., Temple, F., & Burris, N. A. (1993). *The beginnings of writing* (3rd ed.). Needham Heights, MA: Allyn & Bacon.

Thorndyke, E. L. (1977). Cognitive structures in comprehension and memory of narrative discourse. *Cognitive Psychology, 9,* 77–110.

Tierney, R. J., Carter, M. A., & Desai, L. E. (1991). *Portfolio assessment in the reading-writing classroom.* Norwood, MA: Christopher-Gordon.

Tinajero, J., & Calderon, M. (1988). Language experience approach plus. *Educational Issues of Language Minority Students: The Journal, 2,* 31–45.

Tindal, G., Heath, B., Hollenbeck, K., Almond, P., & Harniss, M. (1998). Accommodating students with disabilities on large-scale tests: An experimental study. *Exceptional Children, 64*(4), 439–450.

Truax, R. (1992). Becoming literate: A sketch of a never ending cycle. *Volta Review, 94,* 395–410.

Tunnell, M. O., & Jacobs, J. S. (1989). Using "real" books: Research findings on literature based reading instruction. *Reading Teacher, 42,* 470–477.

Tyson, H., & Woodward, A. (1989). Why students aren't learning very much from textbooks. *Educational Leadership*, 47, 14–17.

Vacca, J. L., Vacca, R. T., & Gove, M. K. (1995). *Reading and learning to read* (3rd ed.). New York: HarperCollins.

Vacca, R. T., & Linek, W. M. (1992). Writing to learn. In J. W. Irwin & M. A. Doyle (Eds.), *Reading/writing connections: Learning from research*. Newark, DE: International Reading Association.

Vacca, R. T., & Vacca, J. (1996). *Content area reading*. New York: HarperCollins.

Valeri-Gold, M., Olson, J., & Deming, M. (1991–92). Portfolios: Collaborative authentic assessment opportunities for college developmental learners. *Journal of Reading*, 35, 298–304.

Van Daalen-Kapteijns, M. M., & Elshout-Mohr, M. (1981). The acquisition of word meaning as a cognitive learning process. *Journal of Verbal Learning Behavior*, 20, 386–391.

Van Horn, B., & Brown, E. (1993). Hurdles in evaluating adult literacy programs . . . a few answers. In B. Hayes & K. Camperell (Eds.), *Reading strategies, practices, and research for the 21st century* (pp. 59–66). Logan: Utah State University.

Van Horn, B., & Guaraldi, R. (1994). Alternative assessment: Use of portfolio assessment in a workplace literacy program. In B. Hayes & K. Camperell (Eds.), *Reading: Putting the pieces together* (pp. 139–152). Logan: Utah State University.

Vars, G. F. (1991). Integrated curriculum in historical perspective. *Educational Leadership*, 49(2), 14–15.

Videen, J., Deno, S. L., & Marston, D. (1982). *Correct word sequences: A valid indicator of proficiency in written expression*. (Research Report No. 84). Minneapolis: University of Minnesota, Institute for Research on Learning Disabilities.

Vivan, B. (1991, January–February). You don't have to hate meetings: Try computer-assisted notetaking. *SHHH Journal*, 25–28.

Vygotsky, L. S. (1978). *Mind in society*. Cambridge, MA: Harvard University Press.

Wagoner, S. A. (1983). Comprehension monitoring: What it is and what we know about it. *Reading Research Quarterly*, 18(3), 328–346.

Waldron, M., & Rose, S. (1996). *GCD: Graphic Communication Device for the Deaf*. Hillsboro, OR: Butte Publications.

Walker, B. (1996). *Diagnostic teaching of reading: Techniques for instruction and assessment*. Englewood Cliffs, NJ: Prentice-Hall.

Waters, G. S., & Doehring, D. G. (1990). Reading acquisition in congenitally deaf children who communicate orally: Insights from an analysis of component reading, language, and memory skills. In T. H. Carr & B. A. Levy (Eds.), *Reading and its development* (pp. 323–373). San Diego, CA: Academic.

Wathum-Ocama, J. (1987). *Use of instructional materials for hearing impaired students in Minnesota Public Schools*. Unpublished master's thesis, University of Minnesota, Minneapolis.

Watts, S. M., & Graves, M. F. (1995). *Fostering word consciousness*. Unpublished manuscript, Minneapolis, MN.

Weaver, C. (1994). *Reading process and practice: From socio-psycholinguistics to whole language*. Portsmouth, NH: Heinemann.

Webster, A., Wood, D., & Griffiths, A. (1981). Reading retardation or linguistic deficit? I. Interpreting reading test performance of hearing impaired adolescents. *Journal of Research in Reading*, 4, 136–147.

Wells, G. (1990). Creating the conditions to encourage literate thinking. *Educational Leadership, 47*, 13–17.

White, T. G., Graves, M. F., & Slater, W. H. (1990). Growth of reading vocabulary in diverse elementary schools: Decoding and word meaning. *Journal of Educational Psychology, 82*, 281–290.

Whorf, B. (1956). *Language, thought, and reality.* Cambridge, MA: MIT Press.

Wiig, E. H., & Semel, E. (1984). *Language assessment and intervention for the learning disabled* (2nd ed). Columbus, OH: Merrill.

Wilbur, R. (1987). *American Sign Language: Linguistic and applied dimensions* (2nd ed.). Boston: Little, Brown.

Williams, J., & Snipper, G. (1990). *Literacy and bilingualism.* New York: Longman.

Williams, L. C. (1994, April–May–June) The language and literacy worlds of three profoundly deaf preschool children. *Reading Research Quarterly*, 125–155.

Williams, P. L., Reese, C. M., Campbell, J. R., Mazzeo, J., & Phillips, G. N. (1995). *1994 NAEP reading: A first look.* Washington, DC: U.S. Department of Education.

Wilson, K. (1979). *Inference and language processing in hearing and deaf children.* Unpublished doctoral dissertation, Boston University, Massachusetts.

Wilson, L. M. (1996). *The effects of student created expert systems on the reasoning and content learning of deaf students.* Unpublished doctoral dissertation, University of Minnesota, Minneapolis.

Wilson, M., & Emorey, K. (1997). Working memory for sign language: A window into the architecture of the working memory system. *Journal of Deaf Studies and Deaf Education, 2*(3), 121–130.

Wittrock, M. C. (1983). Writing and the teaching of reading. *Language Arts, 60*, 600–606.

Wittrock, M. C. (1986). Students' thought processes. In M. C. Wittrock (Ed.), *Handbook of research on teaching* (3rd ed.). New York: Macmillan.

Wittrock, M. C. (1990). Generative processes of comprehension. *Educational Psychologist, 24*, 345–376.

Wolf, K. (1991). The schoolteacher's portfolio: Issues in design, implementation, and evaluation. *Phi Delta Kappan, 73*, 129–136.

Wolf, K. (1993). From informal to informed assessment: Recognizing the role of the classroom teacher. *Journal of Reading, 36*, 518–523.

Wolk, S., & Schildroth, A. (1984). *Consistency of an associational strategy used on reading comprehension tests by hearing-impaired students in special education* (Series R, No. 9). Washington, DC: Gallaudet University, Center for Assessment and Demographic Studies.

Wollman-Bonilla, J. E. (1989). Reading journals: Invitations to participate in literature. *Reading Teacher, 43*, 112–120.

Wollman-Bonilla, J. E. (1991). *Response journals: Inviting students to think and write about literature.* New York: Scholastic.

Wood, A. (1984). *The napping house.* New York: Harcourt Brace & Company.

Wood, K. D., Lapp, D., & Flood, J. (1992). *Guiding readers through the text: A review of study guides.* Newark, DE: International Reading Association.

Woods, D. J., Griffiths, A. J., & Webster, A. (1981). Reading retardation or linguistic deficit? II. Test answering strategies in hearing and hearing impaired school children. *Journal of Research in Reading, 4*, 148–156.

Yarger, C. C. (1996). An examination of the *Test of Written Language–3*. *Volta Review, 98*(1), 211–215.

Yoshinaga, C. (1983). *Syntactic and semantic characteristics in the written language of hearing impaired and*

Author Index

Abruscato, J., 312, 315
Abrutyn, L., 308, 310, 311
Ackerman, D. B., 161
Adams, M. J., 65, 143
Adkins, T., 181
Afflerbach, P., 173
Ahlgren, I., 97, 108–109
Akamatsu, C. T., 53, 85
Albertini, J., 41, 42, 321
Allen, T., 33, 291
Allen, V., 103, 105, 106
Allington, R., 131, 132, 173
Almond, P., 292
Altwerger, B., 165–166
Alvermann, D. E., 78, 282
Ammon, P., 108
Anders, P. L., 38, 268, 270, 283
Anderson, R. C., 11, 22, 24, 64, 77, 139, 143, 264
Anderson, T. H., 189, 240, 265, 276, 279, 282
Andre, M. E. D. A., 279
Andrews, J. F., 52, 53, 77, 84, 85, 291, 301, 302
Anthony, R. J., 128
Applebee, A. N., 146, 254, 262
Areglado, N., 312
Armbruster, B. B., 189, 240, 264, 265, 276, 282, 284
Arnold, P., 102–103
Artley, S. A., 134

Aschbacher, P. R., 160
Atwell, N., 230, 232, 249–250
Au, K. H., 27, 37, 39, 50, 58, 59, 60, 61, 77, 80

Babbidge Committee, 33
Bahan, B., 46
Baker, I., 194
Baker, K., 131
Baker, L., 23, 83, 84
Baldwin, L., 141
Bales, R. J., 281
Ballard, L., 312, 314
Barnes, D., 126
Barton, D., 42
Baston, T., 180
Battle, J., 132
Baum, D. D., 277
Baumann, J. F., 189
Beane, J. A., 157, 161, 162
Beck, I. L., 74, 81, 239, 267
Bell, S., 314
Bellugi, U., 9, 9–10, 46
Bench, R., 7
Bender, R. E., 292
Berglund, R. L., 196
Bernhardt, E., 61, 76, 86
Berry, S. R., 317
Betts, E., 153
Biggs, S. A., 314
Bilsky, L. H., 72
Birch, J., 93
Blair, F., 7
Bloom, B. S., 169
Bochner, J. H., 321

Bodner-Johnson, B., 97
Booher, H., 82
Boothby, P. R., 78
Botel, M., 266
Boyle, P., 91, 92, 98, 99, 100, 107, 108, 109, 110, 112, 163, 164, 166
Braden, J., 94
Bradley-Johnson, S., 287, 305, 317
Bratcher, S., 321, 323
Brewer, L. C., 17, 83
Brewer, W., 23
Bridge, C., 206–207
Bromley, K., 249, 252
Brooks, J., 150
Brooks, M., 150
Brophy, J., 187
Brown, A. L., 23, 76, 83, 84, 102, 158, 190, 279
Brown, B. J., 312, 314, 315
Brown, E., 314
Brown, M. W., 105
Brown, P. M., 17, 83
Brown, T. L., 239
Browning, W. G., 228
Brozo, W., 268, 314
Brueggeman, M. A., 249
Bruer, J. T., 120
Bruffee, K. A., 241
Bruner, J., 146
Bryk, A. S., 174
Buell, E., 48
Burke, C. L., 128, 166
Burris, N. A., 256

Subject Index

ABOUT THE AUTHORS

Patricia L. McAnally, Ph.D., was a classroom teacher for 14 years and taught deaf and hard of hearing students at preschool, elementary, and middle school levels. She taught in the teacher training programs at Illinois State University and the University of Minnesota for the next 11 years, leaving the University of Minnesota to become the reading and language specialist at the Minnesota Academy for the Deaf. Dr. McAnally left Minnesota to accept a position at the Arizona Schools for the Deaf and the Blind at the School for the Deaf in Tucson. After 3 years, she became the principal of the School for the Deaf and continues to work in that position, although she returns to Minnesota every summer to teach in the training program at the university.

Dr. McAnally was one of the authors of the *Reading Bridge* series and also was a primary author in the revision of the *Reading Milestones* series. Along with Dr. Stephen Quigley and Dr. Susan Rose, she wrote the textbook *Language Learning Practices with Deaf Children,* which has recently been revised. Throughout her many years of rich experiences in the field of education of deaf and hard of hearing students, Dr. McAnally has pursued her special interest in the development of language and reading skills in this population.

Susan Rose is an associate professor and coordinator of the graduate studies pro-gram in education for children who are deaf or hard of hearing at the University of Minnesota in Minneapolis. In addition to her extensive experience as a class-room teacher at the elementary, secondary, and postsecondary levels, she has served in numerous national and state professional and community organiza-tions serving deaf and hard of hearing people; conducted research in the areas of communication, reading, writing, and computer technology; and co-authored the *Reading Bridge* series and the revised *Reading Milestones* with Drs. Quigley and McAnally.

Stephen P. Quigley, Ph.D., was associate director of the Institute for Child Behavior and Development in the Graduate College of the University of Illinois at Urbana-Champaign until his retirement in 1987. He held appointments as professor of education and speech and hearing science at the university. Dr. Quigley's major research interests were language development, particularly syn-tactic development, and reading with hearing-impaired learners. Some of his scholarly works are *The Education of Deaf Children* (PRO-ED), *Language Learning Practices with Deaf Children* (2nd ed., PRO-ED), and *Language and Deafness* (2nd ed., Singular Publishing Group). Based on his extensive research on language and reading with hearing-impaired learners, Dr. Quigley and some of his collaborators developed educational materials widely used in the education of hearing-impaired students and with language-delayed, learning-disabled, ESL, and other special learners. These materials include *The Test of Syntactic Abilities Syntax Program*, *Reading Milestones*, and *Reading Bridge*.